Sustained Attention in Human Performance

Wiley Series on
Studies in Human Performance

Series Editor
Dennis H. Holding
University of Louisville
Kentucky, USA

Human Skills
edited by Dennis H. Holding

Biological Rhythms, Sleep, and Performance
edited by Wilse B. Webb

Stress and Fatigue in Human Performance
edited by Robert Hockey

Sustained Attention in Human Performance
edited by Joel S. Warm

Further titles in preparation

Sustained Attention in Human Performance

Edited by

Joel S. Warm

University of Cincinnati
Cincinnati, USA

JOHN WILEY & SONS

Chichester · New York · Brisbane · Toronto · Singapore

Library of Congress Cataloging in Publication Data:
Main entry under title:

Sustained attention in human performance.

   (Wiley series on studies in human performance)
   Includes indexes.
   1. Attention.   2. Vigilance (Psychology)   3. Performance.
I. Warm, Joel S.   II. Series.
BF321.S87   1984   153.7'33   83-19846

ISBN 0 471 10322 5

British Library Cataloguing in Publication Data:

Sustained attention in human performance. —
   (Wiley series on studies in human performance)
   1. Vigilance
I. Warm, Joel S.
   153.7'33   BF325.V5

ISBN 0 471 10322 5

Phototypeset by Dobbie Typesetting Service, Plymouth, Devon and
printed by St. Edmundsbury Press, Bury St. Edmunds, Suffolk

To Eric and Ellen

List of Contributors

EARL A. ALLUISI
Chief Scientist, Air Force Human Resources Laboratory, Brooks Air Force Base Texas, USA

DANIEL B. BERCH
Associate Professor, Department of Psychology, University of Cincinnati, Cincinnati, Ohio, USA.

ANGUS CRAIG
Research Psychologist, MRC Perceptual & Cognitive Performance Unit, University of Sussex, Brighton, Sussex, England.

PETER A. HANCOCK
Assistant Professor, Safety Science Department, Institute of Safety and Systems Management, University of Southern California, Los Angeles, California, USA.

HARRY J. JERISON
Professor, Neuropsychiatric Institute, University of California: Los Angeles, Los Angeles, California, USA.

DONALD R. KANTER
Research Psychologist, Veterans Administration Medical Center, Cincinnati, Ohio, USA.

MICHAEL LOEB
Professor, Department of Psychology, University of Louisville, Kentucky, USA.

TIMOTHY H. MONK
Assistant Professor, Institute of Chronobiology, The New York Hospital—Cornell Medical Center, White Plains, New York, USA.

RAJA PARASURAMAN
Associate Professor, The Catholic University of America, Washington, DC, USA.

JOEL S. WARM
Professor, Department of Psychology, University of Cincinnati, Cincinnati, Ohio, USA.

EARL L. WIENER
Professor, Department of Management Science and Computer Information Systems, University of Miami, Coral Gables, Florida, USA.

Contents

Contents

Series Preface

Research on human performance has made considerable progress during the past forty years, reaching a respectable depth of analysis in several areas while, at the same time, becoming broader in scope. As a result, there have emerged a number of theoretical ideas which impinge on the general progress of experimental psychology and, moreover, a great deal of knowledge has been obtained in ways that encourage direct, practical applications. The series of *Studies in Human Performance* is intended to explain these ideas and their applications in adequate detail.

Some of the books in the series are monographs while most, like the present text, are edited volumes. The edited volumes are not haphazard collections of papers. Rather, they should be viewed as systematically organized texts which have the advantages of multiple authorship. Writing a monograph is often regarded as the more difficult assignment, but producing an edited volume presents a considerable challenge. On one hand, it provides an opportunity to bring to bear a concentration of expertise that is otherwise unattainable; on the other hand, the multiplicity of contributors carries with it the risk that the overall result may be disorganized or, literally, incoherent. In the *Human Performance* series, every effort has been made to counter the potential disadvantages attendant on using the edited format while preserving the positive advantages of drawing upon special knowledge. The chapters have been commissioned in accordance with an integrated plan for each volume, information about each chapter has been circulated among the contributors in order to ensure cohesion, and editorial control has extended to the level of difficulty as well as to the format of each text.

The result of these preparations should be a series of books which combine readability with high standards of scholarship. The aim has been to supply a good deal of content, but within an expository framework that emphasizes explanation rather than mere reporting. Thus, although each volume contains sufficient material for the needs of graduate students or advanced undergraduates in experimental psychology, the books should provide readily accessible information for applied psychologists in many areas. In addition, it is hoped that the books will be useful to practitioners in ergonomics, to persons with interdisciplinary interests in production and industrial engineering, in physical education and in exercise physiology, and to psychologists in other fields.

The present volume deals with the problem of alertness, which is seen as a factor in a wide variety of human activities. It is obvious that any loss of alertness is critical in watch-keeping tasks, but perhaps less obvious that alertness matters in virtually any laboratory or industrial task that requires a person to exert sustained attention over an extended period of time. One of the virtues of the book is that it makes a genuine effort to show what kinds of tasks are most affected by the tendency for human vigilance to decline over time and to make recommendations for overcoming the resulting problems. The chapters on applied problems in industry and defense are preceded by a very thorough treatment of the massive accumulation of laboratory research that has followed the wartime beginnings of concern with sustained attention. The nature of the vigilance task and its sensory input, the physiological underpinnings of sustained performance and the part played by individual differences, as well as their clinical implications, have all been examined before a review of the theories is undertaken. Not unexpectedly, no single theory of human vigilance proves satisfactory in isolation.

Both of the immediately previous volumes in the Series made creative attempts to integrate different fields of study. *Biological Rhythms, Sleep, and Performance* interrelated sleep research with the work on circadian and similar biological rhythms while *Stress and Fatigue in Human Performance*, as its name implies presented fatigue research in addition to studies of environmental and other stresses. The integrative contribution of the present book, apart from its success in coping with the sheer diversity of existing vigilance studies, derives in part from its inclusion of research on search processes. Early vigilance tasks, such as the wartime anti-submarine patrols, contained an element of search that has been omitted in many of the laboratory studies of sustained attention. The book provides a useful reminder of the importance of search processes which may be expected to influence to some extent the future course of vigilance research. Like the two previous volumes, the present book may therefore lay claim to making an appreciable theoretical contribution, despite its primary function as an explanatory text. At the same time, the level of explanation satisfies the overall objective of the series, that each book should be within the grasp of any educated person who has the motivation to study its subject matter.

DENNIS H. HOLDING
Series Editor

Preface

The quotation above is borrowed from the work of Charles Churchill, an 18th century British poet and satirist. In this passage, he gives clear expression to a fundamental aspect of attention—it cannot be maintained indefinitely without cost. Through the years, much has been written on the subject of attention. It was an important topic in the early days of psychology and was featured in the writings of scholars such as James, Pillsbury and Titchener. Nevertheless, the full impact of temporal limitations in attention did not become apparent to experimental psychologists nor to human factors specialists until the development of automated human–machine systems during and after World War II.

In their interaction with such systems, human operators often serve as monitors who must remain alert for indications of malfunctions or changes in operating state and, upon becoming aware of such events, take appropriate action. Monitoring or watchkeeping functions have become integral elements in many civilian and military tasks in which inspection, quality control and surveillance activities are involved. Lapses of attention (or the blotting out of our powers, as Churchill describes it) which may occur over time are potential sources of system failure. As a result, the study of sustained attention or vigilance has become an important topic in the general domain of human performance.

This book serves as a forum in which a number of specialists from Great Britain and the United States provide an in-depth examination of the many factors which control our ability to remain attentive over extended periods of time, of the theoretical mechanisms that might underlie this ability and of the applicability of vigilance research to a variety of real-world operational problems. In sum, it represents a comprehensive and critical survey of this vital aspect of human performance. The book is intended for a broad audience, including advanced undergraduate and graduate students in psychology and professionals concerned with human skills such as those in ergonomics, industrial and human engineering and education.

In editing this book, I was aided by several people. I am grateful to my colleagues William N. Dember and William R. Meyers for the encouragement which supported a sometimes weakening writing imperative. I am also indebted to my students, especially John Bowers, Mark Scerbo, Mary Lynne Dittmar, Debbie Korchmar, Tom Lanzetta, Bob Lysaght, Roger Rosa and Kim Wolk for helping me to refine my understanding of vigilance. Thanks are also due Debbie Korchmar, Bob Lysaght and Roger Rosa for their valuable assistance in preparing the author index. The series editor, Dr. Dennis H. Holding and Ms Celia Bird, Social Sciences Editor, John Wiley and Sons, Ltd., have provided an inordinate measure of patience and understanding and more than a cupful of kindness for which I shall be ever grateful.

JOEL S. WARM
Cincinnati, Ohio, USA
June 1983

Sustained Attention in Human Performance
Edited by J. S. Warm
© 1984 John Wiley & Sons Ltd.

Chapter 1

An Introduction to Vigilance

Joel S. Warm

HISTORICAL BACKGROUND

To observe and perceive not

The time is World War II. A British patrol plane flies over the Bay of Biscay. Inside, an observer peers at a speckled, flickering radar screen looking for a tell-tale spot of light or 'blip' that will signal the presence of an enemy submarine on the surface of the sea. The observer has been on watch for a little over 30 minutes and nothing much has happened. Perhaps this mission, like so many others, will be fruitless. Suddenly, the 'blip' appears but the observer makes no response. The 'blip' appears a few more times. Still the observer fails to respond. Evidently, the signal has gone undetected and, as a result, so has the submarine.

Scenarios such as this, in which a trained observer failed to detect specific cues critical to the effective performance of a military surveillance task, gave impetus to the comprehensive study of an aspect of behavior known as vigilance or sustained attention. The term attention in the definition of vigilance merits special note. It is a term that is applicable to a wide range of activities and one that has a variety of meanings (Dember and Warm, 1979). For example, Moray (1969) has proposed at least six different definitions for the term in current experimental psychology. After careful consideration of this matter, Posner and Boies (1971) have suggested that the concept of attention may encompass three major subdivisions: (1) alertness or the ability to maintain optimal sensitivity to external stimuli; (2) selection or the ability to concentrate awareness upon one source of information rather than another; and (3) limited processing capacity, a term which reflects the difficulty people have in processing two tasks stimultaneously. Davies and Parasuraman (1982) have pointed out that the study of vigilance is concerned predominantly with the first two of these subdivisions. Thus, what is of interest in the study of vigilance is the ability of observers to maintain their focus of attention and to remain alert to stimuli over prolonged periods of time.

Setting the stage

Before World War II, there was some occasional concern about the problems that industrial workers may have have in sustaining attention to prolonged tasks. This concern can be traced to questions of quality control in situations in which workers had to observe the monotonous flow of products on an assembly line and be alert for defects (Adams, 1963; Davies and Tune, 1969; Stroh, 1971; Mackie, 1977). For example, Wyatt and Langdon (1932) described time-related variations in the performance of experienced inspectors who examined cartridge cases for metal flaws and other faults prior to packaging. Accuracy of inspection varied in approximately a U-shaped manner over a 4-hour working spell, reaching its lowest ebb after about 90 minutes on the job. With the advent of the war, interest in vigilance was accelerated by the need to know as much as possible about the capabilities of lookouts and radar and sonar operators who had to sustain attention for relatively infrequent events under monotonous conditions.

Efforts to meet this wartime challenge were initiated at about the same time in Great Britain, the United States and Canada. In England, Ditchburn (1943) undertook a study for the Admiralty of the performance of lookouts and made the rather startling discovery that their ability to detect a target began to decline soon after their work was started. Similarly, in the United States, Anderson and his colleagues (see Lindsley, 1944) studying radar operations and, in Canada, Solandt and Partridge (1946) studying sonar operations, also found that performance efficiency in these attention-demanding tasks dwindled over time. Indeed, Anderson's group recommended that daily operating periods last not longer than 40 minutes.

These investigations, together with others (cf. Lindsley, 1944; Baker, 1962) had begun to uncover an important fact about the nature of sustained attention in human performance—it is fragile in situations requiring watchkeeping or monitoring functions. However, these studies were not programmatic and little attempt was made to coordinate the efforts of different workers. In addition, in some cases, the focus of concern was fatigue not attention (Jerison, 1970). Thus, these investigations are not generally considered as the genesis of vigilance research. As Stroh (1971) has noted, they served mainly to create interest and to set the stage for more productive experimentation.

Mackworth's experiments

Controlled laboratory research on sustained attention is generally considered to date from a series of systematic and ingenious experiments by Norman H. Mackworth (1948, 1950). His seminal studies provided several fundamental findings (which will appear in many chapters of this book) and set the tone for much of the work to follow. He was the first to point out the theoretical as well as the practical implications of watchkeeping behavior (Davies and Tune, 1969) and it was Mackworth (1957) who borrowed the term 'vigilance' from the British neurologist, Sir Henry Head (1926), and used it to describe watchkeeping or monitoring tasks. For Head, vigilance referred to a state of maximum physiological and psychological readiness to react. Mackworth used the term to characterize an observer's ability to detect and respond to small stimulus changes in situations in which one must direct attention to sources of stimulation for long, unbroken periods of time (Davies and Parasuraman, 1982).

Mackworth began his work in response to a request from the Royal Air Force for laboratory experiments to study the problem of U-boat contacts missed by radar observers on anti-submarine patrol. He devised a simulated radar display called the *clock test* in which subjects were asked to view movements of a black pointer along the circumference of a blank-faced clock which contained no scale markings or reference points. Once every second, the pointer would move 0.3 inch to a new position. From time to time, it executed a 'double jump' of 0.6 inch, and this was the critical signal for detection. Mackworth's subjects were required to press a key whenever they spotted a movement of double length during a session which lasted continuously for 2 hours.

Using the clock test in this way, Mackworth was able to chart the course of performance over time. In so doing, he confirmed the suspicions generated in operational settings that the quality of sustained attention in

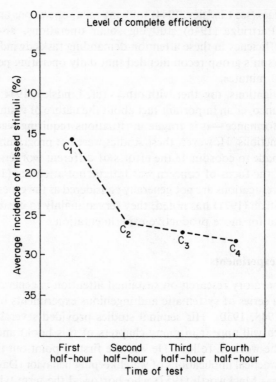

Figure 1.1   The decrement function in vigilance obtained with the clock test in one of Mackworth's early experiments. [After Mackworth (1950). Reproduced by permission of the Controller of Her Majesty's Stationery Office.]

monitoring tasks wanes rapidly. Some of his findings are illustrated in Figure 1.1.

It is evident in the figure that the observers became more inefficient at detecting signals as time on watch progressed. Notice that the incidence of missed signals increased sharply from the first to the second half-hour of the session and then showed a more gradual decline for the remainder of the 2-hour watch. In addition to the clock test, Mackworth also employed an auditory vigilance task in which critical signals for detection were slight increments in the duration of recurrently presented tones. As in the case of the clock test, the incidence of missed signals on the auditory task also increased over time.

The progressive decline in performance with time on task noted in Mackworth's pioneering experiments has since been found in a large number of subsequent investigations. This body of evidence includes experiments in which subjects monitored cutaneous stimulation as well as those in which visual or acoustic stimuli were involved. The progressive decline in performance has been termed the *decrement function* (Dember and Warm, 1979) or the *vigilance decrement* (Davies and Parasuraman, 1982). Although it does not always occur (cf. Jerison, 1963; Richter *et al.*, 1981), the decrement is perhaps the most ubiquitous finding in research on sustained attention.

The fundamental problem

Most of the experiments that have explored the decrement function have charted the temporal course of performance by averaging scores over a group of subjects for several blocks of time (as in Figure 1.1). On the whole, these studies suggest that the vigilance decrement is complete within 20–35 minutes after the initiation of the vigil and that at least half of the final loss is completed within the first 15 minutes (Teichner, 1974). Jerison (1959) has suggested that this typical sort of temporal analysis is 'coarse-grained' and that it might provide a rather conservative estimate of the speed of the waning of performance in vigilance studies. Using a more 'fine-grained' approach in which a signal by signal estimate of performance efficiency was made, Jerison has found evidence for a decline in efficiency from the very first signal onward. As Dember and Warm (1979) have pointed out, the most striking aspect of the decrement function is that it seems to result merely from the necessity of looking or listening (or feeling) for an infrequent signal over a continuous period of time! An understanding of the vigilance decrement and of the factors that influence the absolute level of vigilance performance has been the fundamental problem for most laboratory studies of vigilance.

THE VIGILANCE PARADIGM

Stimulus specification

Since Mackworth's initial investigations, a plethora of experimental tasks has been used in the study of vigilance behavior. Complete descriptions of the spectrum of tasks employed can be found in several sources (McGrath *et al.*, 1968; Mackworth, 1970; Teichner, 1974). In some cases, the tasks have involved relatively simple displays in which observers were required to detect the onset or conclusion of a discrete stimulus event, e.g. the illumination of a small spot of light or a brief interruption in the presentation of a continuous tone. In such cases, all stimulus or non-stimulus occurrences are critical signals for detection. In most cases, however, more complex, dynamic displays have been used in which subjects were required to observe a stream of repetitively presented neutral stimulus events for specified changes that constituted critical stimuli. Mackworth's clock test is an example, as is a case in which subjects must listen to repeated pulses of acoustic stimulation of fixed duration (e.g. 0.5 seconds) for occasional longer pulses (e.g. 1.0 seconds). In these situations, of course, only some stimulus events are critical signals. The discrete–dynamic distinction is important. For one thing, the decrement function has been found to be more pronounced with dynamic as compared to discrete types of tasks (Davies and Tune, 1969). For another, the rate of repetition of neutral events in the dynamic tasks, the background event rate, has a profound effect upon performance efficiency (cf. Dember and Warm, 1979; Parasuraman, 1979).

Davies and Tune (1969) have noted that vigilance tasks can also be categorized along a sensory–cognitive dimension. In sensory tasks, of which those described above would serve as examples, critical signals for detection are specified changes in the physical attributes of stimuli. By contrast, in cognitive tasks, critical signals for detection are more symbolic than sensory. The best known version of this type of task is one devised by Bakan (1959) in which a series of digits is presented and the observer must detect a specified sequence such as three consecutive 'odd' digits all of which are different. Although the vigilance decrement is present in cognitive tasks (cf. Jones *et al.*, 1979), performance with these tasks may differ from that with sensory tasks in important ways (cf. Howe *et al.*, 1976; Sprague, 1981; Lysaght, 1982).

Given the wide variation in the types of tasks that have been used to study sustained attention, it would be prudent to ask if they have features in common which, in sum, are unique to the vigilance situation. The absence of any common characteristics would make it difficult to define 'vigilance' in operational terms and to draw meaningful conclusions about 'vigilant behavior' (McGrath, 1963).

Fortunately, a number of task dimensions can be specified which might be considered to be special features of vigilance situations. As described by Jerison (1970) and by Warm (1977) they include the following: (1) the task is prolonged and continuous, often lasting for half an hour or more; (2) the signals to be detected are usually clearly perceivable when the observer is alerted to them, but would seem 'weak' to most observers because they are not 'compelling changes' in the observer's operating environment; (3) the signals to be detected occur infrequently, aperiodically and without forewarning; and (4) the observer's response typically has no effect upon the probability of appearance of critical signals. It should be emphasized that all vigilance tasks do not conform to these characteristics in a hard and fast manner. There are exceptions, as for example tasks in which critical signals appear quite frequently (cf. Jenkins, 1958) and tasks of very brief duration (Davies, 1968). All in all, however, these four dimensions seem to capture the special characteristics of most vigilance tasks.

Response specification

The measures used as indices of vigilance performance, like the tasks employed, have also varied considerably. Broadbent (1971) has viewed these measures in terms of a 'conventional–non-conventional' classification scheme. Conventional or 'traditional' measures include (1) detection probability or its reciprocal, the probability of errors of omission; (2) errors of commission—false detections or false alarms; (3) the number of times a signal must be repeated before it is detected; (4) changes in threshold sensitivity; and (5) response time to correct signal detection. Of these, the frequency of correct detections and response time to correct detection have been the principal means of gauging performance.

The use of different response measures led to problems in specifying the most appropriate performance index (McGrath, 1963). At this time, however, the bulk of available evidence seems to indicate that the vigilance decrement is revealed by a drop in the number of correct detections and/or by a rise in response time to correct detections and that these measures can be broadly considered as correlated indicies of performance efficiency (Buck, 1966).

The non-conventional aspect of Broadbent's (1971) view of the measurement of vigilance performance involves the application of the theory of signal detection (TSD) to the analysis of vigilance data (Swets and Kristofferson, 1970; Swets, 1977). This approach makes use of the frequencies of correct detections and false alarms to provide independent metrics to assess the observer's behavior in a vigilance experiment as a sensor (the observer did not perceive the signal) and as a decision maker (the observer interpreted a stimulus event as a non-signal). Parasuraman and Davies (1976) have described a method by which a TSD analysis can be extended to response times, thus incorporating detection and latency data within the same framework. The application of the TSD model to vigilance experiments has been viewed with great promise by some investigators (Davies and Parasuraman, 1982) and challenged by others (Long and Waag, 1981). This issue will be discussed in detail in Chapters 2, 3 and 6 of the present volume.

THE SCOPE OF THE VIGILANCE PROBLEM

Psychological processes in sustained attention

At this point, one might wonder why so much interest has been devoted to a problem that surfaced in the performance of military surveillance tasks in a war that ended nearly 40 years ago. The answer lies in the fact that the problem of vigilance occupies a unique niche in psychology—it is the sort of problem that accommodates both basic research and more applied interests.

The capacity to sustain attention is a fundamental element in behavioral adaptation. In regard to animal life for example, Dimond and Lazarus (1974) have pointed out that vigilant behavior plays an integral role in detecting sources of external danger, in exploiting environmental resources and in intraspecies communication. In terms of human endeavors, Jerison (1977) has emphasized that the capacity to maintain some level of alertness during the activities of the day is a primary aspect of perceptual functioning and Broadbent (1971) has noted that the theoretical importance of the vigilance task is that it allows us to study in a controlled situation almost all of the factors that may be considered to influence attention.

The quality of vigilance performance has indeed been found to be related to a wide variety of factors. These include several psychophysical parameters like background event rate and the sensory modality and amplitude of critical signals as well as several neurophysiological parameters as revealed through pupillary responses, electroencephalographic activity, blood catecholamine levels and the actions of pharmacological agents (cf. Dember and Warm, 1979; Davies and Parasuraman, 1982; Beatty, 1982). In addition, sources of environmental stress, such as heat, cold, noise and vibration also contribute to people's ability to sutain attention to a task for prolonged periods of time (cf. Poulton, 1977) and large individual differences in the quality of sustained attention are a common element in vigilance experiments (Buckner, 1963; Smith, 1966; Davies and Parasuraman, 1982). Several personality and organismic dimensions have been related to vigilant behavior and monitoring tasks have been used to study attentional difficulties in clinical populations ranging from the reading disabled (Rugel and Mitchell, 1977) to schizophrenics (Wohlberg and Kornetsky, 1973).

The diversity of vigilance findings is impressive. How might they be explained? In a comment to Harry Jerison, Norman Mackworth observed that an essential feature of the vigilance story is that its origins were without any theoretical base (Jerison, 1970). This state of affairs changed rapidly in the evolution of vigilance research. Mackworth himself appealed to the Hullian notion of response inhibition to explain the vigilance decrement (Mackworth, 1950). Since then, theoretical efforts to account for vigilant behavior have focused upon many psychological processes. Theories of vigilance range from psychophysiological accounts anchored in arousal or habituation notions to accounts invoking motivational principles or operant conditioning principles to cognitive views, featuring concepts such as expectancy formation, attentional filtering, decision making and automatic and controlled processing.

Theories of human performance often fluctuate between 'bottom-up' approaches in which performance is considered to be driven by external factors and 'top-down' approaches in which actions are said to be controlled by internal hypotheses or expectations (Posner, 1978). Vigilance theories reflect both classes of this dichotomy as well as a mixture of the classes. In the past few years, several reviews of the theories of vigilance have appeared (Loeb and Alluisi, 1977, 1980; Warm, 1977; Dember and Warm, 1979; Davies and Parasuraman, 1982). The consensus seems to be that none of these positions is entirely adequate to account for what is now known about vigilant behavior. Clearly, what might have seemed originally to be a relatively simple and limited problem has turned out to be a much more complex issue with dimensions that span the domain of modern experimental psychology.

Ergonomic considerations

In a more practical vein, interest in vigilance remains because the surveillance problems encountered in World War II are still with us in one form or another. Howell and Goldstein (1971) have pointed out that great changes have occurred in man–machine relations since the war. Machines can no longer be considered as the willing but witless servants of human operators. Instead, as a result of automation, they have become our 'partners' and vigilant behavior is an important element in the contribution to this partnership.

More specifically, with the advent of automatic control and computing systems for the acquisition, storage and processing of information, the human operator has been relieved of many of the routine but active controlling activities that were necessary in earlier, less sophisticated systems. The operator's role has evolved along more 'executive' lines in which much time is spent in the passive monitoring of dials, video screens and other sources of information for occasional 'critical' stimuli that demand decision and action (Adams *et al.*, 1961; Adams, 1963; Sheridan and Ferrell, 1974; Kessel and Wickens, 1982).

Today, vigilant behavior is required in the operation of many military surveillance devices and advanced weapons systems. It is an important factor in the reliability of human performance in many industrial quality control operations (Drury and Fox, 1975), as well as in air traffic control (Barnes and Dickson, 1973; Hopkin, 1975; Thackray *et al.*, 1977), seaboard navigation (Davies and Parasuraman, 1982), railway operation (Buck, 1968) and nuclear power plant operations (Rasmussen, 1981). Vigilance has been implicated as a human factors concern in jet and space flight (Hanks, 1961; Eason and Harter, 1972; Johnson *et al.*, 1972), in the operation of agricultural machinery such as tractors (Kaminaka *et al.*, 1981) and in long distance driving (Mackie, 1977). The importance of vigilance even extends to medical settings in which anesthesiologists must monitor electronic equipment displaying a patient's life signs during prolonged surgery (Beatty *et al.*, 1977).

Viewed in the context of an automation-oriented society, in which failures to detect critical signals can often be disastrous, the problem of vigilance assumes considerable significance. The decrement function bears witness to the fact that by placing monitoring responsibilities primarily in the hands of the human components of man–machine systems we may have created work situations for which people are not ideally suited. Letting the machines themselves carry the primary responsibility for monitoring functions is a solution. However, this is not always possible because of task complexities and costs. Thus, the proper design of automated systems to maximize the human operator's vigilance capabilities has been a challenge for human engineering specialists and the problem of vigilance has provided a unique opportunity for the immediate marriage of laboratory and operations research. Whether or not this has been a 'happy' marriage is an interesting aspect of the vigilance story (cf. Kibler,

1965; Mackie, 1977; Nachreiner, 1977; Morgan, 1980; Davies and Parasuraman, 1982). On a broader level, it may also have important implications for the relation between psychological science and psychotechnology.

The scope of this book

From what has been said in this introductory chapter, it should be evident that the study of sustained attention has come a long way since its wartime origins. Pribram (1969) has pointed out that research in a given area usually evolves through a series of phases. First is one of enthusiastic discovery; second, the accumulation of detailed information; third, a phase of deeper understanding and exploration; and fourth, an attempt at synthesis. I have suggested elsewhere (Warm, 1977) that vigilance research may be in the third phase. The purpose of the present volume is to offer an intensive examination of the several facets of vigilance research in the hope that such examination will help to clarify old problems, suggest new avenues of investigation and promote advancement toward Pribram's fourth phase.

To this end, the first six chapters of the book focus upon the psychophysical, psychobiological, environmental and personal determinants of vigilance and upon theories of vigilance. Chapters 7 and 8 take up the practical implications of vigilance and what might be done to improve monitoring efficiency in operational settings. These chapters are complemented by a discussion of visual search in Chapter 9 since search requirements—those in which individuals look for known targets with uncertain spatial locations—and vigilance requirements are often related in 'real-world' settings. In the final chapter, I will endeavor to put what has been said in perspective by summarizing some of the major accomplishments of vigilance research and highlighting possible directions for future investigation.

REFERENCES

Adams, J. A. Experimental studies of human vigilance. Electronic Systems Division Technical Development Report No. ESD-TDR-63-320. Hanscom Field, Bedford, Mass.: Operations Applications Laboratory, Electronic Systems Division, 1963.

Adams, J. A., Stenson, H. H., and Humes, J. M. Monitoring of complex visual displays. II. Effects of visual load and response complexity on human vigilance. *Human Factors*, 1961, **3**, 213–221.

Bakan, P. Extroversion–introversion and improvement in an auditory vigilance task. *British Journal of Psychology*, 1959, **50**, 325–332.

Baker, C. H. *Man and radar displays*. New York: Macmillan, 1962.

Barnes, L. B., and Dickson, D. L. Optimizing the role of the air traffic controller. *Journal of Air Traffic Control*, 1973, **15**, 25–27.

Beatty, J. Phasic not tonic pupillary responses vary with auditory vigilance performance. *Psychophysiology*, 1982, **19**, 167–172.

Beatty, J., Ahren, S. K. and Katz, R. Sleep deprivation and the vigilance of anesthesiologists during simulated surgery. In R. R. Mackie (Ed.), *Vigilance: theory, operational performance and physiological correlates*. New York: Plenum, 1977.

Broadbent, D. E. *Decision and stress*. New York: Academic Press, 1971.

Buck, L. Reaction time as a measure of perceptual vigilance. *Psychological Bulletin*, 1966, **65**, 291–304.

Buck, L. Experiments on railway vigilance devices. *Ergonomics*, 1968, **11**, 557–564.

Buckner, D. N. An individual-difference approach to explaining vigilance performance. In D. N. Buckner and J. J. McGrath (Eds), *Vigilance: a symposium*. New York: McGraw-Hill, 1963.

Davies, D. R. Age differences in paced inspection tasks. In G. A. Talland (Ed.), *Human aging and behavior: recent advances in research and theory*. New York: Academic Press, 1968.

Davies, D. R. and Parasuraman, R. *The psychology of vigilance*. London: Academic Press, 1982.

Davies, D. R. and Tune, G. S. *Human vigilance performance*. New York: American Elsevier, 1969.

Dember, W. N. and Warm, J. S. *Psychology of perception*, 2nd edn. New York: Holt, Rinehart and Winston, 1979.

Dimond, S. and Lazarus, J. The problem of vigilance in animal life. *Brain, Behavior and Evolution*, 1974, **9**, 60–79.

Ditchburn, R. W. Some factors affecting the efficiency of work by lookouts. Admiralty Research Laboratory Report No. ARC/R1/84/46/0. 1943.

Drury, C. G. and Fox, J. G. (Eds). *Human reliability in quality control*. London: Taylor and Francis, 1975.

Eason, R. G. and Harter, M. R. Sensory, perceptual and motor factors. In Space Science Board, National Academy of Sciences, National Research Council (Eds), *Human factors in long-duration spaceflight*. Washington: National Academy of Sciences, 1972.

Hanks, T. G. Human factors related to jet aircraft. In S. B. Sells and C. A. Berry (Eds.), *Human factors in jet and space travel: a medical-psychological analysis*. New York: Ronald Press, 1961.

Head, H. *Aphasia*. Cambridge: Cambridge University Press, 1926.

Hopkin, V. D. The provision and use of information on air traffic control displays. In Advisory Group for Aerospace Research and Development (Ed.), *Conference Proceedings No. 188, Plans and Developments for Air Traffic Control Systems*. North Atlantic Treaty Organization, 1975.

Howe, S. R., Fishbein, H. D., Kindell, L. and Warm, J. S. Enhancing sustained attention through cognitive complexity. Paper presented at the meeting of the Psychonomic Society, St Louis, Mo., 1976.

Howell, W. C., and Goldstein, I. L. Vigilance. In W. C. Howell and I. L. Goldstein (Eds.), *Engineering psychology: Current perspectives in research*. New York: Appleton–Century–Crofts, 1971.

Jenkins, H. M. The effect of signal rate on performance in visual monitoring. *American Journal of Psychology*, 1958, **71**, 647–661.

Jerison, H. J. Experiments on vigilance: V. The empirical model for human vigilance. Wright Air Development Center Technical Report No. WADC-TR-58-526. Wright-Patterson Air Force Base, Ohio: Aero Medical Laboratory, Wright Air Development Center, 1959.

Jerison, H. J. On the decrement function in human vigilance. In D. N. Buckner and J. J. McGrath (Eds), *Vigilance: a symposium*. New York: McGraw-Hill, 1963.

Jerison, H. J. Vigilance, discrimination and attention. In D. I. Mostofsky (Ed.), *Attention: contemporary theory and analysis.* New York: Appleton–Century–Crofts, 1970.

Jerison, H. J. Vigilance: biology, psychology, theory and practice. In R. R. Mackie (Ed.), *Vigilance, theory, operational performance and physiological correlates.* New York: Plenum, 1977.

Johnson, L. C., Williams, H. L., and Stern, J. A. Motivation, cognition, and sleep-work factors; central- and autonomic-nervous-system indices. In Space Science Board, National Academy of Sciences, National Research Council (Eds), *Human factors in long-duration spaceflight.* Washington: National Academy of Sciences, 1972.

Jones, D. M., Smith, A. P., and Broadbent, D. E. Effects of moderate intensity noise on the Bakan vigilance task. *Journal of Applied Psychology,* 1979, **64,** 627–634.

Kaminaka, M. S., Rehkugler, G. E., and Gunkel, W. W. Visual monitoring in a simulated agricultural machinery operation. *Human Factors,* 1981, **23,** 165–173.

Kessel, C. J., and Wickens, C. D. The transfer of failure-detection skills between monitoring and controlling dynamic systems. *Human Factors,* 1982, **24,** 49–60.

Kibler, A. W. The relevance of vigilance research to aerospace monitoring tasks. *Human Factors,* 1965, **7,** 93–99.

Lindsley, D. B. (Ed.). Radar operator 'fatigue': the effect of length and repetition of operating periods on efficiency of performance. Office of Scientific Research and Development Report No. OSRD 3334. 1944.

Loeb, M., and Alluisi, E. A. An update of findings regarding vigilance and a reconsideration of underlying mechanisms. In R. R. Mackie (Ed.), *Vigilance: theory, operational performance and physiological mechanisms.* New York: Plenum, 1977.

Loeb, M., and Alluisi, E. A. Theories of vigilance: a modern perspective. In G. E. Corrick, E. C. Haseltine and R. T. Durst, Jr (Eds), *Proceedings of the Human Factors Society.* Santa Monica, Calif.: Human Factors Society, 1980.

Long, G. M., and Waag, W. L. Limitations on the practical applicability of *d'* and β measures. *Human Factors, 1981,* **23,** 285–290.

Lysaght, R. J. The effects of noise on sustained attention and behavioral persistence. Unpublished doctoral dissertation, University of Cincinnati, 1982.

McGrath, J. J. Some problems of definition and criteria in the study of vigilance performance. In D. N. Buckner and J. J. McGrath (Eds), *Vigilance: a symposium.* New York: McGraw-Hill, 1963.

McGrath, J. J., Harabedian, A., and Buckner, D. N. Human factor problems in anti-submarine warfare. In *Studies of human vigilance: an omnibus of technical reports.* Goleta, Calif.: Human Factors Research, Inc., 1968.

Mackie, R. R. Introduction. In R. R. Mackie (Ed.), *Vigilance: theory, operational performance and physiological correlates.* New York: Plenum, 1977.

Mackworth, J. F. *Vigilance and attention.* Baltimore: Penguin, 1970.

Mackworth, N. H. The breakdown of vigilance during prolonged visual search. *Quarterly Journal of Experimental Psychology,* 1948, **1,** 6–21.

Mackworth, N. H. Researches on the measurement of human performance. Medical Research Council Special Report Series 268. London: HM Stationery Office, 1950. Reprinted in H. W. Sinaiko (Ed.), *Selected papers on human factors in the design and use of control systems.* New York: Dover, 1961.

Mackworth, N. H. Some factors affecting vigilance. *Advancement of Science,* 1957, **53,** 389–393.

Moray, N. *Attention: selective processes in vision and hearing.* New York: Academic Press, 1969.

Morgan, B. B., Jr. Influence of task and situational variables on the applicability of vigilance data to physical security. In G. E. Corrick, E. C. Haseltine and R. T. Durst, Jr. (Eds), *Proceedings of the Human Factors Society*. Santa Monica, Calif.: Human Factors Society, 1980.

Nachreiner, F. Experiments on the validity of vigilance experiments. In R. R. Mackie (Ed.), *Vigilance: theory, operational performance and physiological correlates*. New York: Plenum, 1977.

Parasuraman, R. Memory load and event rate control sensitivity decrements in sustained attention. *Science*, 1979, **205**, 924–927.

Parasuraman, R., and Davies, D. R. Decision theory analysis of response latencies in vigilance. *Journal of Experimental Psychology: Human Perception and Performance*, 1976, **2**, 578–590.

Posner, M. I. *Chronometric explorations of mind*. Hillsdale, N.J.: Lawrence Earlbaum, 1978.

Posner, M. I., and Boies, S. J. Components of attention. *Psychological Review*, 1971, **78**, 391–408.

Poulton, E. C. Arousing stresses increase vigilance. In R. R. Mackie (Ed.), *Vigilance: theory, operational performance and physiological correlates*. New York: Plenum, 1977.

Pribram, K. H. Editorial forward. In J. F. Mackworth, *Vigilance and habituation*. Baltimore: Penguin, 1969.

Rasmussen, J. Models of mental strategies in process plant diagnosis. In J. Rasmussen and W. B. Rouse (Eds), *Human detection and diagnosis of system failures*. New York: Plenum, 1981.

Richter, D. O., Senter, R. J., and Warm, J. S. Effects of the rate and regularity of background events on sustained attention. *Bulletin of the Psychonomic Society*, 1981, **18**, 207–210.

Rugel, R. P., and Mitchell, A. Characteristics of familial and non-familial disabled readers. *Journal of Learning Disabilities*, 1977, **10**, 308–313.

Sheridan, T. B., and Ferrell, W. R. *Man-machine systems: information, control and decision models of human performance*. Cambridge, Mass.: MIT Press, 1974.

Smith, R. L. *Monotony and motivation: a theory of vigilance*. Santa Monica, Calif.: Dunlap and Associates, 1966.

Solandt, D. Y., and Partridge, D. M. Research on auditory problems presented by naval operations. *Journal of the Canadian Medical Service*, 1946, **3**, 323–329.

Sprague, R. L. The cognitive increment function in sustained attention. Unpublished masters thesis, University of Cincinnati, 1981.

Stroh, C. M. *Vigilance: the problem of sustained attention*. Oxford: Pergamon, 1971.

Swets, J. A. Signal detection theory appied to vigilance. In R. R. Mackie (Ed.), *Vigilance: theory, operational performance and physiological correlates*. New York: Plenum, 1977.

Swets, J. A., and Kristofferson, A. B. Attention. *Annual Review of Psychology*, 1970, **21**, 339–366.

Thackray, R. I., Bailey, J. P., and Touchstone, R. M. Physiological, subjective and performance correlates of reported boredom and monotony while performing a simulated radar control task. In R. R. Mackie (Ed.), *Vigilance: theory, operational performance and physiological correlates*. New York: Plenum, 1977.

Teichner, W. H. The detection of a simple visual signal as a function of time of watch. *Human Factors*, 1974, **16**, 339–353.

Warm, J. S. Psychological processes in sustained attention. In R. R. Mackie (Ed.), *Vigilance: theory, operational performance and physiological correlates.* New York: Plenum, 1977.

Wohlberg, G. W., and Kornetsky, C. Sustained attention in remitted schizophrenics. *Archives of General Psychiatry*, 1973, **28**, 533–537.

Wyatt, S., and Langdon, J. N. Inspection processes in industry. Industry Health Research Board Report No. 63. London: HM Stationery Office, 1932.

Sustained Attention in Human Performance
Edited by J. S. Warm
© 1984 John Wiley & Sons Ltd.

Chapter 2

The Psychophysics of Vigilance

Joel S. Warm and Harry J. Jerison

STIMULUS PARAMETERS

Most laboratory studies of vigilance seem to demand little of an observer and to require relatively simple behavior. The observer merely waits patiently for a critical signal and, when it appears, must only press a button to signify its detection. But the apparent simplicity is deceptive. Under analysis, it is clear that complexity not simplicity is the rule that characterizes the behavior of the observer.

Part of this complexity is in the quality of sustained attention, which is determined to a considerable extent by the nature of the stimulus. The study of vigilance, like that of other perceptual phenomena, has profited from the precise determination of the stimulus conditions which influence performance.

In discussing stimulus parameters, Dember and Warm (1979) distinguished between first-order and second-order psychophysical factors. First-order factors involve immediate physical properties of the stimulus; second-order factors refer to characteristics of a signal inferred by the observer on the basis of experience with the task. This distinction provides a convenient way to order the components of the psychophysics of vigilance.

First-order factors

Sensory Modality

A basic element of all vigilance tasks is the transformation of an environmental stimulus into a biological event. Before a critical signal can be detected, energies form the source of stimulation to be monitored must be transformed and encoded into neural messages by the observer's sensory ('transducer') systems. Since different sensory systems have different transduction properties (Uttal, 1973), the sensory modality that carries signals may determine the quality of sustained attention. It is the first concern in the psychophysics of vigilance.

Acoustic, tactile and visual stimuli have been used in vigilance tasks, and the sensory modality of signals has indeed made a difference in performance efficiency. While the decrement function is present in all three modalities, its extent is usually different for different sensory systems. The decrement function has been less steep for acoustic vigilance tasks than for their tactile and visual analogs (Hawkes and Loeb, 1961; Sipowicz and Baker, 1961; Ware, 1961). In terms of the overall level of performance, the speed and accuracy of signal detections tend to be greater for auditory than for visual signals (Baker *et al.*, 1962; Buckner and McGrath, 1963; Colquhoun, 1975; Craig *et al.*, 1976; Jones and Kirk, 1970), and auditory signals are also detected more rapidly and more accurately than tactual signals (Hawkes and Loeb, 1961, 1962; Loeb and Hawkes, 1962). In addition, several studies have indicated that the correlations between monitoring performances in auditory and visual tasks are either low ($r < 0.30$) or nonsignificant (Buckner and McGrath, 1963; Pope and McKechnie, 1963; Gruber, 1964; Buckner *et al.*, 1966; Loeb and Binford, 1968).

Vigilance tasks can involve different sensory modalities, yet can present analogous information in each modality (e.g. increments or reductions in stimulus duration or intensity). Although a reasonable assumption could be that the sustained attention underlying performance on vigilance tasks is a general characteristic of the observer, controlled by similar laws of performance in all sensory modalities, the results just described imply that sustained attention in different modalities may be based on different central properties. This possibility would greatly complicate efforts to understand the mechanisms that underlie sustained attention. Consequently, there have been several attempts to evaluate these sensory differences, particularly for audio-visual performance, and to determine whether they are indeed inconsistent with the notion of a unitary 'factor' of sustained attention.

In a particularly cogent examination of this problem, Hatfield and Loeb (1968) suggested that poor audio-visual correlations in earlier vigilance studies may have resulted from confounding by differential 'coupling' (Elliott, 1960) inherent in these sensory modalities. Visual tasks, in which observers are typically free to make head and eye movements incompatible with observing the display, are 'loosely coupled', in that subjects are free to orient away from the display. Auditory tasks, on the other hand, are 'closely coupled', because observers on those tasks are usually linked to a source of stimulation either through headphones or through an enveloping sound field; their physical orientation does not determine their receptiveness for stimuli.

Hatfield and Loeb (1968) reasoned that audio-visual correlations in vigilance might be improved if a way could be found to couple observer more closely to the visual display. In order to test this notion, they devised a way to minimize the role of eye blinks and eye movements in a visual vigilance task by requiring observers to monitor changes in the illumination level of pulsed stimuli that were detectable when presented through closed eyelids. Eyelids were taped, and head and eye orientations were, thus, irrelevant for performance. Speed and accuracy of performance under these conditions exceeded that under conditions of free observing and closely approximated performance on an analogous auditory task, which also required the detection of increments in the intensity of pulsed stimuli. In addition, correlations between the auditory and the closely coupled visual task were $0.65 < r < 0.76$, values considerably higher than those found earlier.

Hatfield and Loeb (1968) raised another methodological issue in regard to earlier studies of audio-visual differences in vigilance. They pointed out that in these studies there was little effort to equate the difficulty of the discriminations in the auditory and visual tasks, and that disparities in task difficulty may have contributed to the low correlations in the earlier investigations. Hatfield and Loeb's suspicions have been confirmed by several experiments in which discrimination difficulty in auditory and visual monitoring tasks was equated either over groups of observers or for each observer individually. Under these conditions, intermodal correlations were more substantial than in earlier experiments: r values ranged from 0.65 to 0.80 (Gunn and Loeb, 1967; Hatfield and Soderquist, 1970; Loeb and Binford, 1971; Tyler *et al.*, 1972). It is worth noting that studies using relatively strong signals, in which acuity differences between modalities would not be a factor, have also reported substantial intermodal correlations (Sverko, 1968; Kennedy, 1971; Colquhoun, 1975).

We conclude that although modality-specific sensory factors are important, and perhaps distinct, for sustained attention, there is probably a common factor in sustained attention that transcends sensory modalities. Within limits, vigilant behavior is a general characteristic of the observer.

This conclusion is buttressed by two additional sources of evidence. First, vigilance experience in one sensory modality apparently transfers to subsequent vigilance performance in another modality (Gunn and Loeb, 1967; McFarland and Halcomb, 1970; Tyler *et al.*, 1972; Epps, 1973). Second, when required to monitor dual-mode displays with redundant signals (an analogous signal presented simultaneously to the auditory and visual channels), subjects tend to perform better than when they monitor single-mode displays (auditory or visual) under otherwise identical conditions (Buckner and McGrath, 1963; Osborn *et al.*, 1963; Gruber, 1964; Tyler *et al.*, 1972; Colquhoun, 1975). A careful study by Craig *et al.* (1976) indicates that the dual-mode superiority is based upon the integrative action of the auditory and visual systems and is not the result of a fortuitous combination of the independent actions of these systems.

Signal Conspicuity

A common finding in psychophysical experiments under alerted conditions is that the detectability of stimuli is positively related to the amplitude and duration of the signal. These factors are also important in the ability of observers to detect targets under conditions requiring sustained attention.

In general, the speed and accuracy of vigilance performance increases as the signal-to-noise ratio of critical signals increases. This effect is illustrated in a study by Loeb and Binford (1963) in which observers listened for occasional increments in the intensity of recurrent acoustic pulses. Normal pulses had an intensity of 60 dB above the subject's absolute threshold while critical signals were pulses of 2.1, 3.6 or 5.1 dB above this level.

As critical signal amplitude increased, signals became more 'detectable', but the important result is that the vigilance decrement was most pronounced at the lowest level of critical signal amplitude (Figure 2.1). Several studies have reported similar results with a detection probability measure (Adams, 1956; Wiener, 1964; Thurmond *et al.*, 1970; Guralnick, 1972; Tickner *et al.*, 1972; Metzger *et al.*, 1974), while others have shown that response latency for correct detections decreased with increments in critical signal amplitude (Adams, 1956; Hawkes and Loeb, 1962; Loeb and Schmidt, 1963; Lisper *et al.*, 1972).

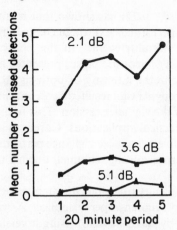

Figure 2.1 Effects of critical signal intensity on the detection of loudness increments in an auditory vigilance task. [Reproduced with permission from Loeb and Binford (1963).]

An important finding in regard to signal amplitude is that an 'adaptive measurement' procedure can eliminate the vigilance decrement, at least as far as detection probability is concerned. Adaptive measurement techniques are closed-loop control systems designed to adjust task difficulty automatically and continuously on the basis of some index of operator performance (Kelley, 1969). Wiener (1973) modified this technique for use in a vigilance task in which subjects monitored trains of brief flashes of horizontally separated dots for pairs of dots (signals) in which the horizontal separation was slightly greater than usual. Each subject's performance was followed continuously by a computer system, and the separation between the 'signal' dots was increased automatically whenever the detection rate fell below a level of about 70% over a block of signals. Under these conditions, the detection rate remained close to 70% throughout a 48-minute vigil, while a typical vigilance decrement was found in the absence of the adaptive procedure. This result is interesting for both theory and practice. Theoretically, it indicates that increments in signal amplitude may compensate for factors such as arousal or habituation, which have been nominated as critical elements in the vigilance decrement (cf. Frankmann and Adams, 1962; Mackworth, 1968). On a practical level, as Wiener (1973) has pointed out, the adaptive measurement approach might be used to attenuate the decrement function in operational settings in which a running check can be made on operator performance through the use of artificial signals.

In addition to the possibility of arresting the vigilance decrement through changes in critical signal amplitude, a recent study by Corcoran and his coworkers (Corcoran *et al.*, 1977) has shown that it is possible to *reverse* the usual course of vigilance performance through changes in the amplitude of both critical and non-critical stimulus events. In this study, subjects listened for increments in the duration of acoustic pulses presented at an intensity of 70 dB SPL. An abrupt increase in the intensity of both signal and non-signal pulses to 90 dB SPL midway through a vigil resulted in an *increment* in signal detections during the second half of the vigilance session. This finding, like that of Wiener (1964), has interesting practical implications. Corcoran and his colleagues have noted that it may be possible to enhance vigilance performance merely by turning up the gain over the transmitting channel during the late periods of a watchkeeping spell.

Increments in the conspicuity of signals through changes in duration can also enhance the efficiency of vigilance performance. A well known example of this effect was reported by Baker (1963b) using a version of the clock test in which a black 'second hand' swept continuously around the plain face of the clock. Critical signals were brief stops of the hand for 200, 300, 400, 600 or 800 milliseconds. Baker found that detection probability in this situation varied directly with signal (stoppage) duration and that the vigilance decrement was more pronounced with brief signals (200 ms) than with those of longer duration (600–800 ms). Similar results have also been reported by Adams (1956) and by Warm *et al.* (1970). In this last experiment, the effects of signal duration were studied over a rather broad range of intervals. As illustrated in Figure 2.2, detection probability increased as a negatively accelerated function of signal duration.

The work on signal conspicuity described thus far has focused upon the efficiency with which a single target can be detected in a sustained attention task. There are a few studies on the impact of conspicuity when an observer has to be alert for several kinds of signals during a vigil, the situation in many operational settings (Craig and Colquhoun, 1977). These studies examined have the effects of signal-mix upon vigilance performance. The central question has been whether a multiple signal condition changes the efficiency with which one of the signals is detected when considered separately.

Loeb and his coworkers compared the ability of observers to detect increments in the intensity of recurrent acoustic pulses under conditions in which the increment that constituted a critical signal was either a single value, or multiple values that bracketed the intensity increment of the unitary critical signal. Performance for the mid-value of critical signal intensity was essentially identical in the fixed- and mixed-intensity conditions (Hatfield and Loeb, 1968; Thurmond *et al.*, 1970). The quality of sustained attention for an auditory target of fixed intensity is apparently not influenced by the need to listen for other targets of different intensities.

On mixing auditory and visual signals, Binford and Loeb (1963) have studied the effects of easy-to-detect auditory signals of the efficiency with which

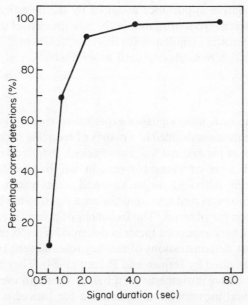

Figure 2.2   The percentage of signals detected in a vigilance task for several values of critical signal duration. [After Warm *et al.* (1970).]

observers could monitor relatively difficult visual signals. They found that the addition of a few of the auditory signals reduced performance efficiency on the visual task while the inclusion of many auditory signals produced the opposite effect.

Craig has developed a visual vigilance task comparing effects of variations on two dimensions of the critical signal. The non-signal stimuli in these experiments were circles with fixed diameter and a radius oriented at a fixed angle relative to the horizontal plane. One type of critical signal was a circle of identical diameter whose radius was set at a sharper angle than the standard. A second type of critical stimulus was a circle of larger diameter than the standard, with a radius set at an angle identical to the standard. Thus, in these studies, critical signals for detection were differentiated on the basis of radius angle or circle diameter. Craig found that the presence of one sort of critical signal degraded performance with the other but only if one of the critical signal types was more difficult to detect than the other and only if signal detection theory measures were used to index performance (Craig and Colquhoun, 1977; Craig, 1979b, 1981).

Loeb and Alluisi (1977) have suggested that the effects of signal-mix on vigilance performance are likely to be intricate. Among the important factors, they mention the difficulty of the discriminations required, the sensory modalities involved and the relative importance assigned by the investigator (or by the observer) to the different types of signals in the mix. In view of their importance for generalizing laboratory vigilance findings to 'real world' settings, these complex mixed-signal effects clearly need more analysis.

Event Rate

As indicated in Chapter 1, most vigilance experiments employ dynamic displays in which critical signals are embedded in a matrix of recurring neutral background events. For example, in the original Mackworth clock test, small movements of a pointer constituted a set of neutral events in which large 'double jumps' occasionally appeared. Although the background events may be neutral in that they usually require no overt response from the observer, they are far from neutral in their influence upon the observer. The frequency of neutral events or the *background event rate* is a very important factor in determining performance efficiency.

One of the earliest demonstrations of the key role of event rate in vigilance performance was provided by Jerison and Pickett (1964). They asked observers to attend to the repetitive movements of a bar of light. An event was defined as a sequence of dual movements in which the bar moved a predetermined distance to the right, snapped back to its start position, again moved the same distance, and returned to its point of origin, where it remained before the next dual movement or event took place. The critical signal for detection was an increment of 4 mm in the second deflection within an event. Two event rates were used: a slow rate of five events per minute and faster rate of 30 events per minute. Equal numbers of critical signals were presented at each event rate. The results of this study are shown in Figure 2.3.

Notice that the percentage of signals correctly detected was considerably higher at the slow than at the fast event rate. In addition, there was a vigilance decrement only for the fast event rate. A substantial number of other investigators have confirmed the finding that the quality of sustained attention is inversely related to the rate of presentation of neutral events (cf. Jerison *et al.*, 1965; Mackworth, 1965b; Johnston *et al.*, 1966; Jerison, 1967a; Guralnick, 1973; Parasuraman and Davies, 1976; Parasuraman, 1979).

The effects of event rate seem paradoxical in two ways. First, they imply that the more one is required to look or to listen for critical signals, the less likely one is to detect such signals. Second, as Jerison and Pickett (1964) have noted, they imply that the detection of a signal in a vigilance task is determined by what is going on when no signal is presented. The paradoxes might be resolved in a simple way by a closer look at the Jerison and Pickett experiment.

In describing the Jerison and Pickett study, we were careful to point out that equal numbers of critical signals were presented in the fast and slow event rate conditions. Such an arrangement, which has often been used in studies on the effects of event rate, confounds the probability of critical signals (the ratio of

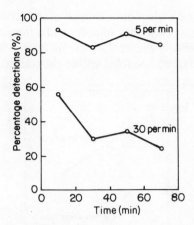

Figure 2.3 Effect of event rate on the detection of critical signals during an 80-minute vigil. Events to be judged as signal or non-signal were repeated at the rate of either five or 30 per minute. Critical signal frequency was constant at 15 per hour. [Reproduced with permission from Jerison and Pickett, *Science*, **143**, 970–971. Copyright 1964 by the AAAS.]

critical signals to neutral events) and event rate. The probability of a critical signal is higher under a slow compared to a fast event rate. Thus, the effects of event rate might simply reflect differences in the likelihood that any stimulus event is a critical signal. Indeed, an early study by Colquhoun (1961) indicated that this might be the case. Colquhoun varied the number of critical signals so that the probability of signals was arranged factorially within slow and fast event rates. In this way, he was able to examine the conjoint effects of event rate and signal probability. Colquhoun found that most of the variance in performance could be attributed to differences in critical signal probability and that when such probability was held constant within event rates, the event rate factor alone had no effect upon signal detections. Later studies, however, did not uphold his findings. These studies have shown that detection probability varies inversely with event rate even when the probability of critical signals is equated within event rates (Jerison, 1965, 1967a, 1970; Loeb and Binford, 1968; Taub and Osborne, 1968; Parasuraman, 1979). Evidently, the effects of event rate transcend factors in the simple probability of signals.

It is important to note that the background event rate not only influences sustained attention in its own right; it also modifies the effects of other stimulus parameters. For example, Metzger *et al.* (1974) have shown that event rate interacts with critical signal amplitude. Using a light bar display similar to that employed by Jerison and Pickett (1964), these investigators compared the effects of incremental excursions of 2 mm (low amplitude) and 8 mm (high amplitude) in the length of the second deflection within an event. Critical signals occurred in the context of a slow (six events per minute) and a fast (21 events per minute) event rate. As can be seen in Figure 2.4, the difference in detection rate for the 2 mm and 8 mm signals was doubled within the context of a fast event rate.

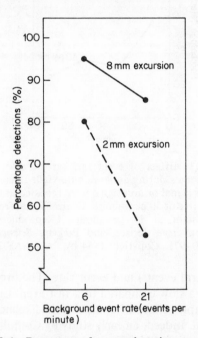

Figure 2.4   Percentage of correct detections as a function of background event rate for two levels of critical signal amplitude in a Jerison moving-light display. Amplitude is expressed in millimeters of incremental excursion. [Reprinted with permission of publisher from Metzger, K. R., Warm, J. S., and Sentor, R. J. Effects of background event rate and critical signal amplitude on vigilance performance. *Perceptual and Motor Skills*, 1974, **38**, 1175–1181, Figure 2.]

The role of accessory stimulation is another vigilance dimension that is modified by variation in background event rate. In most laboratory vigilance tasks, subjects work in a barren and monotonous environment; they are usually tested individually in an isolated chamber in which ambient temperature, lighting and noise levels are held as constant as possible. Increased sensory input in the form of mild exercise or extraneous stimulation to this situation usually makes performance more efficient (Kirk and Hecht, 1963; Zuercher, 1965; Randel, 1968; Davenport, 1974; Tolin and Fisher, 1974). McGrath (1963), however, has demonstrated that added stimulation can degrade as well as enhance performance efficiency, depending upon the background event rate in which critical signals are embedded. McGrath asked subjects to perform a visual monitoring task requiring the detection of slight increments in the brightness of pulses of light. He found that with 20 events per minute, the vigilance decrement was attenuated when subjects were exposed to accessory auditory stimulation in the form of recorded vocal music, mechanical noise and traffic noise. When the event rate was increased to 60 events per minute, however, the vigilance decrement was exacerbated by the accessory auditory stimulation. Results such as these, along with other findings in which event rate modified the effects of important psychophysical parameters (see the section on temporal uncertainty), have confirmed a suspicion articulated by J. F. Mackworth several years ago (Mackworth, 1968, 1969)—background event rate is probably the prepotent psychophysical factor in the maintenance of sustained attention.

In view of its importance, several attempts have been made to specify the mechanisms responsible for the effects of event rate. Mackworth (1968, 1969) has offered an explanation on the basis of habituation, the waning of neural responsiveness as a result of repetitive stimulation. Habituation is differentiated from adaptation or fatigue by the phenomenon of dishabituation, or the sudden reappearance of responsiveness following qualitative or quantitative changes in the pattern of stimulation. In general, the degree of neural responsiveness in a given situation is directly related to the frequency of stimulus presentation (Sharpless and Jasper, 1956; Groves and Thompson, 1970). Mackworth proposed that the repetitive stimulation of neutral background events in sustained attention tasks habituates cortical responses to the stimuli being monitored. Because of the frequency of repetition, habituation accumulates more rapidly at a fast than at a slow event rate, resulting in poorer performance in the context of the fast event rate.

Although based upon a neurophysiological concept, the habituation model lends itself readily to experimental test using psychophysical measures. In one such test, Krulewitz *et al.* (1975) shifted event rates in a high-to-low or a low-to-high direction during a vigilance session. According to the habituation model, any change in stimulus conditions should produce dishabituation and, therefore, improve performance. Shifts in event rate represent rather drastic changes in the pattern of stimulation. Therefore, the habituation model leads to the expectation that any shift in event rate should result in improved performance regardless of the direction of the shift. The results of the study are displayed in Figure 2.5.

Contrary to expectations based upon the habituation model, performance efficiency depended precisely upon the direction of the shift in event rates. The subjects who were shifted in the fast-to-slow direction did exceed the performance of the non-shifted controls under the slow event rate, but the subjects shifted in the slow-to-fast direction eventually performed more poorly than the non-shifted controls under the fast event rate. Further, enhancement in the performance of the subjects shifted in the fast-to-slow direction did not occur until after the shifted group had experienced the new event rate for 20 minutes.

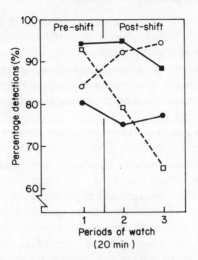

Figure 2.5   The effects of shifts in background event rate during a vigilance task on the detectability of critical signals. Data for pre-shift and post-shift phases are plotted separately in each panel. The shift groups are indicated by open figures and dashed lines (i.e. □———□ , slow-fast; o———o, fast-slow) and the non-shift control groups by filled figures and solid lines (i.e. ■———■ , slow-slow; •———•, fast-fast). [After Krulewitz *et al.* (1975).]

Such a result does not conform to the expected time course of habituation and dishabituation since habituated neural responses tend to dishabituate promptly after a change in stimulus conditions and then rehabituate with continued exposure to the new pattern of stimulation (Cotman and McGaugh, 1980).

Another property of habituation discussed by Mackworth (1968, 1969) is arrested development of habituation when stimuli are presented irregularly. The habituation model, therefore, leads to the expectation that overall performance might be enhanced and the effects of event rate attenuated if critical signals are embedded in a temporally irregular matrix of neutral events instead of the temporally regular matrix that is typically used in vigilance studies. This is contrary to results in Jerison (1965, 1967a), confirmed by Richter *et al.* (1981) and Warm *et al.* (1984), in which an irregular event schedule failed to attenuate the effects of event rate and suppressed rather than enhanced signal detections.

The effects of event rate can also be described from a more cognitive point of view. Jerison (1970) argued that a fast event rate may increase the demands placed upon a subject in a vigilance task by increasing the rate at which the subject must emit observing responses or 'unitary attentive acts' toward the stimuli to be monitored. The point is that there is a cost to observing as well as a benefit for a correct detection of a signal. When it is hard to observe there is also a greater likelihood that observations will be inappropriate—blurred or even misdirected.

A position of this sort, which emphasizes inappropriate observing as the root of the event rate effect, is related to the previous discussion of the role of 'coupling'. Warm *et al.* (1976b) demonstrated that the event rate effect can be attenuated by closely coupling observers to a visual display. In this study, a head restraint was used to restrict subjects' gross head movements while they monitored a Jerison and Pickett light bar display under either fast (21 events per minute) or slow (six events per minute) rates of stimulus presentation. As Figure 2.6 reveals, the effects of a fast event rate were reduced considerably under conditions of restrained as compared to non-restrained viewing.

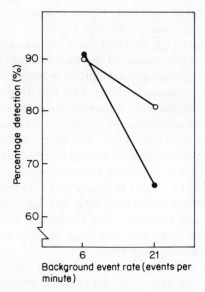

Figure 2.6   The influence of head restraint on the effects of event rate in a Jerison moving-light display. The percentage of correct detections is plotted as a function of event rate under non-restrained (●———●) and restrained (o———o) viewing conditions. [After Warm *et al.* (1976b).]

The elicited observing rate position does not provide a complete account of the effects of event rate on vigilance performance, at least partly because 'observing' is not fully defined. In the experiment carried out by Warm *et al.* (1976), the effects of event rate were attenuated but not eliminated under close coupling conditions. Does this mean that close coupling makes 'observing' easier (less costly)? Intuitively, we would say that it does, but there is no formal statement of that intuition in the Jerison thesis. Similarly, there are studies using eye-movement recordings, in which subjects are known to miss signals in a vigilance task even when the target is visually fixated (Baker, 1960; Mackworth *et al.*, 1964). This 'looking without seeing' is another instance of poorly understood 'observing'. Finally, auditory vigilance tasks, which are more closely coupled than visual tasks, also show strong event rate effects (Loeb and Binford, 1968; Parasuraman, 1979; Richter *et al.*, 1981). Observing responses here may be defined only by neural events in the auditory system.

The most recent attempt to explain the effects of event rate has been made by Posner (1978). He suggested a two-factor model involving general alertness and pathway inhibition. According to this model, fast and slow event rates produce essentially different vigilance tasks, and the vigilance decrement is due to different mechanisms in each task. Under a slow event rate, the decrement comes about from understimulation and a general reduction in arousal or alertness. Fast event rates, on the other hand, do not reduce general alertness because of the high rate of stimulation involved. Instead, the decrement at fast event rates results from accumulated inhibition in the specific pathway carrying information from the monitored display. This line of reasoning led Posner to predict that if probe stimuli were delivered to a different channel from that monitored during a vigilance task, the probes would be detected more readily under a fast than under a slow event rate. To test this notion, Posner and Ogden (Posner, 1978) set up a visual monitoring task in which observers pressed a key whenever a particular letter appeared. Other letters were neutral events. The event rate was either fast (30 events per minute) or slow (five events per minute), and superimposed upon this primary task was a secondary task, in which observers had to detect an auditory probe. Consistent with Posner's reasoning, response times to probe detections were more rapid in the context of a fast as compared to a slow primary task event rate.

Posner and Ogden's findings are unique. They are the sole experimental demonstration that a fast event rate can facilitate performance in a vigilance task in any way. Unfortunately, they have not been confirmed in a subsequent investigation by Bowers (1982). This study was modeled after Posner and Ogden's original experimental design. However, the targets for detection were increments in the length of a repetitively presented line rather than the 'cognitive' stimuli used by Posner and Ogden. Under these conditions, the overall response time to probe detections was faster in the context of a slow as compared to a fast primary task event rate. Such a result is not consistent with a general decline in alertness which Posner suggests is the basis of the vigilance decrement under the slow event rate.

An important methodological feature of Bowers' study was the use of visual as well as auditory probes. He found that response times to the auditory probe were faster than those to the visual probes and that, with regard to the latter, response times to probe detections were faster for probes that differed from neutral events in the primary task than for those that were identical to such events. In sum, as the probe becomes more distinct from the background stimuli of the primary task, the latency for detecting the probe is shorter. Bowers noted that an assumption inherent in Posner's concept of pathway inhibition is that such inhibition is specific to the repeated stimuli. Bowers' findings are consistent with an assumption of stimulus specificity. Consequently, he suggests that the concept of pathway inhibition, alone, may be able to account for the effects of event rate. The greater the rate of stimulus repetition, the greater the build-up of this sort of inhibition and the poorer the efficiency of the monitor's performance.

Second-order factors

In a thoughtful examination of the nature of monitoring tasks, Alluisi (1966) drew a parallel between the position of subjects in vigilance experiments and that of lookouts in the days of sailing vessels. Once in the crow's nest, the lookouts were responsible for sensing anything atypical in their operating environment. Often, they did not know what the atypical event would be or when or where it would occur. Thus, they were faced with several sources of uncertainty in performing their duties. Subjects in vigilance experiments must also detect atypical events in their operating environment. They usually know what the critical signals will be, but they do not know when such signals will appear (temporal uncertainty) and, in some experiments, where they will appear (spatial uncertainty). Subjects come to appreciate these signal characteristics through their experience with the task at hand and modify their behavior accordingly.

Dember and Warm (1979) designated temporal and spatial uncertainty as the major second-order psychophysical factors in vigilance, to emphasize their source as derived from the context of the situation. Subjects must infer these characteristics from task experience. The second-order factors are not less important than those which involve an immediate physical property of the stimulus.

Temporal Uncertainty

One means of experimentally manipulating an observer's temporal uncertainty is through variations in the density or the number of critical signals. The more frequently such signals occur in a fixed time period, the greater the *a priori* signal probability and the less the observer's average uncertainty about when a critical signal will occur. The overall likelihood of detection is markedly affected by the density of critical signals. Many studies have demonstrated that the likelihood of detection varies directly as a function of signal density

(Mackworth, 1950; Deese and Ormond, 1953, Nicely and Miller, 1957; Jenkins, 1958; Kappauf and Powe, 1959; Jerison, 1959; 1967a; Ellis and Ahr, 1960; Wiener, 1963; Martz, 1967; Williges, 1971; Murrell, 1975). This effect is illustrated in Figure 2.7. Note how the percentage of signal detections increases with increments in critical signal density over a broad range of values.

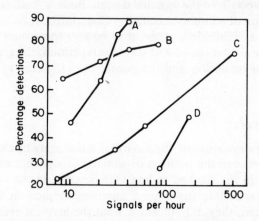

Figure 2.7   Percentage of signals detected as a function of log critical signal frequency in several vigilance experiments. Curve A, Deese and Ormond (1953); curve B, Kappauf and Powe (1959); curve C, Jenkins (1958); curve D, Jerison (1959). The log scale is used for convenience in graphing and has no special theoretical significance. [From *Human Factors*, 1963, **5**, 211–238. Copyright 1963 by the Human Factors Society, Inc., and reproduced by permission.]

The probability of critical signals also has an influence upon the latency with which signals are detected. In general, response time to signal detections varies inversely with signal probability (Martz, 1967; Warm *et al.*, 1976a). Alluisi and his coworkers (Smith *et al.*, 1966; Warm and Alluisi, 1971) were able to describe the speed of signal processing in vigilance with a model from information theory, a mathematical approach that can describe the effects of stimulus probability on a wide variety of perceptual functions (cf. Dember and Warm, 1979). Alluisi's group derived an uncertainty metric, the signal *surprisal* due to density, as a measure of temporal uncertainty determined by density. The surprisal due to density may be expressed as

$$h = -\log_2 P \text{ (signal)}, \tag{2.1}$$

where h is the information, in bits, associated with the signal's occurrence at a specific time and the probability of occurrence of a signal, P (signal), is

$$P \text{ (signal)} = D/D_{\max} \tag{2.2}$$

D is the signal density or actual number of signals per hour and D_{max} is the maximum possible number of signals per hour.

The experiment by Warm and Alluisi (1971) illustrates the approach. Subjects were required to detect increments in the duration of recurrent acoustic or visual pulses during a 1-hour vigil. Neutral events were pulses of 0.5 s duration presented once every 2.0 s, and the critical signals were 1.0 s pulses that occasionally replaced these events. A total of 6, 12, 24, 48 or 96 critical signals were presented. Since stimuli were presented every 2.0 s, the maximum number of critical signals that could have been presented during the hour, D_{max}, was 1800. With signal densities of 6, 12, 24, 48 and 96 signals per hour, the associated probabilities (P values) were 6/1800, 12/1800, 24/1800, 48/1800 and 96/1800, and the surprisals due to density (h values) were 8.23, 7.23, 6.23, 5.23 and 4.23 bits, respectively.

The results were straightforward. Response times for correct detections of both auditory and visual signals increased as a linear function of the temporal uncertainty due to density. The combined results for the auditory and visual signals are shown in Figure 2.8.

An identical result was found in the other study in this series (Smith *et al.*, 1966) using an alternating 'blinking lights' display in which observers were required to detect arrests in the alternation of the lights. On the basis of these findings, Alluisi and his coworkers concluded that an important quantitative

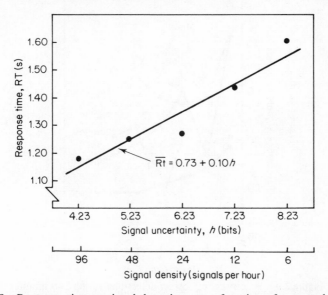

Figure 2.8 Response time to signal detections as a function of temporal uncertainty due to signal density. Signal density values are given for reference. [From Warm and Alluisi (1971). Copyright (1971) by the American Psychological Association. Reprinted by permission.]

generalization about the speed of performance in other perceptual tasks may also be applicable to vigilance tasks. This generalization is Hicks' law, which states that the rate of processing of a signal is a positive linear function of stimulus uncertainty (cf. Dember and Warm, 1979).

The effects of signal probability perseverate. This dramatic effect was first described by Colquhoun and Baddeley (1964) who used either a low ($P = 0.02$) or a high ($P = 0.18$) level of signal probability during training in a vigilance study and then tested their subjects either under the same probability level or under the alternative probability. The results, shown in Figure 2.9, indicated that subjects who practised at the high signal probability performed better during testing than those who practised with the low level of signal probability. Whatever was established during the practice period continued to determine performance during the later vigilance session.

It is natural to think of this as showing a persisting effect of expectancies. These findings have since been replicated by Colquhoun and Baddeley (1967) and by McFarland and Halcomb (1970). In addition to their theoretical significance, they have important practical and methodological implications. As Colquhoun and Baddeley (1964) note, they indicate that care should be taken during the training that usually precedes testing in most vigilance experiments to insure that the levels of signal probability that subjects experience are

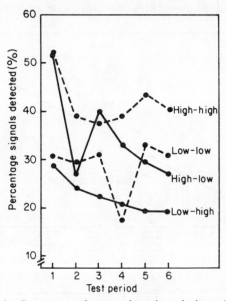

Figure 2.9   Percentage of correct detections during a 40-minute vigilance test for different conditions of critical signal probability during training and test. [From Colquhoun and Baddeley (1964). Copyright (1964) by the American Psychological Association. Reprinted by permission.]

comparable to those that will be experienced during the test itself. Otherwise, performance during the test could be based upon spurious expectancies on the part of subjects about the temporal uncertainty of signals.

Although the general effects of signal probability (Figures 2.7 and 2.8) may appear to be rather straightforward, a number of carefully executed experiments have found negligible effects (Davies and Hockey, 1966; Stern, 1966; Craig, 1981). The reasons are not clear. Davies and Tune (1969) have suggested that signal probability effects may be dependent upon the range of probabilities used in a given experiment. Warm and Alluisi (1971) have noted that probability or density effects were absent in an experiment which employed a range of densities identical to their own but which also used a display in which critical signals were not embedded in a matrix of neutral events—all stimulus events were critical signals for detection (Warm *et al.*, 1970).

Another possibility is that signal probability interacts with event rate. The residual effects of experience with one level of critical signal probability during training on subsequent performance during testing tends to show up only under a fast event rate. These effects do not appear when the experiment is conducted under a slow event rate (Krulewitz and Warm, 1977).

To add to the complexity of signal probability effects, Davies and Tune (1969) have reported several studies which found that performance was superior in low density compared to high density conditions. According to Davies and Tune, this may have been related to the poor discriminability of the signals. These results have not been integrated into the emerging picture of factors that determine vigilance performance.

In addition to variations in the number of critical signals, the observer's temporal uncertainty in a vigilance experiment can also be manipulated through variations in time between critical signals. These intervals can be made perfectly regular and easily predictable or quite irregular and unpredictable. For example, a regular schedule of intervals might be one in which critical signals appear at exactly 1-minute intervals. In an irregular schedule, intersignal intervals might average 1 minute but they might vary from 0.5 to 5 minutes. Both the speed and the accuracy of signal detections have usually been found to be directly related to signal regularity (McCormack and Prysiazniuk, 1961; Dardano, 1962; Baker, 1963a; Adams and Boulter, 1964; McCormack, 1967; Lisper and Törnros, 1974; Warm *et al.*, 1974).

Manipulations of signal regularity do not always produce consistent results, with negligible effects in some cases (Boulter and Adams, 1963; Warm *et al.*, 1980). In a factorial study, signal regularity was found to be much less important than signal density (Smith *et al.*, 1966). The 'slippery' nature of the regularity parameter should not be too surprising. In order to take advantage of a temporally regular schedule of signals, one needs to be able to make accurate judgments of time. Human observers are not very precise estimators of time, especially with durations of 30 s or more (cf. Warm *et al.*, 1975), and these longer durations are the ones used for intersignal intervals in most vigilance experiments.

It is also important to note that the effects of signal regularity, like those of signal density, are closely tied to the background event matrix in which critical signals are embedded. Moore and Gross (1973) have reported that under a fast event rate (30 events per minute) the effects of signal regularity were maximal during the first 30 minutes of a vigilance session and became negligible thereafter. The opposite result was observed under a slow event rate (five events per minute). It is evident that a comprehensive psychophysical account of the effects of temporal uncertainty on vigilance performance will need to include a consideration of the matrix of stimulus events in which critical signals appear.

Spatial Uncertainty

Spatial uncertainty in a vigilance task involves visual search for signals that can appear in different positions in the monitored visual display. In a representative experiment, Nicely and Miller (1957) used a simulated radar scope in which targets were much more probable in one quadrant of the display than in the others. They found that observers learned to bias their attention within the display and detected a higher proportion of signals in the portion of the display in which the likelihood of signal appearances was greatest. Similar results have been described in other experiments (Baker, 1958; Adams and Boulter, 1964; Bell *et al.*, 1974; Milosević, 1974).

Kulp and Alluisi (1967) have related the effects of spatial uncertainty to those of temporal uncertainty by showing that Hick's law in vigilance tasks is applicable when the source of stimulus uncertainty is the spatial location of critical signals. The question of whether the effects of spatial uncertainty also parallel those of temporal uncertainty in terms of sensitivity to the background event rate in which critical signals are embedded remains to be investigated.

SENSING AND DECISION MAKING

Thus far, our discussion of the psychophysics of vigilance has focused upon the signal and non-signal stimuli. A psychophysical analysis is also concerned with the responses made by the observer that reflect judgments about the stimulus. An observer may be confident or uncertain in reporting that a critical signal had been presented. The judgments underlying the reports are based on information about the stimuli and decisions on how to use the information; the observer is both a sensor and a decision maker. The theory of signal detectability (TSD) is concerned with these aspects of performance (Tanner and Swets, 1954; Green and Swets, 1974), and is a major theory for the general study of psychophysics. Efforts to apply its concepts and procedures to vigilance experiments represent an important aspect of the psychophysics of vigilance.

Signal detection theory (TSD): a model

Signals always occur against a background of 'noise' which emanates from several possible sources. These sources include spontaneous firing in the nervous system and changes inherent in the environment or in the equipment used for generating stimuli. According to the model as applied in most studies of vigilance, the sensory effects produced by signals are added to noise, which varies randomly from moment to moment. Noise is usually represented as a normal distribution with unit variance. The addition of a signal to the noise background is assumed to shift the average level of excitation upward in proportion to the magnitude of the signal, without changing the shape of the distribution of sensory effects. Thus, the theory postulates two distributions of sensory effects, which are normally distributed with equal variance — noise alone (N) and signal plus noise (SN). The model in its simplest form is displayed in Figure 2.10.

A detection situation can then be conceptualized as one in which the observer makes an observation during a fixed interval of time and reports his or her judgment whether the experience during the interval was an instance drawn from the distribution of noise alone (N) or signal plus noise (SN). The observer may

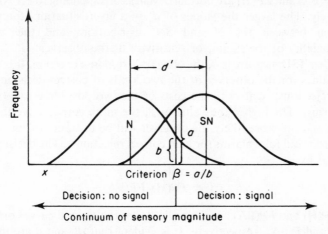

Figure 2.10 Hypothetical distributions of sensory events assumed by signal-detection theory. The magnitude of sensory excitations, x, from weak to strong, is arrayed from left to right along the horizontal axis, while the relative frequency of these excitations is represented along the vertical axis. An observation samples an excitation, x_i, and the observer must decide whether x_i is from distribution N or distribution SN. The decision is based on whether $x_i > \beta$ or $x_i < \beta$. The distribution of effects for noise alone and for signal plus noise are the two normal probability distributions N and SN. Note that the presence of a signal actually shifts the N distribution to the right, transforming it into the SN distribution, but leaves the shape of the distribution unchanged. The indices d' and β represent signal-detection parameters of sensitivity and response bias, respectively.

be pictured as going through the following steps: During the observation interval, the observer assesses the probability that a particular level of excitation x_i was an instance of noise (N) and the probability that it was an instance of signal plus noise (SN). The observer then computes a likelihood ratio, λx, which expresses the odds that the observation arose from SN relative to N alone, i.e., $\lambda x = P(\text{SN})/P(\text{N})$. The observer maintains a decision criterion, β, and if λx equals or exceeds β a response, 'signal', is made. If λx falls below this value, the response is, 'no signal'. This is the complete model of the observer's report, as illustrated in Figure 2.10.

It follows that the observer's responses should be in four categories: correct detections (hits), correct rejections, incorrect 'detections' (false alarms) and incorrect rejections (misses). Using the conditional probabilities of hits, $P(\text{H})$, and false alarms, $P(\text{FA})$, obtained in an experiment, two measures of performance are derived. One of these, d', specifies the distance between signal and noise, and is expressed in terms of their standard deviations. In vigilance applications, it is customary to index discriminability by

$$d' = ZP(\text{FA}) - ZP(\text{H}), \tag{2.3}$$

where $ZP(\text{FA})$ and $ZP(\text{H})$ are normal deviates corresponding to $P(\text{FA})$ and $P(\text{H})$, respectively. The larger the values of d' in a given situation, the greater the separation between the N and SN distributions and the greater the discriminability of the signal, or sensitivity of the observer.

The other TSD measure is β, the observer's response criterion. It is determined by the values for the observer of the two kinds of correct decisions (hits and correct rejections) relative to the costs of the two possible errors (misses and false alarms). The higher the value of β, the more conservative the response criterion and the more likely the observer will be to trade off hits (or misses) in order to avoid false alarms (or gain correct rejections). The decision criterion is indexed by

$$\beta = FP(\text{H})/FP(\text{FA}), \tag{2.4}$$

where $FP(\text{H})$ and $FP(\text{FA})$ are the ordinates of the normal curve corresponding to $P(\text{H})$ and $P(\text{FA})$, respectively. It is evident that d' and β are independent elements that determine the actual reports (responses) of the observer, according to the theory.

The distributions of N and SN do not have to be Gaussian, or even similar in shape, according to the theory. These two conditions make computations much easier, however, and are often assumed for this reason. They are unlikely to be fulfilled in most vigilance situations (Jerison, 1977).

Data from experiments using TSD concepts are frequently displayed in terms of receiver operating characteristic (ROC) curves, in which $P(\text{H})$ is plotted against $P(\text{FA})$. Such a curve is illustrated in Figure 2.11.

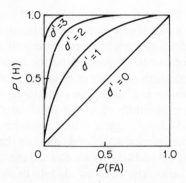

Figure 2.11   Receiver operating characteristic (ROC) curves
for several levels of d'. Based on the assumption that the
distributions of N and SN are normal and of equal variance.
The diagonal line ($d' = 0$) reflects chance performance when
the N and SN distributions are identical.

The ROC curve traces the relation between the conditional probabilities of
hits and false alarms for a fixed degree of detectability (d') as the criterion (β)
is shifted in a conservative to lenient direction. The diagonal line in the figure
represents chance performance ($d' = 0$). When detectability increases, the ROC
curve forms a set of arcs which are displaced further and further from the chance
diagonal. Shifts in response criteria β at a given d' are represented as the various
points on the ROC curve for which that d' is the parameter. Movement in a
left-to-right direction along the curve, reflects shifts from a conservative to a
more lenient response criterion.

More complete treatments of TSD along with empirical support for its
assumptions can be found in Broadbent (1971), Green and Swets (1974),
Gescheider (1976), Baird and Noma (1978) and Dember and Warm (1979).

Applications to vigilance

The possibility that TSD concepts could be applied in a fruitful way to vigilance
experiments was pointed out by Egan *et al.* (1961). They noted that false alarms
as well as correct detections tend to decline over time in vigilance situations.
This led them to suggest that the decrement function could imply a shift to a
more conservative response criterion rather than a decline in the observer's
alertness or sensitivity during a vigil. Their suggestion was supported in
experiments by Broadbent and Gregory (1963, 1965) who reported that the
computed sensitivity index, d', remained stable during a vigil while the response
criterion, β, increased progressively over time. This kind of result has since been
reported by many other investigators (Loeb and Binford, 1964; Jerison *et al.*,
1965; Loeb *et al.*, 1965; Levine, 1966, Colquhoun, 1967; Davenport, 1968, 1969;
McCann, 1969; Colquhoun and Edwards, 1970; Thurmond *et al.*, 1970;
Milosević, 1975; Murrell, 1975).

What might account for the result? Williges (1969) tried to explain it in terms of the TSD concept of an ideal observer — an optimum detector that yields the best possible performance under specified conditions. If one assumes a situation in which the rewards for correct responses and the costs of incorrect responses are symmetrical, the optimum response criterion, β_i, for an observer who tries to maximize expected values is given by the equation $\beta_i = P(N)/P(SN)$, where, as before, $P(N)$ is the probability of a non-signal or noise and $P(SN)$ is the probability of a signal. Williges suggested that at the outset of a vigil, observers begin with β set at some intermediate level, and, as the vigil progresses, they adjust the value of their response criterion toward that of the optimum value, β_i. In most vigilance tasks, the ratio of signals to non-signals is quite low (usually $P(SN) < 0.5$). Williges noted that, in such cases, the value of β_i would be considerably larger than 1.0, and if the observer regarded signals and non-signals as equally likely at the outset of the vigil, the ideal observer hypothesis would predict a rise in β as the vigil continued. Conversely, if the ratio of signals to non-signals is greater than 1.0, the value of β_i would be considerably less than 1.0 and the ideal observer hypothesis would predict a decline in β over time.

To test these possibilities, Williges performed an experiment in which observers were asked to detect periodic reductions in the illumination of a visual target under conditions in which the signal to non-signal ratio was 1:5 or 5:1. Perceptual sensitivity as indexed by d' remained constant throughout the experiment, but the response criterion, β, varied over time. Consistent with the ideal observer hypothesis, β increased over time when non-signals outnumbered signals and decreased over time when signals were more numerous than non-signals. Williges replicated these results in a second experiment (Williges, 1973). On the basis of these findings, he suggested that the vigilance decrement may be viewed from a new perspective; instead of reflecting a decline in performance efficiency over time, it may reflect a tendency toward more optimum decision behavior. It should be noted that signal rates were unusually high in both conditions, much higher than in typical vigilance studies.

Williges' interpretation of the decrement function has not been supported by later research. Recently, Vickers *et al.* (1977) tested the implications of the ideal observer hypothesis by using a ramp technique in which a vigilance session began with a signal probability of 0.5, and this probability gradually declined as the session progressed. Such a procedure should result in a progressive increment in the optimal value of β_i. Consequently, if observers adjust the criterion toward an optimal level as the ideal observer hypothesis maintains, the observers in this experiment would be expected to become more conservative as signal probability declined (β should increase). Contrary to expectation, they showed a strong tendency to become less conservative (β decreased) as signal probability declined during the session. Clearly, observers do not always adopt a value for β that moves toward the optimal value, β_i.

In the experiments just considered, TSD indices permitted the inference that the vigilance decrement is non-perceptual. Other data are available that indicate that under some circumstances, the vigilance decrement is accompanied by a decline in perceptual sensitivity or d'. The initial report of a drop in d' with time on task was by Mackworth and Taylor (1963) who used the continuous clock display described by Baker (1963b) (see p.20 above). Mackworth replicated this finding in later studies using the same and a different display (Mackworth, 1965a,b, 1968), and it has been reported by other investigators as well (Hatfield and Loeb, 1968; Loeb and Binford, 1968; Hatfield and Soderquist, 1969; Deaton *et al.*, 1971; Benedetti and Loeb, 1972; Guralnick, 1972; Parasuraman and Davies, 1976; Parasuraman, 1979). The decrement function appears to involve a decline in d' in tasks in which there is the need for a high rate of observing. We shall examine this issue further in our discussion of task taxonomies.

In addition to the decrement function, TSD measures have also been used to study the effects on performance of major psychophysical parameters such as signal probability and event rate. Baddeley and Colquhoun (1969) sought to determine whether signal probability affects the criterion β as opposed to the observer's ability to discriminate signals from non-signals, indexed by d'. In this study, monitors were required to inspect repetitively presented rows of six small disks and to report whenever a row appeared in which one of the disks was larger than the others. Separate groups of observers were tested at five levels of signal probability: 0.02, 0.06, 0.18, 0.24 and 0.36. The percentage of correct detections varied directly with signal probability, as would be expected. This increase in correct detections was accompanied by a rise in the false alarm rate, and an analysis in terms of TSD revealed that β declined as signal probability increased, while d' remained invariant.

The data provided by Baddeley and Colquhoun (1969) were re-examined by Swets (1977) using an ideal observer approach. He found that the subjects tended to shy away from the extreme values represented by the optimal criteria (β_i) but that there was a perfect rank-order correlation in the data between the empirical values and the optimal values of the response criterion. Swets pointed out that a result of this sort is consistent with the outcome of psychophysical studies performed under alerted conditions in which signal probability is varied.

Baddeley and Colquhoun's (1969) findings have been confirmed by Parasuraman and Davies (1976), who extended a TSD analysis to response latency data in vigilance. Starting from the TSD assumption that the observer's decision about the presence or absence of a signal depends on the value of the likelihood ratio relative to the response criterion, they pointed out that the closer the likelihood ratio is to the criterion, the 'weaker' the evidence the observer would have on which to base a decision. If the time taken to respond is inversely related to the 'strength' of the evidence, 'weaker' evidence should produce longer response times. If d' remains constant, this approach leads to some straightforward predictions in regard to the relation between the response criterion and response latency. Shifts in the criterion in a conservative to risky direction (declines in β) should result in declines in the latencies of 'yes' responses (hits and false alarms) since, on the average, such responses would be distributed further from criterion than before. By contrast, latencies for 'no' responses (correct rejections and misses) should increase since, on the average, these responses would be distributed nearer the response criterion than before.

Parasuraman and Davies (1976) asked their observers to monitor repetitive flashes of light for occasional dimmer flashes. The observers were required to respond as rapidly as possible to any event by pressing either a 'yes' ('signal') or a 'no' ('non-signal') button and they were tested under conditions of either high or low signal probability. In terms of hits and false alarms, an increment in signal probability led to a relaxed response criterion but did not influence d'. Consistent with this outcome and with Parasuraman and Davies' extension of the signal detection model, response times to 'yes' responses (hits and false alarms) declined with increments in signal probability whereas the opposite results occurred for 'no' responses (correct rejections and misses); response times increased with increasing signal probability.

While TSD analyses indicate clearly that signal probability influences decision processes rather than perceptual sensitivity, as these are defined in TSD, the story with respect to event rate is currently equivocal. Some evidence points to the possibility that poorer performance at fast relative to slow event rates results from a lowered ability to discriminate signals from noise at a fast event rate (Guralnick, 1973). On the other hand, evidence is also available to suggest that fast event rates induce the observer to set a more stringent response criterion than slow event rates (Jerison *et al.*, 1965; Taub and Osborne, 1968), and some studies have reported that increments in event rate are associated with both a decline in d' and an elevation in β (Loeb and Binford, 1968; Parasuraman and Davies, 1976). Resolution of these conflicting results remains an important task for the future.

Critique of TSD applications

The theory of signal detection has had considerable impact upon the study of vigilance, as it has upon many other areas of psychological research. Nevertheless, it is important to emphasize that serious difficulties can result from the uncritical acceptance of an extension of the model from its origins in psychophysical detection under alerted conditions to the vigilance situation (Broadbent, 1971; Craig and Colquhoun, 1975; Wiener, 1975).

Vigilance experiments differ considerably from the psychophysical detection tasks in which TSD was developed. Long and Waag (1981), among others, have contrasted the low levels of signal probability that are typical in vigilance experiments with conditions in psychophysical detection tasks in which there may be hundreds of stimulus trials, about equal probabilities of signals and non-signals, and observers who are very familiar with the stimuli. They suggest that a vigilance task with a minimal number of critical signals may not provide the observer with sufficient opportunity to establish the theoretically proposed distributions of noise and signal plus noise against which to apply a decision rule. This line of reasoning questions whether the equal variance assumption underlying the computation of d' and can be met in vigilance situations. As indicated by other investigators, the problem is exacerbated by the fact that false alarm rates in vigilance tasks are often quite low; the observer is uncertain about the time of target arrival, and the time-grain established by the observer to make a decision is unknown and must be estimated by the experimenter (Jerison, 1967b; 1977; Mackworth, 1970; Swets and Kristofferson, 1970; Craig, 1977). These are not factors in alerted detection tasks. In a careful examination of the relation between TSD and vigilance, Taylor (1967) has shown how departures from TSD assumptions can lead to seriously inflated values of d' and β and also to spurious correlations between these indices. Examples of what may be spurious correlations between TSD indices in a vigilance task have been provided recently by Long and Waag (1981).

Jerison (1967b) has pointed out the unreasonably high values of β found in analyzing vigilance data along TSD lines. In psychophysical tasks $\beta > 4.0$ is rare. In vigilance tasks β values ranging from 70 to 500 are not uncommon. Jerison noted that values such as these are psychologically meaningless for they imply that observers require odds of 70:1 or 500:1 before calling a stimulus a signal.

Vigilance tasks are clearly not normal psychophysical settings, not settings that TSD was designed to explain. Jerison and his coworkers (Jerison *et al.*, 1965) have, therefore, cautioned that important and unique processes in vigilance experiments may have little to do with sensing or decision making as assumed by TSD. If these unique processes are overlooked, there can be serious misinterpretations of changes in d' and β as typically computed. Jerison *et al.* (1965) explain the measured variations in d' and β for visual vigilance as results of various mixes of three modes of observing: (1) alert observing or optimal attention; (2) blurred observing—perhaps by inappropriate accommodation or fixation which changes the detectability of the signal; and (3) distracted 'observing', in which information from the display is completely blocked and the observer never responds. During the course of a vigil, if the monitor's observing behavior changes from the alert to the distracted mode, the frequency of 'yes' responses (hits and false alarms) will decline and be accompanied by a large elevation in β. Various mixes of these modes of observing, with fixed and meaningful d' and β during each mode, are shown to generate all of the unusual values of these TSD parameters that are computed from vigilance data.

Jerison (1977) has also pointed out that in the one report on the use of TSD from which judgments about the shape of the N and SN distributions could be made (Broadbent and Gregory, 1963), the evidence favored a change in distribution as the explanation for the decrement. The variance of the SN distribution may have tripled during the course of the vigil. This is consistent with the view that there was more diversity of modes of observing as the vigil proceeded.

The application of TSD to vigilance situations has faced these and other severe criticisms. Does this mean that efforts to interpret vigilance performance along TSD lines should be abandoned? In a strong defense of the use of TSD in vigilance experiments, Swets (1977) has pointed out that it is important to distinguish between the value of TSD postulates for an understanding of vigilant behavior and the question of whether assumptions necessary for the computation of TSD indices are violated in particular experimental situations. Davies and Parasuraman (1982) have also emphasized the necessity for such a distinction, as has Jerison (1967b, 1977).

Problems stemming from the violation of TSD assumptions may be rectified through the use of non-parametric (distribution-free) measures. These measures have been described thoroughly by Craig (1979a). In addition, TSD provides the best approach to describing the elements of any detection task, as is evident from the successful translation of attention variables into effects on the N and SN distributions as well as the obvious utility of distinguishing sensitivity (d') from decision processes (β) in the analysis of detections, false alarms and missed signals. If there has been an error it has been in ignoring the shapes of the distributions, as Taylor (1967) pointed out, and this error is easily corrected.

Vigilance theories run the gamut of 'bottom-up' (data driven) and 'top-down' (conceptually driven) approaches to explain what is known about vigilance, and no single position is entirely satisfactory. The ability to localize changes in performance in terms of perceptual processes, decision processes, and the diversity of observing can be helpful in improving the theoretical models. TSD has been the theory of choice for preparing the framework for understanding mechanisms in vigilance behavior. Further discussions of the relation between TSD and vigilance can be found in Chapters 3 and 6.

SELECTED TASK PARAMETERS

There are general aspects of the vigilance situation, in addition to the stimulus and response parameters, that influence the quality of performance, and some of these may interact with the simpler psychophysics of vigilance. We shall consider three such aspects in this section; task complexity, knowledge of results and task taxonomy.

The experiments described up to this point have required relatively simple perceptual discriminations, such as 'double jumps' in a Mackworth clock or changes in the illumination level, duration or movement of stimuli. In most cases, the vigilance decrement has appeared. One might wonder what would happen to performance efficiency if the sorts of perceptual discriminations required of observers became more intricate. Sustained attention in normal environments is almost never restricted to such simple stimuli. The issue in the concluding section of this chapter is to consider a broader range of tasks and situations and to determine whether they can be understood as sums of their parts, as it were. The first of these questions is on the effect of making the vigilance task more complex.

Task complexity

One of the first experiments to explore the issue of task complexity was reported by Jerison (1963). He asked observers to monitor either one Mackworth clock or two or three such clocks, simultaneously. Unlike the redundant audiovisual displays that were described earlier, the multiple displays in Jerison's experiment were independent. The results of that study, shown in Figure 2.12, indicated that increasing task complexity by increasing the number of displays to be monitored lowered performance efficiency compared to a single display condition but, paradoxically, also seemed to eliminate the vigilance decrement. However, using a fine-grained analysis in which the number of subjects detecting successive signals during the watch was examined, Jerison found that a decrement did indeed appear in the complex tasks but that it was masked in the gross view displayed in Figure 2.12 by a very rapid approach to a plateau.

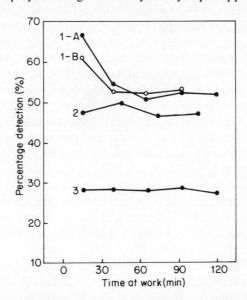

Figure 2.12   Percentage of detections during successive time periods with one, two or three Mackworth clocks in the monitored display. [After Jerison (1963). Reproduced by permission of McGraw-Hill Book Company.]

In this case, then, increasing task complexity by requiring observers to monitor more than one display at a time speeded up the vigilance decrement, with performance dropping to a plateau within the first few minutes of work.

Along similar lines, Fisk and Schneider (1981) have examined the vigilance decrement in terms of two different forms of information processing, which they describe as 'automatic' and 'controlled'. The former refers to fast, fairly effortless, skilled behaviors, the latter to comparatively slow, effortful, capacity-limited activities (cf. Schneider and Shiffrin, 1977). They found that the vigilance decrement occurred only with controlled processing. Automatic processing tasks did not result in a vigilance decrement.

While the work of Jerison (1963) and of Fisk and Schneider (1981) indicated that increments in task complexity degrade vigilance performance, other experiments, using different ways to increase complexity, have shown that increments in complexity are not always paralleled by reductions in performance efficiency. McGrath (1965), for example, asked observers to monitor non-redundant audiovisual displays and found that performance on a display presenting easily detectable signals was enhanced by requiring the observer to monitor another display presenting difficult signals in another sensory modality. This occurred regardless of the modality combinations for easy and difficult signals.

In an extensive series of experiments, Adams and his coworkers employed very complex vigilance tasks with multiple stimulus sources (from six to 36) under conditions in which any one source could present a signal at any moment in time. The vigilance decrement was either absent or minimal in these experiments, even though the vigil lasted for several hours (Adams *et al.*, 1961, 1962, 1963; Adams and Humes, 1963; Webber and Adams, 1964; Montague *et al.*, 1965). In addition, Montague *et al.* (1965) reported that signal probability had no effect upon performance in the complex task that they employed. The absence of a vigilance decrement in complex vigilance tasks has also been reported by Alluisi *et al.* (1977) and by Howell *et al.* (1966), and the negligible effect of signal probability in complex tasks has also been reported recently by Craig (1979b).

As noted in Chapter 1, vigilance tasks can be characterized along a sensory–cognitive dimension. In sensory tasks, the critical signals are changes in the physical attributes of stimuli, whereas in cognitive tasks the critical signals are defined symbolically. Recently, Warm and his coworkers have attacked the problem of task complexity by varying the difficulty of the discriminations to be made on a cognitive dimension.

In one study (Warm *et al.*, 1976c), observers monitored repetitive pairs of visually presented digits under two conditions of signal difficulty. These were, first, a simple condition in which critical signals were digit pairs in which the arithmetic values of the digits differed by no more than ± 1, and, second, a complex condition in which critical signals were pairs of digits which met the difference criterion and also summed to values between 4 and 14. In both the simple and complex conditions, event rates of six and 21 events per minute were used. Typical vigilance results were found in the simple condition—the probability of correct detections was greater under a slow as compared to a fast event rate and performance efficiency declined over time. By contrast, in the complex condition, the event rate effect was eliminated and performance efficiency improved over time, i.e. a cognitive increment function was found. Subsequent studies have replicated the increment in performance over time and demonstrated that it is not a learning 'artifact' reflecting poor task mastery at the ouset of the vigil (Warm *et al.*, 1981; Lysaght, 1981).

If we define task complexity in terms of the intricacy of the discriminations that observers must make, there are several ways to increase discrimination difficulty, and different patterns of results accompany different techniques. Depending upon the approach employed, it is possible to amplify, eliminate or reverse the vigilance decrement and eliminate the effects of signal probability and event rate. Thus, task complexity is an important contextual factor for some of the major psychophysical determinants of vigilant behavior. Unfortunately, work on task complexity has been piecemeal, and there are no systematic investigations of the relation between different dimensions of complexity and the several psychophysical parameters described in this chapter.

Knowledge of results

In many perceptual tasks that are performed under alerted conditions, performance efficiency can be substantially improved by giving the observers information on how well they are doing (Gibson, 1969). Such an effect of knowledge of results was first demonstrated in Mackworth's earliest experiments on vigilance (Mackworth, 1950). He found that this information could prevent the vigilance decrement. Many other experiments have since demonstrated that feedback enhances the frequency and also the speed of signal detections in vigilance experiments (McCormack, 1959; McCormack *et al.*, 1962; Sipowicz *et al.*, 1962; Hardesty *et al.*, 1963; Wiener, 1963, 1964, 1968; Chinn and Alluisi, 1964; Warm *et al.*, 1973).

The consistency of findings with regard to knowledge of results led Jerison and Pickett (1963) to conclude that when there is room to improve in a vigilance task, improvement will occur when knowledge of results is available. However, the manner in which improvement is accomplished has given rise to an interesting debate. Some investigators have taken the position that knowledge of results is effective because it has cue properties which foster the observer's awareness of important task relevant characteristics (Adams and Humes, 1963; Baker, 1963; Williges and North, 1972). Others, however, have maintained that that the facilitative effects of feedback are primarily motivational rather than instructive in character (McCormack, 1967; Mackworth, 1970). When, as in most vigilance tasks, the required discriminations are simple, the latter alternative seems to be the most appropriate. Three lines of evidence form the empirical foundation for this statement.

The first of these relates to the use of false feedback, i.e. feedback that does not reflect the monitor's performance. Evidently, informing observers that they missed a signal when in fact they did not, or giving them information about the speed of signal detections on purely a random basis, seems to improve overall performance efficiency and, in general, does so as well as when veridical information is provided (Weidenfeller *et al.*, 1962; Loeb and Schmidt, 1963; Mackworth, 1964; Antonelli and Karas, 1967).

It is unlikely that observers could learn anything about actual task characteristics under false feedback conditions. On the other hand, the argument for cue properties associated with knowledge of results could be pursued further along the following lines. Observers are already able to distinguish signal and non-signal events at the outset of a vigil, and new information to be learned while performing the task is primarily about the temporal distribution of signals. Since studies using false feedback have followed the usual procedure in vigilance experiments of using highly irregular temporal distributions, it would be very difficult even with feedback to learn to predict the appearance of a critical signal. Thus, the instructional component of knowledge of results could have been masked in these investigations. To test this possibility, Warm *et al.* (1974) compared the effects of true and false knowledge of results under conditions in which signal schedules followed perfectly regular or highly irregular temporal patterns. As might be anticipated from our earlier discussion of temporal uncertainty, response latencies for correct detections were shorter with the regular as compared to the irregular signal schedule. The availability of true and false knowledge of results enhanced the speed of signal detections, but the beneficial effects of true feedback did not exceed those of false feedback even when the signal schedule was regular and, as the data imply, predictable.

Embedded in a motivational view of feedback is the notion that knowledge of results acts as a reinforcing or incentive agent in a vigilance task. Thus, techniques of incentive manipulation that are important in other areas of behavior should also be relevant for vigilant behavior when feedback is manipulated in similar ways. Partial or intermittent reinforcement—reinforcement for some but not all of a subject's responses—constitutes one of the principal ways to vary the delivery of an incentive according to a set pattern. An outstanding finding associated with this technique is the partial reinforcement effect: intermittent reinforcement leads to more stable levels of responding when reinforcement is subsequently withdrawn than does exposure to continuous reinforcement (Cofer and Appley, 1964; Houston, 1981). If knowledge of results acts as a reinforcing agent in vigilance, a partial feedback schedule during the initial portion of a vigil should lead to more stable later performance than a continuous feedback schedule after feedback is withdrawn.

Warm *et al.* (1971) tested this possibility in an experiment in which observers watched for the occasional illumination of a small jewel lamp during a 1-hour vigil. There were five feedback conditions: (1) 100% feedback—feedback about each response—throughout the session (group 100/100); (2) 50% feedback—intermittent knowledge of results for 50% of the observer's responses—throughout the session (group 50/50); (3) 100% feedback during the first two periods of watch and none thereafter (group 100/0); (4) 50% feedback during the first two periods of watch and none thereafter (group 50/0); and (5) a non-feedback control condition (group AC). As can be seen in Figure 2.13, response latencies were slowest in the control group, and there was a continuous vigilance decrement (an increase in response time with time at work) in that group. Groups on either a continuous or partial feedback schedule throughout the watch had similar response times and no vigilance decrement. Withdrawal of knowledge of results during the last two periods of watch was accompanied by a notable vigilance

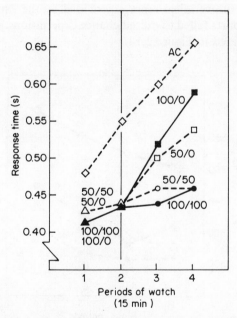

Figure 2.13 The partial reinforcement effect in a vigilance task. Response time is plotted as a function of periods of watch for various knowledge of results conditions. The data for groups experiencing similar feedback schedules during the initial two periods are pooled. Note that knowledge of results is withdrawn after Period 2 for Groups 50/0 and 100/0. Group AC is a control group which received no evaluative information. [Reprinted with permission of publisher from Warm, J. S., Hagner, G. L., and Meyer, D. The partial reinforcement effect in a vigilance task. *Perceptual and Motor Skills*, 1971, **32**, 987–993, Figure 1.]

decrement (increment in response time). Consistent with the partial reinforcement effect, the magnitude of the decrement was greater for observers exposed to continuous than to intermittent feedback during the earlier portion of the session.

The third line of evidence for a motivational interpretation of the effects of knowledge of results in vigilance comes from a study by Warm *et al.* (1972) which compared the effects of accurate experimenter-feedback regarding response latencies with the effects of subject-controlled feedback in the form of self-evaluations of the latency of their responses. The subjects in this study responded to aperiodic disappearances of a visual signal during a 1-hour session. Both feedback procedures enhanced performance compared with that of a control group that received no evaluative information. In addition, the groups of subjects operating under experimenter-controlled or subject-controlled feedback did not differ significantly from each other, despite the fact that the subjects' self-provided information regarding detection latency was considerably less accurate than the veridical reports provided by the experimenter. (The accuracy of self-reports failed to exceed chance expectations.) The outcome of this study is illustrated in Figure 2.14.

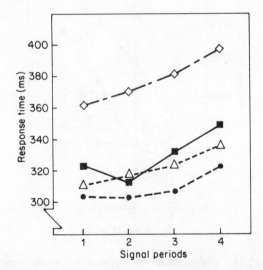

Figure 2.14   Response time to signal detections as a function of watchkeeping periods (15 minutes) for different feedback conditions. Subjects in the acknowledgment condition (◇— - —◇) received no evaluative feedback. Those in the modified KR (△--------△) and regular KR (●------●) conditions received knowledge of results from the experimenter. Subjects in the self-evaluation condition (■————■) provided the experimenter with evaluations of their own performance. [From Warm *et al.* (1972). Copyright (1972) by the American Psychological Association. Reprinted by permission.]

As Dember and Warm (1979) have noted, feedback is clearly important in vigilance performance but since the feedback does not have to be accurate to be effective, it must play a primarily motivational rather than informational role. Beyond their implications for the psychophysics of vigilance, the effects of knowledge of results have important implications for theories of vigilance, particularly the expectancy position. These matters are discussed more fully in Chapter 6.

Task taxonomy

A scientific understanding requires the careful description of phenomena under investigation. This entails the specification of variables and the interrelations among variables that play a role in the phenomena that are being studied (Corso, 1967). One approach to careful description is the development of a comprehensive system of classification, in which entities are ordered into groups or sets on the basis of their relationships. Such an approach is known as a taxonomic analysis and it affords several advantages. Among other things, it offers increased efficiency in organizing empirical information; it enhances our capability to compare different experiments and it leads to more dependable generalizations of research results from one situation to another (Fleishman, 1982).

The development of taxonomic systems has been a major endeavor in the biological sciences, and the need for systems of this sort in psychology, particularly in the geneal area of human performance, has been recognized for many years (Melton, 1964; Alluisi, 1967). Recently, Fleishman and his associates (Fleishman, 1975, 1982) have generated a taxonomic framework for describing performance tasks which is relevant for the study of vigilance. Their work features an 'ability requirements' approach in which tasks are categorized according to the abilities needed to perform them effectively. As part of this line of investigation, Levine *et al.* (1973) conducted an extensive analysis of 58 vigilance experiments and determined that the tasks used in these investigations could be dichotomized into two ability categories. One of these, termed 'perceptual speed', refers to the ability to compare sensory patterns or configurations rapidly for identity or degree of similarity. It is exemplified by situations in which the observer must detect a change in a stimulus relative to a preceding stimulus, such as an increase in the movement of the pointer in a Mackworth clock or an increase in the duration of a tone. The other category is known as 'flexibility of closure'. It involves the ability to detect a specified stimulus in a complex field. Examples are tasks in which observers must detect the presence of a disk of specified saturation in a display of several disks or the presence of a pure tone in a burst of noise.

Levine *et al.* (1973) found that the vigilance decrement seemed to be closely related to these ability categories. For tasks in which the predominant ability was perceptual speed, the decrement occurred primarily within the first hour of a vigil and performance leveled off thereafter. By contrast, in tasks requiring flexibility of closure, the decrement appeared during the first hour of watch and then performance improved spontaneously as the vigil continued. In addition, 'closure' tasks resulted in less performance variability than did 'speed' tasks.

When examined closely, it appears that the tasks that Fleishman and his associates place in the perceptual speed category are essentially absolute judgment tasks in which an observer must decide if a stimulus configuration does or does not differ from a *remembered* standard. On the other hand, tasks that fall in the flexibility-of-closure category are differential discrimination tasks in which the information needed to make a discrimination is present in the stimulus events themselves — either they contain the specified stimulus attribute or they do not. Davies and Parasuraman (1982) have suggested that perceptual speed and flexibility of closure tasks be termed successive and simultaneous discrimination tasks, respectively.

Beginning with the successive/simultaneous distinction, Davies and Parasuraman have developed a more complete taxonomic analysis of vigilance tasks. They use a twofold classification system in which the dimensions are task type (successive or simultaneous) and event rate (fast or slow). On the basis of their own experiments and careful scrutiny of many others, they have brought the vigilance decrement and signal detection theory together within this taxonomic framework. According to these investigators, the vigilance decrement is based upon a decline in perceptual sensitivity (d') in tasks that combine a fast event rate with the requirement for successive discriminations. In all other combinations of task type and event rate, the source of the decrement is an elevation in the response criterion (Parasuraman and Davies, 1977; Parasuraman, 1979; Davies and Parasuraman, 1982). This will be described more completely by Parasuraman in the next chapter.

In addition to their investigations of the decrement function, Davies and Parasuraman have also shown that a taxonomic approach has meaning for the issue of sensory specificity in vigilance discussed earlier in this chapter. They carried out an experiment in which intersensory (audio-visual) correlations and intrasensory (visual-visual) correlations were obtained between vigilance tasks under conditions in which the tasks required categorically similar discriminations, i.e. both successive or both simultaneous, or categorically discordant discriminations, i.e. successive in one task and simultaneous in the other. They found that intersensory correlations were considerably higher when categorically similar discriminations were involved than when the discriminations involved in each modality were categorically discordant. Moreover, intersensory correlations between vigilance tasks featuring categorically similar discriminations exceeded intrasensory correlations between tasks requiring categorically discordant discriminations (Parasuraman and Davies, 1977).

The taxonomic approach advocated by Davies and Parasuraman and by Fleishman and his associates raises some important questions for the psychophysics of vigilance. In addition to issues regarding time on task and the sensory modality of signals, what other psychophysical considerations are linked to the type of discriminations—simultaneous or successive—that observers are faced with in vigilance tasks? Do the precise effects of parameters such as signal conspicuity, signal probability and the event rate context in which signals appear depend upon task type? Further, to what extent does the successive/simultaneous distinction implicate memory functions as critical factors in vigilance performance? As noted previously, successive discrimination tasks require absolute judgments and experiments in classical psychophysics have shown that our ability to make absolute judgments is limited, in part, by the inexactness of memory in comparing a stimulus with previously stored data (cf. Dember and Warm, 1979). Does memory also limit the quality of sustained attention with successive discrimination tasks? These and other questions remain as intriguing issues for future research into the psychophysics of vigilance.

ACKNOWLEDGMENTS

The authors are indebted to John C. Bowers, William N. Dember, David F. Ricks and Donald A. Schumsky for comments on the manuscript.

REFERENCES

Adams, J. A. Vigilance in the detection of low-intensity visual stimuli. *Journal of Experimental Psychology*, 1956, **52**, 204–208.

Adams, J. A., and Boulter, L. R. Spatial and temporal uncertainty as determinants of vigilance performance. *Journal of Experimental Psychology*, 1964, **67**, 127–131.

Adams, J. A., and Humes, J. M. Monitoring of complex visual displays: IV. Training for vigilance. *Human Factors*, 1963, **5**, 147–153.

Adams, J. A., Stenson, H. H., and Humes, J. M. Monitoring of complex visual displays: II. Effects of visual load and response complexity on human vigilance. *Human Factors*, 1961, **3**, 213–221.

Adams, J. A., Humes, J. M., and Stenson, H. H. Monitoring of complex visual displays: III. Effects of repeated sessions on human vigilance. *Human Factors*, 1962, **4**, 149–158.

Adams, J. A., Humes, J. M., and Sieveking, N. A. Monitoring of complex visual displays: V. Effects of repeated sessions and heavy visual load on human vigilance. *Human Factors*, 1963, **5**, 385–389.

Alluisi, E. A. Attention and vigilance as mechanisms of response. In E. A. Bilodeau (Ed.), *Acquisition of skill*. New York: Academic Press, 1966.

Alluisi, E. A. Methodology in the use of synthetic tasks to assess complex performance. *Human Factors*, 1967, **9**, 375–384.

Alluisi, E. A., Coates, G. D., and Morgan, B. B. Effects of temporal stressors on vigilance and information processing. In R. R. Mackie (Ed.), *Vigilance: theory, operational performance and physiological correlates*. New York: Plenum, 1977.

Antonelli, D. C., and Karas, G. G. Performance on a vigilance task under conditions of true and false knowledge of results. *Perceptual and Motor Skills*, 1967, **25**, 129–138.

Baddeley, A. D., and Colquhoun, W. P. Signal probability and vigilance: a reappraisal of the 'signal-rate' effect. *British Journal of Psychology*, 1969, **60**, 169–178.

Baird, J. C., and Noma, E. *Fundamentals of scaling and psychophysics.* New York: Wiley, 1978.

Baker, C. H. Attention to visual displays during a vigilance task. I. Biasing attention. *British Journal of Psychology,* 1958, **49**, 279–288.

Baker, C. H. Observing behavior in a vigilance task. *Science,* 1960, **132**, 674–675.

Baker, C. H. Further toward a theory of vigilance. In D. N. Buckner and J. J. McGrath (Eds), *Vigilance: a symposium,* New York: McGraw-Hill, 1963 (a).

Baker, C. H. Signal duration as a factor in vigilance tasks. *Science,* 1963, **141**, 1196–1197 (b).

Baker, R. A., Ware, J. R., and Sipowicz, R. R. Vigilance: a comparison in auditory, visual and combined audio-visual tasks. *Canadian Journal of Psychology,* 1962, **16**, 192–198.

Bell, C. R., Symington, L. E., and Bevan, W. Watchkeeping performance as a function of certain properties of the viewing situation. *Human Factors,* 1974, **16**, 65–69.

Benedetti, L. H., and Loeb, M. A comparison of auditory monitoring performance in blind subjects with that of sighted subjects in light and dark. *Perception and Psychophysics,* 1972, **11**, 10–16.

Binford, J. R., and Loeb, M. Monitoring readily detected auditory signals and detection of obscure visual signals. *Perceptual and Motor Skills,* 1963, **17**, 735–746.

Boulter, L. R., and Adams, J. A. Vigilance decrement, the expectancy hypothesis and intersignal interval. *Canadian Journal of Psychology,* 1963, **17**, 201–210.

Bowers, J. C. Effects of the rate of repetitive stimulation on probe detection in a vigilance task. Unpublished master's thesis, University of Cincinnati, 1982.

Broadbent, D. E. *Decision and stress.* New York: Academic Press, 1971.

Broadbent, D. E., and Gregory, M. Vigilance considered as a statistical decision. *British Journal of Psychology,* 1963, **54**, 309–323.

Broadbent, D. E., and Gregory, M. Effects of noise and of signal rate upon vigilance analysed by means of decision theory. *Human Factors,* 1965, **7**, 155–162.

Buckner, D. N., Harabedian, A. and McGrath, J. J. Individual differences in vigilance performance. *Journal of Engineering Psychology,* 1966, **5**, 69–85.

Buckner, D. N., and McGrath, J. J. A comparison of performances on single and dual sensory mode vigilance tasks. In D. N. Buckner and J. J. McGrath (Eds), *Vigilance: a symposium.* New York: McGraw-Hill, 1963.

Chinn, R. M., and Alluisi, E. A. Effect of three kinds of knowledge of results information on three measures of vigilance performance. *Perceptual and Motor Skills,* 1964, **18**, 901–912.

Cofer, C. N., and Appley, M. H. *Motivation: theory and research.* New York: Wiley, 1964.

Colquhoun, W. P. The effect of 'unwanted' signals on performance in a vigilance task. *Ergonomics,* 1961, **4**, 42–51.

Colquhoun, W. P. Sonar target detection as a decision process. *Journal of Applied Psychology,* 1967, **51**, 187–190.

Colquhoun, W. P. Evaluation of auditory, visual and dual-mode displays for prolonged sonar monitoring in repeated sessions. *Human Factors,* 1975, **17**, 425–437.

Colquhoun, W. P., and Baddeley, A. D. Role of pretest expectancy in vigilance decrement. *Journal of Experimental Psychology,* 1964, **68**, 156–160.

Colquhoun, W. P., and Baddeley, A. D. Influence of signal probability during pretraining on vigilance decrement. *Journal of Experimental Psychology,* 1967, **73**, 153–155.

Colquhoun, W. P., and Edwards, R. S. Practice effects on a visual vigilance task with and without search. *Human Factors,* 1970, **12**, 537–545.

Corcoran, D. W. J., Mullin, J., Rainey, M. T., and Frith, G. The effects of raised signal and noise amplitude during the course of vigilance tasks. In R. R. Mackie (Ed.), *Vigilance, theory, operational performance and physiological correlates.* New York: Plenum, 1977.

Corso, J. E. *The experimental psychology of sensory behavior.* New York: Holt, Rinehart and Winston, 1967.

Cotman, C. W., and McGaugh, J. L. *Behavioral neuroscience: an introduction.* New York: Academic Press, 1980.

Craig, A. Broadbent and Gregory revisitied: vigilance and statistical decision. *Human Factors*, 1977, **19**, 25–36.

Craig, A. Nonparametric measures of sensory efficiency for sustained monitoring tasks. *Human Factors*, 1979, **21**, 69–78 (a).

Craig, A. Vigilance for two kinds of signal with unequal probabilities of occurrence. *Human Factors*, 1979, **21**, 647–653 (b).

Craig, A. Monitoring for one kind of signal in the presence of another: the effects of signal mix on detectability. *Human Factors*, 1981, **23**, 191–197.

Craig, A., and Colquhoun, W. P. Vigilance: a review. In C. G. Drury and J. G. Fox (Eds), *Human reliability in quality control.* London: Taylor and Francis, 1975.

Craig, A., and Colquhoun, W. P. Vigilance effects in complex inspection. In R. R. Mackie (Ed.), *Vigilance: theory, operational performance and physiological correlates.* New York: Plenum, 1977.

Craig, A., Colquhoun, W. P., and Corcoran, D. W. J. Combining evidence presented simultaneously to the eye and the ear: a comparison of some predictive models. *Perception and Psychophysics*, 1976, **19**, 473–484.

Dardano, J. F. Relationships of intermittent noise, intersignal interval and skin conductance to vigilance behavior. *Journal of Applied Psychology*, 1962, **46**, 106–114.

Davenport, W. G. Auditory vigilance: the effects of costs and values on signals. *Australian Journal of Psychology*, 1968, **20**, 213–218.

Davenport, W. G. Vibrotactile vigilance: the effects of costs and values on signals. *Perception and Psychophysics*, 1969, **5**, 25–28.

Davenport, W. G. Arousal theory and vigilance: schedules for background stimulation. *Journal of General Psychology*, 1974, **91**, 51–59.

Davies, D. R., and Hockey, G. R. J. The effects of noise and doubling the signal frequency on individual differences in visual vigilance performance. *British Journal of Psychology*, 1966, **57**, 381–389.

Davies, D. R., and Parasuraman, R. *The psychology of vigilance.* London: Academic Press, 1982.

Davies, D. R., and Tune, G. S. *Human vigilance performance.* New York: American Elsevier, 1969.

Deaton, M., Tobias, J. S., and Wilkinson, R. T. The effect of sleep deprivation on signal detection parameters. *Quarterly Journal of Experimental Psychology*, 1971, **23**, 449–452.

Deese, J., and Ormond, E. Studies of detectability during continuous visual search. Wright Air Development Center Technical Report No. WADC-TR-53-8, Wright Patterson Air Force Base, Ohio: Wright Air Development Center, 1953.

Dember, W. N., and Warm, J. S. *Psychology of perception*, 2nd edn. New York: Holt, Rinehart and Winston, 1979.

Egan, J. P., Greenberg, G. Z., and Schulman, A. I. Operating characteristics, signal detectability and the method of free response. *Journal of the Acoustical Society of America*, 1961, **33**, 993–1007.

Elliott, E. Perception and alertness. *Ergonomics*, 1960, **3**, 357–364.

Ellis, H. C., and Ahr, A. E. The role of error density and set in a vigilance task. *Journal of Applied Psychology*, 1960, **44**, 205–209.

Epps, B. D. Training for vigilance: intersensory transfer in monitoring performance. Unpublished master's thesis, University of Cincinnati, 1973.

Fisk, A. D., and Schneider, W. Control and automatic processing during tasks requiring sustained attention: a new approach to vigilance. *Human Factors*, 1981, **23**, 737–750.

Fleishman, E. A. Toward a taxonomy of human performance. *American Psychologist*, 1975, **30**, 1127–1149.

Fleishman, E. A. Systems for describing human tasks. *American Psychologist*, 1982, **37**, 821–834.

Frankmann, J. P., and Adams, J. A. Theories of vigilance. *Psychological Bulletin*, 1962, **59**, 257–272.

Gescheider, G. A. *Psychophysics: method and theory*. New York: Erlbaum, 1976.

Gibson, E. J. *Principles of perceptual learning and development*. New York: Appleton–Century–Crofts, 1969.

Green, D. M., and Swets, J. A. *Signal detection theory and psychophysics* (reprinted with corrections). Huntington, N.Y.: Krieger, 1974.

Groves, P. M., and Thompson, R. F. Habituation: a dual process theory. *Psychological Review*, 1970, **77**, 419–450.

Gruber, A. Sensory alternation and performance in a vigilance task. *Human Factors*, 1964, **6**, 3–12.

Gunn, W. J., and Loeb, M. Correlation of performance in detecting visual and auditory signals. *American Journal of Psychology*, 1967, **80**, 236–242.

Guralnick, M. J. Observing responses and decision processes in vigilance. *Journal of Experimental Psychology*, 1972, **93**, 239–244.

Guralnick, M. J. Effects of event rate and signal difficulty on observing responses and decision measures in vigilance. *Journal of Experimental Psychology*, 1973, **99**, 261–265.

Hardesty, D., Trumbo, D., and Bevan, W. Influence of knowledge of results on performance in a monitoring task. *Perceptual and Motor Skills*, 1963, **16**, 629–634.

Hatfield, J. L., and Loeb, M. Sense mode and coupling in a vigilance task. *Perception and Psychophysics*, 1968, **4**, 29–36.

Hatfield, J. L., and Soderquist, D. R. Practice effects and signal detection indices in an auditory vigilance task. *Journal of the Acoustical Society of America*, 1969, **46**, 1458–1463.

Hatfield, J. L., and Soderquist, D. R. Coupling effects and performance in vigilance tasks. *Human Factors*, 1970, **12**, 351–359.

Hawkes, G. R., and Loeb, M. Vigilance for cutaneous and auditory signals. *Journal of Auditory Research*, 1961, **4**, 272–284.

Hawkes, G. R., and Loeb, M. Vigilance for cutaneous and auditory stimuli as a function of intersignal interval and signal strength. *Journal of Psychology*, 1962, **53**, 211–218.

Houston, J. P. *Fundamentals of learning and memory*, 2nd edn. New York: Academic Press, 1981.

Howell, W. C., Johnston, W. A., and Goldstein, I. L. Complex monitoring and its relation to the classical problem of vigilance. *Organizational Behavior and Human Performance*. 1966, **1**, 129–150.

Jenkins, H. M. The effect of signal-rate on performance in visual monitoring. *American Journal of Psychology*, 1958, **71**, 647–661.

Jerison, H. J. Experiments on vigilance: V. The empirical model for human vigilance. Wright Air Development Center Technical Report No. WADC-TR-58-526. Wright-Patterson Air Force Base, Ohio: Aero Medical Laboratory, Wright Air Development Center, 1959.

Jerison, H. J. On the decrement function in human vigilance. In D. N. Buckner and J. J. McGrath (Eds), *Vigilance: a symposium*. New York: McGraw-Hill, 1963.

Jerison, H. J. Human and animal vigilance. *Perceptual and Motor Skills*, 1965, **21**, 580–582.

Jerison, H. J. Activation and long term performance. *Acta Psychologica*, 1967, **27**, 373–389 (a).

Jerison, H. J. Signal detection theory in the analysis of human vigilance. *Human Factors*, 1967, **9**, 285–288 (b).

Jerison, H. J. Vigilance, discrimination and attention. In D. I. Mostofsky (Ed.), *Attention: contemporary theory and analysis*. New York: Appleton–Century–Crofts, 1970.

Jerison, H. J. Vigilance: biology, psychology, theory and practice. In R. R. Mackie (Ed.), *Vigilance: theory, operational performance and physiological correlates*. New York: Plenum, 1977.

Jerison, H. J., and Pickett, R. M. Vigilance: a review and re-evaluation. *Human Factors*, 1963, **5**, 211–238.

Jerison, H. J., and Pickett, R. M. Vigilance: the importance of the elicited observing rate. *Science*, 1964, **143**, 970–971.

Jerison, H. J., Pickett, R. M., and Stenson, H. H. The elicited observing rate and decision processes in vigilance. *Human Factors*, 1965, **7**, 107–128.

Johnston, W. A., Howell, W. C., and Goldstein, I. L. Human vigilance as a function of signal frequency and stimulus density. *Journal of Experimental Psychology*, 1966, **72**, 736–743.

Jones, T. N., and Kirk, R. Monitoring performance on visual and auditory displays. *Perceptual and Motor Skills*, 1970, **30**, 235–238.

Kappauf, W. E., and Powe, W. E. Performance decrement at an audio-visual checking task. *Journal of Experimental Psychology*, 1959, **57**, 49–56.

Kelley, C. R. What is adaptive training? *Human Factors*, 1969, **11**, 547–556.

Kennedy, R. S. A comparison of performance on visual and auditory monitoring tasks. *Human Factors*, 1971, **13**, 93–97.

Kirk, R. E., and Hecht, E. Maintenance of vigilance by programmed noise. *Perceptual and Motor Skills*, 1963, **16**, 553–560.

Krulewitz, J. E., and Warm, J. S. The event rate contest in vigilance: relation to signal probability and expectancy. *Bulletin of the Psychonomic Society*, 1977, **10**, 429–432.

Krulewitz, J. E., Warm, J. S., and Wohl, T. H. Effects of shifts in the rate of repetitive stimulation on sustained attention. *Perception and Psychophysics*, 1975, **18**, 245–249.

Kulp, R. A., and Alluisi, E. A. Effects of stimulus–response uncertainty on watchkeeping performance and choice reactions. *Perception and Psychophysics*, 1967, **2**, 511–515.

Levine, J. M. The effects of values and costs on the detection and identification of signals in auditory vigilance. *Human Factors*, 1966, **8**, 525–537.

Levine, J. M., Romashko, T., and Fleishman, E. A. Evaluation of an abilities classification system for integrating and generalizing human performance research findings: an application to vigilance tasks. *Journal of Applied Psychology*, 1973, **58**, 149–157.

Lisper, H. O., and Törnros, J. Effects of inter-signal interval regularity on increases in reaction time in a one hour auditory monitoring task. *Acta Psychologica*, 1974, **38**, 455–460.

Lisper, H. O., Kjellberg, A., and Melin, A. Effects of signal intensity on increase of reaction time on an auditory monitoring task. *Perceptual and Motor Skills*, 1972, **34**, 439–444.

Loeb, M., and Alluisi, E. A. An update of findings regarding vigilance and a reconsideration of underlying mechanisms. In R. R. Mackie (Ed.), *Vigilance: theory, operational performance and physiological correlates.* New York: Plenum, 1977.

Loeb, M. and Binford, J. R. Some factors influencing the effective auditory intensive difference limen. *Journal of the Acoustical Society of America,* 1963, **35**, 884–891.

Loeb, M., and Binford, J. R. Vigilance for auditory intensity changes as a function of preliminary feedback and confidence level. *Human Factors,* 1964, **6**, 445–458.

Loeb, M., and Binford, J. R. Variation in performance on auditory and visual monitoring tasks as a function of signal and stimulus frequencies. *Perception and Psychophysics,* 1968, **4**, 361–367.

Loeb, M., and Binford, J. R. Modality, difficulty, and 'coupling' in vigilance behavior. *American Journal of Psychology,* 1971, **84**, 529–541.

Loeb, M., and Hawkes, G. R. Detection of differences in duration of acoustic and electrical cutaneous stimuli in a vigilance task. *Journal of Psychology,* 1962, **54**, 101–111.

Loeb, M., and Schmidt, E. A. A comparison of the effects of different kinds of information in maintaining efficiency on an auditory monitoring task. *Ergonomics,* 1963, **6**, 75–81.

Loeb, M., Hawkes, G. R., Evans, W. O., and Alluisi, E. A. The influence of *d*-amphetamine, benactyzine and chlorpromazine on performance in an auditory vigilance task. *Psychonomic Science,* 1965, **3**, 29–30.

Long, G. M., and Waag, W. L. Limitations on the practical applicability of d' and β measures. *Human Factors,* 1981, **23**, 285–290.

Lysaght, R. J. The effects of noise on sustained attention and behavioral persistence. Unpublished doctoral dissertation, University of Cincinnati, 1982.

McCann, P. H. Variability of signal detection measures with noise type. *Psychonomic Science,* 1969, **15**, 310–311.

McCormack, P. D. Performance in a vigilance task with and without knowledge of results. *Canadian Journal of Psychology,* 1959, **13**, 68–71.

McCormack, P. D. A two-factor theory of vigilance in the light of recent studies. *Acta Psychologica,* 1967, **27**, 400–409.

McCormack, P. D., and Prysiazniuk, A. W. Reaction time and regularity of interstimulus interval. *Perceptual and Motor Skills,* 1961, **13**, 15–18.

McCormack, P. D., Binding, F. R. S., and Chylinski, J. Effects on reaction-time of knowledge of results of performance. *Perceptual and Motor Skills,* 1962, **14**, 367–372.

McFarland, B. P., and Halcomb, C. G. Expectancy and stimulus generalization in vigilance. *Perceptual and Motor Skills,* 1970, **30**, 147–151.

McGrath, J. J. Irrelevant stimulation and vigilance performance. In D. N. Buckner and J. J. McGrath (Eds), *Vigilance: a symposium.* New York: McGraw-Hill, 1963.

McGrath, J. J. Performance sharing in an audio-visual vigilance task. *Human Factors,* 1965, **7**, 141–153.

Mackworth, J. F. The effect of true and false knowledge of results on the detectability of signals in a vigilance task. *Canadian Journal of Psychology,* 1964, **18**, 106–117.

Mackworth, J. F. Decision interval and signal detectability in a vigilance task. *Canadian Journal of Psychology,* 1965, **19**, 111–117 (a).

Mackworth, J. F. Deterioration of signal detectability during a vigilance task as a function of background event rate. *Psychonomic Science,* 1965, **3**, 421–422 (b).

Mackworth, J. F. Vigilance, arousal and habituation. *Psychological Review,* 1968, **75**, 308–322.

Mackworth, J. F. *Vigilance and habituation.* Baltimore, Md: Penguin, 1969.

Mackworth, J. F. *Vigilance and attention.* Baltimore, Md: Penguin, 1970.

Mackworth, J. F., and Taylor, M. M. The d' measure of signal detectability in vigilance-like situations. *Canadian Journal of Psychology,* 1963, **17**, 302–325.

Mackworth, N. H. *Researches on the measurement of human performance.* Medical Research Council Special Report Series 268, London: HM Stationery Office, 1950. Reprinted in H. W. Sinaiko (Ed.), *Selected papers on human factors in the design and use of control systems.* New York: Dover, 1961.

Mackworth, N. H., Kaplan, I. T., and Metlay, W. Eye movements during *vigilance. Perceptual and Motor Skills,* 1964, **18**, 397–402.

Martz, R. L. Auditory vigilance as affected by signal rate and intersignal interval variability. *Perceptual and Motor Skills,* 1967, **24**, 195–203.

Melton, A. W. (Ed.). *Categories of human learning.* New York: Academic Press, 1964.

Metzger, K. R., Warm, J. S., and Senter, R. J. Effects of background event rate and critical signal amplitude on vigilance performance. *Perceptual and Motor Skills,* 1974, **38**, 1175–1181.

Milošević, S. Effect of time and space uncertainty on a vigilance task. *Perception and Psychophysics,* 1974, **15**, 331–334.

Milošević, S. Changes in detection measures and skin resistance during an auditory vigilance task. *Ergonomics,* 1975, **18**, 1–8.

Montague, W. E., Webber, C. E., and Adams, J. A. The effects of signal and response complexity on eighteen hours of visual monitoring. *Human Factors,* 1965, **7**, 163–172.

Moore, S. F., and Gross, S. J. Influence of critical signal regularity, stimulus event matrix and cognitive style on vigilance performance. *Journal of Experimental Psychology,* 1973, **99**, 137–139.

Murrell, G. A. A reappraisal of artificial signals as an aid to a visual monitoring task. *Ergonomics,* 1975, **18**, 693–700.

Niceley, P. E., and Miller, G. A. Some effects of unequal spatial distribution on the detectability of radar targets. *Journal of Experimental Psychology,* 1957, **53**, 195–198.

Osborn, W. C., Sheldon, R. W., and Baker, R. A. Vigilance performance under conditions of redundant and non-redundant signal presentation. *Journal of Applied Psychology,* 1963, **47**, 130–134.

Parasuraman, R. Memory load and event rate control sensitivity decrements in sustained attention. *Science,* 1979, **205**, 924–927.

Parasuraman, R., and Davies, D. R. Decision theory analysis of response latencies in vigilance. *Journal of Experimental Psychology: Human Perception and Performance,* 1976, **2**, 578–590.

Parasuraman, R., and Davies, D. R. A taxonomic analysis of vigilance performance. In R. R. Mackie (Ed.), *Vigilance: theory, operational performance and physiological correlates.* New York: Plenum, 1977.

Pope, L. T., and McKechnie, D. F. Correlation between visual and auditory vigilance performance. Aerospace Medical Research Laboratory Technical Report No. AMRL-TR-63-57. Wright-Patterson Air Force Base, Ohio: Aerospace Medical Research Laboratory, 1963.

Posner, M. I. *Chronometric explorations of mind.* Hillsdale, N.J.: Lawrence Erlbaum, 1978.

Randel, J. M. Attentuation of the vigilance decrement through stimulation in a second modality. *Human Factors,* 1968, **10**, 505–512.

Richter, D. O., Senter, R. J., and Warm, J. S. Effects of the rate and regularity of background events on sustained attention. *Bulletin of the Psychonomic Society,* 1981, **18**, 207–210.

Schneider, W., and Shiffrin, R. M. Controlled and automatic human information processing: I. Detection, search and attention. *Psychological Review,* 1977, **84**, 1–66.

Sharpless, S., and Jasper, H. H. Habituation of the arousal reaction. *Brain,* 1956, **79**, 655–680.

Sipowicz, R. R., and Baker, R. A. Effects of intelligence on vigilance: a replication. *Perceptual and Motor Skills,* 1961, **13**, 398.

Sipowicz, R. R., Ware, J. R., and Baker, R. A. The effects of reward and knowledge of results on the performance of a simple vigilance task. *Journal of Experimental Psychology*, 1962, **64**, 58–61.

Smith, R. P., Warm, J. S., and Alluisi, E. A. Effects of temporal uncertainty on watchkeeping performance. *Perception and Psychophysics*, 1966, **1**, 293–299.

Stern, R. M. Performance and physiological arousal during two vigilance tasks varying in signal presentation rate. *Perceptual and Motor Skills*, 1966, **23**, 691–700.

Sverko, B. Intermodal correlations in vigilance performance. *Proceedings of the 16th International Congress of Applied Psychology*, 1968, 341–346.

Swets, J. A. Signal detection theory applied to vigilance. In R. R. Mackie (Ed.), *Vigilance: theory, operational performance and physiological correlates*. New York: Plenum, 1977.

Swets, J. A., and Kristofferson, A. B. Attention. *Annual Review of Psychology*, 1970, **21**, 339–366.

Tanner, W. P., Jr, and Swets, J. A. A decision-making theory of visual detection. *Psychological Review*, 1954, **61**, 401–409.

Taub, H. A., and Osborne, F. H. Effects of signal and stimulus rates on vigilance performance. *Journal of Applied Psychology*, 1968, **52**, 133–138.

Taylor, M. M. Detectability theory and the interpretation of vigilance data. *Acta Psychologica*, 1967, **27**, 390–399.

Thurmond, J. B., Binford, J. R., & Loeb, M. Effects of signal-to-noise variability over repeated sessions in an auditory vigilance task. *Perception and Psychophysics*, 1970, **7**, 100–102.

Tickner, A. H., Poulton, E. C., Copeman, A. K., and Simmonds, D. C. V. Monitoring 16 television screens showing little movement. *Ergonomics*, 1972, **15**, 279–291.

Tolin, P., and Fisher, P. G. Sex differences and effects of irrelevant auditory stimulation on performance of a visual vigilance task. *Perceptual and Motor Skills*, 1974, **39**, 1255–1262.

Tyler, D. M., Waag, W. L., and Halcomb, C. G. Monitoring performance across sense modes: an individual differences approach. *Human Factors*, 1972, **14**, 539–547.

Uttal, W. R. *The psychobiology of sensory coding*. New York: Harper and Row, 1973.

Vickers, D., Leary, J., and Barnes, P. Adaptation to decreasing signal probability. In R. R. Mackie (Ed.), *Vigilance: theory, operational performance and physiological correlates*. New York: Plenum, 1977.

Ware, J. R. Effects of intelligence on signal detection in visual and auditory monitoring. *Perceptual and Motor Skills*, 1961, **13**, 99–102.

Warm, J. S., and Alluisi, E. A. Influence of temporal uncertainty and sensory modality of signals on watchkeeping performance. *Journal of Experimental Psychology*, 1971, **87**, 303–308.

Warm, J. S., Loeb, M., and Alluisi, E. A. Variations in watchkeeping performance as a function of the rate and duration of visual signals. *Perception and Psychophysics*, 1970, **7**, 97–99.

Warm, J. S., Hagner, G. L., and Meyer, D. The partial reinforcement effect in a vigilance task. *Perceptual and Motor Skills*, 1971, **32**, 987–993.

Warm, J. S., Kanfer, F. H., Kuwada, S., and Clark, J. L. Motivation in vigilance: effects of self-evaluation and experimenter-controlled feedback. *Journal of Experimental Psychology*, 1972, **92**, 123–127.

Warm, J. S., Riechmann, S. W., Grasha, A. F., and Seibel, B. Motivation in vigilance: a test of the goal-setting hypothesis of the effectiveness of knowledge of results. *Bulletin of the Psychonomic Society*, 1973, **1**, 291–292.

Warm, J. S., Epps, B. D., and Ferguson, R. P. Effects of knowledge of results and signal regularity on vigilance performance. *Bulletin of the Psychonomic Society*, 1974, **4**, 272–274.

Warm, J. S., Stutz, R. M., and Vassolo, P. A. Intermodal transfer in temporal discrimination. *Perception and Psychophysics*, 1975, **18**, 281–286.

Warm, J. S., Schumsky, D. A., and Hawley, D. K. Ear asymmetry and the temporal uncertainty of signals in sustained attention. *Bulletin of the Psychonomic Society*, 1976, **7**, 413–416 (a).

Warm, J. S., Wait, R. G., and Loeb, M. Head restraint enhances visual monitoring performance. *Perception and Psychophysics*, 1976, **20**, 299–304 (b).

Warm, J. S., Fishbein, H. D., Howe, S., and Kindell, L. Effects of event rate and the cognitive complexity of critical signals on sustained attention. Paper presented at the meeting of the Psychonomic Society, St Louis, November, 1976 (c).

Warm, J. S., Richter, D. O., Sprague, R. L., Porter, P. K., and Schumsky, D. A. Listening with a dual brain: hemispheric asymmetry in sustained attention. *Bulletin of the Psychonomic Society*, 1980, **15**, 229–232.

Warm, J. S., Sprague, R. L., and Dember, W. N. The cognitive increment function in sustained attention. Paper presented at the meeting of the Psychonomic Society, Philadelphia, November, 1981. Based upon Sprague, R. L. The cognitive increment function in sustained attention. Unpublished master's thesis, University of Cincinnati, 1981.

Warm, J. S., Thompson, L. A., and D'Ambrosio, D. A. Memory load and event regularity in vigilance performance. Paper in preparation, University of Cincinnati, 1982.

Webber, C. E., and Adams, J. A. Effects of visual display mode on six hours of visual monitoring. *Human Factors*, 1964, **4**, 13–20.

Weidenfeller, E. W., Baker, R. A., and Ware, J. R. Effects of knowledge of results (true and false) on vigilance performance. *Perceptual and Motor Skills*, 1962, **14**, 211–215.

Wiener, E. L. Knowledge of results and signal rate in monitoring: a transfer of training approach. *Journal of Applied Psychology*, 1963, **47**, 214–222.

Wiener, E. L. Transfer of training in monitoring: signal amplitude. *Perceptual and Motor Skills*, 1964, **18**, 104.

Wiener, E. L. Training for vigilance: repeated sessions with knowledge of results. *Ergonomics*, 1968, **11**, 547–556.

Wiener, E. L. Adaptive measurement of vigilance decrement. *Ergonomics*, 1973, **16**, 353–363.

Wiener, E. L. Individual and group differences in inspection. In C. G. Drury and J. G. Fox (Eds), *Human reliability in quality control*. London: Taylor and Francis, 1975.

Williges, R. C. Within-session criterion changes compared to an ideal observer criterion in a visual monitoring task. *Journal of Experimental Psychology*, 1969, **81**, 61–66.

Williges, R. C. The role of payoffs and signal ratios in criterion changes during a monitoring task. *Human Factors*, 1971, **13**, 261–267.

Williges, R. C. Manipulating the response criterion in visual monitoring. *Human Factors*, 1973, **15**, 179–185.

Williges, R. C., and North, R. A. Knowledge of results and decision-making performance in visual monitoring. *Organizational Behavior and Human Performance*, 1972, **8**, 44–57.

Zuercher, J. D. The effects of extraneous stimulation on vigilance. *Human Factors*, 1965, **7**, 101–105.

Sustained Attention in Human Performance
Edited by J. S. Warm
© 1984 John Wiley & Sons Ltd.

Chapter 3

The Psychobiology of Sustained Attention

Raja Parasuraman

INTRODUCTION

The role of the brain in the regulation of consciousness and attention has been the subject of inquiry and speculation for many hundreds of years. In the 19th century, J. Hughlings Jackson and William James were among those scientists attempting to give further substance to such speculation in their work. The concept of sustained attention, or 'vigilance', appears in the writings of Hughlings Jackson (1884), but the latter term was first used in a technical sense by the British neurologist Sir Henry Head (1923). Head defined vigilance as a 'state of high grade efficiency of the central nervous system' (Head, 1926, p.486). Norman Mackworth, who was originally trained as a neurologist, subsequently redefined vigilance as a 'state of readiness to detect and respond to certain small changes occurring at random time intervals in the environment' (Mackworth, 1957, pp.389–390). The origins of modern research on vigilance and sustained attention can be traced to Mackworth's classic studies of performance degradation in radar operators (Mackworth, 1944, 1948), and to related wartime studies of radar fatigue (Lindsley, 1944).

The terms 'sustained attention' and 'vigilance' are used interchangeably in this chapter. Neurologists and physiologists tend to use vigilance as a synonym for 'physiological efficiency' or 'arousal', and indeed the French word *vigilance* does have the latter meaning. Vigilance and arousal, however, although related, should not be treated as identical concepts. Vigilance is an aspect of *attention*, which can be divided into its *selective* and *intensive* components (Posner and Boies, 1971; Warm, Chapter 1 in this volume); vigilance is thus sustained attention as opposed to selective attention (Broadbent and Gregory, 1963a; Jerison, 1977). The term sustained attention is preferable in some respects to vigilance but the latter term has such a long history of use that it cannot now be easily replaced.

Despite a long tradition of interest in vigilance as an aspect of brain function, research on the brain mechanisms underlying attention, and sustained attention in particular, has a much shorter history. One reason for this is that the study of attention was itself more or less neglected during the first part of this century, particularly in the 1930s and 1940s, largely due to the behaviorist tradition in psychology which was then dominant. But with the resurgence of interest in the internal mechanisms of human behavior, and against a background of rapid developments in the neurosciences, research into the psychobiology of attention, vigilance and related mental phenomena began to flourish after World War II.

The problem of sustained attention is examined from three different but related standpoints in this chapter. First, the relationship of sustained attention to arousal, as indicated by various signs of central and autonomic nervous system activity, is examined. The major question of interest here is whether these signs reflect specific aspects of central processing underlying vigilance, or whether they provide only some indication of the general level of arousal. Second, vigilance is considered in relation to information processing and decision making. The evidence suggests that two functionally distinct mechanisms are responsible for the vigilance decrement, each operating in different types of task and at different stages in the flow of information through the nervous system. Third, the possible brain systems responsible for the control and maintenance of vigilance are briefly examined. There are conceptual and methodological differences between these three approaches, and the findings consistent with one approach may be at variance with those of another. Nevertheless, the complexity of the vigilance problem and its practical significance demands that it be studied using different methods and languages. As Posner (1978) has demonstrated recently, such a strategy may be particularly effective in developing an understanding of the neural bases of mental events.

Throughout this chapter, a distinction is made between the vigilance decrement, which refers to the reduction in performance with time spent on some task, and the overall level of performance. The distinction is important for both theoretical and practical reasons. Factors that influence the vigilance decrement may not affect overall performance, and vice versa; and thus theories of vigilance must be evaluated for their ability to deal with both these aspects of performance. The distinction is important in the practical sense because the overall level of performance in many settings may be a cause for concern, even though no vigilance decrement as such can be found, as is often the case in industrial situations such as quality control inspection (A. Craig, personal communication; Davies and Parasuraman, 1982). In other situations demanding sustained attention there may be serious deficiencies in both these components of vigilance performance (Mackie, 1977; Davies and Parasuraman, 1982).

AROUSAL AND SUSTAINED ATTENTION (VIGILANCE)

The term arousal refers to a variety of physiological and behavioral states characterized by a degree of excitation or energy mobilization (Duffy, 1962). The unity of the arousal concept is open to query (Lacey, 1967; Pribram and McGuinness, 1975). Nevertheless, it has been customary to identify arousal states as varying in a continuum between the extremes of coma and excited emotion. Transitions between these states are accompanied by a number of changes in the autonomic and the central nervous systems (ANS and CNS), especially in the passage from alert wakefulness to deep sleep. Changes in the electrical activity of the brain, as measured by the electroencephalogram (EEG), are particularly important (Lindsley, 1952), but various changes also occur in other physiological indices such as the heart rate, blood pressure, muscle tone and so on. The pattern of change varies from person to person, and from task to task (Duffy, 1962; Lacey, 1967).

Tasks requiring sustained attention, being prolonged and often monotonous, may sometimes induce drowsiness or feelings of boredom in the subject. Not surprisingly, therefore, many investigators have examined whether physiological signs of lowered arousal are related to the performance decrements typically found in such tasks. In general, only weak or inconsistent relationships have been noted between ANS measures and vigilance performance. More robust findings have been obtained with the EEG and related measures of CNS activity. But these studies indicate that a theory of the vigilance decrement based on a reduction in arousal only accounts for the most general findings on vigilance. Lowered arousal is clearly a concomitant of the decrement, and it probably plays a contributory role in tasks performed under extremes of arousal, such as after a period without sleep or after ingestion of a stimulant (see Davies and Parasuraman, 1982). However, recent findings indicating that more than one mechanism is responsible for the vigilance decrement (Parasuraman, 1976, 1979; see also Warm, 1977) suggest the need for a more detailed and specific theory.

Autonomic arousal

Two requirements appear mandatory for the vigilance decrement to be attributed to a reduction in arousal. First, the decrement should be accompanied by some change in a physiological index indicative of a reduction in arousal. Second, there should be a relationship between the physiological index and behavioral performance, either in the form of inter- or intra-subject correlations, or in different patterns of physiological activity for correct and incorrect responses.

Unfortunately most autonomic measures fail to meet these minimum criteria. The mean heart rate, for example, either decreases or remains stable during a vigilance task, but is uncorrelated with performance (Griew *et al.*, 1963; Thackray *et al.*, 1974). Heart rate variability, on the other hand, increases over time and is moderately correlated with performance (O'Hanlon, 1970; Thackray *et al.*, 1974; Riemersma *et al.*, 1977). The skin conductance is another index which declines over time, but its correlation with performance is weak or unstable (Davies and Krkovic, 1965; Eason *et al.*, 1965; O'Hanlon, 1970). Negative or inconsistent findings have been reported for other variables such as muscle tone and respiration rate (Stern, 1966; O'Hanlon, 1970).

More encouraging results have been obtained with biochemical measures, particularly adrenalin and noradrenalin. Apart from its function as a regulatory hormone released in conditions of rage or fear, adrenalin has been related to coping behavior in a variety of 'stressful' situations (Frankenhaeuser, 1971). The amount of adrenalin in the blood or urine generally decreases during a period of continuous performance. Adrenalin concentration is also positively correlated with performance in both vigilance and complex motor tasks (O'Hanlon, 1965; Frankenhaeuser *et al.*, 1971; O'Hanlon and Beatty, 1976). Although vigilance tasks, being by definition continuous, present some special problems for catecholamine sampling, these results are encouraging, and they raise some important questions regarding the nature of the vigilance decrement and its possible control through manipulation of catecholamine levels (see also p.89). For example, it would be interesting to examine the effects of amphetamine using this methodology. Amphetamine is a stimulant which improves vigilance performance (Mackworth, 1950), and some of its effects are similar to those of adrenalin.

Apart from this work, the results using physiological measures of ANS activity are inconsistent, and provide only marginal evidence that the vigilance decrement is due to a decline in physiological arousal over time. Furthermore, the implications of these studies for the *central* mechanisms controlling vigilant behavior are unclear.

Electrocortical arousal

The EEG is commonly used as an index of central nervous system activity, since it is sensitive to changes in cortical arousal (Lindsley, 1951). In an alert person, the EEG shows a predominance of low-amplitude waves which are desynchronized, and, if some critical stimulus is being awaited, there is usually also a slow negative shift in the baseline activity. This pattern changes to one of regular low-frequency waves interspersed with 'sleep spindles' as the person becomes drowsy and falls asleep.

EEG studies of vigilance show that brain wave activity shifts to lower frequencies during the task. Most studies also report significant correlations between performance and the abundance of EEG activity in the alpha (7–13 Hz) and theta (3–7 Hz) frequency bands (Davies and Krkovic, 1965; Gale *et al.*, 1977; O'Hanlon and Beatty, 1977). In O'Hanlon and Beatty's (1977) study, subjects performed a 2-hour simulation of a radar monitoring task. The EEG activity in different frequency bands was recorded from the occipital and parietal regions of the scalp. A significant decrement in detection efficiency was obtained and this was accompanied by a reliable increase in alpha and theta activity (see Figure 3.1). Detection performance was also significantly correlated with the level of alpha and theta activity. These findings are especially significant as subjects have been noted to miss critical signals when theta activity is predominant in the EEG record (Horvath *et al.*, 1975); and recent findings showing that operant suppression of posterior theta rhythms improves vigilance performance provide further evidence of a relationship between EEG theta signs of electrocortical activation and vigilance (Beatty, 1977; see also pp.89–90).

Arousal theory of vigilance

The changes in electrocortical activity and performance observed during vigilance tasks can be taken to support an arousal theory of vigilance. Nevertheless, these findings do not warrant any strong conclusions regarding the mechanisms of the decrement. A unitary state concept of arousal cannot easily

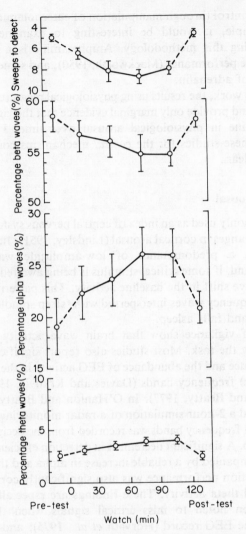

Figure 3.1 Mean detection performance (± standard error), assessed in terms of the number of display sweeps required for target detection, and the amount of EEG activity in three frequency bands, as a function of time on task. Pre- and post-task scores are also shown. [From O'Hanlon and Beatty (1977). Copyright © 1977 Plenum Press, Inc. Reprinted with permission.]

accommodate the array of behavioral, psychophysiological and neuropsychological findings indicating that the vigilance decrement is not a unitary process (Posner, 1975, 1978; Parasuraman, 1976, 1979; Warm, 1977).

Several reviewers have suggested that a multi-state arousal theory may be more successful in accounting for the discrepant findings in the literature (Gale, 1977; Loeb and Alluisi, 1977), but the elements of such a theory have not been detailed. A major problem with arousal theory is that a reduction in arousal is compatible with quite different behavioral outcomes. For example, similar declines in electrocortical arousal are noted (1) when a reliable vigilance decrement occurs (Haider *et al.*, 1964; Davies and Krkovic, 1965); (2) when there is no decrement in performance (Hink *et al.*, 1978); (3) when a decrement occurs in a condition of high target probability but not in a condition of low target probability (Wilkinson and Haines, 1970); or (4) when the decrement is attributable to such functionally distinct mechanisms as a criterion change or a change in sensitivity (see Davies and Parasuraman, 1977). There is also a decline in electrocortical activity if the subject relaxes and performs no task for a comparable period, as Fruhstorfer and Bergstrom (1969) and Roth and Kopell (1969) have found for auditory evoked potentials. Indeed, the only prerequisite for obtaining a reduction in electrocortical activity seems to be that the experimental situations be prolonged and monotonous (Davies *et al.*, 1983). In such conditions, EEG signs of lowered arousal are observed not only in the discrimination and monitoring tasks usually studied in vigilance, but also in long-term tracking tasks (Kornfeld and Beatty, 1977). These findings suggest that while it is indisputable that arousal declines during a vigilance task, it cannot be said that the decrement in detection performance is wholly dependent on lowered arousal.

The vigilance decrement refers not only to the decrement in detection rate that is most commonly reported in vigilance studies, but also to the decrement in speed of response (Davies and Tune, 1970). Detection latency is regarded as a performance measure strongly related to the detection rate, and governed by similar underlying mechanisms. Buck (1966) proposed that a declining state of 'perceptual vigilance' can account for both a fall in the detection rate and a concomitant rise in detection latency; such an interpretation is, of course, consistent with arousal theory. But if latency data for response categories other than detections are considered, an arousal interpretation no longer seems tenable. Parasuraman and Davies (1976) had subjects respond to both target and non-target events in a 45-minute visual vigilance task. While the latencies of positive responses (correct detections and false alarms) increased with time on task, the latencies of negative responses (correct rejections and omission errors) decreased or remained stable with time (see Figure 3.2). It is difficult to account for these differential trends in terms of a reduction in arousal, if, as is generally the case, speed of response is a monotonic function of arousal level. The results are, on the other hand, compatible with a decision theory view that latency of response is related to the strictness of the response criterion for reporting targets (Parasuraman and Davies, 1976). With an increase in the response criterion with time on task, positive responses increase in latency because the subject becomes less confident and more cautious about responding positively; negative responses,

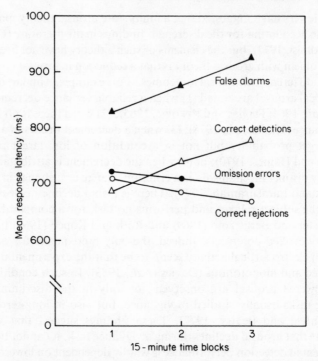

Figure 3.2   Mean latencies of positive (correct detections and false alarms) and negative responses (correct rejections and omission errors) in consecutive 15-minute time blocks of a vigilance task. [From Parasuraman and Davies (1976). Copyright © 1976 The American Psychological Association. Reprinted with permission.]

on the other hand, decrease in latency because, at the same time, the subject becomes less cautious about responding negatively (see also pp.72–73).

Posner (1975) has pointed out that the concept of arousal had its origins in the view that a general energizing state drives all behavior. As such, it is compatible more with a stimulus–response view of the organism than with the information processing view that has currency today. The emphasis in the information processing approach is on different modes and stages of processing in the flow of information from stimulus to response. These stages may differ in the optimum level of 'arousal' necessary for efficient processing, and thus it cannot be assumed that a single general state is optimum for all stages (Routtenberg, 1971; Posner, 1975).

Arousal and the level of vigilance

While a unitary state concept of arousal is unsatisfactory in the analysis of the vigilance decrement, such a conceptualization accounts for differences in the overall level of vigilance performance. Evidence from a number of different sources points to a monotonic relationship between the level of arousal and the level of vigilance. Detection efficiency is reduced by stresses which lower arousal, such as moderate heat (Poulton, 1977). Alcohol-induced drowsiness also lowers the overall level of vigilance, there being little or no effect on the vigilance decrement (Erwin *et al.*, 1978). Moreover, stimulants such as amphetamine (Mackworth, 1965a; Rapaport *et al.*, 1978), and stresses which increase arousal, such as low-frequency vibration (Poulton, 1978), improve vigilance. The evidence in favor of the so-called inverted-U relationship between arousal and performance is less convincing, and will not be dealt with here (see Näätänen, 1973; Davies and Parasuraman, 1982).

Arousal differences have been reported between individuals differing in temperament. Byrne (1976, 1977) found that neurotic and psychotic depressive patients had lower performance levels on an auditory vigilance task, due apparently to individual differences in chronic arousal. Introverted persons are thought to be more highly aroused than extraverts, and to have greater resistance to inhibitory influences (Eysenck, 1957). This suggests that introverts should perform better on vigilance tasks than extraverts. The results generally bear out this prediction, and suggest further that the superiority of introverts is based on a higher d', a measure of perceptual efficiency (Harkins and Geen, 1975). However, early findings indicating that only extraverts show a vigilance decrement (Bakan *et al.*, 1963) have not been fully replicated (see Davies and Parasuraman, 1982, for a review).

Studies of circadian rhythms and work–rest schedules also indicate that fluctuations in the level of arousal are accompanied by consistent changes in the level of vigilance performance. Blake (1967a) found that performance on a letter-cancellation vigilance task covaried with body temperature at different times of day; performance and oral temperature were lowest at 8 a.m., and highest at 9 p.m. Other studies have reported reliable improvements in vigilance from morning to afternoon testing (Colquhoun, 1960; Davies and Davies, 1975). This is thought to be due to an improvement in d' (Colquhoun, 1971), although Craig (1979) has recently reported that, for a short-duration discrimination task at least, the improvement is due to the use of a more liberal response criterion later in the day. Circadian effects on performance in real world operations involving vigilance have also been noted; in one study on vehicle operation, over 50% of a sample of accidents thought to be due to loss of alertness occurred between midnight and 8 a.m., when arousal is generally at its lowest level (Harris, 1977).

There are individual differences in circadian rhythms that may make some individuals more susceptible to the adverse effects of loss of alertness. For example, the body temperature of introverts is higher than that of extraverts during the normal working day (from about 8 a.m. to 5 p.m.), the reverse being true in the evening, thus suggesting a distinction between 'morning types' and 'evening types' (Blake, 1967b; Horne and Ostberg, 1977). One would therefore predict that introverts should be more vigilant than extraverts during the day, and that extraverts should be superior in the evening and at night. Unfortunately, most studies have been conducted during normal working hours, so that only the first prediction has been tested. On the whole, introverts perform better than extraverts during the day (Davies and Parasuraman, 1982).

Although most tasks requiring a direct response to stimulus input show the usual afternoon over morning superiority effect, tasks involving memory generally show the reverse effect. Performance on short-term memory tasks has been found to decline with time of day in a number of studies (Blake, 1967a; Baddeley *et al.*, 1970; Folkard, 1979; for an exception, see Jones *et al.*, 1978). A low level of arousal is thought to be conducive to efficient short-term memory and thus the time of day effect could be due to an increase in the general level of arousal over the working day (Hockey and Colquhoun, 1972). A recent study by Davies *et al.* (1980) supports this hypothesis and extends it to vigilance tasks. They found that the normal afternoon superiority in vigilance performance is reversed if target discrimination is changed from one not involving memory to one which incorporates a memory load (see also pp.74–78 for a further discussion of the effects of memory load).

Habituation theory of vigilance

The habituation theory of vigilance is a variant of arousal theory, and was first proposed by J. F. Mackworth (1968, 1969). A physiological or behavioral response may be said to habituate if it is reduced in amplitude or eliminated as a result of repeated stimulation (Groves and Thompson, 1970). The EEG desynchronization response, for example, habituates with regular presentation of the same stimulus. Sharpless and Jasper (1956) were among the first to report this phenomenon, and they also suggested that the performance decrements found in vigilance and other monotonous tasks may be due to habituation processes.

A factor that is closely related to habituation as well as to vigilance is the rate of presentation of stimulus events, or the event rate. Generally speaking, habituation is greater at higher event rates; and it is also known that vigilance performance is lower at higher event rates (Jerison and Pickett, 1964). Mackworth (1968) therefore suggested that the repetitious nature of the background events in a vigilance task serves to habituate the neural responses to these stimuli, as a result of which the observer's ability to detect signals in the background neural 'noise' is impaired; this is a process which unfolds over time, so that there is a progressive drop in the detection rate. Mackworth suggested that the habituation in the EEG arousal response (desynchronization) and in the cortical evoked responses leads to the performance decrements found in a variety of prolonged tasks. Unfortunately, empirical support for this simple and elegant theory has not yet emerged (Harkins, 1974; Gale, 1977; Gale *et al.*, 1977). At the time the theory was proposed, supporting evidence was drawn mainly from Mackworth's own studies with the continuous clock task, which is a modification of the clock test used originally by Norman Mackworth (1944). Mackworth (1969) reported an approximately exponential decay in detection efficiency (d') in this task; this appears to simulate a habituation process, which is usually a negatively accelerated function of the number of stimulus presentations per unit time (Thompson and Spencer, 1966). However, this result is specific to this task alone, and is probably due to the continuous visual pursuit required by the task. In most other vigilance tasks, d' does not decay exponentially, and the time course of habituation appears too short to account for vigilance decrements which cover periods from 30 minutes to 4 hours (Jerison, 1977).

Habituation can be distinguished from passive processes such as fatigue, or general adaptation, by the phenomenon of *dishabituation*, or the immediate restoration of response following some sudden change in the pattern of stimulation. Although the effects of factors such as rest pauses and task

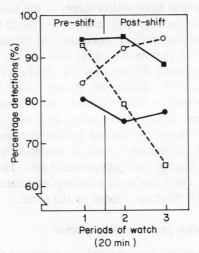

Figure 3.3 Mean percentage of correct detections as a function of 20-minute periods of watch for low and high event rate, and 'shifted' and 'non-shifted' groups of subjects (see text). *Key:* ●———● *and* ■———■ *represent the non-shifted groups (fast and slow event rate groups, respectively);* o-----o *and* □----□ *represent the fast-to-slow and slow-to-fast shifted groups, respectively.* [From Krulewitz *et al.* (1975). Copyright © 1975 The Psychonomic Society, Inc. Reprinted with permission.]

interruption, which improve vigilance (Mackworth, 1950), may be interpreted as dishabituation effects, a study which specifically examined the effects of dishabituation failed to support the habituation theory (Krulewitz *et al.*, 1975). In this study, a shift paradigm was used in which the event rate was increased or decreased suddenly halfway through a vigilance session. Shifts from slow to fast and from fast to slow were made for separate groups, and two non-shifted groups were also run. The results are illustrated in Figure 3.3. According to Mackworth's (1968) theory, improved performance due to the dishabituating effect of the shift should be observed for both shifted groups. Figure 3.3 shows, however, that the slow to fast group performed poorly compared to the non-shifted control at the fast event rate. For the fast to slow group, performance improved after the shift compared to the non-shifted group, but did so only after the shifted group had experienced the new event rate for about 20 minutes. These results are at odds with known facts about the time course of habituation and dishabituation (Thompson and Spencer, 1966; see also Warm, 1977; and Chapter 2, pp.25–26).

INFORMATION PROCESSING AND SUSTAINED ATTENTION

J. F. Mackworth's neural habituation theory is the most recent of a number of theories of vigilance, among which are theories based on arousal, inhibition, expectancy and related constructs (Frankmann and Adams, 1962). Warm (1977) has recently pointed out that each of these theories can account for only part of the data, thus suggesting the need for a multi-factor theoretical approach to sustained attention. The distinction already made between the vigilance decrement and the overall level of vigilance, and the suggestion that these are influenced by different factors, is consistent with this idea. A distinction can also be made between the perceptual and decision processes that affect changes in vigilance. Once this distinction is made, it becomes clear that more than one mechanism is responsible for the vigilance decrement. This in turn suggests that theoretical constructs which can explain findings associated with one mechanism may not accommodate findings related to the other.

Perceptual and decision processes in vigilance

The rate of presentation of stimulus events, or the event rate, is one of the most important of the many variables that affect the vigilance decrement. The marked event rate effects found in the study by Krulewitz *et al.* (1975) were first described by Jerison and Pickett (1964), although Mackworth (1957) had earlier alluded to their importance. Following Jerison and Pickett's seminal work, several investigators have shown that an increase in the event rate results in a substantial reduction in vigilance performance, primarily due to an increased performance decrement (Mackworth, 1965b; Taub and Osborne, 1968; Metzger *et al.*, 1974; Warm, 1977). There has been some dispute as to whether the event rate effect represents a genuine reduction in performance efficiency, or is a by-product of response criterion changes induced by a reduction in conditional target probability, which is inversely proportional to the event rate (Colquhoun, 1961; Jerison, 1967a); but by using signal detection measures it is possible to show that the reduction in efficiency is independent of response criterion changes (Loeb and Binford, 1968; Parasuraman, 1979).

According to signal detection theory, a distinction should be made between the observer's *perceptual sensitivity* and his *response* or *decision* criterion (Green and Swets, 1966). The former refers to the observer's efficiency in detecting a target; the latter reflects his bias for reporting a target as opposed to a non-target. The d' and β parameters are commonly used as measures of these two characteristics, although a number of other indices are also used (Swets, 1973; Swets and Green, 1978).

Until fairly recently, it was unclear whether the vigilance decrement results primarily from a decline in sensitivity or from changes in the response criterion (Swets and Kristofferson, 1970). As the decrement in the detection rate is normally also accompanied by a decline in the *false* detection rate, the vigilance decrement could be due either to a deterioration in the observer's ability to detect targets (Mackworth and Taylor, 1963) or to a response process in which the observer becomes more cautious about reporting a target with time (Broadbent and Gregory, 1963b).

It now appears that the vigilance decrement results from a decrement in perceptual sensitivity only when the observer has to discriminate a target from a non-target represented in memory, and stimulus events are presented rapidly. In contrast, if the discrimination does not load memory, or if the event rate is low, the decrement results from changes in decision criteria, with no change in sensitivity. This is true irrespective of whether the observer has to look for or listen for targets (Parasuraman and Davies, 1977; Parasuraman, 1979).

These findings suggest that the vigilance decrement may result from one of two functionally distinct mechanisms — a sensitivity shift or a response criterion shift. It must be noted, however, that the use of the d' and β measures to distinguish between these two processes may not always be appropriate (Jerison, 1967b; Taylor, 1967; see also Davies and Parasuraman, 1982). Most psychophysical measures of perceptual sensitivity and response criterion are derived on the assumption that signals arrive in a relatively well-defined observation interval; when this is not the case, and signals can occur randomly at any point in time, reaction time-based estimates of sensitivity may be used (Egan *et al.*, 1961). Watson and Nichols (1976) have outlined a modification of Egan *et al.*'s free-response method whereby an estimate of d' can be obtained from reaction time distributions. If some of the assumptions of parametric signal detection theory are suspect, nonparametric measures and/or receiver operating characteristics (ROCs) should be examined. Analyses using these techniques also reveal that the vigilance decrement reflects one of two underlying, independent mechanisms (Swets, 1977; Parasuraman, 1979). What are the limiting conditions associated with each of these mechanisms? One view is that sensitivity decrements occur only for visual displays, especially those demanding a high rate of observation (Mackworth, 1970; Broadbent, 1971). However, there are examples of auditory tasks showing sensitivity decrements and high event rate tasks which do not show such decrements (Swets, 1977).

A closer examination of the discrimination tasks used in studies of sustained attention suggests a division of these tasks into two general categories: successive-discrimination tasks and simultaneous-discrimination tasks. In the first type of task, a target is specified as a change in some feature of a repetitive standard stimulus, the standard value being absent when the non-standard value is given; examples include the discrimination of an increase in the brightness of a visual display, or a change in the intensity or duration of an auditory stimulus. In tasks belonging to the second category, the target is specified fully within a stimulus event, as in the detection of a target element in a display containing many elements, or of a specified auditory signal within a more complex noisy background. The important distinguishing feature between these tasks is the memory load imposed by the successive-discrimination target, since target and non-target features are not present simultaneously. Both intra-modal and cross-modal correlations in performance are large within but not across these task categories, further testifying to the validity of this dichotomy (Parasuraman, 1976). These categories are also known by the terms 'perceptual speed' and 'flexibility of closure' (Parasuraman, 1976; see also Levine *et al.*, 1973; Fleishman, 1975). However, in the present context, the terms successive-

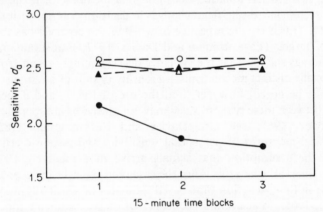

Figure 3.4 Mean values of perceptual sensitivity in consecutive 15-minute time blocks of a vigilance task, for successive and simultaneous discrimination tasks at low and high event rates. o-----o , Successive discrimination at low event rate; ●————● , successive discrimination at high event rate; ▲-----▲ , simultaneous discrimination at low event rate; △————△ , simultaneous discrimination at high event rate. [From Parasuraman, *Science*, **205**, 924–927. Copyright 1979 by the AAAS.]

discrimination and simultaneous-discrimination are more suggestive of the information processing differences between these two types of task.

Parasuraman (1979) examined the effects of event rate on two auditory vigilance tasks, a successive-discrimination task and a simultaneous-discrimination task. In the former, the target was a 2.1 dB increase in the intensity of an intermittent 1000 Hz tone. In the latter, a 1000 Hz tone had to be detected within an intermittent noise burst. Performance was compared at event rates of 5 and 30 events per minute. As Figure 3.4 shows, a sensitivity decrement in d_a (an ROC-based measure which is more robust than d') was obtained only for the high event rate successive-discrimination task combination, although a vigilance decrement (detection rate) was obtained in all conditions. These findings were confirmed and extended to visual stimulation in a further experiment. Stimuli (circular light flashes) were presented intermittently at two adjacent locations on a visual display. When dependence on short-term retention was eliminated by presenting target and non-target items (dimmer and brighter flashes, respectively) on the two sources at the same time, a sensitivity decrement

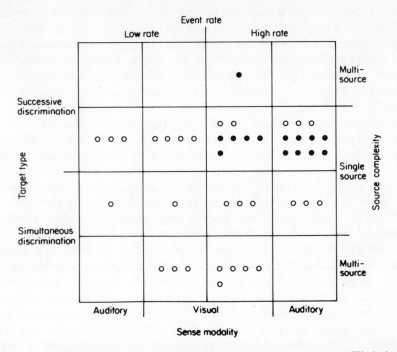

Figure 3.5 Taxonomic classification of vigilance tasks by the presence (filled circles) or absence (open circles) of a reliable decrement in perceptual sensitivity over time. Each circle represents a task used in a study of sustained attention in which sensitivity was indexed by d' or a related measure. [From Parasuraman (1979). Copyright © 1979 The American Association for the Advancement of Science. Reprinted with permission.]

was no longer obtained at a high event rate. Given the modality-specific nature of many vigilance phenomena (Davies and Tune, 1970), the congruence of the findings between visual and auditory stimulation provides strong support for the distinction between successive and simultaneous discrimination in the context of vigilance. As a further test of the generality of the results, they were compared to the findings of 27 previous studies reporting sensitivity data for a wide range of vigilance tasks. The results of a taxonomic analysis of this data set revealed that all instances of sensitivity decrement occurred only for successive-discrimination tasks at high event rates, and not otherwise, as indicated in Figure 3.5.

Mental effort and sensitivity decrement

The results of the studies by Parasuraman (1979) suggest that peformance decrements in sustained attention result either from a reduction in sensitivity or from changes in response criteria over time, depending on the task parameters. The first mechanism may be conceived to be operative at an early stage in the flow of information through the nervous system and probably involves the efficiency of neural units concerned with the detection of critical signals in the environment. The decrement in sensitivity occurs only if the detection system has to utilize information from short-term stores that are subject to interference at high stimulation rates. This effect may also be due to a modification of the neural pathways concerned with the registration and early analysis of stimulus input (Posner, 1978). The second underlying mechanism is associated with the decision processes leading to the selection of a response, and may therefore operate at a later stage. Changes in factors such as subjective probability affect the decision process, which is largely independent of the earlier detection system. Which of these two systems contributes to changes in vigilance performance with time depends on the task or, more specifically, on the processes involved in target discrimination and the required stimulus processing rate.

These processes may be data-limited, or processes for which performance cannot be improved beyond a certain level by increasing processing resources because of the relatively poor quality of the data (Norman and Bobrow, 1975). The available data may be of poor quality either because of the stimulus itself, as in the detection of a weak signal in noise, or because of its representation in memory, as in delayed-comparison memory tasks and successive-discrimination vigilance tasks. Tasks which combine these limitations with the demands of a high processing rate will be likely to yield decrements in sensitivity. For tasks which do not demand this sustained level of 'effort' (Kahneman, 1973; Pribram and McGuinness, 1975), sensitivity remains stable over time, and the vigilance decrement reflects variations in decision criteria. The criterion increases that occur may be due to changes in the subjective probability of the occurrence of a target, or to related changes in response strategy (Broadbent, 1971; Craig, 1978; Davies and Parasuraman, 1982).

Delayed-comparison tasks are similar in some respects to successive-discrimination tasks, since in each task a target has to be discriminated by comparing it to a previously presented standard. Sensitivity (d') decreases as the delay interval between the standard and the comparison stimulus increases, and a number of models of the decay in the memory trace for the standard stimulus may be proposed to account for this result (Kinchla and Smyzer, 1967; Baddeley, 1976). This apparently contradicts the finding in vigilance that an increase in event rate (which corresponds to a decrease in the inter-stimulus or 'delay' interval) reduces d'. But this effect interacts with time on task, and the reduction in d' is due mainly to the decrement in d' found at a high event rate. Event rate effects are not marked under 'alerted' detection conditions, at the beginning of a vigil (Parasuraman, 1979), or immediately following a sudden shift in event rate (Krulewitz *et al.*, 1975). Also in delayed-comparison tasks, the decay in d' is much less marked when there is only one standard stimulus (Aiken and Lau, 1966), as in most vigilance tasks.

A taxonomic analysis of vigilance data provides broad support for a two-process model of the vigilance decrement that distinguishes between perceptual and decision processes that affect performance. Physiological evidence for such a distinction is not as strong, although this is partly because of the limited number of relevant studies which have been carried out. Studies of ANS activity have been concerned for the most part with state variables (arousal, motivation, etc.) and not with concepts of information processing and decision making, although psychophysiological correlates of 'mental effort' have been reported (Kahneman, 1973). Beatty (1982a) has shown that changes in pupillary dilation, time-locked to the presentation of a stimulus, or to the execution of a response, can provide a sensitive index of the momentary effort required to perform a mental operation. Task-evoked pupillary responses should therefore decline in amplitude in a vigilance task in which sensitivity declines over time. This was reported in a recent study by Beatty (1982b), who found that the sensitivity decrement over time for a 40-minute auditory successive discrimination task was related to a significant decline in the amplitude of the task-evoked (phasic) pupillary response. There was no change in the amplitude of the basal (tonic) pupillary diameter, which is a good index of the general level of arousal (Yoss *et al.*, 1970). The results reject the view that the vigilance decrement is due to a drop in arousal and provide physiological confirmation that the decrement is related to the combined demands on mental effort of a high event rate and memory load.

Although one's subjective experience of performance of most vigilance tasks might lead to the conclusion that such tasks do not require much mental effort, the behavioral and physiological evidence suggests that high event rate vigilance tasks, despite their superficial lack of difficulty, are especially demanding. The amount of mental effort exerted can be measured by the amount of circulating catecholamines released into the blood. As discussed on pp.64–65, changes during task performance in the blood and urine concentration of adrenalin, noradrenalin and related hormones have been investigated by Frankenheuser (1971) and Frankenheuser *et al.* (1971). These studies have shown that the release of adrenalin is related to the effort exerted to perform a given task, and that adrenalin is released during the performance of vigilance tasks (characterized as monotonous, low subject control tasks), as well as during tasks clearly identifiable as more challenging, such as choice-reaction time and problem solving.

Event-related brain potentials and sustained attention

While the spontaneous electrical activity of the brain is usually analyzed in the frequency domain (alpha, theta, frequency bands, etc.), the event-related potentials (ERPs) which are present in the EEG are usually analyzed in the time domain. A variety of such potentials has been discovered, each being characterized by the length of time over which the EEG response is averaged. These range from the very short latency brainstem potentials (Jewett and Williston, 1971) to the longer latency contingent negative variation (Walter *et al.*, 1964) and P300 (Donchin *et al.*, 1978). The neural substrates of these potentials are still largely unknown, although several possible mechanisms have been outlined (Goff *et al.*, 1978).

Of the various types of event-related potential, the longer-latency potentials, and in particular the CNV and P300 waves, have aroused greatest psychological interest (Donchin *et al.*, 1978; Posner, 1978). The substantial literature on these components indicates that P300 and other late ERP components are related to different aspects of human information processing. The better controlled and analyzed studies suggest that P300 is not a unitary process, but may represent a complex of brain activity that is differentially related to such factors as subjective probability or expectancy, task relevance and decision confidence (Tueting, 1978; Donchin *et al.*, 1978). It is likely that since some of these factors are implicated in vigilance, a conceptualization of the electrocortical basis of sustained attention in terms of P300 and related ERP components will prove more satisfactory than the more superficial framework of a generalized state of arousal (but see Wilkinson and Seales, 1978, for a dissenting view).

Changes in ERP components in signal detection and vigilance tasks have been examined in a number of studies (Haider *et al.*, 1964; Ritter and Vaughan, 1969; Parasuraman and Davies, 1975; Squires, 1975a,b; Davies and Parasuraman, 1976, 1977). In an influential study, Haider *et al.* (1964) reported that the principal negative wave of the ERP to visual stimuli declined in amplitude during the course of a vigilance task. ERP amplitude was also greater for detected targets than for omissions. Similar findings were reported by Wilkinson *et al.* (1966), using an auditory task. A different ERP component was affected in this latter study, but given the different sensory modalities employed, both findings may be interpreted as showing that the decrement is accompanied by a reduction in electrocortical arousal (Davies and Parasuraman, 1977).

A study by Hink *et al.* (1978) is an interesting variant to the typical study showing parallel declines in arousal and vigilance performance. Hink *et al.* had subjects listen to a series of tones presented to each ear (or 'channel'), and detect a designated target in a specified ear. The ear to be attended was alternated over a vigil lasting about 70 minutes. In this type of situation, it is known that the N100 component of the ERP is larger in amplitude when attention is focussed on a channel than when attention is either divided between channels (Hink *et al.*, 1977; Parasuraman, 1978), or directed to another channel (Hillyard *et al.*, 1973). It is thought that this apparent modulation of N100 is due to a long-lasting slow negative wave which displaces N100 (see Näätänen and Michie, 1979). The magnitude of the effect is related to factors which affect the ability to allocate attentional resources selectively, such as the presentation rate (Schwent *et al.*, 1976a; Parasuraman, 1978) and the distinctiveness of the cues separating attended and unattended material (Schwent *et al.*, 1976b). It has also been observed that the size of the effect is dependent on the difficulty of target discriminations in the attended channel (Parasuraman, 1980). Hink *et al.* reasoned that if the vigilance decrement reflects changes in selective attention, the N100 amplitude difference between attended and unattended channels should change with time on task; on the other hand, if the decrement is related to changes in general state (arousal), there should be a decrement in the ERP amplitudes of both attended and unattended channels. The latter hypothesis was supported, but it is weakened by the failure to obtain a significant decrement in detection rate over time, probably because rest periods were used. Moreover, the results conflict with a similar study by Donald and Young (1980), who found differential long-term (but not short-term) habituation of N100 amplitude for attended and unattended channels, albeit using a different signal-averaging procedure. Nevertheless the study is an interesting attempt to separate the effects of arousal and attention, and the results support Jerison's proposal of a fundamental distinction between selective attention and sustained attention (Jerison, 1977).

Other studies of ERPs and vigilance have focused on longer latency components such as the P300. Ritter and Vaughan (1969) repeated the study by Haider *et al.* (1964) using both visual and auditory discrimination tasks. They noted that Haider *et al.*'s failure to obtain a late positive component (P300) could be accounted for by their usage of a bipolar linkage between the vertex and occipital leads, P300 being common to both these 'active' leads. With 'monopolar' recording between the vertex and a relatively inactive site (the ear), Ritter and Vaughan found that detected signals were associated with a large P300 component, which was reduced or absent following missed signals or non-signals. Since P300 was present both when subjects withheld motor responses for 1 second following detection and also when they responded to both signal and non-signal events, Ritter and Vaughan concluded that P300 is unrelated to central processes underlying motor response. It should be noted, though, that the extent to which P300 overlaps with potentials associated with motor preparation is currently a matter for further investigation. In tasks where P300 latency and reaction time overlap in the same range, multivariate statistical techniques (see Donchin and Heffley, 1978) may be useful in separating decision- and motor-related potentials in the ERP. On the other hand, earlier components such as N200 may provide correlates of the decision process in these situations (Ritter *et al.*, 1979). In delayed-response tasks or in tasks where P300 precedes the response, the problem may be less serious. (For a discussion of P300 and potentials associated with expectancy and motor preparation, see Donchin *et al.* (1975) and Friedman *et al.* (1978), who have distinguished between different P300-like waves on the basis of reaction time distributions.) Cooper *et al.* (1977) have also reported that the detection of an infrequent event in a visual display continuously scanned for 1.5 hours is accompanied by a large positive potential which is independent of motor response. The positive component observed in this study is similar to the P300 component found in other vigilance studies, but changes in this component with time on task were not reported.

Ritter and Vaughan's (1969) study suggests the possibility that the late ERP components may provide neurophysiological signs of the time course of the decision process underlying detection performance in vigilance tasks. This was explored further by Parasuraman and Davies (1975), who examined the relationship between the latencies of late ERP components and response latencies in a visual monitoring task. The latencies of N200 and P300 for ERPs averaged to correct detections and false alarms discriminated between the latencies of these responses as well as between response latencies in the first and second halves of the task. The differences in response latency are consistent with a decision process in which the time of response is related to the criterion level above which the response is elicited (Parasuraman and Davies, 1976; see also pp.72–76). The peak latencies of N200 and P300 are apparently related to this process, slower, less confident responses being associated with ERP components which peak later. This interpretation receives further support from a study in which ERPs were recorded selectively to responses varying in confidence level (Davies and Parasuraman, 1977). ERPs averaged to correct detections had longer latency P300s for doubtful responses than for confident responses, and these responses also had longer decision latencies.

A number of signal detection studies have also examined P300–decision criteria relationships. Paul and Sutton (1972), for example, varied the decision criterion by manipulating either the stimulus–response payoff matrix or the target porbability in an auditory signal detection task. Both manipulations affected the decision criterion and P300, the latter being related to the strictness of the criterion. Similar results were reported by Hillyard *et al.* (1971) and by

Squires *et al.* (1975a,b). The amplitude of P300 is closely related to decision confidence and the relative probability of response (Squires *et al.*, 1975a). Squires *et al.* (1975b) averaged ERPs selectively in accordance with the criterion cutoff in an auditory signal detection task and found a remarkably close covariation between both the amplitude and latency of P300 and the observer's decision criterion. The same relationship was preserved whether the criterion cutoff value was derived from confidence ratings or from variations in signal probability (see Figure 3.6).

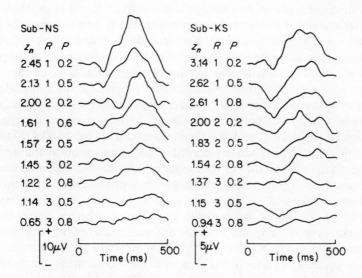

Figure 3.6   Relationship between criterion cutoff (z_n) and ERP waveforms for correct detections in an auditory signal detection task. Also shown are the confidence rating (*R*) and the *a priori* signal probability (*P*). [From Squires *et al.* (1975b). Copyright © 1975 Academic Press. Reprinted with permission.]

The P300 findings provide converging evidence pointing to the importance of criterion shifts in sustained attention. Yet, the ERP studies have yet to distinguish between criterion and sensitivity shifts, nor do ERP components provide diagnostic measures to evaluate such shifts independently of performance. In principle, such a distinction should be possible; if variations in sensitivity are associated with the efficiency of neural activity which precedes the decision process, there could be changes in early or middle latency components (e.g. N100). Unfortunately, the effects of changes in sensitivity may often be confounded with changes in decision confidence or response probability (Hillyard *et al.*, 1971). Thus a differentiation of sensitivity and criterion changes using ERP components may be possible only insofar as these changes can be manipulated independently.

BRAIN SYSTEMS IN SUSTAINED ATTENTION

EEG and ERP studies in humans have provided an informative picture of changes in brain electrical activity in sustained attention. Ultimately, the value of this information will depend on its successful integration with other findings from neuropsychology and animal neurophysiology. These disciplines have contributed significantly to our understanding of the brain systems involved in the higher cortical functions of attention, memory and thought (Pribram, 1971; Luria, 1973). Much of this knowledge is still evolving, but this research holds out the promise of translating the concepts of cognitive psychology into identifiable areas of the brain that are anatomically and functionally related.

Pribram and McGuinness (1975) have recently proposed a theory of attention that attempts to integrate a diverse range of findings related to this topic. The theory identifies three different but interacting neural systems that control arousal, activation and effort. Neural circuitry located in the amygdala and in related structures of the frontal cortex is proposed to control arousal, defined in terms of phasic response to stimulus input. Activation, or tonic preparedness to respond, is associated with basal ganglia circuits in this model. Finally, the control of effort, or the activity needed to coordinate arousal and activation, is proposed to be a function of the hippocampus. Since the arousal, activation (expectancy), and effort constructs have been implicated with different aspects of vigilance (the overall level of vigilance, criterion shifts and sensitivity shifts, respectively), it should be possible to examine whether these facets of performance can be 'mapped' onto the different brain regions identified in the Pribram and McGuinness model. There are some studies of vigilance in patients who have sustained injuries to one or more of these brain areas, but these studies face special problems of interpretation (see below). Electrophysiological and lesion studies of animals in vigilance situations (e.g. Goodman, 1970; Donchin *et al.*, 1971; Spevack and Pribram, 1973) should provide some indication of the relative importance of these brain areas. The current evidence is sparse, since most of the relevant research has not been concerned with sustained attention *per se*. This is also true of neuropsychological research, although at least one researcher has used the vigilance task as a 'model' task (see Posner, 1978) for studying hemispheric organization in the brain (Dimond, 1976). Consequently, it is possible here only to make what may appear to be rather crude generalizations based on very limited evidence.

The ascending reticular activating system

The reticular formation is a core of neural tissue occupying the lower regions of the brainstem and mid-brain. It receives sensory information that is en route to the cortex, as well as projections from the spinal cord, the cerebellum and the cortex. The diversity of these connections attests to the importance of this brain region, which plays an important role in the regulation of arousal (Moruzzi and Magoun, 1949). The destruction of the reticular formation or its functional disablement can produce an enduring loss of consciousness. On the other hand, electrical stimulation of this area awakens a sleeping animal and produces the familiar EEG pattern of desynchronization. Due to these properties the reticular formation has been likened to a sentinel which serves to arouse the cortex, forming part of an alarm system called the ascending reticular activating system or ARAS (Lindsley, 1960).

Since the level of vigilance is related to the level of arousal, this aspect of vigilance performance is probably controlled by neural circuits forming part of a frontal cortex–ARAS network. Skinner and associates (Skinner and Lindsley, 1973; Skinner and Yingling, 1977; Skinner, 1978) have recently outlined a neural model of attention and arousal in which the combined influence of the mesencephalic reticular formation (MRF) and the mediothalamic-frontocortical system on the thalamic reticular nucleus controls sensory input to the cortex. They proposed that the thalamic reticular nucleus is inhibited by activity in the MRF and stimulated by frontal cortex activity, thus providing mechanisms for the control of both general arousal and selective attention. This model can explain many of the neurophysiological findings on selective attention, but its applicability to sustained attention is limited to an interpretation of the overall level of performance. Evidence from other studies also points to a relationship between the MRF and the level of vigilance. (Studies of brain-injured patients are considered below.) One relevant animal study was reported by Goodman (1970), who trained monkeys to respond to visual targets in a vigilance-like task. Multiple-unit neuronal activity in the MRF was correlated with both the speed and the accuracy of target detection over a 4–6 hour period. A complementary finding is the improvement in discrimination accuracy and speed found in monkeys after electrical stimulation of the MRF (Fuster, 1958).

Pribram and McGuinness (1975) have reviewed evidence suggesting that the arousal system includes the MRF as well as more rostral and caudal structures, from the medial parts of the spinal cord up to and including the hypothalamus. They refer to this group of structures as the corebrain arousal system, and suggest that it is coordinated by excitatory and inhibitory circuits centered on the amydala. The control of the level of vigilance by such circuits is a hypothesis without firm evidence, but at present the hypothesis is plausible and has heuristic value.

The effects of brain injury

Impairments in concentration and the ability to sustain attention for even relatively short periods of time are common in persons who have suffered various forms of brain injury. Performance decrements are commonly noted for the continuous performance test (CPT), a 15-minute discrimination task developed by Rosvold *et al.* (1956) as a diagnostic aid in the assessment of brain damage. Patients with either diffuse or localized brain damage perform poorly on the CPT and related vigilance tasks (Mirsky, 1960; Mirsky and Orren, 1977).

The relationship between the location of the damage and the type of performance affected is not clear, although there are some suggestive findings. Patients with epileptic foci in the MRF perform poorly on the CPT compared to those with frontal or temporal lobe foci (Mirsky *et al.*, 1960), while unilateral removal of the frontal or temporal lobes does not affect CPT performance (Mirsky and Rosvold, 1960). Mirsky and associates (Bakay-Pragay *et al.*, 1975; Mirsky *et al.*, 1977) have also shown that simulating an epileptic discharge by electrically stimulating the mesopontine reticular formation in monkeys produces performance impairments on the CPT. These findings point to the involvement of the MRF in the overall level of vigilance. It should be noted, however, that patients with senile dementia (Alexander, 1973) or with EEG signs of generalized subcortical epilepsy (Bruhn, 1970) also show poor CPT performance. Evidence pointing to the importance of specific brain regions is difficult to come by, although some findings reported by McDonald and Burns (1964) are interesting in this regard. They reported that the characteristic low performance levels and large vigilance decrements found in a brain-damaged population were contributed primarily by patients with basal ganglia lesions. Psychomotor regulation is one of the functions of the basal ganglia, and these findings are consistent with other evidence showing impairment in response speed in patients with basal ganglia damage and in the aged (Hicks and Birren, 1970). Pribram and McGuinness' (1975) suggestion that the basal ganglia control changes in expectancy and tonic activation is also consonant with these results. This raises the intriguing possibility that this brain system may control changes in vigilance performance arising from fluctuations in the subject's expectancy that a critical target will occur.

The effects of brain injury are clear insofar as performance effects are concerned. Vigilance is reduced following damage to the MRF and other areas of the brain; and in tasks like the CPT, performance impairment takes the form of reduced accuracy and response slowing. Further research should reveal more specific relationships between the area of brain damage and the aspect of performance affected, but some problems with this general approach should be noted. First, the exact location and extent of the damage may be uncertain in many patients. This is especially true of tumors and closed head injuries, but the problem is less severe for missile and gunshot wounds, since these usually produce localized damage and, because they receive early treatment, the possibility of infection and generalized damage is reduced (Newcombe, 1969). Second, in patients with functional disturbances of particular brain regions (e.g. focal epilepsy), there may be subtle changes in neural organization as a result of the condition. Furthermore, it is usually impossible to make a comparison of performance on the same task before and after the injury occurred, except in cases where surgical intervention is necessary to relieve a patient's condition. Finally, patients may recover at different rates following brain injury, and this will affect the extent of any performance deficit observed.

The frontal cortex and related structures

The role the frontal cortex plays in the control of complex behavior has been known since Jacobson (1935) showed that monkeys with resections of the anterior part of this brain region were unable to perform delayed-response tasks. Almost all forms of higher mental activity are associated with the frontal cortex, which appears to play an 'executive' role in the purposeful planning and organization of such activity (Luria, 1965; Pribram, 1973; for a recent review of frontal cortex functions, see Walsh, 1978).

Changes in perceptual sensitivity and in stimulus registration have been found after lesions and electrical stimulation of parts of the frontal cortex. Spinelli and Pribram (1967), for example, examined the effects of electrical stimulation on the efficiency of visual registration in monkeys. The cortical evoked responses to pairs of light flashes were recorded from implanted electrodes, and the inter-flash interval was varied to yield a recovery function indicating the amount of visual capacity available for processing the second flash of each pair. Recovery was significantly enhanced by frontal stimulation, suggesting that the frontal cortex is involved in the registration of stimulus input. Changes in the efficiency of this process will affect perceptual sensitivity. Pribram and McGuinness (1975) suggest that registration is a process that requires effort, and that the hippocampus coordinates this process. This control system may possibly also play a role in performance decrements arising from decrements in perceptual sensitivity.

In summary, despite some suggestive findings in the literature, the brain mechanisms regulating vigilance remain something of a mystery. With the development of new models of brain function, new clues may emerge. Two current models of attention, proposed by Pribram and McGuinness (1975) and by Skinner (1978) provide some clues, but evidence for their applicability to vigilance is limited. It is tempting to draw a parallel between the Pribram and McGuinness model and the tripartite model of vigilance described in this chapter. They distinguish between arousal, activation (expectancy) and effort, processes controlled respectively by the amygdala and 'corebrain', the basal ganglia and the hippocampus; here a distinction is drawn between the level of vigilance, which is a function of arousal, vigilance decrements resulting from expectancy-related criterion changes, and decrements due to effort-related decrements in sensitivity. (If these brain structures alone, and excluding the cortex, prove to be the most important brain systems in vigilance, it appears that Jerison's suggestion that sustained attention is a very primitive function, in the evolutionary sense, will have been confirmed (Jerison, 1973, 1977; see also

Dimond and Lazarus, 1974).) Irrespective of the validity of this admittedly tenuous association, it seems clear that a differentiation of brain systems, and of the mechanisms underlying independent aspects of vigilance performance, are both steps in the right direction toward the goal of understanding the neural basis of sustained attention.

Cerebral laterality

Vigilance may be impaired following damage to either half of the brain. The same is not true of other functions. Speech, for example, tends to be impaired following damage to particular areas of the left cerebral hemisphere, but not to comparable areas of the right hemisphere. This was first noted by Broca in 1865, and a 'speech area' localized in the left hemisphere has come to be known as Broca's area. There are considerable individual variations in the size and localization of this area (Ojemann, 1979), and left hemisphere specialization for speech is less marked for left-handed persons. Much evidence has been gathered since Broca's observations which has confirmed his findings and indicated that the two cerebral hemispheres have different functions. At the same time, the evidence suggests that there is an integration of function between hemispheres, and that each hemisphere may have facilitatory and inhibitory influences over the other (Sperry, 1973; Broadbent, 1974; Kinsbourne, 1974).

Hemisphere differences in vigilance have been studied by Dimond (1977). The results show some differences in the capacities of each hemisphere. Dimond (1976) compared the performance of split-brain patients with total or partial sectioning of the corpus collusum (a procedure known as commissurotomy) to that of normal subjects in a 30-minute task in which stimuli were presented to either the left or the right visual fields. The total commissurotomy group showed a marked vigilance decrement and poor overall performance, while the other two groups hardly missed any signals (96–100% detection). The total commissurotomy group detected targets projected to the right hemisphere more often than those projected to the left hemisphere, but the right hemisphere also made more false alarms. Essentially similar findings were obtained in a further study in which visual, tactile and auditory vigilance tasks were used (Dimond, 1979a,b).

In a study with normal subjects using the same visual task, Dimond and Beaumont (1971) found no hemisphere differences in correct detections but more left hemisphere false alarms. However, in a second experiment, in which targets were projected to each hemisphere separately in different subjects, the left hemisphere gave more detections but fewer false alarms than the right hemisphere (Dimond and Beaumont, 1973). This conflicts with the results of Dimond (1979a,b), where a right hemisphere superiority in detection rate was obtained with split-brain patients. Unfortunately, the pattern of results obtained for the false detection rate further complicates the picture, as the visual task used in this study elicited more right hemisphere false alarms, while the reverse was true for the tactile and auditory tasks.

Warm and colleagues have carried out a more recent series of laterality studies of auditory vigilance performance. Warm *et al.* (1976) had subjects listen to noise bursts (presented to each ear alternately every 5 minutes) in order to detect infrequent targets (slightly longer noise bursts) over a period of 1 hour. The *a priori* target probability was varied from 24 to 96 targets per hour. Response time to targets was found to be a function of the interaction between target probability and ear of presentation. At a low probability of target presentation, a right ear superiority in detection latency was observed; at a high probability the left ear was superior; and no differences were obtained at an intermediate target probability. No ear differences in the vigilance decrement (changes in detection latency over time) were reported. In a subsequent study, however, in which a similar task was used, Warm *et al.* (1980) reported that reaction time to left ear signals increased over time on task while reaction time to right ear signals, although higher, remained stable over time. The difference between the studies was attributed to the use of a more fine-grained assessment of performance changes over time in the 1980 study (four 20-minute periods) than in the 1976 study (two 30-minute periods). These studies suggest the view that the right hemisphere is faster (or more accurate) at detecting signals than the left hemisphere but also 'fatigues' quickly, whereas the left hemisphere, while not quite so fast or accurate, shows little fatigue over time. This hypothesis has already attracted attention in popular left brain/right brain accounts (Krugman, 1980), but further experiments aimed specifically at investigating this hypothesis are clearly needed before it can be accepted uncritically.

Currently, no firm conclusions regarding cerebral laterality and vigilance seem possible. Jerison (1977) has suggested that the functions of selective and sustained attention are lateralized to opposite halves of the brain, with the right hemisphere controlling sustained attention, a conclusion echoed by Dimond (1979a,b). Although there is some evidence that supports this view, it is also clear that each hemisphere possesses a capacity for sustained attention. While the right hemisphere may dominate in maintaining attention over time, overall performance must depend upon an efficient integration of the capacities of the two cerebral hemispheres (Warm *et al.*, 1980). The overall organization of vigilance behavior must also include other brain structures, such as the limbic system, and the ascending reticular activating system, given that these areas of the brain play an intimate role in controlling different aspects of vigilance performance.

PHYSIOLOGICAL REGULATION OF AROUSAL AND VIGILANCE

As the preceding sections show, a fairly large data base of results on the psychophysiology of vigilance has been built up over the last two decades or so. Only some of these findings are applicable, even indirectly, to the problem of regulating arousal and vigilance in real settings. Efforts to control vigilance in the field have focused on a variety of both behavioral and psychophysiological techniques. Three psychophysiological methods are briefly considered here—physiological alerting devices, pharmacological methods and biofeedback training. (For a more detailed discussion of these and related efforts, see Davies and Parasuraman (1982).)

Alerting devices

Loss of vigilance may be an important safety problem in jobs where the operator has to monitor some display or control process for a prolonged period of time. To counter the potentially hazardous consequences of operator failure, alerting devices may sometimes be introduced into the job. These devices may consist of 'synthetic' targets (for which knowledge of performance can be given), or 'secondary' tasks imposed on the primary task. The reaction time devices for train drivers used in many railways systems is an example of a secondary task (Buck, 1968; Cox, 1973).

Since many of these devices cannot be transferred from one job to another (say from vehicle operation to air traffic control), many attempts have been made to devise physiological 'alertness indicators'. The earliest such attempt used neck EMG activity as the index (Travis and Kennedy, 1947), but this proved to be impractical, and in more recent investigations heart rate variability and EEG measures (Lecret and Pottier, 1971; O'Hanlon, 1971; Carriero, 1977) have been studied. EEG findings indicating that missed signals are preceded by periods of lowered electrocortical activation (see pp.65–66) may have implications for the design of alerting devices. A recent finding that train drivers can successfully operate a secondary task vigilance monitoring device even when their EEG record indicates the presence of stage 1 sleep (Fruhstorfer *et al.*, 1977) suggests that many existing devices are poorly designed. Carriero (1977) has also suggested that physiological measures may enable the construction of a new type of alertness indicator; in his view, it should be possible to obtain physiological profiles corresponding to optimum performance under operational conditions, which could then be used as a 'template' to test on-going physiological activity during actual working conditions for deviations from optimum levels. The feasibility of this suggestion is somewhat open to question, not only because it may be difficult to control the artifacts produced by the innumerable factors affecting bodily activity in actual working conditions, but also because of the inconvenience to the worker of being constantly wired-up for physiological recording (unless expensive telemetric methods are used.)

Drugs and vigilance

As discussed earlier, amphetamine, a central nervous system stimulant, is known to improve vigilance performance when administered in small doses. This was first demonstrated by Mackworth (1950), and has since been confirmed in subsequent studies (Talland and Quarton, 1966; Rapoport *et al.*, 1978). Improvements in vigilance performance have also been reported for other stimulant drugs, such as caffeine (Keister and McLaughlin, 1972) and methylphenidate (Anderson *et al.*, 1974). The latter drug has been used extensively in controlling problems of sustained attention in hyperactive and learning-disabled children.

Although stimulant drugs have marked beneficial effects on vigilance performance, their use in regulating vigilance in real settings may be limited because of the side effects of such drugs, which include elevated heart rate, decreased appetite and possible physiological and psychological dependence.

The field of psychopharmacology has recently witnessed an upsurge of research interest on the effects of peptides and hormones on human behavior. The recent discovery of endogenous opiates and the delineation of their role as neurotransmitters (Martinez *et al.*, 1981) has boosted research into the effects of analogs of endogenous chemicals on human performance. Although only a few studies have begun to investigate the effects of neuropeptides on vigilance, the results are encouraging. O'Hanlon *et al.* (1978) found that administration of 40 mg of ORG 2766, an analog of adrenocorticotropic hormone (ACTH 4-9), eliminated the decrement in performance (in detection rate) over a 105 minute period on a visual vigilance task. Gaillard and Varey (1979) found that 20 mg of ORG 2766 counteracted a decrement in response speed (for slow responses) over time in a 30 minute serial-reaction task. Although many of these preliminary results need to be replicated and extended, the evidence suggests that fairly low dosages of peptides and peptide analogs can aid in the maintenance of performance under monotonous conditions.

Biofeedback

The possibility of using biofeedback of physiological activity to control performance decrements in vigilance situations has been explored recently. Beatty *et al.* (1974) were the first to demonstrate the potential utility of biofeedback techniques for controlling the vigilance decrement. They tested undergraduate students on a 2-hour simulation of a radar monitoring task and found that performance was reliably improved in subjects trained to supress EEG theta activity, and impaired with theta augmentation. This imaginative and well-conducted experiment has aroused considerable interest in EEG operant control techniques, but the practical usefulness of theta suppression training is still a matter for debate. Alluisi *et al.* (1977) employed EEG theta- and auto-regulation methods in alternating 2-hour periods of a 48-hour cycle of work and sleep loss. There was some indication that theta suppression prevented performance decrements due to sleep loss, but no within-session effects were obtained, there being no significant decrements in performance within each 2-hour work period.

O'Hanlon *et al.* (1976) repeated the Beatty *et al.* (1974) study using highly experienced radar operators and air traffic controllers in three separate experiments. The results of the first two studies generally confirmed the finding that detection efficiency improves with theta suppression and deteriorates with theta augmentation. In the third experiment, actual radar equipment was used, with synthetic targets being inserted into background air traffic of the Los Angeles area. In this study the effects of theta suppression were not dramatic, although there was a small improvement in detection efficiency in the final hour of the task. In the last experiment of this series, it was found that although subjects were able to maintain control of EEG theta in subsequent nonfeedback sessions following a feedback (training) session, the behavioral effects of transfer of training were not marked (Beatty and O'Hanlon, 1979). No within-session decrements were obtained, probably because a shorter task duration was used than in the previous studies. This may account for the small size of the behavioral effects of EEG theta training obtained in this study, as in the study by Alluisi *et al.* (1977).

SUMMARY AND CONCLUSIONS

Psychobiological research pertaining to vigilance, arousal and attention is reviewed from three different but related standpoints: (1) information processing and decision making; (2) autonomic and electrocortical activity in the nervous system; (3) neural systems and hemispheric organization in the brain. Vigilance is related to arousal and attention, but it is also distinct from each of these constructs; vigilance is sustained attention, as opposed to selective attention, while arousal is primarily related to only one aspect of vigilance, the overall level of vigilance. Unitary theories of the *vigilance decrement*, for example those based on physiological arousal and neural habituation, are evaluated, and it is concluded that they can account for only part of the data, thus suggesting the need for a multi-factor theoretical approach to sustained attention. Two functionally distinct mechanisms, sensitivity shifts and criterion shifts, appear to be responsible for the vigilance decrement, each operating in different types of task and at different stages in the flow of information in the nervous system. Thus three facets of vigilance performance can be distinguished: (1) the overall level of vigilance, which is a function of arousal; (2) vigilance decrements which result from changes in expectancy, subjective probability, and other factors related to the response criterion; (3) vigilance decrements due to decrements in perceptual sensitivity in tasks having high event rates and targets which load memory. Autonomic and electrocortical measures of arousal provide sensitive indices of changes in the level of vigilance, while event-related potential and reaction time measures provide converging evidence pointing to the importance of criterion changes underlying the vigilance decrement. Different neural systems which are associated with each of these aspects of vigilance performance are tentatively identified. Finally, some possible techniques for regulating arousal and vigilance in real settings are briefly discussed.

ACKNOWLEDGMENTS

The author would like to thank Roy Davies, Donald Lindsley and Michael Posner for their useful comments on previous drafts of this chapter.

REFERENCES

Aiken, E. G., and Lau, A. W. Memory for the pitch of a tone. *Perception and Psychophysics*, 1966, **1**, 232–233.

Alexander, D. A. Attention dysfunction in senile dementia. *Psychological Reports*, 1973, **32**, 229–230.

Alluisi, E. A., Coates, G. D., and Morgan, B. B., Jr. Effects of temporal stressors on vigilance and information processing. In R. R. Mackie (Ed.), *Vigilance: theory, operational performance and physiological correlates*. New York: Plenum, 1977, pp.361–421.

Anderson, R. P., Halcomb, C. G., Gordon, W., and Ozolins, D. A. Measurement of attentional distractability in LD children. *Academic Therapy*, 1974, **9**, 261–266.

Baddeley, A. D. *The psychology of memory*. New York: Basic Books, 1976.

Baddeley, A. D., Hatter, J. E., Scott, D., and Snashall, A. Memory and time of day. *Quarterly Journal of Experimental Psychology*, 1970, **22**, 605–609.

Bakan, P., Belton, J. A., and Toth, J. C. Extraversion–introversion and decrement in an auditory vigilance task. In D. N. Buckner and J. J. McGrath (Eds), *Vigilance: a symposium*. New York: McGraw-Hill, 1963, pp.22–28.

Bakay-Pragay, E., Mirsky, A. F., Fullerton, B. C., Oshima, H. I., and Arnold, S. W. Effect of electrical stimulation of the brain on visually controlled (attentive) behavior in the *Macaca mulatta*. *Experimental Neurology*, 1975, **49**, 203–220.

Beatty, J. Learned regulation of alpha and theta activity in the human electro-encephalogram. In G. E. Schwartz and J. Beatty (Eds), *Biofeedback: theory and research*. New York: Academic Press, 1977, pp.351–370.

Beatty, J. Task-evolved pupillary responses, processing load, and the structure of processing resources. *Psychological Bulletin*, 1982, **91**, 276–292 (a).

Beatty, J. Phasic not tonic pupillary responses vary with auditory vigilance performance. *Psychophysiology*, 1982, **19**, 167–172 (b).

Beatty, J., and O'Hanlon, J. F. Operant control of posterior theta rhythms and vigilance performance: repeated treatments and transfer of training. In N. Birbaumer and H. D. Kimmel (Eds), *Progress in operant conditioning of physiological events*. Hillsdale, N.J.: Lawrence Erlbaum, 1979, pp.235–246.

Beatty, J., Greenberg, A., Diebler, W. P., and O'Hanlon, J. F. Operant control of occipital theta rhythm affects performance in a radar monitoring task. *Science*, 1974, **183**, 871–873.

Blake, M. J. F. Time of day effects in a range of tasks. *Psychonomic Science*, 1967, **9**, 349–350 (a).

Blake, M. J. F. Relationships between circadian rhythm of body temperature and introversion-extraversion. *Nature*, 1967, **215**, 896–897 (b).

Broadbent, D. E. *Decision and stress*. London: Academic Press, 1971.

Broadbent, D. E. Division of function and integration of behavior. In F. O. Schmitt and F. G. Worden (Eds), *The neurosciences: third study program*. Cambridge, Mass.: MIT Press, 1974, pp.31–41.

Broadbent, D. E., and Gregory, M. Division of attention and the decision theory of signal detection. *Proceedings of the Royal Society B*, 1963, **158**, 221–231 (a).

Broadbent, D. E., and Gregory, M. Vigilance considered as a statistical decision. *British Journal of Psychology*, 1963, **54**, 309–323 (b).

Broca, P. Sur la faculté du language articule. *Bulletin Societe Anthropologie, Paris*, 1865, **6**, 493–494.

Bruhn, P. Disturbances of vigilance in subcortical epilepsy. *Acta Neurologica Scandinavica*, 1970, **46**, 442–454.

Buck, L. Reaction time as a measure of perceptual vigilance. *Psychological Bulletin*, 1966, **65**, 291–308.

Buck, L. Experiments on railway vigilance devices. *Ergonomics*, 1968, **11**, 557–564.

Byrne, D. G. Vigilance and arousal in depressive states. *British Journal of Social and Clinical Psychology*, 1976, **15**, 267–274.

Byrne, D. G. Affect and vigilance performance in depressive illness. *Journal of Psychiatric Research*, 1977, **13**, 185–191.

Carriero, N. Physiological correlates of performance in a long duration repetitive task. In R. R. Mackie (Ed.), *Vigilance: theory, operational performance and physiological correlates*. New York: Plenum, 1977, pp.307–330.

Colquhoun, W. P. Temperament, inspection efficiency, and time of day. *Ergonomics*, 1960, **3**, 377–378.

Colquhoun, W. P. The effect of unwanted signals on performance in a vigilance task. *Ergonomics*, 1961, **4**, 41–52.

Colquhoun, W. P. Circadian variations in mental efficiency. In W. P. Colquhoun (Ed.), *Biological rhythms and human performance*. London: Academic Press, 1971.

Cooper, R., McCallum, W. C., Newton, P., Papakostpolous, D., Pocock, P. V., and Warren, W. J. Cortical potentials associated with the detection of visual events. *Science*, 1977, **196**, 74–77.

Cox, J. J. Train control, stress, and vigilance. In *Proceedings of the annual conference of the Ergonomics Society of Australia and New Zealand*, 16.1–16.22.

Craig, A. Is the vigilance decrement simply a response adjustment towards probability matching? *Human Factors*, 1978, **20**, 441–446.

Craig, A. Discrimination, temperature, and time of day. *Human Factors*, 1979, **21**, 61–68.

Davies, A. D. M., and Davies, D. R. The effects of noise and time of day upon age differences in performance at two checking tasks. *Ergonomics*, 1975, **18**, 321–326.

Davies, D. R., and Krkovic, A. Skin conductance, alpha-activity, and vigilance. *American Journal of Psychology*, 1965, **78**, 304–306.

Davies, D. R., and Parasuraman, R. Vigilanz, Antwortlatenzen, und kortikale evozierte Potentiale. *Probleme und Ergebnisse der Psychology*, 1976, **59**, 95–99.

Davies, D. R., and Parasuraman, R. Cortical evoked potentials and vigilance: a decision theory analysis. In R. R. Mackie (Ed.), *Vigilance: theory, operational performance and physiological correlates*. New York: Plenum, 1977, pp.285–306.

Davies, D. R., and Parasuraman, R., 1982. *The psychology of vigilance*. London: Academic Press.

Davies, D. R., Shackleton, V. J., and Parasuraman, R. Monotony and boredom. In G. R. J. Hockey (Ed.), *Stress and fatigue in human performance*. Chichester: John Wiley, 1983.

Davies, D. R., Toh, K., and Parasuraman, R. Time of day, memory load, and vigilance performance. Unpublished manuscript, University of Aston, Birmingham, 1980.

Davies, D. R., and Tune, G. S. *Human vigilance performance*, London: Staples Press, 1970.

Dimond, S. J. Depletion of attentional capacity after total commisurotomy in man. *Brain*, 1976, **99**, 347–356.

Dimond, S. J. Vigilance and split-brain research. In R. R. Mackie (Ed.), *Vigilance: theory, operational performance and physiological correlates*. New York: Plenum, 1977, pp.341–355.

Dimond, S. J. Tactual and auditory vigilance in split-brain man. *Journal of Neurology, Neurosurgery, and Psychiatry*, 1979, **42**, 70–74 (a).

Dimond, S. J. Performance by split-brain humans on lateralized vigilance tasks. *Cortex*, 1979, **15**, 43–50 (b).

Dimond, S. J., and Beaumont, J. G. Hemisphere function and vigilance. *Quarterly Journal of Experimental Psychology*, 1971, **23**, 443–448.

Dimond, S. J., and Beaumont, J. G. Differences in the vigilance performance of the right and left hemispheres. *Cortex*, 1973, **9**, 259–265.

Dimond, S. J., and Lazarus, J. The problem of vigilance in animal life. *Brain, Behavior, and Evolution*, 1974, **9**, 60–79.

Donald, M. W., and Young, M. Habituation and rate decrements in the auditory vertex potential during selective listening. In H. Kornhuber and L. Deeke (Eds), *MOSS V: Proceedings of the 5th International Congress on Electrical Potentials related to Motivation, Motor, and Sensory Processes of the Brain*. Amsterdam: Elsevier, 1980.

Donchin, E., and Heffley, E. Multivariate analysis of ERP data: a tutorial review. In D. A. Otto (Ed.), *Multidiscplinary perspectives in event-related brain potential research*. Environmental Protection Agency Report No. EPA-600/9-77-043. Washington, D.C.: US Government Printing Office, 1978, pp.555–572.

Donchin, E., Otto, D., Gerbrandt, L. K., and Pribram, K. H. While a monkey waits: electrocortical events recorded during the fore-period of a reaction time study. *Electroencephalography and Clinical Neurophysiology*, 1971, **31**, 115–127.

Donchin, E., Tueting, P., Ritter, W., Kutas, M., and Heffley, E. On the independence of the CNV and P300 components of the human averaged evoked potential. *Electroencephalography and Clinical Neurophysiology*, 1975, **38**, 449–461.

Donchin, E., Ritter, W., and McCallum, W. C. Cognitive psychophysiology: The endogenous components of the ERP. In E. Callaway, P. Tueting and S. H. Koslow (Eds), *Event-related brain potentials in man*. New York: Academic Press, 1978, pp.349–411.

Duffy, E. *Activation and behavior*. New York: John Wiley, 1962.

Eason, R. G., Beardshall, A., and Jaffee, S. Performance and physiological indicants of activation in a vigilance situation. *Perceptual and Motor Skills*, 1965, **20**, 3–13.

Egan, J. P., Greenberg, G. Z., and Schulman, A. I. Operating characteristics, signal detectability, and the method of free response. *Journal of the Acoustical Society of America*, 1961, **33**, 993–1007.

Erwin, C. W., Wiener, E. L., Linnoila, M. I., and Truscott, T. R. Alcohol induced drowsiness and vigilance performance. *Journal of Studies of Alcohol*, 1978, **39**, 565–576.

Eysenck, H. J. *The dynamics of anxiety and hysteria*. New York: Praeger, 1957.

Fleishman, E. A. Toward a taxonomy of human performance. *American Psychologist*, 1975, **30**, 1127–1149.

Folkard, S. Time of day and level of processing. *Memory and Cognition*, 1979, **7**, 247–252.

Frankenhaeuser, M. Behavior and circulating catecholamines. *Brain Research*, 1971, **31**, 241–262.

Frankenhaeuser, M., Nordheden, B., Myrtsen, A. L., and Post, B. Psychophysiological reactions to understimulation and overstimulation. *Acta Psychologica*, 1971, **35**, 298–308.

Frankmann, J. P. and Adams, J. A. Theories of vigilance. *Psychological Bulletin*, 1962, **59**, 257–272.

Friedman, D., Vaughan, H. G., and Erlenmeyer-Kimling, L. Stimulus and response related components of the late positive complex in visual discrimination tasks. *Electroencephalography and Clinical Neurophysiology*, 1978, **45**, 319–330.

Fruhstorfer, H., and Bergstrom, R. M. Human vigilance and auditory evoked potentials. *Electroencephalography and Clinical Neurophysiology*, 1969, **27**, 346–365.

Fruhstorfer, H., Langanke, P., Meinzer, K., Peter, J. H., and Pfaff, U. Neurophysiological vigilance indicators and operational analysis of a train vigilance device: A laboratory and field study. In R. R. Mackie (Ed.), *Vigilance: theory, operational performance and physiological correlates*. New York: Plenum, 1977, pp.147–162.

Fuster, J. M. Effects of stimulation of brain stem on tachistocopic perception. *Science*, 1958, **127**, 150.

Gaillard, A. W. K. and Varey, C. A. Some effects of an ACTH4-9 analog (ORG 2766) on human performance. *Physiology and Behavior*, 1979, **23**, 79–84.

Gale, A. Some EEG correlates of sustained attention. In R. R. Mackie (Ed.), *Vigilance: theory, operational performance and physiological correlates*. New York: Plenum, 1977, pp.263–283.

Gale, A., Davies, R., and Smallbone, A. EEG correlates of signal rate, time in task, and individual differences in reaction time during a five-stage sustained attention task. *Ergonomics*, 1977, **20**, 363–376.

Goff, W. R., Allison, T., and Vaughan, H. G. The functional neuroanatomy of event-related potentials. In E. Callaway, P. Tueting and S. H. Koslow (Eds), *Event-related brain potentials in man*. New York: Academic Press, 1978, pp.1–79.

Goodman, S. J. Vigilance, the psychological refractory period, and brain-stem multiple-unit activity. *Experimental Neurology*, 1970, **27**, 139–150.

Green, D. M., and Swets, J. A. *Signal detection theory and psychophysics*. New York: John Wiley, 1966.

Griew, S., Davies, D. R., and Treacher, A. Heart rate during auditory vigilance performance. *Nature*, 1963, **200**, 1026.

Groves, P. M., and Thompson, R. F. Habituation: a dual process theory. *Psychological Review*, 1970, **77**, 419–450.

Haider, M., Spong, P., and Lindsley, D. B. Attention, vigilance, and cortical evoked potentials in humans. *Science*, 1964, **145**, 180–182.

Harkins, S. W. Aspects of the psychobiology of attention: visual evoked potentials and performance in a task demanding sustained attention. *Dissertation Abstracts International*, 1974, **36B**, 471–472.

Harkins, S. G. and Geen, R. G. Discriminability and criterion differences between extraverts and introverts during vigilance. *Journal of Research in Personality*, 1975, **9**, 335–340.

Harris, W. Fatigue, circadian rhythm, and truck accidents. In R. R. Mackie (Ed.), *Vigilance: theory, operational performance and physiological correlates*. New York: Plenum, 1977, pp.133–146.

Head, H. The conception of nervous and mental energy. II. Vigilance: a physiological state of the nervous system. *British Journal of Psychology*, 1923, **14**, 126–147.

Head, H. *Aphasia and kindred disorders of speech*. New York: Macmillan, 1926.

Hicks, L. H., and Birren, J. E. Aging, brain damage, and psychomotor slowing. *Psychological Bulletin*, 1970, **74**, 377–396.

Hillyard, S. A., Squires, K. C., Bauer, J. W., and Lindsay, P. H. Evoked potential correlates of auditory signal detection. *Science*, 1971, **172**, 1357–1360.

Hillyard, S. A., Hink, R. F., Schwent, V. L., and Picton, T. P. Electrical signs of selective attention in the human brain. *Science*, 1973, **182**, 177–180.

Hink, R. F., Van Voorhis, S. T., and Hillyard, S. A. The division of attention and the human auditory potential. *Neuropsychologia*, 1977, **15**, 597–605.

Hink, R. F., Fenton, W. H., Tinklenberg, J. R., Pfefferbaum, A., and Kopell, B. S. Vigilance and human attention under conditions of methylphenidate and secobarbital intoxication: an assessment using brain potentials. *Psychophysiology*, 1978, **15**, 116–125.

Hockey, G. R. J., and Colquhoun, W. P. Diurnal variation in human performance: A review. In W. P. Colquhoun (Ed.), *Aspects of human efficiency*. London: English University Press, 1972, pp.1–24.

Horne, J. A., and Ostberg, O. Individual differences in human circadian rhythms. *Biological Psychology*, 1977, **5**, 179–190.

Horvath, M., Frantik, E., Kopriva, K., and Meissner, J. EEG theta activity increase coincides with performance decrement in a monotonous task. *Activitas Nervosa Superior*, 1975, **18**, 207–210.

Hughlings Jackson, J. On the evolution and dissolution of the nervous system. *Lancet*, 1884, **1**, 555–558, 649–652, 739–744.

Jacobson, C. F. Functions of the frontal association areas in primates. *Archives of Neurology and Psychiatry*, 1935, **33**, 558–569.

Jerison, H. J. Activation and long-term performance. In A. F. Sanders (Ed.), *Attention and performance*. Amsterdam: North Holland, 1967, pp.373–389 (a).

Jerison, H. J. Signal detection theory in the analysis of human vigilance. *Human Factors*, 1967, **9**, 285–288 (b).

Jerison, H. J. *Evolution of the brain and intelligence*. New York: Academic Press, 1973.

Jerison, H. J. Vigilance: biology, psychology, theory and practice. In R. R. Mackie (Ed.), *Vigilance: theory, operational performance and physiological correlates*. New York: Plenum, 1977, pp.27–40.

Jerison, H. J., and Pickett, R. M. Vigilance: the importance of the elicited observing rate. *Science*, 1964, **143**, 970–971.

Jewett, D. L., and Williston, J. S. Auditory evoked far fields averaged from the scalp of humans. *Brain*, 1971, **94**, 681–696.

Jones, D. M., Davies, D. R., Hogan, K. M., Patrick, J., and Cumberbatch, W. G. Short-term memory during the normal working day. In M. M. Gruneberg, P. E. Morris, and R. N. Sykes (Eds), *Practical aspects of memory*. New York: Academic Press, 1978.

Kahneman, D. *Attention and effort*. Englewood Cliffs, N.J.: Prentice-Hall, 1973.

Keister, M. E. and McLaughlin, R. J. Vigilance performance related to introversion-extraversion and caffeine. *Journal of Experimental Research in Personality*, 1972, **6**, 5–11.

Kinchla, R., and Smyzer, F. A diffusion model of perceptual memory. *Perception and Psychophysics*, 1967, **2**, 219–229.

Kinsbourne, M. Mechanisms of hemisphere interaction in man. In M. Kinsbourne and W. L. Smith (Eds), *Hemispheric disconnection and cerebral function*. Springfield, Ill.: Charles C. Thomas, 1974.

Kornfeld, C. M., and Beatty, J. EEG spectra during a long-term compensatory tracking task. *Bulletin of the Psychonomic Society*, 1977, **10**, 46–48.

Krugman, H. E. Sustained viewing of television. *Journal of Advertising Research*, 1980, **20**, 65–68.

Krulewitz, J. E., Warm, J. S., and Wohl, T. H. Effects of shifts in the rate of repetitive stimulation on sustained attention. *Perception and Psychophysics*, 1975, **18**, 245–249.

Lacey, J. I. Somatic response patterning and stress: some revisions of activation theory. In M. H. Appley and R. Trumbull (Eds), *Psychological stress*. New York: Appleton-Century-Crofts, 1967, pp.14–37.

Lecret, F., and Pottier, M. La vigilance, facteur de securité dans la conduite automobile. *Le Travail Humain*, 1971, **34**, 51–68.

Levine, J. M., Romashko, T., and Fleishman, E. A. Evaluation of an abilities classification system for integrating and generalizing human performance: an application to vigilance tasks. *Journal of Applied Psychology*, 1973, **58**, 149–157.

Lindsley, D. B. (Ed.). Radar operator 'fatigue': the effects of length and repetition of operating periods on efficiency of performance. Office of Scientific Research and Development Report No. OSRD 33334. 1944.

Lindsley, D. B. Emotion. In S. S. Stevens (Ed.), *Handbook of experimental psychology*. New York: John Wiley, 1951.

Lindsley, D. B. Psychological phenomena and the electroencephalogram. *Electroencephalography and Clinical Neurophysiology*, 1952, **4**, 443–456.

Lindsley, D. B. Attention, consciousness, sleep, and wakefulness. In J. Field, H. W. Magoun and V. E. Hall (Eds), *Handbook of physiology*, Section 1, Vol. 3. Baltimore, Md: Williams and Wilkins, 1960, pp.1553–1593.

Loeb, M., and Alluisi, E. A. An update of findings regarding vigilance and a reconsideration of underlying mechanisms. In R. R. Mackie (Ed.), *Vigilance: theory, operational performance and physiological correlates*. New York: Plenum, 1977, pp.719–749.

Loeb, M., and Binford, J. R. Variation in performance on auditory and visual monitoring tasks as a function of signal and stimulus frequencies. *Perception and Psychophysics*, 1968, **4**, 361–366.

Luria, A. R. *Higher cortical functions in man*. London: Tavistock Press, 1965.

Luria, A. R. The frontal lobes and regulation of behavior. In K. H. Pribram and A. R. Luria (Eds), *Psychophysiology of the frontal lobes*. New York: Academic Press, 1973, pp.3–26.

McDonald, R. D., and Burns, S. B. Visual vigilance and brain damage: an empirical study. *Journal of Neurology, Neurosurgery, and Psychiatry*, 1964, **27**, 206–209.

Mackie, R. R. Introduction. In R. R. Mackie (Ed.), *Vigilance: theory, operational performance and physiological correlates*. New York: Plenum, 1977, pp.1–25.

Mackworth, J. F. Effect of amphetamine on the detectability of signals in a vigilance task. *Canadian Journal of Psychology*, 1965, **19**, 104–110 (a).

Mackworth, J. F. Deterioration of signal detectability during a vigilance task as a function of background event rate. *Psychonomic Science*, 1965, **3**, 421–422 (b).

Mackworth, J. F. Vigilance, arousal, and habituation. *Psychological Review*, 1968, **75**, 308–322.

Mackworth, J. F. *Vigilance and habituation*. Baltimore, Md: Penguin Books, 1969.

Mackworth, J. F. *Vigilance and attention*. Baltimore, Md: Penguin Books, 1970.

Mackworth, J. F., and Taylor, M. M. The *d'* measure of signal detectability in vigilance-like situations. *Canadian Journal of Psychology*, 1963, **17**, 302–325.

Mackworth, N. H. Notes on the clock test — a new approach to the study of prolonged perception to find the optimum length of watch for radar operators. Air Ministry FPRC Report No. 586. 1944.

Mackworth, N. H. The breakdown of vigilance during prolonged visual search. *Quarterly Journal of Experimental Psychology*, 1948, **1**, 6–21.

Mackworth, N. H. Researches on the measurement of human performance. Medical Research Council Special Report No. 268. London: HMSO, 1950.

Mackworth, N. H. Some factors affecting vigilance. *Advancement of Science*, 1957, **53**, 389–393.

Martinez, J. L., Jensen, R. A., Messing, R. B., Rigter, H. and McGaugh, J. L. (Eds), *Endogenous peptides and learning and memory processes*. New York: Academic Press, 1981.

Metzger, K. R., Warm, J. S., and Senter, R. J. Effects of background event rate and artificial signals on vigilance performance. *Perceptual and Motor Skills*, 1974, **38**, 1175–1181.

Mirsky, A. F. The relationship between paroxysmal EEG activity and performance on a vigilance task in epileptic patients. *American Psychologist*, 1960, **15**, 486.

Mirsky, A. F., and Orren, M. M. Attention. In L. H. Miller *et al.* (Eds), *Neuropeptide influences on the brain and behavior*. New York: Raven Press, 1977, pp.233–267.

Mirsky, A. F., and Rosvold, H. E. The use of psychoactive drugs as a neurophysiological tool in studies of attention in man. In L. Uhr and J. G. Miller (Eds), *Drugs and Behavior*. New York: Wiley, 1960.

Mirsky, A. F., Primac, D. W., Ajmone-Marsan, C., Rosvold, H. E., and Stevens, J. R. A comparison of the psychological test performance of patients with focal and non-focal epilepsy. *Experimental Neurology*, 1960, **2**, 75–89.

Mirsky, A. F., Bakay-Pragay, E., and Harris, S. Evoked potential correlates of stimulation-induced impairment of attention in *Macaca mullata*. *Experimental Neurology*, 1977, **57**, 242–256.

Moruzzi, G., and Magoun, H. W. Brain stem reticular formation and activation of the EEG. *Electroencephalography and Clinical Neurophysiology*, 1949, **1**, 455–473.

Näätänen, R. (1973). The inverted-U relationship between activation and performance: a critical review. In S. Kornblum (Ed.), *Attention and performance IV*. New York: Academic Press, 1973, pp.155–174.

Näätänen, R., and Michie, P. T. Early selective attention effects on the evoked potential: a critical review and reinterpretation. *Biological Psychology*, 1979, **8**, 81–136.

Newcombe, F. *Missile wounds of the brain*. Oxford: Oxford University Press, 1969.

Norman, D. A., and Bobrow, D. G. On data-limited and resource-limited processes. *Cognitive Psychology*, 1975, **7**, 46–64.

O'Hanlon, J. F. Adrenaline and noradrenaline: relation to performance in a visual vigilance task. *Science*, 1965, **150**, 507–509.

O'Hanlon, J. F. Vigilance, the plasma catecholamines, and related biochemical and physiological variables. Human Factors Research Inc. Technical Report No. 787-2. Goleta, Calif.: Human Factors Research Inc., 1970.

O'Hanlon, J. F. Heart rate variability: a new index of driver alertness/fatigue. Human Factors Research Inc. Technical Report No. 1712-1, Goleta, Calif.: Human Factors Research Inc., 1971.

O'Hanlon, J. F., and Beatty, J. Catecholamine correlates of radar monitoring performance. *Biological Psychology*, 1976, **4**, 293–304.

O'Hanlon, J. F., and Beatty, J. Concurrence of electroencephalographic and performance changes during a simulated radar watch and some implications for the arousal theory of vigilance. In R. R. Mackie (Ed.), *Vigilance: theory, operational performance and physiological correlates.* New York: Plenum, 1977, pp.189–201.

O'Hanlon, J. F., Royal, J. W., and Beatty, J. EEG theta regulation and radar vigilance performance of professional radar operators and air traffic controllers under laboratory and controlled field conditions. In J. Beatty and H. Legewie (Eds), *Biofeedback and behavior.* New York: Plenum, 1976, pp.147–165.

O'Hanlon, J. F., Fussler, C., Sancin, E., and Grandjean, E. Efficacy of an ACTH4-9 analog, relative to that of a standard drug (*d*-amphetamine) for blocking the vigilance decrement. Unpublished report, Swiss Federal Institute for Technology, 1978.

Ojemann, G. A. Individual variability in cortical localization of language. *Journal of Neurosurgery, 1979,* **50**, 164–169.

Parasuraman, R. Consistency of individual differences in human vigilance performance: an abilities classification analysis. *Journal of Applied Psychology*, 1976, **61**, 486–492.

Parasuraman, R. Auditory evoked potentials and divided attention. *Psychophysiology*, 1978, **15**, 460–465.

Parasuraman, R. Memory load and event rate control sensitivity decrements in sustained attention. *Science*, 1979, **205**, 924–927.

Parasuraman, R. Effects of information processing demands on auditory evoked potential correlates of selective and divided attention. *Biological Psychology*, 1980, **11**, 217–233.

Parasuraman, R., and Davies, D. R. Response and evoked potential latencies associated with commission errors in visual monitoring. *Perception and Psychophysics*, 1975, **17**, 465–468.

Parasuraman, R., and Davies, D. R. Decision theory analysis of response latencies in vigilance. *Journal of Experimental Psychology: Human Perception and Performance*, 1976, **2**, 569–582.

Parasuraman, R., and Davies, D. R. A taxonomic analysis of vigilance performance. In R. R. Mackie (Ed.), *Vigilance: theory, operational performance and physiological correlates.* New York: Plenum, 1977, pp.559–574.

Paul, D. D., and Sutton, S. Evoked potential correlates of response criterion in auditory signal detection. *Science*, 1972, **177**, 362–364.

Posner, M. Psychobiology of attention. In M. S. Gazzaniga and C. Blakemore (Eds), *Handbook of psychobiology.* New York: Academic Press, 1975, pp.441–480.

Posner, M. *Chronometric explorations of mind.* Hillsdale, N.J.: Lawrence Erlbaum, 1978.

Posner, M., and Boies, S. J. Components of attention. *Psychological Review*, 1971, **78**, 391–408.

Poulton, E. C. Arousing stresses increase vigilance. In R. R. Mackie (Ed.), *Vigilance: theory, operational performance and physiological correlates.* New York: Plenum, 1977, pp.423–459.

Poulton, E. C. Increased vigilance with vertical vibration at 5 Hz: an alerting mechanism. *Applied Ergonomics*, 1978, **9**, 73–76.

Pribram, K. H. *Languages of the brain.* Englewood Cliffs, N.J.: Prentice-Hall, 1971.

Pribram, E. C. The primate frontal cortex—executive of the brain. In K. H. Pribram and A. R. Luria (Eds), *Psychophysiology of the frontal lobes.* New York: Academic Press, 1973, pp.293–314.

Pribram, K. H., and McGuinness, D. Arousal, activation, and effort in the control of attention. *Psychological Review*, 1975, **82**, 116–149.

Rapoport, J. L., Buchsbaum, M. S., Zahn, T. P., Weingarter, H., Ludlow, C., and Mikkelsen, E. J. Dextroamphetamine: cognitive and behavioral effects in normal prepubertal boys. *Science*, 1978, **199**, 560–563.

Riemersma, J. B. J., Sanders, A. F., Wildervanck, C., and Gaillard, A. W. Performance decrement during prolonged night driving. In R. R. Mackie (Ed.), *Vigilance: theory, operational performance and physiological correlates*. New York: Plenum, 1977, pp.41–58.

Ritter, W., and Vaughan, H. G., Jr. Averaged evoked responses in vigilance and discrimination: a reassessment. *Science*, 1969, **164**, 326–328.

Ritter, W., Simson, R., Vaughan, H. G., Jr, and Friedman, D. A brain event related to the making of a sensory discrimination. *Science*, 1979, **203**, 1358–1361.

Rosvold, H. E., Mirsky, A. F., Sarason, I., Bransome, E. D., Jr, and Beck, L. N. A continuous performance test of brain damage. *Journal of Consulting Psychology*, 1956, **20**, 343–350.

Roth, W. T., and Kopell, B. S. The auditory evoked response to repeated stimuli during a vigilance task. *Psychophysiology*, 1969, **6**, 301–309.

Routtenberg, A. Stimulus processing and response execution: A neurobehavioral theory. *Physiology and Behavior*, 1971, **6**, 589–596.

Schwent, V. L., Hillyard, S. A., and Galambos, R. Selective attention and the auditory vertex potential. I. Efforts of stimulus delivery rate. *Electroencephalography and Clinical Neurophysiology*, 1976, **40**, 604–614 (a).

Schwent, V. L., Snyder, E., and Hillyard, S. A. Auditory evoked potentials during multichannel selective listening: Role of pitch and localization cues. *Journal of Experimental Psychology: Human Perception and Performance*, 1976, **2**, 313–325 (b).

Sharpless, S., and Jasper, H. H. Habituation of the arousal reaction. *Brain*, 1956, **79**, 655–680.

Skinner, J. E. A neurophysiological model for regulation of sensory input to the cortex. In D. A. Otto (Ed.), *Multidisciplinary perspectives in event-related brain potential research*, Environment Protection Agency Report No. EPA-600/9-77-043, Washington, D.C.: US Government Printing Office, 1978, pp.616–625.

Skinner, J. E., and Lindsley, D. B. The nonspecific mediothalamic fronto-cortical system: Its influence on electrocortical activity and behavior. In K. H. Pribram and A. R. Luria (Eds), *Psychophysiology of the frontal lobes*. New York: Academic Press, 1973, pp.185–234.

Skinner, J. E., and Yingling, C. D. Central gating mechanisms that regulate event-related potentials and behavior: a neural model for attention. In J. E. Desmedt (Ed.), *Attention, voluntary contraction, and event-related cerebral potentials*. Basel: Karger, 1977, pp.30–69.

Sperry, R. W. Lateral specialization of cerebral function in the surgically separated hemispheres. In F. J. McGuigan (Ed.), *The psychophysiology of thinking*. New York: Academic Press, 1973, pp.209–229.

Spevack, A., and Pribram, K. H. A decisional analysis of the effects of limbic lesions in monkeys. *Journal of Comparative and Physiological Psychology*, 1973, **82**, 211–226.

Spinelli, D. N. and Pribram, K. H. Changes in visual recovery function and unit activity produced by frontal and temporal cortex stimulation. *Electroencephalography and Clinical Neurophysiology*, 1967, **22**, 143–149.

Squires, K. C., Squires, N., and Hillyard, S. A. Decision-related cortical potentials during an auditory signal detection task with cued observation intervals. *Journal of Experimental Psychology: Human Perception and Performance*, 1975, **1**, 268–279 (a).

Squires, K. C., Squires, N., and Hillyard, S. A. Vertex evoked potentials in a rating-scale detection task: relation to signal probability. *Behavioral Biology*, 1975, **13**, 21–34 (b).

Stern, R. M. Performance and physiological arousal during two vigilance tasks varying in signal presentation rate. *Perceptual and Motor Skills*, 1966, **23**, 691–700.

Swets, J. A. The relative operating characteristic in psychology. *Science*, 1973, **182**, 990–1000.

Swets, J. A. Signal detection theory applied to vigilance. In R. R. Mackie (Ed.), *Vigilance: theory, operational performance and physiological correlates*. New York: Plenum, 1977, pp.705–718.

Swets, J. A., and Green, D. M. Applications of signal detection theory. In H. L. Pick *et al.* (Eds), *Psychology: from research to practice*. New York: Plenum, 1978, pp.311–331.

Swets, J. A., and Kristofferson, A. B. Attention. *Annual Review of Psychology*, 1970, **21**, 339–366.

Talland, G. A. and Quarton, G. The effects of drugs and familiarity on performance in continual search. *Journal of Nervous and Mental Disorders*, 1966, **143**, 266–274.

Taub, H. A., and Osborne, H. Effects of signal and stimulus rates on vigilance performance. *Journal of Applied Psychology*, 1968, **52**, 133–138.

Taylor, M. M. Detectability theory and the interpretation of vigilance data. In A. F. Sanders (Ed.), *Attention and performance*. Amsterdam: Elsevier, 1967, pp.390–399.

Thackray, R. I., Jones, K. N., and Touchstone, R. M. Personality and physiological correlates of performance decrement on a monotonous task requiring sustained attention. *British Journal of Psychology*, 1974, **65**, 351–358.

Thompson, R. F., and Spencer, W. A. Habituation: a model phenomenon for the study of neuronal substrates of behavior. *Psychological Bulletin*, 1966, **73**, 16–43.

Travis, R. C., and Kennedy, J. L. Prediction and automatic control of alertness. I. Control of lookout alertness. *Journal of Comparative and Physiological Psychology*, 1947, **40**, 457–461.

Tueting, P. Event-related potentials, cognitive events, and information processing. In D. Otto (Ed.), *Multidisciplinary perspectives in event-related brain potential research*, Environmental Protection Agency Report No. EPA-600/9-77-043. Washington, D.C.: US Government Printing Office, 1978, pp.157–169.

Walsh, K. W. *Neuropsychology: a clinical approach*. Edinburgh: Churchill Livingstone, 1978.

Walter, W. G., Cooper, R., Aldridge, V. J., McCallum, W. C., and Winter, A. L. Contingent negative variation: an electrical sign of sensorimotor association and expectancy in the human brain. *Nature*, 1964, **203**, 380–384.

Warm, J. S. Psychological processes in sustained attention. In R. R. Mackie (Ed.), *Vigilance: theory, operational performance and physiological correlates*. New York: Plenum, 1977, pp.623–644.

Warm, J. S., Schumsky, D. A., and Hawley, D. K. Ear assymmetry and temporal uncertainty in sustained attention. *Bulletin of the Psychonomic Society*, 1976, **7**, 413–416.

Warm, J. S., Richter, D. O., Sprague, R. L., Porter, P. K., and Schumsky, D. A. Listening with a dual brain: hemispheric asymmetry in sustained attention. *Bulletin of the Psychonomic Society*, 1980, **15**, 229–232.

Watson, C. S., and Nichols, T. L. Detectability of auditory signals presented without defined observation intervals. *Journal of the Acoustical Society of America*, 1976, **59**, 655–668.

Wilkinson, R. T. and Haines, E. Evoked response correlates of expectancy during vigilance. *Acta Psychologica*, 1970, **33**, 402–413.

Wilkinson, R. T., and Seales, D. M. EEG event-related potentials and signal detection. *Biological Psychology*, 1978, **7**, 13–28.

Wilkinson, R. T., Morlock, H. C., and Williams, H. L. Evoked cortical response during vigilance. *Psychonomic Science*, 1966, **4**, 221–222.

Yoss, R. E., Moyer, N. J., and Hollenhorst, R. W. Pupil size and spontaneous pupillary waves associated with alertness, drowsiness and sleep. *Neurology*, 1970, **201**, 545–554.

Sustained Attention in Human Performance
Edited by J. S. Warm
© 1984 John Wiley & Sons Ltd.

Chapter 4

Environmental Stressors

Peter A. Hancock

INTRODUCTION

Scope of the chapter

This chapter examines the effect of environmental stressors upon the performance of tasks requiring sustained attention. Variations in capability due to changes in the thermal, acoustic and sensory environment are reviewed. For the purpose of clarity, details pertaining to specific experimental investigations are presented mostly in tabular form. Previous reviews have adopted a largely empirical (Davies and Tune, 1970) or theoretical (Poulton, 1977a) emphasis. In the current work, the effects of operator- and task-related factors which influence performance across a variety of stressful conditions are examined. The effects of drug, time of day and sleep loss manipulations which affect the state of the performer but are not environmental stressors *per se* are not detailed in the present chapter. The effects that these variables exert upon vigilance performance have been reviewed recently by Davies and Parasuraman (1982). Wherever possible the general trends of experimental evidence concerning particular stressors are summarized and some indication of importance for practical task performance given.

Definitions of stress

An initial and important concern in examining the effect of any form of stress upon performance is an understanding and definition of the stress concept. Although the term possesses a precise connotation in the physical sciences, an equivalent and unambiguous definition has yet to be found for behavioral enquiry. The classic work of Selye (1950) has been central in the formation of a definition of stress as *the nonspecific response of the organism to any demand made upon it* (see also Selye, 1973). Wilkinson (1969a) pointed out that from this work, environmental conditions which are abnormal in any way should be referred to as *stressors* rather than the more common but less accurate term stress. Variations in both input to the organism which require compensatory response and changes in behavior to effect such response have been suggested as reflections of stress and an interesting discussion of such indices has been given by Ruff (1963). However, the purpose of the present section is to provide neither a comprehensive definition nor exhaustive discussion of such a complex problem. Rather, a practical definition is sought from which subsequent research on vigilance performance in different environmental conditions may be viewed. A simplistic and somewhat practical concept of stressors is that they are those environmental conditions which act to change the comfort of the performer in his attempt to sustain attention.

Prior to analyzing results concerning the action of individual stressors, it is pertinent to examine certain elements common to performance in many conditions. One point which is rarely emphasized in reviews of stress and performance (e.g. Corkindale, 1965; Fraser, 1957a), is that environmental stressors interfere with performance through certain coarse-grained actions. For example, in extreme heat, profuse sweating causes interruptions to vision independent of the more central effects of high temperature. While these problems might be regarded as mundane and somewhat peripheral by those concerned with theoretical research, such factors may be most influential in reducing performance efficiency in real-life tasks. Also, in operational environments it is often the case that a combination of stressors fluctuating in composition and intensity is imposed upon the worker. Investigations concerning the effect of multiple stressors in combination are relatively rare (although see Loeb and Jeantheau, 1958; Grether *et al.*, 1971; Poulton and Edwards, 1974a,b, for exceptions).

A problem which transcends the effect of any particular stressor is the methodology utilized to measure such action. Stressor effects may be masked due to the use of insensitive measures, or results may be contaminated by using subjects in multiple exposure designs without regard for the possibility of performance transfer. This latter problem has been the focus of some attention, particularly in the interpretation of results in studies where single or multiple stressors have been employed (see Poulton and Kerslake, 1965; Poulton, 1973, 1977a, 1982).

The following sections consider the effects that individual stressors have exerted on people's ability to sustain attention. In addition, proposals concerning the mechanisms through which such stressors act are analyzed. Several factors are identified as influential in such action and two of these, task composition and the skill of the performer are examined in some detail.

STRESSORS AND SUSTAINED ATTENTION TASK PERFORMANCE

The thermal environment

The effect exerted by the thermal environment upon vigilance task performance has been of concern since the earliest investigations (Mackworth, 1950; Pepler, 1953) and forms the focus of some current empirical research (e.g. Mackie and O'Hanlon, 1977; Angus *et al.*, 1979). Table 4.1 provides a summary of studies which have examined vigilance efficiency in both heat and cold conditions. Such variations in ambient temperature have elicited improvement (Poulton and Kerslake, 1965), decrement (Fraser, 1957b) and no change (Colquhoun, 1969) in performance efficiency. These contradictory results are not due merely to experimental error. Rather, they reflect the result of complex interactions between several impinging factors. The specific structure of the sustained attention task, the severity of the thermal condition, the length of temporal exposure and differences in individual subjects all contribute to overall performance variation. Wilkinson (1969a) has identified several factors which influence performance under a variety of environmental stressors. In the sections which follow, the potency of such factors will be examined in an attempt to reconcile certain ambiguous research findings.

Table 4.1 Thermal stress and performance on sustained attention tasks

Investigation	Temperature (°C) ET	DB	N	Sustained attention task	Performance measures	Practice	Results
Mackworth (1950)	21 26 31 36	24 29 35 40	20 23 24 22	Monitoring for irregular two-step jumps in one per second single jumps	Signals detected Response latency	One 2 hour practice session; lookouts vs non-lookouts	Optimum performance at 26 °C ET; superior ability mitigated decrement at two highest temperatures
Fraser (1957)	Control 29† 31 33 35	30† 33 36 38	72 20 20 20 12	Monitoring irregularly large lights in lights presented at one per 5 seconds; duration of task 15 minutes; first observation on event rate	Missed signals	No prior task practice	Missed signals greatest at 31 °C; temperature effect confounded in time of exposure
Pepler (1953, 1958)	19 28 33	24 32 49	18‡	As Mackworth above	Signals detected	Task naive subjects who improved with practice	Minimal signal omissions at 28 °C ET; confirmation of Mackworth's findings
Loeb and Jeantheau (1958)	— —	21 47	12‡	Twenty dials monitoring	Median response times	Task naive subjects	No effect for heat alone; confounded in time of day
Fine et al. (1960)	20 34	21 35	10‡	Identical discrimination of two tones from three; task duration 20 minutes	Error committed in discrimination	One practice prior to performance	No temporal effect for repeated trials on errors; non-viable inter-temperature comparison

Study	Temperatures	N	Task	Measures	Practice	Findings
Carlson (1961)	20 — 25 — 40 — 50 —	9‡	Visual monitoring in quadrant and octant displays	Omitted signals	Naive subjects	Decrement at highest combined temperature and event rate
Bell et al. (1964)	29.5 to 56.0	8‡ 8‡	Twenty dials and auditory analog	Median response time percentage signals missed	Practice by days	Visual vigilance, no effect for heat, confounded in days and practice; little effect for auditory performance
	Oral temperatures <37 37–37.49 37.5–37.99 >38					Possible relationship between ascending body temperature and decreasing performance efficiency
Wilkinson et al. (1964)	Oral temperatures 37.3 37.9 38.5	12‡	Monitoring prolonged 900 ms tones in one per 3.3 s presentations 650ms, 1000Hz tones.	Response detection rate response time	No practice reported	Improved performance at 38.5 °C compared to control condition
Poulton and Kerslake (1965)	30 45 19 25	6 6	Concurrent monitoring of five dials and repeated letters in sequence; duration of task 20 minutes.	Mean percent error	Minimal practice	Entry to warm environment stimulates perceptual efficiency

(continued)

Table 4.1 (continued)

Investigation	Temperature (°C) ET	Temperature (°C) DB	N	Sustained attention task	Performance measures	Practice	Results
Colquhoun (1969)	19 28 33	24 32 49	9 9	Monitoring bright flashes in background of light presentations; duration 120 minutes	Percentage detections	Several hours of practice at three event rates, KR given	No effect on efficiency for thermal manipulation
Benor and Shvartz (1971)	— — — — —	30 35 40 45 50	7[‡]	Monitoring of 1000 Hz tones at 2 second intervals; targets 1120 Hz tones; maximum duration 120 minutes	Percentage omitted responses	No recorded practice	Decreasing efficiency with heat; confounded in exposure time; body cooling mitigated deleterious heat-induced effects
Colquhoun and Goldman (1972)	— —	24 39	12[‡]	Monitoring variations in light presentation; 300 ms duration presented once per 3.3 seconds	Percentage signals detected Percentage signals detected, false reports, response latency	Colquhoun's (1969) subjects	No performance change with heat
Mortagy and Ramsey (1973)	23 28 32	27 33 39	108	Monitoring movements of oscilloscope dot	Percentage correct detection, i.e. percentage correct	No practice noted	No simple temperature effect; decrement in highest temperature longest work period condition

Study				Task	detections and observed size of signal		Result
Poulton and Edwards (1974a)	19 / 34	20 / 38	12‡	Visual analog of Wilkinson auditory vigilance task	False detections and d'	Practice control condition prior to Latin square manipulation	Heat increased false detections; trend attenuated by addition of low frequency noise
Poulton et al. (1974)	19 / 33	20 / 38	10‡	Monitoring 500 ms tones presented at one per 2 seconds for a foreshortened 370 ms tone	Percentage detections false detections; mean response time	No practice condition reported	Deterioration in detections with heat
Poulton and Edwards (1974b)	20 / 38	19 / 34	12‡	As above	As above	Practice prior to stress imposition	Significant deterioration in detections with heat
Mackie and O'Hanlon (1977)	20§ / 32§	— / —	20‡	Driving along a set freeway route	Steering corrections >10°; technical errors	No experience metric noted	Heat affected both measures adversely and eliminated four subjects
Fine and Kobrick (1978)	33.3 / 19	35 / 21	28‡	Performance on fire command translation; 7 hours task duration	Accuracy of translation	Task naive subjects; one week training	Performance degradation magnified by temporal exposure

(continued)

Table 4.1 (continued)

| Investigation | Temperature (°C) | | N | Sustained attention task | Performance measures | Practice | Results |
	ET	DB					
Kissen et al. (1964)	—	4	5‡	Matching of simultaneously presented pattern pairs	Correct responses errors commission omission	No practice recorded	Hypnosis mitigated performance decrement; equivocal whether cold effect or temporal effect is offset by hypnotic state
Poulton et al. (1965)	— —	−2 3	16‡	Monitoring for light illumination; seven in a 30 minute period	Delayed; + 2.0 second responses	No practice	Detection deterioration in cold, also with wind and rain; suggestion of relationship between body temperature fall and performance degradation
Angus et al. (1979)	—	0–5	6‡	Wilkinson visual vigilance task	Percentage correct detection	Progressive practice; straight 16 day cold exposure	Cold-induced inefficiency mitigated partly by practice; possible interaction with sleep loss

†Estimated temperatures.
‡Within subject design.
§Wet bulb globe thermometer (WBGT) temperature measures.
A dash (—) indicates that the equivalent effective temperature was not recorded

Heat

In his seminal investigation, Mackworth (1950) examined the effects of increasing environmental temperature upon watchkeeping ability. Artificially acclimatized subjects engaged in a single 2 hour practice session with the clock test prior to performance at one of four elevated effective temperatures (ET).[†] He found that minimal signal omission occurred at an intermediate 26 °C ET condition and optimal performance at this temperature was affirmed by combining response times with missed signals which were regarded as long latency responses. The resultant median response times are shown in Figure 4.1 which describes an inverted U-shape function between performance and environmental temperature. Performance efficiency was reduced during the second hour of watch and the vigilance decrement was magnified by the imposition of increasing ambient heat.

The interaction between heat and the vigilance decrement is also illustrated in Figure 4.2. In this case, the incidence of missed signals at the optimal 26 °C ET condition and the combined values for 31 and 36 °C ET are shown for the four progressive half-hour periods on watch. However, this effect differed depending upon whether the subject had prior experience on watchkeeping-type tasks. To test for experience, Mackworth had assigned an equal number of lookouts and non-lookouts to each temperature condition. At 21 and 26 °C ET there were no performance differences between the two groups. However, at 31 °C ET and above, those subjects with prior experience manifested superior ability in resisting the deleterious impact of the heat stressor. Figure 4.2 shows this effect to be dependent on time of watch, as may be seen from a comparison of lookouts and non-lookouts at 31–36 °C ET.

Although Pepler (1953, 1958) subsequently confirmed Mackworth's findings with naturally acclimatized personnel in a tropical location, the inverted U-shape function relating vigilance efficiency and temperature was not found by Fraser (1957b). In a simulation of a practical work setting, he reported that missed signals were *greatest* at an intermediate temperature and performance improved with a decrease or increase in effective temperature around a 31 °C ET value. However, there are several important procedural differences between Fraser's

---

[†]The most familiar measure of temperature is a simple dry-bulb value. However, this is insufficient as an indicator of overall thermal conditions. Mackworth (1950) rightly employed the effective temperature (ET) scale as a measure of environmental heat. This scale was developed by Houghten and Yaglogou (1923) to synthesize values of air temperature, relative humidity and air velocity. There have been subsequent amendments to this scale to include other factors, notably the addition of a radiant heat assessment. No present scale encompasses all variables which affect human thermal response. However, the interested reader is directed to the work of Rohles *et al.* (1982) for their development of a new psychrometric chart for thermal comfort and to Mutchler and Vecchio (1977) for empirical comparison of different heat stress indices. Effective temperature remains in common usage in psychological experimentation as investigators usually report sufficient information to construct an ET measure. However, more recently developed indices such as wet bulb globe temperature (WBGT) (Yaglou and Minard, 1957) and Botsball (Botsford, 1971) may be more pertinent for such investigations. For a comparison of the latter scales see Beshir (1981).

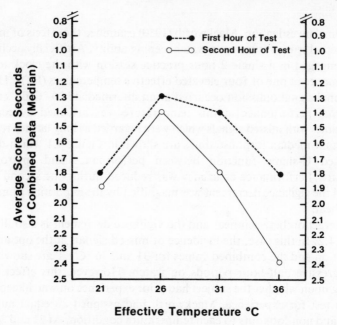

Figure 4.1   Environmental effective temperature versus combined responses scores on a watchkeeping task. [Data redrawn from Mackworth (1950). Reproduced by permission of the Controller of Her Majesty's Stationery Office.]

study and the previous two investigations. First, performance was measured prior to and following exposure to the heat stressor. Second, temporal exposure to the stressor was varied according to the intensity of the heat and the work regimen demanded in each condition. Finally, Fraser varied both event rate and performance time such that a curtailed 15-minute monitoring period was required. For these reasons, it is difficult to compare his results with those of the previous studies. Fraser concluded that the vigilance decrement is a function of the joint effects of temperature intensity, exposure duration and the imposed workload. He postulated that there were two different kinds of vigilance tasks, one of which requires subjects to observe occasional signals in a long watch period and a second in which stimuli are presented at high speed in a comparatively short time. These task differences alter the manner in which the heat stressor affects performance.

The effects of heat and additional environmental stressors in realistic operational conditions were also investigated by Loeb and Jeantheau (1958). They found that noise, vibration and heat in combination reduced efficiency in a 20-dials monitoring task. However, they found no effect on performance when subjects were exposed to environmental heat load alone. Bell and Provins (1962) criticized this finding. They suggested that the null effect was due to the use of an inappropriate night-time control condition which confounded the

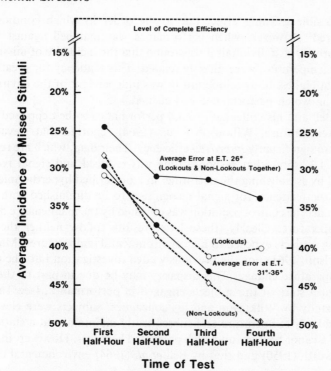

Figure 4.2 Incidence of signal omission against temporal exposure in a watchkeeping task. The effect of experience and its interaction with high atmospheric temperature is illustrated. [Data redrawn from Mackworth (1950). Reproduced by permission of the controller of Her Majesty's Stationery Office.]

effects of heat with those of time of day. In contrast to the above, Carlson (1961) found that elevated temperature exerted a deleterious effect upon monitoring capability. In a test of the activation hypothesis, Carlson reasoned that information input and heat would combine to provide either operator overload or underload, depending upon precise conditions. Using different event rates, in quadrant and octant displays, Carlson found that error incidence was elevated greatly under the highest input and most severe temperature condition. He suggested that a result of this sort was due to an interaction between physiological and psychological inputs represented by the stressor and the task.

Following attempts to relate performance and the temperature of the environment, Bell *et al.* (1964) demonstrated the importance of considering the body temperature of the performer. Initially, they found no change in visual vigilance and little effect for auditory vigilance in subjects sequentially exposed to progressively higher environmental heat loads (see also Bell, 1964). However, these results were confounded with the time spent in each heating condition, which grew shorter as temperature was increased and, as Grether (1973) noted, with a possible learning effect due to the order in which conditions were administered. However, when performance was matched against the body temperature of the individuals it was found that the incidence of missed signals and body temperature were directly related. This tendency for greatest signal omission at highest body temperatures was independent of the environmental condition in which performance was elicited.

While Bell and his colleagues found performance to be depressed by a rise in body temperature, Wilkinson *et al.* (1964) reported that elevated body temperature significantly *improved* efficiency. Their data, which are reproduced in Figure 4.3, show that response time was reduced and signal recognition facilitated by establishing the performer in a prescribed hyperthermic state. In addition, the tendency for signal recognition to be diminished with repeated sessions under the control condition was obviated by the maintenance of elevated body temperature. Clearly, these latter results follow neither the findings concerning subjects exposed to high environmental temperatures (Mackworth, 1950; Carlson, 1961) nor the previously cited investigation into the effects of body temperature change. This disparity may be due in part to the thermo-physiological state of the subjects engaged in performance, (see Table 4.1).

In the study by Wilkinson and his colleagues, subjects were elevated to a prescribed body temperature and subsequently maintained at a static level by the use of a vapor barrier suit which prevented heat loss. However, in the study by Mackworth (1950) and that by Bell *et al.* (1964) environmental conditions

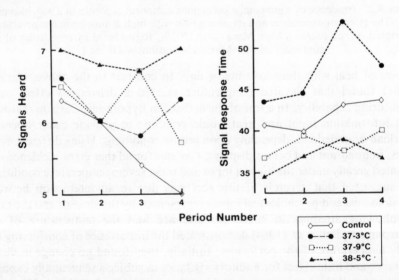

Figure 4.3   Repeated sessions of watchkeeping at prescribed body temperatures. Results illustrated for signals responded to and response latency. [Data redrawn from Wilkinson *et al.* (1964).]

were such that body temperature was consistently ascending in the higher heat exposures (Houghten and Yaglogou, 1923; Lind, 1963). Wilkinson and his collaborators invoked the concept of arousal as a possible mediator of performance improvement. They suggested that the optimal level for the vigilance task was only reached with the addition of an uncomfortable and arousing stressor. The relationship between environmental stressors, arousal and performance upon vigilance tasks has been fully elaborated by Poulton (1977a). The results of the studies concerning body temperature indicate that the physiological state of the performer and the characteristics of the sustained attention task interact to affect performance efficiency.

Although most studies involve prolonged exposure, Poulton and Kerslake (1965) examined the immediate effects of entry into a hot environment. Subjects performed two concurrent monitoring tasks for 20 minutes, and although possible methodological pitfalls are examined (see also Poulton, 1973, 1982), the authors concluded that immediate entry into heat may have a stimulating effect on perceptual efficiency. These results do not appear to accord with those of Carlson (1961), who found that high information rate and temperature summated to depress performance. However, the temporal length of the exposure differed and may have contributed to the difference in findings. From the results of their experiment, Poulton and Kerslake (1965) advanced a description of performance variation with time in a heated environment.

First, entry into a warm environment is stimulating and consequently improves efficiency, while continuation in equivalent conditions results in adaptation, reduced arousal and the depression of performance. With continued exposure the temperature of the body rises and becomes uncomfortably hot, these conditions reactivate arousal and increase capability. Finally, the performer reaches a stage of imminent heat collapse. (Jones, 1970). Theoretical accounts of the relation between upper thermal tolerance and performance have been given by Wing (1965) and by Hancock (1981, 1982a).

In light of this time course, it is somewhat surprising that Colquhoun (1969) found no effect on performance for a 2 hour exposure at 33 °C ET and similarly, that in a subsequent experiment, Colquhoun and Goldman (1972) reported no change in efficiency when body temperature was elevated to 38.6 °C. Although the response criterion was altered in the hyperthermic state, a trend affirmed by the work of Allnutt and Allan (1973), there was no difference in detection rate due to changes in body temperature. The latter finding is in direct contrast to previous reports of either improvement (Wilkinson *et al.*, 1964) or decrement (Bell *et al.*, 1964) at similar body temperatures. The key factor which appears to differentiate the studies is the performance level of the subject prior to the heat manipulation. While previous investigators utilized relatively naive performers, Colquhoun (1969) explicitly states that subjects received several hours of practice prior to the experiment and the same subjects were utilized in the later experiment by Colquhoun and Goldman (1972). Norman Mackworth (1950) has provided an empirical demonstration of the potent effects of prior experience and a possible account of such variation has been offered by Hancock (1982b).

Recent research has focused on performance in more practical work situations and has explored methods by which the effect of the heat stressor may be curtailed. For example, Benor and Shvartz (1971) tested a body cooling technique for the maintenance of performance efficiency in heat. Their data, shown in Figure 4.4, depict some interesting trends. First, without cooling they found an approximately linear relationship between the percentage of signals missed and ascending dry-bulb temperature up to 50 °C. Second, the effect for a progressive time of exposure factor is shown by comparing the second-half results with total performance. However, as with previous studies (Fraser, 1957b; Bell *et al.*, 1964), the time spent in each heat condition covaried with the severity of the stressor. In cooling-aided conditions all subjects completed the 2 hours of exposure with essentially no change in performance. The authors concluded from their data that detection rate is dependent upon environmental rather than body temperature, although this position is somewhat equivocal when the differing time of exposure factor is considered.

Mortagy and Ramsey (1973) draw attention to the fact that, in practical situations, activity may be structured to include rest from the vigilance task. Consequently, they examined visual vigilance under three lengths of work period,

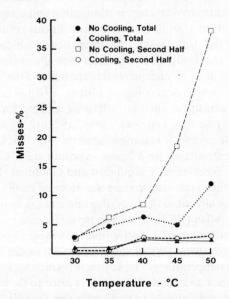

Figure 4.4 Percentage signals missed against environmental temperature. The effect of augmented cooling and temporal exposure are illustrated. [Data redrawn from Benor and Shvartz (1971).]

and two work/rest ratios in three different ET conditions (see Table 4.1). Significant performance decrement was found only in the longest work period, highest temperature combination. Recommendations were offered which were designed to moderate the deleterious effects of heat and time on watch in real-life tasks.

A somewhat similar and highly practical investigation was conducted by Mackie and O'Hanlon (1977). They examined vehicle control during prolonged freeway driving in high ambient temperature. Several parameters of performance were measured, together with indices of physiological strain which was induced by the environmental conditions. One parameter, frequency of corrective steering wheel movements, is shown in Figure 4.5 for both a hot and a cool exposure. In the initial portion of the journey, there is a small and progressive decrease in the frequency of corrective steering, although a significantly larger number of movements are made in the heat. In the latter segment of the journey both temperature conditions resulted in an increase in corrective steering over time. However, the frequency of corrective steering increased at a significantly faster rate in the 32 °C condition. Similar results were reported for technical driving errors composed of a measure of legal infringements and violations of safe driving procedure. Although these results are influenced by traffic conditions on any particular test day, they illustrate the adverse effect that elevated temperature may have on commonplace but important vigilance-type tasks. The interactive effect noted between time on task and heat was also found recently

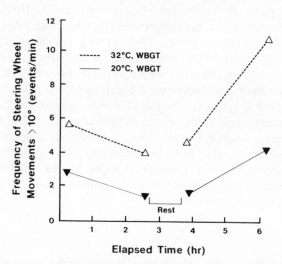

Figure 4.5 Frequency of steering movements above 10° in amplitude against elapsed performance time. The effect of an interpolated rest on both heat and control conditions is illustrated. [Data redrawn from Mackie and O'Hanlon (1977).]

by Fine and Kobrick (1978) using a militarily oriented fire-command translation task.

In a series of experiments by Poulton and his colleagues, the effects of heat have been examined singly and in conjunction with other environmental stressors, i.e. noise (Poulton and Edwards, 1974a) and agents which act to affect the state of the individual, i.e. a drug manipulation (Poulton and Edwards, 1974b) and the loss of a night's sleep (Poulton *et al.*, 1974). The effect of heat alone was to reduce detection efficiency in two experiments and significantly to depress the signal detection *d'* measure in each of the studies. Poulton (1977a) concluded that the decrements reflected the reduction of arousal by the lassitude-inducing temperature condition.

Summary   The current weight of empirical evidence suggests that vigilance performance is impaired by exposure to temperatures greater than 32 °C ET (Benor and Shvartz, 1971; Poulton and Edwards, 1974b; Mackie and O'Hanlon, 1977). This temperature represents a value for environmental heat load, which induces a progressive rise in human body temperature by simple exposure alone (see Lind, 1963; Grether, 1973; Hancock, 1982a). In contrast, there are circumstances in which heat facilitates performance such as the immediate entry into a hot environment (Poulton and Kerslake, 1965).

The relationship between body temperature and performance allows further insight into the effect of heat. In cases where body temperature is increasing, performance appears to suffer (cf. Bell *et al.*, 1964). However, if the performer is established in a *static* hyperthermic state, vigilance performance is facilitated (cf. Wilkinson *et al.*, 1964). Using the latter manipulation, Colquhoun and Goldman (1972) found no change in performance and similarly Colquhoun (1969) reported no effect for an exposure above 32 °C ET. However, on each occasion their performers were highly practised upon the sustained attention task and it is suggested that this skill level mitigated variation induced by the heat stressor (see also Mackworth, 1950; Hancock, 1982b). In summary, conditions which act to elicit dynamically increasing body temperature degrade performance, while a stable hyperthermic state may prove beneficial. In environments which do not produce changes in the performer's body temperature, heat above a thermoneutral condition can aid performance efficiency.

Cold

There have been few studies which have examined the effect of cold upon vigilance efficiency. One reason for this might be that personnel and institutions in countries with cold climates specifically guard against prolonged activity outdoors. One result, as Kreyberg (1949) pointed out, is that cases of frostbite are rare in very cold climatic locations as inhabitants are particularly aware of the potential for injury. In a similar manner tasks are not structured to require an operator to sustain attention in cold conditions for a prolonged period.

One exception, as noted by Poulton *et al.* (1965), is the performance of lookout duties on a vessel operating in Arctic conditions. In their experimental procedure, they exposed subjects once to a cold and once to a more mild temperature condition (see Table 4.1). Their data are reproduced in Figure 4.6 and show an interesting but somewhat complex result. With the exception of the first trial, there is a gradual increase in long latency responses through the watch for the group initially exposed to cold. This group, however, performed significantly more efficiently than a group in milder conditions who experienced the more interruptive effects of wind and rain. Results from the second watch are influenced by prior practice. However, a combination of results from the cold exposures indicates a significant time on watch effect under this stressor. The authors suggest that in cold conditions there is a possible relationship between decreasing body temperature and performance decrement. Although this proposal is consistent with the position concerning heat and monitoring efficiency, it has yet to receive further experimental attention.

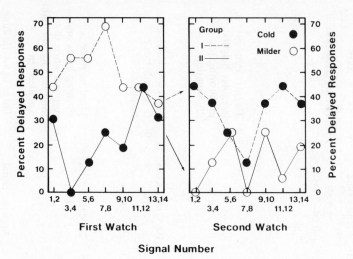

Figure 4.6   Mean percentage of delayed responses (greater than 2.0 seconds) in cold and mild conditions. [Redrawn from Poulton *et al.* (1965).]

Kissen *et al.* (1964) reported changes in physiological response to cold at 4 °C, ambient air temperature, through the imposition of an hypnotic state. Hypnotized subjects also performed a vigilance task better than non-hypnotized controls in the cold. However, from their data it is difficult to determine whether hypnotism enhanced performance by mitigating the effects of the cold stressor

Table 4.2 The effect of noise on sustained attention performance

Investigation	SPL (dB)	Noise type	N	Sustained attention task	Performance	Practice	Results
Broadbent (1954)	70 100	±3 dB 0.04–5 kHz	10‡	Twenty dials task	Pointer deflection reported	Task amenable to practice effect; five sessions noise on third and fourth session	Performance worse in noise
Broadbent (1954)			10*	Twenty lights at irregular heights; monitoring for illumination	Proportion of 'quick founds', i.e. identification.	Dichotomized least vs markedly improving groups	Individuals most susceptible to noise show largest early practice effects
Jerison (1959, Experiment I)	83 114	0.6<max<0.3 kHz	9‡	Mackworth clock task with three displays	Percentage correct detections	One 1-hour training session	No main effect for noise but a significant interaction between noise and time on task
Jerison (1959, Experiment II)	77.5 111.5	2.4<max<1.2 kHz	14‡	Monitor three flashing lights and respond when the total on any one light equalled ten	Percentage correct responses	One 2-hour training session	No effect for noise but an effect for order of presentation
Broadbent and Gregory (1963)	75 100	Approx. equal level 0.1–5 kHz	13‡	Three lights flashing simultaneously for 300 ms once per 1400 ms; monitoring for occasional bright	d', β	10 minutes with KR; Signal refreshment before exposure	No effect for noise during last 30 minutes of exposure on raw detection rate; improvement for most

Study		Noise condition	N	Task	Measure	Practice	Results
McGrath (1963, Experiment I)	72	White noise Varied noise	28‡	Monitoring for increments in brightness of a light, on for 1 second and off for 2 seconds	Percentage signals detected detected	Warm-up session of 2 minutes pre- and post-test; improvement with practice	Performance in variety audio superior to white noise; above effect interacts with time on watch
McGrath (1963, Experiment III)	72	Conditions as in Experiment I	24‡	Task as in Experiment I and faster event rate; light on for 333 ms, off for 666 ms	Percentage detections	Practice as in Experiment I	Slow event rate variety of noise improves over white noise; effect reversed under fast event rate
Kirk and Hecht (1963)	61 64.5 64.5	Quiet Constant noise Variable noise	30‡	Monitor CRT display for 0.525 inch horizontal deflections of 0.25 inch horizontal light beam	Percentage detections; log reaction time	No practice; 30 minute quiet period before performance	Improvement in detection in varied noise compared to other two conditions
Ware et al. (1964)	112	Control; radio program contingent and noncontingent on performance	112	Aperiodic interruptions of an illuminated lamp; 72 signals per 3 hour watch	Percentage detections	No practice noted	Improvement with radio contingent and noncontingent over control; radio contingent provides knowledge of results
Woodhead (1964)	Control 70 110	Recorded rocket firing 1 second bursts	48	Ten digit row presented every 2 seconds; subject crosses out a remembered digit, which is replaced by subsequent ringed digit presentation	Perseverance with a previous number	Instruction given; two unpaced practices, one paced	No main effect for noise condition; some effects in critical 30 seconds following noise

Table 4.2 *(continued)*

Investigation	SPL (dB)	Noise type	N	Sustained attention task	Performance	Practice	Results
Broadbent and Gregory (1965)	75 100	Valve noise flat 0.1–5 kHz	36	Monitoring 300 ms light flashes for occasional brighter signal; two event rates and two displays utilized	Percentage detections, sure and unsure categories	Practice with KR prior to testing	Reduced number of intermediate confidence responses with noise; little effect of noise on slow event rate
Davies and Hockey (1966)	70 95	White noise	48	Monitoring for differences in digits presented for 600 ms comparison time.	Correct detections	Two short practice periods of 2 and 8 minutes	Commission errors greater for extroverts in noise, vice versa for introverts; extroverts improved in noise at low signal rate
McCann (1969)	50	0.52 kHz continuous and 1.5 second bursts interspersed	20	Visual vs auditory number checking	Errors of omission and commission	No practice recorded	Some evidence of reduced omission errors with intermittent noise; noise conditions not compared to quiet
Warner (1969)	80 90 100	White noise for first 70% of each 5 second cycle	24	Search 16 letter displays for target letter; 16 minute total duration	Detection latency and errors	No practice performance in control and each noise condition	No effect of noise on detection latency; reduction of error rate with noise

Study	Intensity (dB)	Noise	N	Task	Measure	Practice	Results
Blackwell and Belt (1971)	50 75 90	White noise	27	Visual monitoring for irregular events; 48 signals in 40 minute exposure	Misses and false alarms	No practice noted	Intensity level of ambient white noise no effect on performance
Warner and Heimstra (1971)	100	White noise on-off ratios 30, 70, 100% of 5 second cycle	22‡	Search in displays of eight and 32 letters for heterogeneous targets	Detection time	Eight test sessions; no prior practice noted	Apparent improvement for detection in large array for noise conditions; decrement due to noise in small array with exception of 30% noise condition
Gulian (1971)	70 90	Both continuous and intermittent conditions	15	Monitoring for specific tones in a background of alternate tones; 70 minute sessions	Percentage correct detections mean RT	No practice noted	No effect on errors; suggestion of increasing RT from continuous to intermittent condition, confounded in exposure order
Childs and Halcomb (1972)	90	Intermittent 2 seconds at 5 second intervals and continuous	140	Monitor moving light for aperiodic large movements	Percentage correct detections false alarms	No practice noted	No effect of noise on performance
Warner and Heimstra (1972)	0 80 90 100	White noise	20‡	See Warner and Heimstra (1971); with addition of 16 letter display.	Detection latency; detection error	Twelve conditions; random order	Interaction noise intensity complexity; 80 dB condition most interruptive, particularly in two most complex displays

Table 4.2 (Continued)

Investigation	SPL (dB)	Noise type	N	Sustained attention task	Performance	Practice	Results
Warner and Heimstra (1973)	0 80 90 100	White noise 30% intermittent in 5 second cycles	20‡	As Warner and Heimstra (1972)	Detection time	As above	Main effect for noise and complexity; interacting effects are complex, based on increments of each
Poulton and Edwards (1974a)	102	C scale attenuated 7.5 dB per octave	12‡	Wilkinson visual vigilance task	Percentage detections false detections	Practice condition prior to exposure	Noise increases number of "certain" category detections
Benignus et al. (1975)	42 80	Low frequency 0.01–0.04 kHz 0.09–0.35 kHz	27	Monitoring digits displayed for 50 ms at rate of one per second; response made to three consecutive odd or even digits	Miss rate false alarms	30–60 minute training session in quiet conditions	More signals missed in noise than quiet conditions
Jones et al. (1979, Experiments I and II)	55 85 From 0.125 to 4 kHz	C scale ±1 dB	14 16	Digits displayed for 750 ms, one per second; monitoring for three successive odd digits	Omission and commission errors	Practice of 129 seconds containing two targets	Omission errors increase in noise; commission errors greater in quiet conditions
Jones et al. (1979, Experiments III and IV)	55 80 85	As above	18 16	As above with pause of one second after group of three digits; targets were odd–even-odd sequences within and between groups of three digits	As above	Practice effect, i.e. noise × order significant	No effect for noise on detections; no difference for commission errors

‡Within subject design.

or those due to time on task, or both. In a recent study, Angus *et al.* (1979) found a fall in performance efficiency for men sleeping in Arctic conditions. Fluctuations in performance capability on a day by day basis were tentatively related to overnight temperature, although one covariate as noted by the authors was differential sleep quality, a factor previously suggested as influential in the performance of sustained attention tasks (Wilkinson, 1960). The gradual recovery toward baseline level over the 16 days of exposure may have been due in part to learning over repeated performances. This might account for the observation that while REM sleep remained 25% below normal levels at the end of the exposure, monitoring efficiency recovered to baseline level by the end of the experiment.

Summary The above study represents a practical investigation into watch-keeping ability in Arctic conditions. However, this is one of a highly restricted number of such investigations. Until further research is undertaken the relationship between reduced ambient temperature and sustained attention remains somewhat unclear. As a general statement, each of the above studies affirm a suggestion that cold *per se* impairs vigilance performance.

The acoustic environment

A summary of studies describing the effects of noise on sustained attention task performance is given in Table 4.2. However, due to the large number of investigations pertaining to the acoustic stressor, only a selection of experiments employing both continuous and intermittent noise have been presented. There have been many reviews concerning the effects of noise upon human performance. Early research was summarized by Diserens (1926) and Harmon (1933) and more recent research has been synthesized by several investigators (see Hockey, 1978; Broadbent, 1979; Loeb, 1980; Cohen and Weinstein, 1981). While these accounts have considered differing aspects of performance capability, the specific effects of noise on vigilance performance have been reported by Broadbent (1953), Mirabella and Goldstein (1967) and Davies and his colleagues (i.e. Davies and Tune, 1970; Davies and Parasuraman, 1982).

Continuous noise

As with performance under thermal stress, individual studies using continuous noise have elicited improvement, decrement and no change in vigilance efficiency. To structure such ambiguous findings, Lysaght (1982) advanced a taxonomic approach dividing performance upon the basis of three parameters. Figure 4.7 gives a diagrammatic representation of this proposal, where the three axes represent noise quality, noise level and degree of processing demand. The latter two measures are dichotomized into high and low levels, high noise being

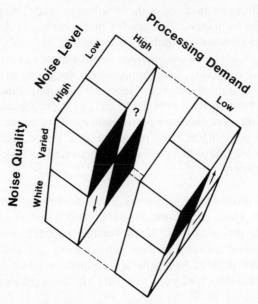

Figure 4.7 Three-factor taxonomic approach to describe continuous noise effects on vigilance performance. ↑ represents improved performance efficiency; ↓ represents depressed performance efficiency; − represents no change in performance efficiency. Equivocal (?) results and areas of little empirical investigation (■) are also illustrated. [After Lysaght (1982).]

above 90 dB SPL while high demand reflects the difficulty of determining critical events. The third axis divides noise according to its quality, whether white or varied.

The figure illustrates the general trend of results in differing noise and task combinations. For example, in the performance of sensory vigilance tasks requiring a high processing demand, the effect of white noise above 90 dB SPL has been to reduce monitoring capability. In his early work, Broadbent (1954) showed that performance in the 20-dials monitoring task was significantly degraded by the introduction of 100 dB white noise. Similar effects have subsequently been reported by Jerison (1959) and Hockey (1973), although certain findings (Jerison, 1959, Experiment II; Broadbent and Gregory, 1963, 1965) have suggested that this may not be a simple relationship. In addition, Davies and Hockey (1966) reported that the decrement was at least in part dependent upon the nature of the subject engaged in the monitoring task.

There has been little reported concerning the effect of low level white noise on highly demanding sensory vigilance tasks. However, such conditions have been found to depress more cognitive vigilance performance. Benignus *et al.*

(1975) found that monitoring digits for consecutive odd or even patterns was disrupted by the introduction of 80 dB SPL white noise, while the results of Warner and Heimstra (1972) suggest that this value may be most interruptive of performance since increases to 90 and 100 dB SPL actually benefited performance on a letter-searching task (see Table 4.2). This position was supported recently by Jones *et al.* (1979), who found slightly depressed performance at 85 dB SPL.

There is little evidence that white noise affects performance on sensory vigilance tasks of low processing demand. In a noise level above 90 dB the absence of effect has been reported by Jerison (1957) and also by others (Broadbent and Gregory, 1965; Blackwell and Belt, 1971). In common with their observation at a high processing demand, Davies and Hockey (1966) suggest that introverts and extraverts respond differently, such that extraverts tend to benefit from the addition of 95 dB white noise in the low demand situation. At noise levels lower than 90 dB no performance change has been found (Kirk and Hecht, 1963; McCann, 1969; Blackwell and Belt, 1971; Davenport, 1972).

In contrast to the disruptive effect of white noise, it has been observed that low level varied noise facilitates performance under low demand monitoring conditions. Support for this contention may be found in several studies (McBain, 1961; Kirk and Hecht, 1963; Watkins, 1964; Watkins and Feehrer, 1965). However, a recent study by Thackray and Touchstone (1979) found no change under these conditions. Subjects were required to search a radar display for differing signals. In the low difficulty condition signals were the occurrence of the figure 999 alongside a radar blip, while in difficult conditions numbers higher than 550 and lower than 150 required response. Quiet conditions (57 dB) were compared with varied noise (78–80 dB) produced by recordings taken in operational air traffic control rooms. Results showed no effect of noise in either the high or low difficulty conditions. This finding leaves equivocal the effect of low level varied noise on high processing demand vigilance tasks. While Davies *et al.* (1973) reported improvement under such conditions, McGrath (1963) intimated that variety audio depressed performance compared to quiet conditions. However, McGrath's comparison is confounded by both variation in event rate and length of watch and firm conclusions on the effect of low level varied noise may not be drawn at the present time.

Summary   While continuous white noise generally degrades performance where processing demand is high in sensory vigilance tasks and may exert a similar effect at lower intensity levels upon cognitive vigilance tasks, there is little evidence for any change in simple sensory monitoring in such acoustic conditions. In contrast, varied noise may improve performance in simple tasks although its effect on more complex performance is somewhat equivocal at the present time. Clearly, such results are dependent, in part, upon the state of the performer (Davies and Hockey, 1966) and upon the ability of the individual to learn in quiet and noisy conditions (Broadbent, 1954).

Intermittent Noise

Compared to continuous noise, relatively few studies have examined the effect of intermittent noise upon vigilance performance (see Table 4.2). Yet, as Woodhead (1964) indicated, in many operational environments there are bursts of noise which have no connection with the performance task. Teichner *et al.* (1963) suggested that such bursts of sound might either facilitate or disrupt performance depending on subject adaption and on–off ratio. They proposed that an equilibrium on–off ratio would occur where performance would neither improve nor decline. At a sound intensity level of 100 dB they found this ratio to be 70%.

Warner (1969) confirmed that at a 70% on–off ratio there was no effect on response latency for differing noise intensity. In a second experiment, Warner and Heimstra (1971) found that a 30% on–off ratio improved detection speed in a difficult target-detection task, while 70% and 100% on–off ratios impaired performance in an easy but not in a difficult task condition. To explore the nature of facilitated performance, Warner and Heimstra (1973) retained the 30% on–off ratio but varied noise and task difficulty. They found that variation in noise intensity had little effect upon performance in simple processing demand conditions and that intermittent noise below 90 dB exerted no appreciable effects. Finally, they reported that variations in performance at 90 dB and above were complex and that facilitation and impairment depended upon the interaction of noise and task complexity.

Woodhead (1964) had previously reported that while bursts of low frequency rocket noise at 110 dB had a detrimental effect, a similar noise regimen at 70 dB was instrumental in reducing errors compared to a quiet condition. Using a comparable number checking test, Benignus *et al.* (1975) found that at a 45% on–off ratio, noise intensity at 80 dB reduced monitoring efficiency and McCann (1969) suggested that intermittent noise at 50 dB interrupted performance (comparison was only made between continuous and intermittent noise conditions and the independent effects of the intermittent manipulation cannot be assessed).

In the above studies the noise manipulation has been made independent of the task under consideration. However, some investigations have related the presence or absence of noise to some parameter of operator efficiency. While some studies have used noise merely as an alerting process, others have used change in acoustic stress as reward or punishment for good or poor performance. For example, Pollack and Knaff (1958) found that performance improved in conditions where a loud noise was used to punish signal omissions. Ware *et al.* (1964) made the presence of a radio program contingent upon operator efficiency. Both a group which performed with the radio continuously on and a radio-contingent group performed significantly better than a control group. However, the radio-contingent group did not show the usual vigilance decrement, while the decrement did appear in the continuous radio condition. Ware and his colleagues attributed this finding to the knowledge of results (KR) which the contingent condition provided. The ability of knowledge of results to minimize the vigilance decrement has been demonstrated in several other experiments (see Chapter 2).

Summary   Changes in performance capability in intermittent noise appears to depend upon four main factors. The first two, noise intensity and on–off ratio, are parameters of the acoustic stressor. When on–off ratio is high, low intensity noise appears to facilitate performance while high intensity noise is antagonistic to monitoring efficiency. At lower on–off ratios the effect of intensity appears less important. Interacting with the two characteristics of the stressor is the complexity of the task at hand. For a discussion of this latter factor see Warner and Heimstra (1973). There is insufficient evidence with which to construct a taxonomy as in the case of continuous noise. When the presence or absence of noise is contingent upon response, performance improves. However, the effects of noise and knowledge of results are confounded in such cases.

The sensory environment

Stimulus deprivation and social isolation

Research into the effects of drastic reductions in stimulation was prompted, in part, by reports that vigilance performance grew progressively poorer with prolonged exposure to monotonous environmental conditions (Zubek, 1964). Experimental investigations have examined the effects of sensory deprivation, where the overall level of input is reduced, and perceptual deprivation, which interrupts the organization and patterning of impinging stimuli.

Following the original work of Hebb and his colleagues, various methods of inducing these deprivational states were adopted. Zubek *et al.* (1961) had subjects recline on a mattress in darkness and silence for 7 days. The subjects were given auditory and visual vigilance tests prior to and following deprivation. Sensory deprivation had no effect on auditory monitoring. On the other hand, visual vigilance was significantly poorer after a week of sensory deprivation. It is not clear from this study, however, whether deprivation itself or a reaction to the re-establishment of normal levels of stimulation resulted in poorer post-deprivation performance.

Some subsequent work by Smith *et al.* (1967) suggested that vigilance performance improves if the task is performed during the time the subjects are in the deprived environment. Davies and Tune (1970) suggested that this latter result is due to the maintenance of alertness by the kinesthetic feedback which subjects receive from their own restless behavior in the deprived condition. This position is supported in a study by Zuercher (1965), who found that feedback from verbal and physical activity improved performance over a control condition.

In contrast, Zubek and MacNeill (1966) found that prolonged immobilization or the reduction of kinesthetic feedback for a period of days also aided efficiency. They compared visual and auditory vigilance in immobilized subjects with that in ambulatory and recumbent controls. Auditory vigilance was depressed for the recumbent subjects relative to the others. With the visual vigilance task, the immobilized subjects were significantly better than both control groups. In these procedures, in which sensory stimuli are drastically curtailed for a considerable period, subjects report that any stimulation still present, e.g. heart beat, takes on magnified importance. Consequently, it is not surprising that the stimulus-seeking subject should produce better sustained attention performance during deprivation. Following such stressful conditions, adjustment to normal intensity stimuli may continue for up to 24 hours after the cessation of exposure (Fiske, 1961). Tests made during this time may confound the effect of deprivation with that of readjustment.

Typically, stimulus deprivation studies using prolonged exposures have denied information to all sensory modalities. However, some researchers have addressed the problem of modality specific performance when stimulation to a competing sense is reduced. Bakan and Manley (1963) reported upon the auditory vigilance of subjects temporarily deprived of vision. They found that male subjects increased detection efficiency when light deprived but that this manipulation had no effect on female subjects. Moreover, Davies (1961) has reported that subjects in normal visual conditions were better at an auditory vigilance task than those temporarily deprived of sight. In practical terms, these results do not encourage the reduction of competing visual information in order to improve auditory vigilance.

Summary Drastic reduction of all environmental stimulation magnifies stimulus-seeking in the individual and consequently improves detection efficiency during exposure. Performance immediately following liberation from such conditions may be depressed due to competition between signals in a vigilance task and readjustment to normal levels of stimulation, although this effect may be specific to the visual modality. Evidence relating performance change in auditory vigilance when competition from vision is reduced is somewhat equivocal at the current time.

Vibration and other environmental stressors

In many practical work situations it is necessary to monitor displays in environmental conditions which inherently contain some degree of vibration.

Airborne and land vehicle systems introduce vibration to the operator who may be required to sustain attention for a considerable period. Given this, it is somewhat surprising that few studies have addressed the problem of vigilance efficiency under vibration stress. Grether (1971) has provided a detailed review of the effect of vibration upon human performance. He notes that vibration typically refers to sinusoidal or random oscillation in the range between 1 and 30 Hz. From subjective estimates of discomfort, Magid *et al.* (1960) established that minimal tolerance to vibration was found in the range 4–7 Hz and subsequently, Shoenberger and Harris (1971) reported that discomfort was greatest at 5 Hz. This value, as Grether (1971) noted, is the frequency at which the resonance of large organs of the body is most severe.

One problem in measuring the effect of vibration upon visual monitoring is that physical interference may prevent the reception of visual signals even in the alerted operator. This problem is most severe in the range 10–25 Hz (Snyder, 1965), although the effect appears to be modality specific, as a study by Holland (1967) on auditory vigilance found no essential change in detection efficiency. Indeed, most studies on the effect of vibration have found little performance variation. Schohan *et al.* (1965) reported no effect on target identification and instrument monitoring for vibration approximating turbulent air conditions on a 3-hour simulated flight. Similarly, Parks (1961) found visual monitoring unaffected by random and sinusoidal oscillation at 0.75 and 2.5 Hz, a result confirmed for both visual and auditory vigilance by Weisz *et al.* (1965) at 5 Hz.

Shoenberger (1967) investigated performance on several tasks where subjects were exposed to 30 minutes' vibration at differing frequency and accelerational values. Tasks requiring some form of central processing ability were mostly unaffected by the stressor, which, however, caused poorer performance on tasks with greater motoric components. In one exception to the former conclusion, Shoenberger reported that a probability monitoring task was better at 5 Hz (± 0.30 Hz) than in a control condition. However, in contrast to Poulton (1978a), Shoenberger suggested that this result was due to an initially poor control performance and was not the result of arousal due to the stressor imposed.

Wilkinson and Gray (1974) utilized an auditory vigilance task in which subjects were required to detect foreshortened tones in a continuous series presented at the rate of one every 2 seconds. Subjects experienced 5 Hz vibration and an acceleration of $1.2 \mathrm{~m~s}^{-2}$, for 3 hours. The vigilance task was of 1 hour's duration and was presented at 23 and 107 minutes into the session. The main effect for vibration was not significant, but the stressor was responsible for partly reducing the vigilance decrement. Wilkinson and Gray manipulated knowledge of results (KR) and suggested that vibration impairs performance with time in motivating conditions, i.e. with KR, but has no effect when KR is not presented.

There have been several studies concerning the effects of variations in atmospheric constitution upon vigilance performance. Cahoon (1970) indicated that sensitivity (d') decreased progressively as subjects breathed oxygen levels simulating increasing altitude. Impaired detection was also found in a subsequent study using auditory vigilance (Cahoon, 1973). Christensen *et al.* (1977) reported that fewer signals were detected when the oxygen content of the breathing mixture was reduced to 17%. However, the addition of carbon monoxide (CO) in a concentration of 113 parts per million (p.p.m.) to the latter breathing mixture resulted in no difference in performance from an initial control. Christensen *et al.* speculated that the additional CO stressor activated a compensatory mechanism which obviated the decrement induced by the reduction of oxygen. The effects of CO itself are somewhat equivocal. While some investigators have found performance impairment as CO in the body increases (e.g. Horvath *et al.*, 1971), others have found no change (e.g. Benignus *et al.*, 1977). For a fuller discussion of the effects of this stressor see Davies and Parasuraman (1982). Finally, and also equivocal, are the effects of air ionization. While Halcomb and Kirk (1965) reported a beneficial effect for the increase in concentration of negative ions, insufficient empirical work has been conducted to elucidate any systematic relationship.

Summary Many practical performance conditions inherently contain vibration as a stressor. Of the studies examined concerning vibration, no report of decrement has been found. Poulton (1978a) has suggested that vibration at 5 Hz may be employed as an alerting mechanism to increase vigilance efficiency; however, evidence suggests that by itself vibration elicits no systematic change in performance on tasks requiring sustained attention. While the reduction of oxygen in breathing mixtures has been found to reduce efficiency, the concomitant effects on performance through variation in CO level, although operating upon the same physiological function, are somewhat more equivocal.

THEORETICAL ACCOUNTS

Unitary

There have been many investigations concerning the effect of environmental stressors on the performance of sustained attention tasks. Various appeals have been made to one or other of several theories of vigilance (Frankmann and Adams, 1962; Stroh, 1971) in an effort to explain the results of these studies. However, little of substance has emerged. The one exception concerns the concept of behavioral arousal which has been presented in most detail by Poulton (1976; 1977a). He has proposed that certain degrees of differing stressors increase or depress behavioral arousal, which subsequently induces performance change. For example in the thermal stressor, initial exposure to hot conditions, or to heat which causes discomfort, both act to increase arousal and improve performance. In contrast, mild heat produces lassitude which depresses monitoring capability through the reduction of arousal. Poulton buttressed this argument through reference to studies concerning noise, isolation and vibration.

There are, however, objections to the concept that a single mediator, which reflects some state of central activation, can account for performance variation under the discrete or interactive effects of individual environmental stressors. First, the nature of arousal as a unitary entity has recently been challenged. Qualitatively different states of activation depending on the nature of the task and the imposed stressor have been suggested (Davies and Parasuraman, 1982). This position reflects the inability to define satisfactorily and consequently to manipulate the arousal metric. As a result, few studies have specifically addressed the predictions of the arousal theory, independent of contaminants due to task or subject characteristics. Consequently, arousal has been largely a *post hoc* invocation which accounts for but does not permit the accurate prediction of performance variation.

Studies which have attempted to examine the arousal position are often difficult to interpret due to methodological problems of asymmetric transfer, as elaborated by Poulton (1973, 1982). In addition, some studies have reported the interactive effects between agencies which alter the state of the performer and some degree of a particular environmental stressor. The manner in which such an amalgam acts upon different individuals under varying task demands is largely unknown. Finally, in addition to the problem of interpretation of individual studies, the arousal theory of stressor action requires occasional adjuncts to account for prescribed results under specific conditions. Poulton (1977a) only proposes one such process, namely the masking of auditory feedback or inner speech by high intensity noise. The efficacy of such a proposal has been the subject of some contention, see the discussions of Broadbent (1978) and Poulton (1977b; 1978b).

Elemental

The unitary account presented above sought to utilize a single concept about which to frame an explanation of performance variation. In contrast, the elemental approach which is outlined below focuses on the specific effects of certain individual factors which are posited as influential upon performance in a variety of environmental stressors. Wilkinson (1969a) identified six of these factors, namely duration of performance, familiarity of the worker with both the stressor and the task, level of operator incentive, presence or absence of additional stressors, kind of work undertaken, and those aspects of that work which are most important. Although this list is not exhaustive (for example, the presence or absence of evaluative others or coworkers on the same task both play a role), it provides a solid foundation from which to review studies previously outlined. In the current work, attention is directed particularly toward two of these factors, namely the composition of the sustained attention task and the familiarity or skill level of the performer, as well as their potential interaction in the context of different stressors. This does not necessarily exclude the possibility that some alternative factors listed above may exert as potent or more potent effects in prescribed conditions.

In a recent approach to the problem of sustained attention, Fisk and Schneider (1981) have suggested that monitoring capability may depend upon the precise nature of the vigilance task. They indicated that when task characteristics foster the development of an automatic process, little decrement in performance might be expected after practice. By contrast, tasks in which conditions inhibit the development of such a process would continue to produce a vigilance decrement even after extensive repetition. To understand this proposal, it is necessary to outline what automatic processing and its companion, control processing, are. Briefly, automatic processes are fast in terms of processing speed, may operate at the same time as other automatic processes, require little effort from the performer, but require considerable practice with consistent responding to develop. Control processes are slow and effortful and do not benefit greatly from prolonged practice. They are used when the operator is required to deal with novel or inconsistent information. A full discussion of these processes is given in Schneider and Shiffrin (1977) (see also the discussions in Chapters 2 and 6 of this volume).

Fisk and Schneider (1981) presented a series of hypothetical curves which describe vigilance performance under each of these processes. These curves are reproduced in Figure 4.8. The vigilance decrement after initial practice is given in Figure 4.8(c). However, when the task is amenable to the development of automated processing, three degrees of which are shown in Figure 4.8(d), the vigilance decrement function does not appear with progressive temporal exposure. Fisk and Schneider (1981) report two experiments which provide empirical support for their hypotheses.

Hancock (1982b) utilized the proposal concerning automated processing to account for observations that skilful performers are able to maintain performance efficiency even in extremes of heat. Clearly, the development of skilful performance is dependent upon both task and performer. In practical tasks certain elements may be more or less amenable to the development of automated responses, while other elements may only be accomplished by the use of controlled processes. Skilled performance, through the repetition of action, may take advantage of those elements in which automatic responses can occur. Hancock (1982b) suggested that automated responses were relatively insensitive to the effects of heat, while Fisk and Schneider (1982) have demonstrated such a result after alcohol administration.

This proposal may account for the data of Mackworth (1950) which are reproduced in Figure 4.2. He showed that prior experience on monitoring tasks was beneficial in reducing heat-induced decrement with time on task. In addition, performer skill level may be an important variant in the studies by Colquhoun

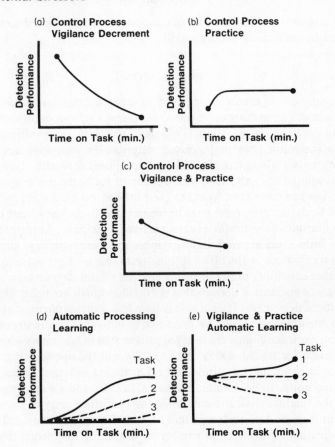

Figure 4.8 Hypothesized components of vigilance curves in control and automated processing conditions. [From Fisk and Schneider, *Human Factors*, 1981, **23**, 737–750. Copyright (1981) by The Human Factors Society, Inc., and reproduced by permission.]

(1969) and Colquhoun and Goldman (1972). They subjected their well-practised subjects to considerable thermal stress and increasing body temperature and yet found little performance change.

Certain investigators are careful to describe the conditions of practice that were imposed by their experimental manipulations (e.g. Colquhoun, 1969; Fine and Korbrick, 1978), while others also report the task-related experiences of their subjects (e.g. Mackworth, 1950). Such details are necessary for *post hoc* analysis concerning the effect of practice and skill upon performance in stressful conditions. Although it is not always possible to reconstruct conditions of training and subject experience from original investigations, future research may be easily structured to test the assertion concerning the mitigation of stress-induced performance decrement by increasing operator skill.

CONCLUSIONS

On occasions the operator is required to sustain attention in non-optimal environmental circumstances. Such conditions may be constituted by an individual stressor or a number of such stressors in combination. The general affirmation that performance deteriorates with exposure to these conditions is not always confirmed by experimental results. Low intensity noise and immediate entry into heat appear to facilitate performance, while vibration has generally been found to exert little effect on the ability to sustain attention. Such interpretations must be tempered with the knowledge that under these circumstances the performer is an active participant. At the present time relatively little is understood about changes in covert strategy, allocation of attentional resources or the effect of long-term repeated exposure in changing performance capability under differing environmental stressors. In conditions which degrade vigilance it appears that skilful individuals are better able to resist stress-induced decrement. If such skill is founded upon automation of response, sustained attention tasks might be structured to mitigate harmful stressor effects.

Practical work conditions are rarely approximated in laboratory investigations (see Loeb and Jeantheau, 1958). In the real world the operator may have the chance for intermittent rest, drink coffee if available and mask or actively elicit background noise. In performance indoors, heating and air-conditioning may regulate the thermal environment, while the performer may be highly skilled or a recent trainee. Although a picture of the efficiency of sustained attention under individual environmental stressors is beginning to emerge, the complex problems of practical performance under multiple stressor conditions await a more complete understanding.

ACKNOWLEDGEMENTS

The author would like to thank Dr Joel Warm and Dr Karl Newell for comments on an earlier version of this chapter.

REFERENCES

Allnutt, M. F., and Allan, J. R. The effects of core temperature elevation and thermal sensation on performance. *Ergonomics*, 1973, **16**, 189–196.
Angus, R. G., Pearce, D. G., Buguet, A. G. C., and Olsen, L. Vigilance performance of men sleeping under arctic conditions. *Aviation, Space and Environmental Medicine*, 1979, **50**, 692–696.
Bakan, P., and Manley, R. Effect of visual deprivation on auditory vigilance. *British Journal of Psychology*, 1963, **54**, 115–119.

Bell, C. R. Climate, body temperature and vigilance performance. *Proceedings of the Second International Congress on Ergonomics*, 1964, 169–172.

Bell, C. R., and Provins, K. A. Effects of high temperature environmental conditions on human performance. *Journal of Occupational Medicine*, 1962, **4**, 202–221.

Bell, C. R., Provins, K. A., and Hiorns, R. W. Visual and auditory vigilance during exposure to hot and humid conditions. *Ergonomics*, 1964, **7**, 279–288.

Benignus, V. A., Otto, D. A., and Knelson, J. H. Effect of low frequency random noises on performance of a numeric monitoring task. *Perceptual and Motor Skills*, 1975, **40**, 231–239.

Benignus, V. A., Otto, D. A., Prah, J. D., and Benignus, G. Lack of effects of carbon monoxide on human vigilance. *Perceptual and Motor Skills*, 1977, **45**, 1007–1014.

Benor, D., and Shvartz, E. Effect of body cooling on vigilance in hot environments. *Aerospace Medicine*, 1971, **42**, 727–730.

Beshir, M. Y. A comprehensive comparison between WBGT and Botsball. *American Industrial Hygiene Association Journal*, 1981, **42**, 81–87.

Blackwell, P. J., and Belt, J. A. Effect of differential levels of ambient noise on vigilance performance. *Perceptual and Motor Skills*, 1971, **32**, 734.

Botsford, J. H. A wet globe thermometer for environmental heat measurement. *American Industrial Hygiene Association Journal*, 1971, **32**, 1–10.

Broadbent, D. Noise, paced performance and vigilance tasks. *British Journal and Psychology*, 1953, **44**, 295–303.

Broadbent, D. E. Some effects of noise on visual performance. *Quarterly Journal of Experimental Psychology*, 1954, **6**, 1–5.

Broadbent, D. E. The current state of noise research: reply to Poulton. *Psychological Bulletin*, 1978, **85**, 1052–1067.

Broadbent, D. E. Human performance in noise. In Harris, C. (Ed.), *Handbook of noise control*. New York: McGraw-Hill, 1979.

Broadbent, D. E., and Gregory, M. Vigilance considered as a statistical decision. *British Journal of Psychology*, 1963, **54**, 309–323.

Broadbent, D. E., and Gregory, M. Effects of noise and of signal rate upon vigilance analyzed by means of decision theory. *Human Factors*, 1965, **7**, 155–162.

Buckner, D. N., and McGrath, J. J. (Eds). *Vigilance: a symposium*. New York: McGraw-Hill, 1963.

Cahoon, R. L. Vigilance performance under hypoxia. *Journal of Applied Psychology*, 1970, **54**, 479–483.

Cahoon, R. L. Auditory vigilance under hypoxia. *Journal of Applied Psychology*, 1973, **57**, 350–352.

Carlson, L. D. Human performance under different thermal loads. USAF Aerospace Medical Center Technical Report No. 61-43. Brooks Air Force Base, Tx: USAF Aerospace Medical Center, 1961.

Childs, J. M., and Halcomb, C. G. Effects of noise and response complexity upon vigilance performance. *Perceptual and Motor Skills*, 1972, **35**, 735–741.

Christensen, C. L., Gliner, J. A., Horvath, S. M., and Wagner, J. A. Effects of three kinds of hypoxias on vigilance performance. *Aviation, Space and Environmental Medicine*, 1977, **48**, 491–496.

Cohen, S., and Weinstein, N. Nonauditory effects of noise on behavior and health. *Journal of Social Issues*, 1981, **37**, 36–70.

Colquhoun, W. P. Effects of raised ambient temperature and event rate on vigilance performance. *Aerospace Medicine*, 1969, **40**, 413–417.

Colquhoun, W. P., and Goldman, R. F. Vigilance under induced hyperthermia. *Ergonomics*, 1972, **15**, 621–632.

Corkindale, K. G. The effect of environmental stress on performance. In J. A. Gillies (Ed.), *A textbook of aviation physiology*. Oxford: Pergamon Press, 1965.

Craig, A., Wilkinson, R. T., and Colquhoun, W. P. Diurnal variation in vigilance efficiency. *Ergonomics*, 1981, **24**, 641–651.

Dardano, J. F. Relationships of intermittent noise, intersignal interval, and skin conductance to vigilance behavior. *Journal of Applied Psychology*, 1962, **46**, 106–114.

Davenport, W. E. Vigilance and arousal: effects of different types of background stimulation. *The Journal of Psychology*, 1972, **82**, 339–346.

Davies, D. R. Vigilance and arousal. *Ergonomics*, 1961, **4**, 283.

Davies, D. R., and Hockey, G. R. J. The effects of noise and doubling the signal frequency on individual differences in visual vigilance performance. *British Journal of Psychology*, 1966, **57**, 381–389.

Davies, D. R., and Parasuraman, R. *The psychology of vigilance*. London: Academic Press, 1982.

Davies, D. R., and Tune, G. S. *Human vigilance performance*. London: Staples Press, 1970.

Davies, D. R., Lang, L., and Shackleton, V. J. The effects of music and task difficulty on performance at a visual vigilance task. *British Journal of Psychology*, 1973, **64**, 383–389.

Diserens, C. M. *The influence of music on behavior*. Princeton, N.J.: Princeton University Press, 1926.

Fine, B. J., and Kobrick, J. L. Effects of altitude and heat on complex cognitive tasks. *Human Factors*, 1978, **20**, 115–122.

Fine, B. J., Cohen, A., and Crist, B. Effect of exposure to high humidity at high and moderate ambient temperature on anagram solution and auditory discrimination. *Psychological Reports*, 1960, **7**, 171–181.

Fisk, A. D., and Schneider, W. Control and automatic processing during tasks requiring sustained attention: a new approach to vigilance. *Human Factors*, 1981, **23**, 737–750.

Fisk, A. D., and Schneider, W. Type of task practice and time-sharing activities predict deficits due to alcohol ingestion. Paper presented to the 26th Annual Meeting of the Human Factors Society, October 1982.

Fiske, D. W. Effects of monotonous and restricted environments. In D. W. Fiske and S. R. Maddi (Eds), *Functions of varied experience*, Dorsey Press: Homewood, Ill., 1961.

Frankmann, J. P., and Adams, J. A. Theories of vigilance. *Psychological Bulletin*, 1962, **59**, 257–272.

Fraser, D. C. Environmental stress and its effects on performance. *Occupational Psychology*, 1957, **31**, 248–255 (a).

Fraser, D. C. Some effects of heat stress on performance of a vigilance task under speed stress. In *Reactions of Mines Research Personnel to Work in Hot Environments*, National Coal Board Medical Research Memorandum No. 1. London: National Coal Board, 1957, pp.50–63 (b).

Grether, W. F. Vibration and human performance. *Human Factors*, 1971, **13**, 203–216.

Grether, W. F. Human performance at elevated environmental temperatures. *Aerospace Medicine*, 1973, **44**, 747–755.

Grether, W. F., Harris, C. S., Mohr, G. C., Nixon, C. W., Ohlbaum, M., Sommer, H. C., Thaler, V. H., and Veghte, J. H. Effect of combined heat, noise and vibration stress on human performance and physiological functions. *Aerospace Medicine*, 1971, **42**, 1092–1097.

Gulian, E. Auditory vigilance under noise conditions: psychophysiological correlations. *Studia Psychologica*, 1971, **8**, 114–119.

Halcomb, C. G., and Kirk, R. E. Effects of air ionization upon the performance of a visual task. *Journal of Engineering Psychology*, 1965, **4**, 120–126.

Hancock, P. A. Heat stress impairment of mental performance: a revision of tolerance limits. *Aviation, Space and Environmental Medicine*, 1981, **52**, 177–180.

Hancock, P. A. Task categorization and the limits of human performance in extreme heat. *Aviation, Space and Environmental Medicine*, 1982, **53**, 778–784 (a).

Hancock, P. A. Mitigation of performance decrement in transient extreme heat. Paper presented to the 26th Annual Meeting of the Human Factors Society, October 1982 (b).

Harmon, F. L. The effects of noise upon certain psychological and physiological processes. *Archives of Psychology*, 1933, **147**, 5–81.

Hockey, G. R. J. Effect of loud noise on attentional selectivity. *Quarterly Journal of Experimental Psychology*, 1970, **22**, 28–36.

Hockey, G. R. J. Changes in information-selection patterns in multi-source monitoring as a function of induced arousal shifts. *Journal of Experimental Psychology*, 1973, **101**, 35–42.

Hockey, G. R. J. Effects of noise on human work efficiency. In D. N. May (Ed.), *Handbook of noise assessment*. New York: Van Nostrand Reinhold, 1978.

Holland, C. L. Performance effects of long-term random vertical vibration. *Human Factors*, 1967, **9**, 93–104.

Horvath, S. M., Dahms, T. E., and O'Hanlon, J. F. Carbon monoxide and human vigilance: a deleterious effect of present urban concentrations. *Archives of Environmental Health*, 1971, **23**, 343–349.

Houghten, F. C., and Yaglogou, C. P. Determining lines of equal comfort. *Transactions of the American Society of Heating and Ventilating Engineers*, 1923, **29**, 163–176.

Jerison, H. J. Performance on a simple vigilance task in noise and quiet. *Journal of the Acoustical Society of America*, 1957, **29**, 1163–1165.

Jerison, H. J. Effects of noise on human performance. *Journal of Applied Psychology*, 1959, **43**, 96–101.

Jerison, H. J. Vigilance: biology, psychology, theory and practice. In R. R. Mackie (Ed.), *Vigilance: theory, operational performance and physiological correlates*. New York: Plenum, 1977.

Jones, D. M., Smith, A. P., and Broadbent, D. E. Effects of moderate intensity noise on the Bakan vigilance task. *Journal of Applied Psychology*, 1979, **64**, 627–634.

Jones, R. D. Effects of thermal stress on human performance: a review and critique of existing methodology. US Army Technical Memorandum No. 11-70. Aberdeen Proving Ground, Md: US Army, 1970.

Kirk, R. E., and Hecht, E. Maintenance of vigilance by programmed noise. *Perceptual and Motor Skills*, 1963, **16**, 553–560.

Kissen, A. T., Reifler, C. B., and Thaler, V. H. Modification of thermoregulatory responses to cold by hypnosis. *Journal of Applied Physiology*, 1964, **19**, 1043–1050.

Kreyberg, L. Development of acute tissue damage due to cold. *Physiological Review*, 1949, **29**, 156–167.

Lind, A. R. A physiological criterion for setting thermal environmental limits for everyday work. *Journal of Applied Physiology*, 1963, **18**, 51–56.

Loeb, M. Noise and performance: do we know more now? In *Proceedings of the International Congress, Noise as a Public Health Problem, Freiberg, Germany, 1978*. Washington, D.C.: American Speech and Hearing Reports, 1980.

Loeb, M., and Jeantheau, G. The influence of noxious environmental stimuli on vigilance. *Journal of Applied Psychology*, 1958, **42**, 47–49.

Lysaght, R. J. The effects of noise on sustained attention and behavioral persistence. Unpublished PhD dissertation, University of Cincinnati, 1982.

Mackie, R. R. (Ed.). *Vigilance: theory, operational performance and physiological correlates*. New York: Plenum, 1977.

Mackie, R. R., and O'Hanlon, J. F. A study of the combined effects of extended driving and heat stress on driver arousal and performance. In R. R. Mackie (Ed.), *Vigilance: theory, operational performance and physiological correlates*. New York: Plenum, 1977.

Mackworth, N. H. *Researches on the measurement of human performance*. Medical Research Council Special Report Series No. 268. London: HM Stationery Office, 1950. Reprinted in H. W. Sinaiko (Ed.), *Selected papers on human factors in the design and use of control systems*. New York: Dover, 1961, pp.174–331.

Magid, E. B., Coermann, R. R., and Ziegenruecker, G. H. Human tolerance to whole body sinusoidal vibration. *Aerospace Medicine*, 1960, **31**, 915–924.

McBain, W. N. Noise, the 'arousal hypothesis' and monotonous work. *Journal of Applied Psychology*, 1961, **45**, 309–317.

McCann, P. H. The effects of ambient noise on vigilance performance. *Human Factors*, 1969, **11**, 251–256.

McGrath, J. J. Irrelevant stimulation and vigilance performance. In D. N. Buckner and J. J. McGrath (Eds), *Vigilance: a symposium*. McGraw-Hill, New York, 1963, pp.3–21.

Mirabella, A., and Goldstein, D. A. The effects of ambient noise upon signal detection. *Human Factors*, 1967, **9**, 227–284.

Mortagy, A. K., and Ramsey, J. D. Monitoring performance as a function of work/rest schedule and thermal stress. *American Industrial Hygiene Association Journal*, 1973, **34**, 474–480.

Mutchler, J. E., and Vechhio, J. L. Empirical relationships among heat stress indices in 14 hot industries. *American Industrial Hygiene Association Journal*, 1977, **38**, 253–259.

Parks, D. L. A comparison of sinusoidal and random vibration effects on performance. Boeing Corporation Report No. D3-3512-2. Seattle: Boeing Corporation, 1961.

Pepler, R. D. The effect of climatic factors on the performance of skilled tasks by young European men living in the tropics. 4. A task of prolonged visual vigilance. Medical Research Council, Royal Naval Research Committee, Applied Psychology Unit Report No. 156/53. London: Medical Research Council, 1953.

Pepler, R. D. Warmth and performance: an investigation in the tropics. *Ergonomics*, 1958, **2**, 63–88.

Pollack, I., and Knaff, P. R. Maintainence of alertness by a loud auditory signal. *Journal of the Acoustical Society of America*, 1958, **30**, 1013–1016.

Poulton, E. C. Unwanted range effects from using within-subject experimental designs. *Psychological Bulletin*, 1973, **80**, 113–121.

Poulton, E. C. Arousing environmental stresses can improve performance, whatever people say. *Aviation, Space and Environmental Medicine*, 1976, **47**, 1193–1204.

Poulton, E. C. Arousing stresses increase vigilance. In R. R. Mackie (Ed.), *Vigilance: theory, operational performance and physiological correlates*. New York: Plenum, 1977 (a).

Poulton, E. C. Continuous noise intensity masks auditory feedback and inner speech. *Psychological Bulletin*, 1977, **84**, 997–1001 (b).

Poulton, E. C. Increased vigilance with vertical vibration at 5 Hz: an alerting mechanism. *Applied Ergonomics*, 1978, **9**, 73–76 (a).

Poulton, E. C. A new look at the effects of noise: a rejoinder. *Psychological Bulletin*, 1978, **85**, 1068–1075 (b).

Poulton, E. C. Influential companions: effects of one strategy on another in the within-subjects designs of cognitive psychology. *Psychological Bulletin*, 1982, **91**, 673–690.

Poulton, E. C., and Edwards, R. S. Interactions and range effects in experiments on pairs of stresses: mild heat and low frequency noise. *Journal of Experimental Psychology*, 1974, **104**, 621–628 (a).

Poulton, E. C., and Edwards, R. S. Interactions, range effects, and comparisons between tasks in experiments measuring performance with pairs of stresses: mild heat and 1 mg of L-hyoscine hydrobromide. *Aerospace Medicine*, 1974, **45**, 735–741 (b).

Poulton, E. C., and Kerslake, D. McK. Initial stimulating effect of warmth upon perceptual efficiency. *Aerospace Medicine*, 1965, **36**, 29–32.

Poulton, E. C., Hitchings, N. B., and Brooke, R. B. Effect of cold and rain upon the vigilance of lookouts. *Ergonomics*, 1965, **8**, 163–168.

Poulton, E. C., Edwards, R. S., and Colquhoun, W. P. The interaction of the loss of a night's sleep with mild heat: task variables. *Ergonomics*, 1974, **17**, 59–73.

Rohles, F. H., Konz, S. A., and Munson, D. A new psychrometric chart for thermal comfort. *American Society of Heating, Refrigerating and Air-Conditioning Engineers Journal*, **1982**, 85–87.

Ruff, G. E. Psychological and psychophysiological indices of stress. In N. M. Burns, R. M. Chambers and E. Hendler (Eds), *Unusual environments and human behavior*. London: Free Press, 1963.

Schneider, W., and Shiffrin, R. M. Controlled and automatic human information processing: I. Detection, search and attention. *Psychological Review*, 1977, **84**, 1–66.

Schohan, B., Rawson, H. E., and Soliday, S. M. Pilot and observer performance in simulated low-altitude high-speed flight. *Human Factors*, 1965, **7**, 257–265.

Selye, H. *The physiology and pathology of exposure to stress: a treatise based on the concepts of the general-adaptation syndrome and the diseases of adaptation*. Montreal: Acta Inc., 1950.

Selye, H. Stress and aerospace medicine. *Aerospace Medicine*, 1973, **44**, 190–193.

Shoenberger, R. W. Effects of vibration on complex psychomotor performance. *Aerospace Medicine*, 1967, **12**, 1265–1269.

Shoenberger, R. W., and Harris, C. S. Psychophysical assessment of whole-body vibration. *Human Factors*, 1971, **13**, 41–50.

Smith, S., Myers, T. I., and Murphy, D. B. Vigilance during sensory deprivation. *Perceptual and Motor Skills*, 1967, **24**, 971–976.

Snyder, F. W. Vibration and vision. In C. A. Baker (Ed.), *Visual capabilities in the space environment*. London: Pergamon Press, 1965, pp.183–201.

Stroh, C. M. *Vigilance: the problem of sustained attention*. New York: Pergamon Press, 1971.

Thackray, R. I., and Touchstone, R. M. Effects of noise exposure on performance of a simulated radar task. FAA Civil Aeromedical Institute Report No. FAA-AM-79-24. 1979.

Ware, J. R., Kowal, B., and Baker, R. A. The role of experimenter attitude and contingent reinforcement in a vigilance task. *Human Factors*, 1964, **6**, 111–115.

Warner, H. D. Effects of intermittent noise on human target detection. *Human Factors*, 1969, **11**, 245–250.

Warner, H. D., and Heimstra, N. W. Effects of intermittent noise on visual search tasks of varying complexity. *Perceptual and Motor Skills*, 1971, **32**, 219–226.

Warner, H. D., and Heimstra, N. W. Effects of noise intensity on visual target-detection performance. *Human Factors*, 1972, **14**, 181–185.

Warner, H. D., and Heimstra, N. W. Target-detection performance as a function of noise intensity and task difficulty. *Perceptual and Motor Skills*, 1973, **36**, 439–442.

Watkins, W. H. Effect of certain noises upon detection of visual signals. *Journal of Experimental Psychology*, 1964, **67**, 72–75.

Watkins, W. H., and Feehrer, C. E. Acoustic facilitation of visual detection. *Journal of Experimental Psychology*, 1965, **70**, 332–333.

Weisz, A. A., Goddard, C., and Allen, R. W. Human performance under random and sinusoidal vibration. Aerospace Medical Research Laboratories Report No. AMRL-TR-65-209. Wright-Patterson Air Force Base, Ohio: Aerospace Medical Research Laboratories, 1965.

Wilkinson, R. T. The effect of lack of sleep on visual watch-keeping. *Quarterly Journal of Experimental Psychology*, 1960, **12**, 36–40.

Wilkinson, R. T. Some factors influencing the effect of environmental stressors upon performance. *Psychological Bulletin*, 1969, **72**, 260–272 (a).

Wilkinson, R. T. Sleep deprivation: performance tests for partial and selective sleep deprivation. In L. A. Abt and B. F. Reiss (Eds), *Progress in clinical psychology*, Vol. 7, New York: Grune and Stratton, 1969 (b).

Wilkinson, R. T., and Gray, R. Effects of duration of vertical vibration beyond the proposed ISO fatigue-decreased proficiency time, on the performance of various tasks. In H. E. Von Gierke (Ed.), *Vibration and combined stress in advanced systems*, AGARD Conference Proceedings No. 145. 1974.

Wilkinson, R. T., Fox, R. H., Goldsmith, R., Hampton, I. F. G. and Lewis, H. E. Psychological and physiological responses to raised body temperature. *Journal of Applied Physiology*, 1964, **19**, 287–291.

Wing, J. F. Upper thermal tolerance limit for unimpaired mental performance. *Aerospace Medicine*, 1965, **36**, 960–964.

Woodhead, M. M. Searching a visual display in intermittent noise. *Journal of Sound and Vibration*, 1964, **1**, 157–161.

Yaglou, C. P., and Minard, D. Control of heat casualties at military training centers. *Archives of Industrial Health*, 1957, **16**, 302–316.

Zubek, J. P. Effects of prolonged sensory and perceptual deprivation. *British Medical Bulletin*, 1964, **20**, 38–42.

Zubek, J. P., and MacNeill, M. Effects of immobilization: behavioral and EEG changes. *Canadian Journal of Psychology*, 1966, **20**, 316–366.

Zubek, J. P., Pushkar, D., Sansom, W., and Gowing, J. Perceptual changes after prolonged sensory isolation (darkness and silence). *Canadian Journal of Psychology*, 1961, **15**, 83–100.

Zuercher, J. D. The effects of extraneous stimulation of vigilance. *Human Factors*, 1965, **7**, 101–105.

Sustained Attention in Human Performance
Edited by J. S. Warm
© 1984 John Wiley & Sons Ltd.

Chapter 5

Individual Differences

Daniel B. Berch and Donald R. Kanter

INTRODUCTION

As with any psychological process, one might expect the ability to sustain attention to vary among individuals. What kinds of characteristics are associated with efficient watchkeeping? Do more intelligent people make better monitors? Are certain personality traits related to good vigilance performance? Does the ability to sustain attention change with increasing chronological age? As Cronbach (1957) has noted, individual differences traditionally have been annoying to experimental psychologists rather than challenging. This is because greater variability within treatment groups leads to larger error variance, thus reducing the likelihood of obtaining a statistically significant treatment effect. In contrast, differential psychologists regard such variation as important and worthy of study in its own right. In Cronbach's words, 'The correlational psychologist is in love with just those variables the experimentalist left home to forget' (Cronbach, 1957, p.674).

Perhaps because the laboratory study of sustained attention arose from practical concerns regarding the deterioration of watchkeeping behavior in tasks such as radar target-detection, most experimental psychologists studying vigilance have been keenly aware of the importance of understanding the role of individual differences in monitoring performance. Clinical psychologists have also been interested in how individuals differ in maintaining attention. However, in their research, sustained attention is usually treated as a psychological trait or ability that individuals may possess to varying degrees. The aim of the clinical researcher is often to determine the extent to which individuals with different types of psychological disorders suffer from an attentional deficit.

In that the present chapter is a survey of experimental, clinical and other related approaches to the study of individual differences in sustained attention, it covers a potpourri of variables that do not fit neatly under any other chapter headings in this book. As a result, the reader will encounter an amalgam of such seemingly disparate topics as hypnotic states, mental retardation and sex-related performance differences. Moreover, it should be pointed out that researchers in many of these subareas have been largely unaware that the other areas even exist. They often ask different questions, have different objectives, employ subjects from radically different populations, use different types of vigilance procedures, have differing theoretical views regarding the construct of sustained attention, and publish in different types of journals (e.g. *Human Factors, Archives of General Psychiatry* and the *Texas Tech Journal of Education*). It is hoped that by bringing these various approaches under one umbrella, this chapter will, at the very least, enhance the awareness of all types of vigilance researchers as to the variety of studies that have been carried out. This is a necessary step if the diversity of findings reviewed here are ever to be integrated in any coherent fashion.

Overview

The first section contains a summary of findings regarding the consistency of monitoring performance within and across watchkeeping sessions and between different vigilance tasks. This is followed by a review of studies concerning the relationship between monitoring efficiency and personality characteristics, such as temperament, field dependence and locus of control. Next, we trace the development of the ability to sustain attention from early childhood through senescence. We also examine the extent to which vigilance performance is correlated with other organismic factors, such as sex and intelligence. In addition to these more traditional categories of individual-differences research, the influence of subjective states on watchkeeping behavior is described, including the effects of boredom, meditation and hypnosis.

The major section of the paper contains a review and appraisal of studies in which vigilance-type tasks have been used for identifying possible attentional deficiencies in individuals with some sort of handicap or psychological disorder, including mental retardation, learning disability and schizophrenia. This is followed by an examination of educational applications of vigilance research with children. The latter portion of the paper will be devoted in part to a critical analysis of methodological issues pertaining to the study of individual differences in monitoring performance. This section includes a discussion of problems concerning the attribution of poor performance by clinical populations to an attentional deficit. Following this, an individual-differences approach is described that can be used for initially testing the viability of theoretical models of sustained attention. Finally, some conclusions are drawn regarding our current understanding of this inherently complex, often unwieldy, yet certainly intriguing area of individual differences.

PERFORMANCE CONSISTENCY

Within- and across-session reliability

While dramatic differences in vigilance performance have been found to exist between individuals, available evidence indicates that within- subject performance is consistent over time. Individual performance levels have been found to be highly correlated within sessions (Mackworth, 1950; Buckner, 1963; Bucker *et al.* 1966; Teichner, 1974). Others have found that individual performance is also highly correlated between sessions (Jenkins, 1958; Buckner *et al.*, 1960, 1966; Loeb and Binford, 1971; Benedetti and Loeb, 1972).

Inter-task reliability

Early studies revealed low correlations in individual performance levels between different vigilance tasks, particularly if different sensory modalities were involved (Baker, 1963a; Pope and McKechnie, 1963; Buckner *et al.*, 1966). However, as Davies and Parasuraman (1982) have noted, recent evidence indicates that performance is highly correlated across tasks that are equated for the types of discriminations and sensory coupling factors involved (Gunn and Loeb, 1967; Hatfield and Loeb, 1968; Tyler *et al.*, 1972; Parasuraman and Davies, 1977). In short, it appears that performance is consistent within and across sessions, and that individual differences are consistently maintained across different vigilance tasks that are equated for certain psychophysical parameters.

PERSONALITY FACTORS

One of the more traditional areas of individual-differences research deals with personality correlates of vigilance performance. Much of this work has been atheoretical in nature, with the objective often consisting of determining a personality measure that would provide a reliable predictor of watchkeeping behavior. In this section, we begin with a discussion of findings regarding the most extensively researched personality dimension, introversion–extraversion. Next, the relationship between cognitive style (field dependence/independence) and monitoring performance is examined. Finally, we describe the results of studies concerning the relationship between watchkeeping behavior and other personality factors, including locus of control (internal–external), coronary-prone behavior pattern and achievement motivation.

Introversion–extraversion

One of the most widely studied personality dimensions with regard to performance in vigilance tasks is that of introversion–extraversion. The monitoring performance of introverts and extraverts might be expected to differ for a number of reasons. First, introverts have been shown to be more sensitive to stimulation. In a study of auditory thresholds, Smith (1968) found that introverts consistently detected signals at weaker levels than did extraverts. In related studies, extraverts have been shown to tolerate higher intensities of noise better than introverts (DiScipio, 1971; Elliot, 1971). These findings indicate that individuals who differ on the introversion–extraversion dimension may have different ranges of stimulus sensitivity.

Second, Eysenck (1967) has theorized that extraverts develop reactive inhibition more rapidly than introverts during a vigil; hence, extraverts should have more frequent lapses in attention and subsequently more omission errors. Since impulsivity is postulated to be a central characteristic of the extravert (Eysenck and Eysenck, 1969; Farley and Farley, 1970), it might also be expected that extraverts would be more prone to make commission errors. Both of these predictions have been supported (omissions by Bakan *et al.*, 1963; Carr, 1971; Krupski *et al.*, 1971; Thackray *et al.*, 1974; commissions by Tune, 1966; Carr, 1969; Krupski *et al.*, 1971). By conducting a signal-detection analysis of their data, Harkins and Geen (1975) found that the superior monitoring performance of introverts reflects a higher level of sensitivity. Other investigators, however, have failed to find significant correlations between vigilance and extraversion in adults (Das, 1964; Gale *et al.*, 1972) or in children (Gale and Lynn, 1972; Medeiros and McManis, 1974). It seems plausible that further study of the differential effects of factors such as impulsivity, task demands and criterion for group inclusion employed in these studies may clarify these discrepancies.

Field dependence/independence

Witkin's field-dependence/independence dimension characterizes individuals by the degree to which they are influenced by cues in the perceptual field. Individuals are typically classified by their performance on the 'embedded figures test' and/or the 'rod and frame test'. According to Witkin *et al.* (1954), field-independent individuals are better able to focus on relevant aspects of the environment and ignore the irrelevant aspects. Consequently, it would be expected that field-independent subjects would perform better on vigilance tasks than field-dependent subjects. Most available evidence appears to support this expectation (Cahoon, 1970; Moore and Gross, 1973; Ware and Baker, 1977).

Other personality factors

Locus of Control

According to Rotter (1966), individuals with an internal locus of control believe that rewards are obtained primarily through their own activities, while externals believe that rewards are contingent on forces outside their control. A number of studies suggest that internals may be superior in processing and utilizing environmental information (Rotter and Mulry, 1965; Phares, 1968; Pines and Julian, 1972). Consequently, internals would be expected to respond more efficiently to task demands. This hypothesis was supported in a vigilance study by Sanders *et al.* (1976), who found that internals made more correct detections and fewer omission errors than externals.

Coronary-prone Behaviour Pattern

Type A (coronary-prone) individuals are characterized by a rushed, competitive, achievement-oriented lifestyle. In a recent study, the vigilance performance of Type A individuals was compared with that of their more relaxed, Type B, counterparts in a 1-hour visual vigilance task (Lundberg *et al.* 1979). It was expected that Type A individuals would experience the task as more stressful and that this stress would have a deleterious effect on their performance. Although the Type A subjects perceived the task as more stressful (as revealed by a measure of mood change), they detected more signals than Type B subjects. Lundberg *et al.* speculated that superior monitoring performance in Type A individuals may be due to a heightened state of arousal and/or greater ability to resist internal distractions.

Achievement Motivation

In an effort to test the predictions of two theories of achievement motivation, Schneider and Eckelt (1975) examined the effects of manipulating success and failure on subsequent vigilance performance. The Atkinson–Weiner theory predicts that in a task viewed as relatively easy, success-oriented individuals (more motivated to achieve success than to avoid failure) will be more achievement motivated after experiencing failure than after success, while the converse is predicted for failure-oriented individuals (those more motivated to avoid failure than to achieve success) (Atkinson, 1964; Weiner, 1970). In contrast, an extension of Ach's (1937) difficulty law of motivation predicts that all individuals will expend greater effort following failure as compared with success. Schneider and Eckelt tested these predictions with high school students, using a Mackworth clock test. Following the first watchkeeping period, the subjects were told (through headphones) how well they had done as compared with their peers. Contrary to the Atkinson–Weiner theory and in support of Ach, the performance of subjects receiving failure feedback declined less than that of subjects experiencing either success or no outcome.

ORGANISMIC FACTORS

This section begins with a review of developmental changes in monitoring performance, covering a range from the study of preschool children to the elderly. Next, investigations of sex-related performance differences are described, followed by a discussion of the relationship between intellectual status and the maintenance of attention. Finally, evidence is examined from studies comparing the vigilance performance of children of different socioeconomic backgrounds and different ethnic groups.

Developmental changes

The number of studies exploring developmental changes in sustained attention at different stages across the life span forms a frequency distribution that is skewed in a direction opposite to that of most developmental research with other types of psychological processes. That is, the majority of such experiments have investigated the monitoring performance of elderly individuals in comparison with that of middle-aged and young adults, fewer have compared adolescents with children, and still fewer have examined the maintenance of attention in preschool-aged youngsters.

Preschoolers

Using an auditory vigilance task, Locke (1970) found a significant performance decline in preschool children over a 5½-minute session. In a more recent experiment with a visual monitoring task, no such decline was demonstrated with preschoolers over a 15-minute session (Simon, 1982). However, children above the mean age (5½ years) of the sample in the latter study produced more correct detections than those below the mean age. In addition, vigilance performance (correct detections) was shown to be significantly predictive of scores on a psychometric test of school readiness.

Early Childhood through Middle Adolescence

For the most part, researchers investigating age-related changes in monitoring performance from early childhood through middle adolescence have had as their primary objective the comparison of clinical and normal populations (e.g. learning disabled, mentally retarded, schizophrenic). A review of the findings from these and other studies reveals rather clearly that vigilance performance (overall detection rate) improves with increasing chronological age (Semmel, 1975; Gale and Lynn, 1972; Sykes *et al.*, 1973; Anderson *et al.*, 1974; Kupietz, 1976; Kupietz and Richardson, 1978; Kirby *et al.*, 1979). The one study in which decrement functions have been compared (Kirby *et al.*, 1979, for 7 and 12 year olds) demonstrated that the rate of decline becomes less steep with age.

Young Adulthood through Senescence

Developmental changes have also been assessed from young adulthood through senescence. A wide variation in ages has been tested, ranging from approximately 18 to 75 years. A number of such studies have failed to show any age-related differences in watchkeeping behavior (Griew and Davies, 1962; York, 1962; Davies and Griew, 1963; Thompson *et al.*, 1963; Neal and Pearson, 1966). Contrary to these findings, however, other studies have demonstrated significant, albeit small, deteriorations in monitoring performance with increasing age (Griew and Davies, 1962; Canestrari, 1963; Thompson *et al.*, 1963; Surwillo and Quilter, 1964, 1965; Surwillo, 1966; Talland, 1966; Harkins *et al.*, 1974; Davies and Davies, 1975). In reviewing these findings, Davies and Parasuraman (1982) concluded that age differences in vigilance are not exhibited when the task requires the simple detection of only one type of critical signal. However, older adults tend to perform more poorly under any of the following conditions: (a) detection of more than one signal is required; (b) the event rate is high; (c) a visual search is involved; (d) an increased memory load is required for reporting or discriminating the critical signal.

Sex

Davies and Tune (1969) critically reviewed vigilance studies in which the performance of males and females had been compared. They noted that although some investigators have found men to be superior to women, the bulk of the evidence suggests that monitoring efficiency is unrelated to the sex of the observer. Consistent with this conclusion, more recent experiments have also failed to provide evidence of sex-related differences in vigilance performance in either children (Locke, 1970; Sykes *et al.*, 1972; Margolis, 1973; Kirchner and Knopf, 1974; Herman *et al.*, 1980) or adults (Gale *et al.*, 1972; Tolin and Fisher, 1974; Parasuraman, 1976). One exception, however, is an experiment by Waag *et al.* (1973) involving a comparison of large samples of men and women. Although a significant sex-related difference was demonstrated, in favor of the males, the magnitude of the difference was quite small. Another noteworthy exception is a study by Gale and Lynn (1972) who found that girls at ages 7, 8 and 12 (but not at 9, 10, 11 or 13) had a higher detection rate than boys in an auditory monitoring task. Noting that the superiority of the girls disappeared at the older ages in the sample, these authors suggested that their results may reflect general sex-related differences in rate of development.

Despite the occasional demonstration of sex-related differences in vigil-ance, Davies and Parasuraman (1982) have pointed out that these differences are usually quite small, and consequently of little practical or theoretical importance.

Intelligence

There have been a number of attempts to determine whether vigilance performance is related to general intellectual ability, with the latter usually being measured by means of a standardized (group or individual) intelligence test. Although a few studies have demonstrated a positive correlation (Kappauf and Powe, 1959; Cahoon, 1970), the majority of experiments in which intelligence (within normal limits) was the primary variable of interest have shown that there is essentially no relationship between IQ and monitoring efficiency (McGrath, 1960; Sipowicz and Baker, 1961; Ware, 1961; Halcomb and Kirk, 1965). As Davies and Parasuraman (1982) pointed out, this result is supported by ancillary findings from other experiments (Mackworth, 1950; Jenkins, 1958; Bakan, 1959; Colquhoun, 1959, 1962; Wilkinson, 1961).

More recently, the lack of a relation between IQ and vigilance has also been found to hold for children aged 7–15 years (Mabel, 1968; Anderson *et al.*, 1969; Gale and Lynn, 1972; Margolis, 1973; Ricks and Mirsky, 1974; Kupietz and Richardson, 1978). In contrast, Herman *et al.* (1980) have provided some evidence that IQ and monitoring performance are positively related for preschool children. These authors suggest that an IQ score may reflect a young child's ability to attend to a long task, and that the significance of this factor may decline with age.

Socio-economic status

Mabel (1968) and Knopf and Mabel (1975) assessed the effects of socioeconomic status (SES) on the visual watchkeeping performance of second- and third-grade white males. High and low SES groups were formed on the basis of the following criteria: parents' occupation, parents' education and residential area. In both of these studies, the high SES group made significantly more correct detections than the low SES group.

Ethnic factors

In a recent study, Anderson *et al.* (1977) examined the vigilance performance of four groups of children: Mexican-American learning disabled, Mexican-American normals, Anglo-American learning disabled and Anglo-American normals. Comparisons of correct detections showed that both learning-disabled groups performed more poorly than normal controls of their own ethnic group. Normal Anglo-American children detected more critical signals than the other three groups. Anglo-American learning-disabled children performed better than

Mexican-American learning-disabled children, but did not differ from Mexican-American normals. However, it remains unclear whether the differences between Mexican-American and Anglo-American children were due to ethnic factors since these groups also differed with regard to reading ability and socioeconomic status, both of which, as is noted elsewhere in this chapter, have been implicated in differential vigilance performance.

SUBJECTIVE STATES

Ware and Baker (1977) have recently noted with concern the relative paucity of systematic research regarding relationships between internal or subjective states and vigilance performance. Nevertheless, a number of interesting experiments have been carried out that are certainly suggestive of such relationships. In this section, we examine first the influence of mental set on monitoring performance. Then the subjective reaction of boredom and the manner in which it appears to relate to watchkeeping behavior is assessed. This is followed by a discussion of studies purportedly demonstrating connections between sustained attention and the internal states of daydreaming and 'transcendental meditation'. The section concludes with a review of findings concerning the relationship between vigilance performance and hypnotic suggestibility as well as effects on monitoring behavior of a post-hypnotic suggestion to increase alertness.

Mental set

Some investigators have assessed the effects of one's 'mental set' and subsequent monitoring performance. In this type of study, the experimenter usually attempts to induce an expectancy concerning the nature or purpose of the task that will be encountered. For example, Jerison (1958) found that subjects who were told to expect a long vigil (2½ hours) exhibited a steeper decrement function than those expecting a short vigil (27 minutes). Lucaccini *et al.* (1968) told one group of subjects that vigilance tasks are considered 'monotonous' by most observers; they told a second group that such tasks are usually considered 'challenging'. This one-word difference in pretask instructions produced a significant performance difference in favor of the latter group. Unfortunately, a neutral-word control condition was not included. Consequently, it is unclear as to whether the performance difference resulted from a facilitating effect of the 'challenging' instruction, or a debilitating effect of the 'monotonous' instructions, or from a combination of both.

In a related study, Neal (1967) gave the following instructions to college students concerning the vigilance task they were about to undertake: (1) the task was a class requirement (required chore); (2) the task was part of a training program for a space project (important task); (3) their freshman orientation test scores indicated that they should perform extremely well on this task (subject important); or (4) a combination of the 'important task' and 'subject important' instructions. Subjects who received either 'important task' or 'combined treatment' instructions made significantly more correct detections than subjects in the other two groups.

Ware *et al.* (1964) showed that exposure to a 'democratic' experimenter as compared with an 'autocratic' one led to significantly better overall monitoring performance. However, the fact that the observers were military personnel (armor trainees) raises a question as to the generalizability of these results to individuals who typically function in a more democratic atmosphere.

Boredom

As one might expect, most subjects consider vigilance tasks to be boring and monotonous. Nevertheless, some find it interesting and even challenging. A number of investigators have attempted to determine relationships between vigilance performance and attitudes toward the task. Most of these studies have used self-report techniques, although with conflicting results. Buckner *et al.* (1960) found no relationship between attitude (positive, negative, or neutral) and performance. In contrast, Bakan (1963) found that subjects who viewed the task as interesting performed significantly better than those who did not. Similarly, Thackray *et al.* (1977) showed that subjects reporting a high degree of boredom produced longer latencies in a complex monitoring task. Jerison *et al.* (1965) noted a significant correlation between degree of boredom and performance, but in the opposite direction of most studies. That is, they found that although subjects under slow event rates reported experiencing greater boredom than subjects under fast event rates, they still performed better. Finally, Durham and Nunnally (1973) showed that participating in a vigilance task under a fast event rate leads to subsequently greater visual exploration than performing under a slow event rate. Nonetheless, contrary to their prediction, these conditions did not produce a difference in the reported amount of boredom experienced while monitoring.

Daydreaming

Antrobus *et al.* (1967) explored the possibility of a relationship between daydreaming and sustained attention. Employing a self-report scale of frequency of daydreaming, they divided subjects into high and low daydreaming groups and then administered a relatively brief auditory detection task. Although the groups did not differ significantly in their overall performance levels, the high daydreaming group exhibited a significant decrement over trials, while the low group showed essentially no change. Moreover, the high group reported the occurrence of significantly more 'task-irrelevant thoughts' during the watch than did the low group. This latter finding is consistent with the results of

Bakan (1963). He found that following their participation in an auditory vigilance task, subjects agreeing with the statement 'I was completely lost in my daydreaming' performed more poorly overall than subjects who disagreed.

Meditation

Warm *et al.* (1977) used a visual vigilance task to test the claim that the practice of 'transcendental meditation' (TM) enhances attentiveness. They found that experienced meditators produced a higher detection rate overall (with no higher false alarm rates) than either novice meditators or nonmeditators. The inclusion of a novice group was of critical importance in demonstrating that the results could not be attributed to unspecified characteristics peculiar to individuals who are attracted to meditation training.

Hypnosis

Ware and Baker (1977) hypothesized that if monitors can be helped to maintain a state of 'hyper-alertness', better vigilance performance might ensue. To test this hypothesis, Barabasz (1980) gave a group of US Navy personnel post-hypnotic suggestions for increased alertness as they experienced visual deprivation. Analysis of pre-test/post-test changes in performance on a simulated radar target-detection task revealed a significant decrease in errors for these subjects. A no-treatment control condition showed no change in performance, while two other control conditions, post-hypnotic suggestion to decrease alertness and visual deprivation, only showed a significant increase in errors. There was a significant positive correlation between degree of suggestibility of the men in the hypnosis augment group and the amount of improvement in monitoring following hypnosis. However, none of the correlations for the other three groups were significant, suggesting that hypnotic susceptibility *per se* may not be associated with the ability to sustain attention.

In contrast, Das (1964) reported a significant negative correlation between hypnotic susceptibility and performance on the Bakan cognitive vigilance task, indicating that good hypnotic subjects may be less vigilant than poor hypnotic subjects (see Chapter 2). However, as Smyth (1979) has noted, this finding should be viewed skeptically because Das used a nonstandardized scale of suggestibility, and because of the differential treatment purportedly given to resistant subjects.

In addition to its utility for investigating the effects of post-hypnotic suggestions, the vigilance paradigm has been instrumental in assessing the nature of attentional processes during hypnosis. For example, Kissen *et al.* (1964) examined the watchkeeping performance of five men during both hypnotic and nonhypnotic states under conditions of extreme cold (approximately 4°C) in an environmental chamber. Although there were no differences in false alarms, the number of correct detections was significantly higher under hypnotized than nonhypnotized conditions. Moreover, whereas a decrement occurred under the nonhypnotized condition, performance actually improved somewhat under the hypnotized condition during the last half of the watch. Concomitantly, there was less shivering, higher basal-skin resistance, and a lower heart rate under the hypnotized conditions. Certainly, the generally higher performance under hypnosis could be due to greater ease of lever-pressing with a lower level of shivering, rather than to an enhancement of attentional processes. However, improved performance under the hypnotic state cannot be attributed to such indirect factors.

Fehr and Stern (1967) investigated the effect of hypnosis on sustained attention in a visual vigilance task. They found that the reaction times of the hypnotized subjects were significantly longer than those of waking controls when there was no extraneous stimulation. In reviewing this finding, Smyth (1979) noted that the longer reaction times could be attributed to either the lethargic motility that often accompanies hypnosis (Ham and Edmonston, 1971) or to more time for processing the information, possibly due to unfocused attention. In any event, since there were no significant differences between the groups in either resting skin resistance or heart rate, the results cannot be attributed to lowered arousal. Fehr and Stern also found that while extraneous auditory stimulation enhanced the performance of the controls, it had a distracting effect for the hypnotized subjects.

In a recent review of research in this area, Smyth (1977, 1979) described two major hypotheses that have emerged regarding the role of attentional processes during hypnosis: (a) the *concentration hypothesis,* according to which the subject's attention becomes narrowed and sustained, focused on the words of the hypnotist or stimuli to which the hypnotist directs the subject's attention (Barber, 1960; White, 1965); (b) the *reduction hypothesis,* according to which the subject's attention becomes diffuse, unfocused and rigid (unsustained), and his/her overall attention capacity (to all environmental stimuli, including the hypnotist's words) is reduced (Hilgard, 1965). Smyth noted that numerous studies have demonstrated that the arousal levels of good hypnotic subjects during hypnosis are either greater or equal to that of waking controls. He concluded that these results contradict the notion that the attentive capacity of good hypnotic subjects is reduced. Nevertheless, Smyth's review also led him to conclude that the other components of the reduction hypothesis (diffuse, unfocused and unsustained) have received considerable confirmation.

In a test of what he renamed as the *diffuse-unfocused* hypothesis, Smyth (1977) hypnotized subjects while requiring them to perform two auditory vigilance tasks simultaneously. One task involved detecting specific digits, and the other required detecting the word 'relax' whenever it was spoken by the hypnotist. Smyth found significant negative correlations between hypnotic suggestibility and vigilance; that is, the good hypnotic subjects were less vigilant than the poor hypnotic subjects both to the hypnotist's words and to other environmental stimuli. Smyth contended that these findings contradict the concentration hypothesis and support the diffuse-unfocused hypothesis. To provide a further test of these hypotheses, Smyth and Lowy (1979) administered two auditory vigilance tasks while subjects were being hypnotized. The neutral events were tones of 500 Hz, with a critical signal of 600 Hz for the easy task and 550 Hz for the hard task. As predicted by both theories, hypnotic suggestibility and performance on both the hard and easy tasks were negatively correlated. However, in support of the diffuse-unfocused hypothesis, it was found that the good hypnotic subjects detected significantly more easy than hard signals.

In review, there is some evidence to indicate that a post-hypnotic suggestion can induce a state of hyper-alertness and consequently enhance vigilance performance. However, the more suggestible subjects are, the less vigilant they will be *during* hypnosis, both to the hypnotist's words and to other environmental stimuli. Tentatively, this seems to result from attention becoming diffuse and unfocused rather than concentrated.

CLINICAL POPULATIONS

Clinical researchers have long had an interest in attentional problems associated with various psychological disorders and developmental learning difficulties. They have employed vigilance tasks as part of a battery of measures designed to help them determine whether such individuals suffer some sort of attentional deficit. The following sections contain a relatively extensive review and critique of this type of research. We begin with an analysis of the relationship between reading ability and sustained attention. Next, findings regarding the monitoring performance of children diagnosed as hyperactive are examined. This is followed by a review of vigilance research with mentally retarded children and adolescents. We then discuss some findings pertaining to the relationship between watchkeeping behavior and sensory impairments, such as blindness. Next, we describe evidence regarding the monitoring performance of both children and adults suffering from different types of neurological impairment. The remaining sections are concerned with the relationship between sustained attention and various psychological disorders, including behavioral deviance, depression and schizophrenia.

A task that is often employed in clinical studies as a measure of sustained attention is the continuous performance test (CPT), devised by Rosvold *et al.* (1956). The CPT requires the visual detection of a letter (usually 'X') or a letter sequence ('X' following 'A') occurring intermittently within a 31-letter series. Subjects are usually tested over two 10-minute periods, receiving the X task during the first period and the AX task during the second. The letters are typically shown at a rate of one per second, resulting in the presentation of 600 letters during each 10-minute period. The critical signal appears 160 times on a random basis in the X task and 120 times in the AX task.

Subsequent modifications of the CPT have included an auditory version, shorter letter sequences (e.g. 12 letters), longer presentation rates (e.g. one letter per 1.5 seconds), lower proportions of critical signals, briefer watchkeeping periods and, most recently, an alternate form in which stimulus presentation rate is adapted to the subject's error rate on a trial-to-trial basis (Buchsbaum and Sostek, 1980).

As compared with standard laboratory vigilance tasks, the CPT is of shorter duration overall, involves very high critical signal probabilities (20% and 27%), an extremely fast background event rate (60 events per minute) and is often presented in a manner that does not permit an unequivocal assessment of performance changes over time (since the two 10-minute periods confound type of task (X and AX) with time periods).

Reading disabled

The majority of children who experience learning difficulties in mathematics, language-based tasks or other related educational activities are also likely to have reading problems. Indeed, according to a leading authority in the field of learning disorders, 'reading difficulties are far and away the most crucial component of any learning-disability syndrome' (Farnham-Diggory, 1978, p.16). In an effort to evaluate the role of psychological processes involved in reading disabilities, a variety of perceptual mechanisms have been implicated. Among these, the study of attention has received considerable emphasis from researchers. To date, the bulk of the empirical work pertaining to this topic has been concerned with the process of *selective* attention. Despite what would appear to be a potentially fruitful avenue of research, only scattered attempts have been made to determine whether children with a reading disability have difficulty in *maintaining* their attention.

Although two studies have found no relation between monitoring efficiency and reading ability (Knopf and Mabel, 1975: Kupietz and Richardson, 1978), the majority of investigations have shown that poor readers exhibit lower overall detection rates than average readers in both visual and auditory modes (Birch, 1968; Noland and Schuldt, 1971; Margolis, 1973; Kirchner and Knopf, 1974; Ricks and Mirsky, 1974; Rugel and Mitchell, 1977). However, in most of these experiments, the reading groups did not differ significantly in their rate of performance decline with time on task. Taken together, these findings indicate that despite inferior monitoring during the initial period of a vigil, reading-disabled children do not differ from average readers in the extent to which their attention is maintained throughout the remainder of the watch (see pp.166–167 for a more detailed assessment of related methodological issues).

Hyperactives

Hyperactivity is a generalized symptom used to describe a heterogenous group of children who experience learning difficulties, presumably because of impaired attentional abilities and impulsivity. It is noteworthy that difficulties in maintaining attention are considered to play such an important role in this disorder that recent revisions in the official diagnostic nomenclature now employ 'attention deficit disorder' as the diagnostic descriptor for these children (American Psychiatric Association, 1980). The scope of this problem is considerable, as reflected by the estimate that 5–10% of all school-age children are hyperactive (Shaywitz *et al.*, 1978).

For many years, it has been common practice for physicians to base a diagnosis of hyperactivity on an outcome of improved attention (typically measured by global impressions or parent/teacher questionnaires) following the administration of a stimulant drug. The apparent calming and attention enhancing effects of stimulant drugs have often been referred to as the 'paradoxical response' because it seemed counterintuitive that a stimulant should have a calming effect. Until recently, it was presumed that only hyperactive children exhibit a paradoxical response to stimulant drugs and that, consequently, this response is somehow reflective of underlying pathology, despite the fact that the effects of psychostimulants had never been examined in normal children. The ethical problems involved in making such a comparison had precluded an adequate test of this assumption. Surprisingly, a research group at the National Institute of Mental Health (NIMH) subsequently managed to surmount these difficulties by testing children of NIMH staff, who clearly understood the risks involved (Rapoport *et al.*, 1978, 1980). These investigators found that the administration of the stimulant, *d*-amphetamine, did not differentially affect hyperactive and normal children, but rather that performance on a test of sustained attention (the CPT) (in addition to other relevant indices) was enhanced for both groups. These findings have raised serious doubts concerning the validity of using improved attentional performance as a criterion for the diagnosis of hyperactivity.

It is ironic that while one of the central characteristics thought to distinguish hyperactive from normal children is difficulty with tasks requiring sustained attention, there is relatively little empirical evidence to substantiate this premise unequivocally. Studies using the continuous performance test (CPT) have generally found that hyperactive children make fewer correct detections and more false alarms when tested in an unmedicated as compared with a medicated state or as compared with normal controls (Conners, 1966, 1972; Conners and Rothschild, 1968; Sykes *et al.*, 1971, 1972, 1973; Werry and Aman, 1975; Kupietz, 1976). Unfortunately, many of these investigations have been seriously flawed by a number of methodological shortcomings. For example, several studies have not used control groups, subjects typically have not been pretested under alerted conditions, and test sessions have been extremely brief in duration (ranging from 2 to 15 minutes). As a result, the relatively poor CPT performance of hyperactive children cannot be clearly attributed to an inability to maintain attention over time (as has been generally assumed).

Despite problems concerning the interpretation of studies using the CPT, several interesting investigations have been conducted with hyperactive children in which standard laboratory vigilance tasks have been used. For example, two studies have demonstrated that the monitoring performance of hyperactive children improves substantially when knowledge of false alarms is provided (Mack, 1976; Ozolins and Anderson, 1980). This finding is consistent with results obtained from experiments using normal adult observers.

Performance on laboratory monitoring tasks has also been examined as a function of activity level in normal children and in learning-disabled children whose primary diagnosis was not hyperactivity. Kirchner (1976) reported that highly active normal children make fewer correct detections and exhibit a steeper decrement than their normally active counterparts. Similarly, it has been shown that highly active learning-disabled children make fewer correct detections and more false alarms than underactive learning-disabled children or normal controls (Doyle *et al.*, 1976). These findings suggest that vigilance tasks may be sensitive to a continuum of attentional abilities and an activity dimension that apparently span many of the diagnostic distinctions characterized by learning difficulties.

Mentally retarded

As noted earlier in this chapter, within normal limits of measured intelligence, intellectual level appears to bear no relation to efficiency of watchkeeping behavior. In contrast, studies with mentally retarded children and adults have provided some evidence that these individuals perform more poorly on vigilance measures as compared with controls whose intelligence levels are considered normal. The bulk of this research has been conducted with individuals categorized as *mildly* mentally retarded, whose standardized IQ scores range from approximately 55 to 69.

The majority of studies to date indicate that chronological age is a critical factor affecting normal–retardate performance differences on vigilance tasks. This view is generally supported by findings showing that although pre-adolescent retardates detect fewer critical signals overall than normal controls (Semmel, 1965; Johnson, 1977; Kirby *et al.*, 1979), this difference disappears by late adolescence (Ware *et al.*, 1962; Jones, 1971; Kirby *et al.*, 1978).

An adequate interpretation of these findings requires an examination of some methodological tenets concerning the use of appropriate comparison groups. In particular, as Stanovich (1978) has noted, the demonstration of a difference between retardates and normal chronological age (CA) controls is by itself insufficient for inferring a *deficit* in some underlying process. If retardates do as well as their mental age (MA) controls, then performance inferior to that of CA controls should be interpreted as reflecting a developmental lag. Stanovich also points out that retardate performance inferior to that of MA controls cannot be interpreted as clear-cut evidence for a deficit unless it can be shown that the groups are matched on all extraneous factors that could affect the dependent variable in use (Zigler, 1973). In the vigilance studies cited above, retardates performed at least equal to but never poorer than their MA controls. By this criterion, then, there is little evidence to indicate that mildly retarded individuals suffer from a deficit in sustained attention. Although pre-adolescent retardates detect fewer critical signals overall than pre-adolescent normals, the fact that adolescent retardates perform at a level comparable to that of their CA controls suggests, at worst, a developmental lag in the ability to maintain attention.

In an attempt to explain the normal–retardate differences in monitoring performance that have been reported, researchers have invoked two competing theoretical positions: arousal and distractibility. According to the former, mentally retarded individuals suffer from a more rapid decay in arousal than their intellectually normal counterparts, while according to the latter, retardates are more distractible than normals. To date, neither position has received unequivocal empirical support. In fact, two studies have provided evidence that is directly contrary to arousal theory (Jones, 1971; Kirby *et al.*, 1978), and three studies have produced findings that are clearly inconsistent with distractibility theory (Crosby, 1972; Johnson, 1977; Kirby *et al.*, 1978). Thus, at least with regard to performance on vigilance tasks, the extant data suggest that the mentally retarded are neither less aroused nor more distractible than intellectually normal individuals.

At this point the reader may be questioning whether any practical implications have emerged from laboratory vigilance research with the mentally retarded. Though there have been few investigations that lend themselves easily to such interpretations, the results of several studies suggest that the visual monitoring of retarded individuals can be improved through the use of various training techniques. For example, researchers have shown that knowledge of results for missed signals as well as for correct detections increases the overall detection rate of adolescent retardates (Ware *et al.*, 1962, and Griffin *et al.*, 1974, respectively). Furthermore, it has been demonstrated recently that a comparatively elaborate conditioning program can greatly enhance the monitoring efficiency of retarded adolescents and young adults. This was achieved in a study by Perryman *et al.* (1981) who employed a specialized multi-method training program that included multiple practice sessions, decreasing of the critical signal probability during training, response prompting, knowledge of results (for both correct detections and false alarms), use of tokens and material back-up reinforcers. Not only did the overall detection rate of the subjects improve as a result of this program, but even more importantly, their vigilance decrement was virtually eliminated. It is especially noteworthy that this high level of performance was demonstrated under transfer conditions involving no knowledge of results.

Sensorily impaired

In sharp contrast to the generally poor vigilance performance exhibited by the other types of clinical populations described in this chapter, findings concerning adults suffering from severe congenital impairment of a major sensory modality suggest that the monitoring efficiency of such individuals is actually enhanced by their disability, albeit indirectly. In the first published study designed specifically to assess the maintenance of attention in sensorily impaired individuals, Benedetti and Loeb (1972) compared the auditory vigilance performance of blind adults with that of sighted controls in both light and dark. The blind subjects produced a higher proportion of detections and significantly higher sensitivity (d') scores. Although all groups exhibited a decrement, there was no interaction with visual status. One might first attribute these findings to what has classically been referred to as 'sensory compensation' (Hayes, 1933). However, Benedetti and Loeb found no differences between the blind and sighted subjects in either absolute or differential thresholds or in performance levels on an altered signal detection task. The authors concluded that the superior monitoring performance of the blind may be more properly ascribed to 'perceptual' compensation. They suggested that blind persons have had more practice in learning to discriminate critical aspects of auditory stimulation under conditions of temporal uncertainty, and as a result are more efficient in their use of sensory information.

Given recent evidence that deaf individuals are either equal or inferior to hearing controls in visual perception tasks, such as brightness discrimination and critical flicker fusion (Bross, 1979a, b; Bross and Sauerwein, 1980), one might not expect the deaf to outperform the hearing in a visual monitoring task. Nevertheless, Dittmar *et al.* (1982) have reported a small but reliable difference in favor of the deaf in just such a task (light-bar display of Jerison and Pickett, 1964). In that there were no differences under alerted conditions, the better watchkeeping performance of the deaf could not be attributed to an initially superior ability to discriminate signal from noise.

The findings of these two studies suggest that the vigilance paradigm has much potential utility for assessing the attentional capabilities of the sensorily impaired.

Neurologically impaired

Available evidence indicates that vigilance performance is sensitive to a wide range of conditions in which neurological integrity has been compromised. The use of the vigilance paradigm in the study of brain damage dates from the work of Rosvold *et al.* (1956), who developed the continuous performance test (CPT).

In this seminal experiment, Rosvold *et al.* demonstrated that vigilance-type tasks could be used to distinguish brain-damaged individuals from normal controls. Subsequent research has confirmed these initial findings in both adults (McDonald and Burns, 1964) and children (Campanelli, 1970; Grassi, 1970; Kaspar *et al.*, 1971). In another study using the CPT, Schein (1962) found that individuals with cortical brain damage performed more poorly than normals, while patients with subcortical damage did not differ from normals, suggesting at least some specificity for the relationship between sustained attention and brain damage.

In addition to the study of individuals with gross brain pathology, watchkeeping performance has been examined in children having more subtle dysfunctions of the central nervous system including aphasia, phenylketonuria and seizure disorders. In assessing the monitoring performance of children with the central language disturbance, receptive–expressive aphasia, Wiig and Austin (1972) found that these children performed more poorly and were more adversely affected by visual distractions as compared with normal controls. Anderson *et al.* (1969) found that children with phenylketonuria (PKU) made fewer correct detections and exhibited a steeper decrement than normal controls. PKU is a disorder that has been linked to a defect in the enzyme which metabolizes phenylalanine and has been associated with neuropsychological consequences. Finally, several vigilance studies have been conducted with children who have seizure disorders. Petit mal is perhaps the best-known type of generalized seizure disorder in children, and characteristically consists of brief losses of consciousness (usually lasting less than 30 seconds) without loss of posture or gross involuntary movements. Findings generally indicate comparatively poor monitoring performance by children with such disorders (Fedio and Mirsky, 1969; Stores *et al.* 1978). Furthermore, it has been suggested recently that vigilance tasks may provide an appropriate index for the assessment of therapeutic drug effects with these children (Dekaban and Lehman, 1975).

Behavior disordered

Behavior-disordered children are typically characterized as markedly aggressive, severely hostile, easily frustrated, dishonest, distractible and impulsive. Noting Eysenck's (1964) previous suggestion that behavior-disordered children should accumulate more reactive inhibition than normals, Grassi (1970) predicted that such children should detect fewer critical signals than normal controls in a vigilance task. This prediction was supported, with both groups showing comparable decrement functions. Using an auditory version of the CPT, Kupietz (1976) also provided evidence that children with behavior disorders are poorer monitors than their normal peers.

Depressives

Depression is a mental disorder, the severity of which spans the spectrum of psychopathology. Although the study of attentional characteristics of depressed individuals has not been of primary concern to clinical researchers, evidence relating arousal level to severity of depression has provided a possible link between this disorder and a prominent theory of monitoring efficiency. Specifically, the use of both electrodermal and pharmacological indices has revealed that while psychotic depressives exhibit lower levels of arousal than normals (hypo-arousal), neurotic depressives exhibit higher levels (hyper-arousal). Coupling these findings with Welford's (1962) theory that vigilance performance is an inverted U-shaped function of arousal level, Byrne (1976) hypothesized that (1) both psychotic and neurotic depressives should detect fewer critical signals than normal controls; (2) psychotic depressives should exhibit lower false alarm rates than controls; and (3) neurotic depressives should exhibit higher false alarm rates than either psychotic depressives or normals. Using a 30-minute auditory vigilance task, Byrne provided evidence in support of all three predictions. In addition, the psychotic depressives were found to have a significantly steeper decrement function than the controls.

Schizophrenics

A breakdown of perceptual filtering has long been noted as a prominent feature of schizophrenia. Recent research suggests that schizophrenics with poor prognosis require longer stimulus durations for identification of critical signals than do normal controls or individuals with depressive disorders (Saccuzzo *et al.*, 1974; Braff and Saccuzzo, 1981). Additional evidence from backward masking studies suggests a relative slowness of information processing in schizophrenics as compared with controls (Saccuzzo *et al.*, 1974; Braff *et al.*, 1981).

As a consequence of these findings, one might expect that the ability to sustain attention would also be impaired in schizophrenics. In support of this expectation, Orzack and Kornetsky (1966) found that schizophrenics made more omission errors on the CPT than normal controls and hospitalized alcoholics. However, it remains unclear whether this difference was due to impaired attentional ability of the schizophrenic group or simply to motivational factors, since the three groups received different types of incentives for successful performance. A later study by Wohlberg and Kornetsky (1973) compared the CPT performance of *remitted* schizophrenics with that of normal controls under basal conditions, and finally, a recovery condition (no distraction). Although there were no differences in *omission* errors under baseline or recovery conditions, the schizophrenics performed more poorly than the controls under distraction conditions and also made more *commission* errors than the controls under both baseline and distraction conditions.

Another line of research has examined the effect on CPT performance of various drugs used in the treatment of schizophrenia. Latz and Kornetsky (1965) found that single doses of chlorpromazine and secobarbital impaired CPT performance in schizophrenic patients. This finding is not surprising, in view of the fact that while single doses of these drugs are sometimes used for rapid tranquilization in the treatment of schizophrenia, true clinical improvement is rarely (if ever) noted in response to a single dose. However, in a later study using chronically administered phenothiazines, Orzack et al. (1967) found improved CPT performance in schizophrenic individuals. While present evidence is inconclusive, it suggests that schizophrenics with poor prognosis exhibit relatively low performance on the CPT, perhaps because of impaired ability to discriminate critical signals.

A popular, though controversial theme in recent research with schizophrenics concerns the premise that genetic factors play a role in the etiology of this disorder (cf. Lidz et al., 1981). Consistent with the notion of a genetically important factor in schizophrenia, at least two research groups have examined the CPT performance of children of schizophrenics (who are presumably at risk to develop schizophrenia) (Grunebaum et al., 1974; Rutschmann et al., 1977). Both studies provided some support for the prediction of poorer CPT performance (more omission errors) in children of schizophrenic parents. Moreover, a signal detection analysis indicated that the poorer monitoring performance of children of schizophrenic parents may reflect a difference in discriminability rather than response bias (Rutschmann et al., 1977). However, it should be noted that the etiological underpinnings of these differences remain obscure since alternative explanations based on environmental influences are equally plausible. An example of an environmentally-based alternative to the genetic hypothesis is that attentional difficulties in children *may*, in part, be due to the extreme stress and unpredictability of growing up in a chaotic family environment with a psychotic parent (Kanter, 1982). Furthermore, carefully controlled adoptive studies are needed to clarify the possible contribution of genetic influences to the etiology of schizophrenia and related attentional difficulties.

EDUCATIONAL APPLICATIONS

If empirical research concerning the monitoring behavior of children is to have any practical benefits, it is likely to be in the realm of educational applications. Yet to date, there has been relatively little examination of the relation between laboratory measures of vigilance performance and observational assessments of classroom attentiveness. In this section we consider findings from studies that represent some initial attempts to explore the relevance of vigilance research to educational settings. Kupietz and Richardson (1978) examined the relationship between children's performance on a vigilance task and their ability to maintain attention in a classroom setting. The subjects, drawn from remedial reading classes in a public (i.e. state-run) school, ranged in age from 7½ to 12½ years. Classroom observations were carried out first, followed by administration of the AX form of the CPT (both auditory and visual versions). The following 'off-task' behaviors were considered as reflective of classroom inattentiveness: head turning, body turning, leaving table or seat, playing with objects, playing with lesson materials, physical contact, irrelevant responses, and vocalizations. Correlational analyses revealed significant positive relationships between off-task behavior and number of omission and commission errors on the visual CPT. Although the group as a whole exhibited a significant decrement on both the auditory and visual tests, individual decrement scores were not significantly related to off-task behavior. Kupietz and Richardson concluded that their findings support the general hypothesis that vigilance performance is correlated with children's attentiveness in the classroom.

Could procedures that have been shown to facilitate laboratory monitoring be adapted for practical usage in the classroom? Anderson *et al.* (1977) attempted to do this by developing a technique based on data indicating that feedback regarding false alarms improves vigilance performance in hyperactive children (Ozolins, 1975; Mack, 1976). They tried to teach hyperactive children to 'pay attention' by providing them with feedback information regarding nonattending behavior during daily, 30-minute sessions. The experimenter flashed a light on a box mounted on the child's desk whenever any of the following behaviors occurred: moving out of chairs, talking aloud, taking eyes off work, or doodling on the worksheet or desk. A control group received comparable assignments in the same special education classroom, but were not given feedback regarding their nonattending behavior. During the three-week training period, the hyperactive children's nonattending time decreased significantly, with no substantial loss in accuracy. Although teachers subjectively reported some improvement in classroom attending behaviors following training, ratings by independent observers revealed no significant change from pretraining levels.

An alternative approach for improving classroom attentiveness has been described by Keogh and Margolis (1976). They suggest that poor performance in a dull, repetitive vigilance task (or classroom assignment) may reflect an unwillingness rather than an inability to sustain attention. According to this point of view, remediation of attentional difficulties may best be accomplished through modification of task parameters, rather than simply trying to bring about changes within the child. Keogh and Margolis state this rather eloquently:

'To infer that their problem in maintaining attention is evidence of an underlying attentional disturbance may be a disservice to the child, shifting the responsibility for remediation from the instructional problem to the child alone. It seems more productive to approach difficulties in maintaining attention as evidence of a lack of an appropriate match between the child and the assignment, and to attempt to modify aspects of the task to improve the child's ability to sustain attentional effort' (Keogh and Margolis, 1976, p.25).

METHODOLOGICAL CONSIDERATIONS

One of the major problems associated with individual-differences research involves the attribution of comparatively poor, overall vigilance performance to a deficit in sustained attention. Suppose that a group of reading-disabled children produced significantly fewer correct detections than a control group of average readers in a vigilance study in which the task was not divided into watchkeeping periods. With no measure of performance changes over time, no meaningful interpretation could be made regarding group differences in the 'maintenance' of attention. That is, the different overall performance levels could have resulted simply from a difference in the ability to discriminate the critical signals from the background events. Unfortunately, most researchers using clinical populations have failed to pretest their subjects under alerted conditions (see Kirby *et al.*, 1979, for a noteworthy exception). Now suppose that periods of watch were employed and that the reading-disabled and control groups exhibited the same rate of decline, despite superior performance overall by the controls. This result would indicate that although the groups might have differed in their ability to discriminate signal from noise, they did not differ in the extent to which their attention was maintained over time (Kennedy, 1977). However, what if the groups also had shown no differences under alerted conditions? A fine-grained analysis (Jerrison, 1959) might have revealed a steeper decline for the reading-disabled group during the very early portion of the vigil.

Suppose it were found that the reading-disabled group performed as well as the controls during the first period of watch, but exhibited a steeper decrement over the later periods. This would constitute much stronger evidence of poorer monitoring ability. Nevertheless, it would be inappropriate to attribute a steeper vigilance decrement to an 'attentional deficit' (Kupietz, 1976). One must distinguish between the operational definition of sustained attention (i.e. a decline in performance over time) and theoretical explanations of the decrement function. The fact that the psychological and/or physiological processes underlying the vigilance decrement are not yet completely understood often precludes any meaningful interpretation of the factor(s) responsible for differential rates of decline exhibited by different subject populations.

Theoretically, the decrement function typically found in vigilance studies could result from any one of a variety of distinct psychological processes (see Chapter 6). Consequently, the steeper decrement function exhibited by our hypothetical reading-disabled group may reflect a difference in any number of underlying processes, including a lower arousal level, a faster build-up of inhibition, the development of a more conservative response criterion, and a more rapid accumulation of habituation.

Space limitations preclude any further detailed examination of other methodological problems typically associated with the individual-differences approach (see Baron and Treiman, 1980, for an excellent analysis of such problems along with concrete suggestions for their resolution). Nevertheless, the following suggestions are offered for improving this type of vigilance research, especially when clinical populations are involved: (a) subjects should be pretested under alerted conditions; (b) the vigil should be divided into separate watchkeeping periods in order that decrement functions may be compared; (c) standard psychophysical parameters should be manipulated (e.g. event rate and signal density); (d) a taxonomic approach to the vigilance tasks employed should be used (Parasuraman and Davies, 1977); (e) where possible, a signal-detection analysis should be performed on the data.

INDIVIDUAL DIFFERENCES AND THEORY CONSTRUCTION

Unfortunately, much of what constitutes the study of individual differences in vigilance performance bears no formal relationship to the testing of general theoretical models of sustained attention. However, there is a unique way in which an individual differences approach can be incorporated into the process of constructing such theories. Underwood (1975) has suggested that in choosing a theoretical process to explain a given phenomenon, one should, if possible, attempt to devise a construct that could yield an individual differences interpretation. This would consist of a mechanism that can be measured reliably in a situation different from the one it was devised to explain. Individuals would then vary along some dimension such as the magnitude or speed of the proposed characteristic. For the theoretical process to remain a viable explanation of the phenomenon, the scores on the two measures must be highly correlated. As Underwood notes, such a finding provides a go-ahead signal and nothing more. However, if a theory fails this individual-differences test (i.e. either a very low or no correlation), then the theory should be dropped (assuming an adequately designed and executed experiment). Underwood's major goal in proposing this approach was to halt the proliferation of mentalistic models in the field of cognitive psychology. Nevertheless, his approach could prove fruitful for theory construction in other areas as well. The following examples illustrate its applicability to vigilance research.

Mackworth (1969, 1970) theorized that the vigilance decrement results in part from habituation of the orienting response produced by the repetitive background events. If this process mediates vigilance performance, then individual differences in detection should covary with performance on some independent measure of speed of habituation. Noting that there are large individual differences in speed of habituation as measured by changes in the galvanic skin response (Lynn, 1966), Siddle (1972) reasoned that fast habituators should display a steeper vigilance decrement function than slow habituators. Subjects were divided into groups of fast or slow habituators on the basis of time to reach a preset criterion of habituation of the GSR to a 1000 Hz tone. Three or four weeks later, the subjects were tested in an auditory vigilance task. As predicted, the fast habituators showed a steeper decrement.

Baker (1963b) proposed what is known as the expectancy theory of vigilance. Basically, the theory posits that subjects develop expectancies regarding the appearance of critical signals based on the time course of previously experienced intersignal intervals. Specifically, Baker hypothesized that subjects perform a continuous averaging process on these intervals, extrapolating from them to predict the occurrence of the subsequent signal. The level of expectancy determines the observer's readiness to detect a signal. Therefore, it would seem to follow that the better an individual is at estimating temporal intervals, the more accurate should be his/her expectancy levels, and thus the better the vigilance performance. To test such a prediction, one might measure the ability of subjects to estimate short time intervals and see whether this ability is correlated with detection performance in a vigilance task. McGrath and O'Hanlon (1967) conducted just such an investigation. They found that neither the accuracy nor consistency with which observers estimated time intervals was related to any of four different measures of vigilance performance.

Recently, Craig (1978) theorized that the vigilance decrement results from a process of 'probability matching'. He noted that the ratio of the number of detection responses (both false alarms and correct detections) to the number of signals usually tends to be much greater than 1.00 early in a vigil and declines as the watch progresses. Craig's explanation is that as naive subjects become more familiar with the task, they learn to appreciate the low critical-signal probability. To our knowledge, this theory has yet to be put to Underwood's individual-differences test. In order to do this, one would first have to provide an independent measure of probability matching behavior. There exists just such a task involving the prediction of the relative occurrence of two (or more) events (Estes and Straughan, 1954). In this so-called probability learning task, the relative frequencies of the events are preprogrammed by the experimenter and the events occur randomly (i.e. they are not contingent upon a subject's prediction responses). The occurrence of the events constitutes feedback or reinforcement for the prediction responses.

Rather than maximizing correct predictions in this situation, most subjects eventually adjust their responses so as to match the relative frequencies. Naturally, they exhibit individual differences in the speed with which they develop this strategy. Recall that according to Craig (1978), the vigilance decrement reflects the use of a probability matching strategy. Thus if Craig is correct, subjects who develop a matching strategy quickly in a probability learning task should, as compared with slower subjects, exhibit a steeper decline in correct detections during the early portion of a vigil.

We suggest that Underwood's (1975) individual-differences test ought to become a prerequisite for initially assessing the viability of vigilance theories.

CONCLUDING REMARKS

For more than twenty years, vigilance researchers have explored possible relations between psychological traits and monitoring performance with the intention of finding a measure that would provide a reliable predictor of watchkeeping behavior. Unfortunately, no one factor has emerged yet from this type of research that accounts for any sizeable portion of the variance in standard, laboratory vigilance experiments. Moreover, as Davies and Parasuraman (1982) have pointed out, it is unlikely that a single global selection test can be devised that would successfully predict an individual's monitoring behavior in different watchkeeping situations.

One might ask, then, whether it is at least possible to integrate the results of individual differences studies so as to specify the optimal characteristics of an efficient monitor. Toward that end, we have developed a fictitious advertisement based on findings described in this chapter.

HELP WANTED

For auditory monitoring position–Prefer a blind, introverted, middle-class male or female, with an average to above average IQ, who exhibits a coronary-prone behavior pattern, is field independent, has an internal locus of control, does not daydream, is a good reader and an experienced meditator.

It is important to realize that this *mélange* of abilities, personality traits and other characteristics was culled from separate studies with different subjects who participated under different environmental conditions in different types of vigilance tasks in which different psychophysical parameters were operative. At present, there are no data indicating how these factors would influence sustained attention when consolidated within the same individual. It is quite possible, for example, that certain traits would offset one another rather than combine to enhance watchkeeping performance. Furthermore, it is doubtful that one could find enough subjects possessing various trait combinations to make any meaningful inferences regarding the monitoring efficiency of such individuals.

Given that the characterization of an 'ideal' monitor is impractical, if not unrealistic, what then should be the objective(s) of individual-differences research? We have offered some suggestions, such as using this type of approach to provide an initial test of the viability of theoretical models of sustained attention. Nevertheless, we believe that the study of individual differences must be given a higher priority if further contributions from this area are to be forthcoming. At a minimum, this calls for more thorough investigations concerning the role of personality traits, organismic factors and subjective states in vigilance performance. Even more critical is the need for innovative methodological techniques and theoretical approaches to the study of individual differences. Despite the complexities associated with these endeavors, it should be recognized that individual variations in monitoring efficiency must be explained if we are ever to achieve a complete understanding of sustained attention.

ACKNOWLEDGEMENTS

The preparation of this manuscript was supported in part by Grant MCH-000-912-16-0, awarded to the Bureau of Community Health Services, Health Services Administration, Public Health Service, DHEW, and by Grant 59-P-25297/5-08, awarded by Region V, Social and Rehabilitation Service, DHEW. The authors are grateful to Mrs Jennifer Garthwaite for her assistance in conducting literature searches pertaining to this chapter. In developing some of the ideas presented in this chapter, we profited greatly from discussions with Joel Warm. Finally, we are indebted to Lisa Reidel for typing the manuscript and providing many helpful comments regarding technical editing. The first and second authors are also affiliated with the Cincinnati Center for Developmental Disorders and the Cincinnati VA Medical Center, respectively.

REFERENCES

Ach, N. Zur neueren Willenslehre. In *Berichte der 15. Kongress der Deutsche Gesellschaft für Psychologie, Jena, 1936*. Jena: Fischer, 1937, pp.125–156.

American Psychiatric Association. *Diagnostic and statistical manual*, 3rd edn. Washington, D.C.; American Psychiatric Association, 1980.

Anderson, R. P., Halcomb, C. G., Gordon, W., and Ozolins, D. A. Measurement of attention distractibility in LD children. *Academic Therapy*, 1974, **9**, 261–266.

Anderson, R. P., Williamson, G. A., and Sherman, C. F. Relationships between ethnic/cultural variables and attentional deficits. *Texas Tech Journal of Education*, 1977, **4**, 29–37.

Anderson, V. E., Siegel, F. S., Fisch, R. O., and Wirt, R. D. Responses of phenylketonuric children on a continuous performance test. *Journal of Abnormal Psychology*, 1969, **74**, 358–362.

Antrobus, J. S., Coleman, R., and Singer, J. L. Signal-detection performance by subjects differing in predispositions to daydreaming. *Journal of Consulting Psychology*, 1967, **31**, 487–491.

Atkinson, J. W. *An introduction to motivation*. Princeton, N.J.: Van Nostrand, 1964.

Bakan, P. Extraversion–introversion and improvement in an auditory vigilance task. *British Journal of Psychology*, 1959, **50**, 325–332.

Bakan, P. An analysis of retrospective reports following an auditory vigilance task. In D. N. Buckner and J. J. McGrath (Eds), *Vigilance: a symposium*. New York: McGraw-Hill, 1963.

Bakan, P., Belton, J. A., and Toth, J. C. Extraversion–introversion and decrement in an auditory vigilance task. In D. N. Buckner and J. J. McGrath (Eds), *Vigilance: a symposium*. New York: McGraw-Hill, 1963.

Baker, C. H. Consistency of performance in two visual vigilance tasks. In D. N. Buckner and J. J. McGrath (Eds), *Vigilance: a symposium*. New York: McGraw-Hill, 1963 (a).

Baker, C. H. Further toward a theory of vigilance. In D. N. Buckner and J. J. McGrath (Eds), *Vigilance: a symposium*. New York: McGraw-Hill, 1963 (b).

Barabasz, A. F. Effects of hypnosis and perceptual deprivation on vigilance in a simulated radar detection task. *Perceptual and Motor Skills*, 1980, **50**, 19–24.

Barber, T. X. The necessary and sufficient conditions for hypnotic behavior. *American Journal of Clinical Hypnosis*, 1960, **3**, 31–42.

Baron, J., and Treiman, R. Some problems in the study of differences in cognitive processes. *Memory and Cognition*, 1980, **8**, 313–321.

Benedetti, L. H., and Loeb, M. A comparison of auditory monitoring performance in blind subjects with that of sighted subjects in light and dark. *Perception and Psychophysics*, **11**, 10–16.

Birch, R. W. Attention span, distractibility and inhibitory potential of good and poor readers. (Doctoral dissertation, University of Wisconsin, 1967.) *Dissertation Abstracts International*, 1968, **28**, 4742B. (University Microfilms, No. 67–16,894.)

Braff, D. L., and Saccuzzo, D. P. Information processing dysfunction in paranoid schizophrenia: a two-factor deficit. *American Journal of Psychiatry*, 1981, **138**, 1051–1056.

Bross, M. Response bias in deaf and hearing subjects as a function of motivational factors. *Perceptual and Motor Skills*, 1979, **49**, 779–782(a).

Bross, M. Residual sensory capacities of the deaf: a signal detection analysis of a visual discrimination task. *Perceptual and Motor Skills*, 1979, **48**, 187–194 (a).

Bross, M., and Sauerwein, H. Signal detection analysis of visual flicker in deaf and hearing individuals. *Perceptual and Motor Skills*, 1980, **51**, 839–843.

Buchsbaum, M. S., and Sostek, A. J. An adaptive-rate continuous performance test: vigilance characteristics and reliability for 400 male students. *Perceptual and Motor Skills*, 1980, **51**, 707–713.

Buckner, D. N. An individual-difference approach to explaining vigilance performance. In D. N. Bucker and J. J. McGrath (Eds), *Vigilance: a symposium*. New York: McGraw-Hill, 1963.

Buckner, D. N., Harabedian, A., and McGrath, J. J. *A study of individual differences in vigilance performance*. Human Factors Research Technical Report No. 2. Los Angeles, Calif.: Human Factors Research, Inc., 1960.

Buckner, D. N., Harabedian, A., and McGrath, J. J. Individual differences in vigilance performance. *Journal of Engineering Psychology*, 1966, **5**, 69–85.

Byrne, D. G. Vigilance and arousal in depressive states. *British Journal of Social and Clinical Psychology*, 1976, **15**, 267–274.

Cahoon, R. L. Vigilance performance under hypoxia: II. Effect of work–rest schedule. *Perceptual and Motor Skills*, 1970, **31**, 619–626.

Campanelli, P. A. Sustained attention in brain damaged children. *Exceptional Children*, 1970, **36**, 317–323.

Canestrari, R. E., Jr. The relationship of vigilance to paced and self-paced learning in young and elderly adults. *Dissertation Abstracts*, 1963, **24**, 2130–2131.

Carr, G. *Introversion–extraversion and vigilance performance.* Unpublished doctoral dissertation, Tufts University, 1969.

Colquhoun, W. P. The effect of a short rest pause on inspection efficiency. *Ergonomics*, 1959, **2**, 367–372.

Colquhoun, W. P. Effects of a small dose of alcohol and certain other factors on the performance of a vigilance task. *Bulletin du Centre d'Études et Recherches Psychologiques*, 1962, **11**, 27–44.

Conners, C. K. The effect of dexedrine on rapid discrimination and motor control of hyperkinetic children under mild stress. *The Journal of Nervous and Mental Disease*, 1966, **142**, 429–433.

Conners, C. K. Psychological effects of stimulant drugs in children with minimal brain dysfunction. *Pediatrics*, 1972, **49**, 702–708.

Conners, C. K., and Rothschild, G. Drugs and learning in children. In *Learning disorders*, Vol. 3. Seattle: Special Child Publications. 1968.

Craig, A. Is the vigilance decrement simply a response adjustment towards probability matching? *Human Factors*, 1978, **20**, 441–446.

Cronbach, L. J. The two disciplines of scientific psychology. *The American Psychologist*, 1957, **12**, 671–684.

Crosby, K. G. Attention and distractibility in mentally retarded and intellectually average children. *American Journal of Mental Deficiency*, 1972, **77**, 46–53.

Das, J. P. Hypnosis, verbal satiation, vigilance, and personality factors: A correlational study. *Journal of Abnormal and Social Psychology*, 1964, **68**, 72–78.

Davies, A. D. M., and Davies, D. R. The effects of noise and time of day upon age differences in performance at two checking tasks. *Ergonomics*, 1975, **18**, 321–336.

Davies, D. R., and Griew, S. A further note on the effect of aging on auditory vigilance performance: the effect of low signal frequency. *Journal of Gerontology*, 1963, **18**, 370–371.

Davies, D. R., and Parasuraman, R. *The psychology of vigilance.* London: Academic Press, 1982.

Davies, D. R., and Tune, G. S. *Human vigilance performance.* New York: American Elsevier, 1969.

Dekaban, A. S., and Lehman, E. J. Effects of different dosages of anticonvulsant drugs on mental performances in patients with chronic epilepsy. *Acta Neurologica Scandinavica*, 1975, **52**, 319–330.

DiScipio, W. J. Psychomotor performance as a function of white noise and personality variables. *Perceptual and Motor Skills*, 1971, **33**, 82.

Dittmar, M. L., Berch, D. B., and Warm, J. S. Sustained visual attention in deaf and hearing adults. *Bulletin of the Psychonomic Society*, 1982, **19**, 339–342.

Doyle, R. B., Anderson, R. P., and Halcomb, C. G. Attention deficits and the effects of visual distraction. *Journal of Learning Disabilities*, 1976, **9**, 48–54.

Durham, R. L., and Nunnally, J. C. The effects of low and high levels of vigilance on subsequent visual exploratory behavior in humans. *Bulletin of the Psychonomic Society*, 1973, **1**, 313–315.

Elliot, C. D. Noise tolerance and extraversion in children. *British Journal of Psychology*, 1971, **62**, 375–380.

Estes, W. K., and Straughan, J. H. Analysis of a verbal conditioning situation in terms of statistical learning theory. *Journal of Experimental Psychology*, 1954, **47**, 225–234.

Eysenck, H. J. *Crime and personality.* Boston: Houghton-Mifflin, 1964.

Eysenck, H. J. *The biological basis of personality.* Springfield, Ill.: Charles C. Thomas, 1967.

Eysenck, H. J., and Eysenck, S. B. G. *Personality structure and measurement*. London: Routledge and Kegan Paul, 1969.

Farnham-Diggory, S. *Learning disabilities: a psychological perspective*. Cambridge, Mass.: Harvard University Press, 1978.

Farley, F. H., and Farley, S. U. Impulsiveness, sociability, and the preference for varied experience. *Perceptual and Motor Skills*, 1970, **31**, 47–50.

Fedio, P., and Mirsky, A. F. Selective intellectual deficits in children with temporal lobe or centrencephalic epilepsy. *Neuropsychologia*, 1969, **7**, 287–300.

Fehr, F. S., and Stern, J. A. The effect of hypnosis on attention to relevant and irrelevant stimuli. *The International Journal of Clinical and Experimental Hypnosis*, 1967, **15**, 134–143.

Gale, A., Bull, R., Penfold, V., Coles, M., and Barraclough, R. Extraversion, time of day, vigilance performance, and physiological arousal: failure to replicate traditional findings. *Psychonomic Science*, 1972, **29**, 1–5.

Gale, A., and Lynn, R. A developmental study of attention. *British Journal of Educational Psychology*, 1972, **42**, 260–266.

Grassi, J. R. Auditory vigilance performance in brain damaged, behavior disordered, and normal children. *Journal of Learning Disabilities*, 1970, **3**, 302–305.

Griew, S., and Davies, D. R. The effect of aging on auditory vigilance performance. *Journal of Gerontology*, 1962, **17**, 88–90.

Griffin, J. C., Perryman, R., Landers, W. F., and Patterson, E. T. *The influence of knowledge-of-results with mental retardates on a simple vigilance task*. Lubbock, Texas: Texas Tech University, 1974. (ERIC Document Reproduction Service No. ED 085 953.)

Grunebaum, H., Weiss, J. L., Gallant, D., and Cohler, B. J. Attention in young children of psychotic mothers. *American Journal of Psychiatry*, 1974, **131**, 887–891.

Gunn, W. J., and Loeb, M. Correlation of performance in detecting visual and auditory signals. *American Journal of Psychology*, 1967, **80**, 236–242.

Halcomb, C. G., and Kirk, R. E. Organismic variables as predictors of vigilance behavior. *Perceptual and Motor Skills*, 1965, **21**, 547–552.

Ham, M. W., and Edmonston, W. E. Hypnosis, relaxation, and motor retardation. *Journal of Abnormal Psychology*, 1971, **77**, 329–331.

Harkins, S., and Geén, R. G. Discriminability and criterion differences between extraverts and introverts during vigilance. *Journal of Research in Personality*, 1975, **9**, 335–340.

Harkins, S. W., Nowlin, J. B., Ramm, D., and Schroeder, S. Effects of age, sex, and time-on-watch on a brief continuous performance task. In E. Palmore (Ed.), *Normal aging II*. Durham, N. C.: Duke University Press, 1974.

Hatfield, J. L., and Loeb, M. Sense mode and coupling in a vigilance task. *Perception and Psychophysics*, 1968, **4**, 29–36.

Hayes, S. P. New experimental data on the old problem of sensory compensation. *Teachers' Forum*, 1933, **5**, 22–26.

Herman, C. S., Kirchner, G. L., Streissguth, A. P., and Little, R. E. Vigilance paradigm for preschool children used to relate vigilance behavior to IQ and prenatal exposure to alcohol. *Perceptual and Motor Skills*, 1980, **50**, 863–867.

Hilgard, E. R. *Hypnotic susceptibility*. New York: Harcourt, Brace and World, 1965.

Jenkins, H. M. The effect of signal-rate on performance in visual monitoring. *American Journal of Psychology*, 1958, **71**, 647–661.

Jerison, H. J. *Experiments on vigilance: IV. Duration of vigil and the decrement function*. Wright Air Development Center Technical Report No. WADC-TR-58-369. Wright-Patterson Air Force Base, Ohio: Wright Air Development Center, 1958.

Jerison, H. J. *Experiments on vigilance: V. The empirical model for human vigilance*. Wright Air Development Center Technical Report No. WADC-TR-58-526.

Wright-Patterson Air Force Base, Ohio: Wright Air Development Center, 1959.

Jerison, H. J., and Pickett, R. M. Vigilance: The importance of elicited observing rate. *Science*, 1964, **143**, 970–971.

Jerison, H. J., Pickett, R. M., and Stenson, H. H. The elicited observing rate and decision processes in vigilance. *Human Factors*, 1965, **7**, 107–123.

Johnson, W. H. Sustained auditory attention and distraction in mentally retarded and brain damaged children. (Doctoral dissertation, Columbia University, 1977.) *Dissertation Abstracts International*, 1977, **38**, 202–203. (University Microfilms No. 77-14,729.)

Jones, F. L. *Vigilance performance of normals and mental retardates: the effects of age and extraneous stimulation.* Unpublished doctoral dissertation, University of Cincinnati, 1971.

Kanter, D. R. Etiological considerations in childhood hyperactivity. In P. Karoly, J. J. Steffen and D. O'Grady (Eds), *Child health psychology*. New York: Pergamon Press, 1982.

Kappauf, W. E., and Powe, W. E. Performance decrement at an audio-visual checking task. *Journal of Experimental Psychology*, 1959, **57**, 49–56.

Kaspar, J. C., Millichap, J. G., Backus, R., Child, D., and Schulman, J. L. A study of the relationship between neurological evidence of brain damage in children and activity and distractibility. *Journal of Consulting and Clinical Psychology*, 1971, **36**, 329–337.

Kennedy, R. S.. The relationship between vigilance and eye movements induced by vestibular stimulation. In R. R. Mackie (Ed.), *Vigilance: theory, operational performance and physiological correlates*. New York: Plenum, 1977.

Keogh, B. K., and Margolis, J. Learn to labor and to wait: attentional problems of children with learning disorders. *Journal of Learning Disabilities*, 1976, **9**, 276–286.

Kirby, N. H., Nettelbeck, T., and Bullock, J. Vigilance performance of mildly mentally retarded adults. *American Journal of Mental Deficiency*, 1978, **82**, 394–397.

Kirby, N. H., Nettelbeck, T., and Thomas, P. Vigilance performance of mildly mentally retarded children. *American Journal of Mental Deficiency*, 1979, **84**, 184–187.

Kirchner, G. L. Differences in the vigilance performance of highly active and normal second-grade males under four experimental conditions. *Journal of Educational Psychology*, 1976, **68**, 696–701.

Kirchner, G. L., and Knopf, I. J. Differences in the vigilance performance of second-grade children as related to sex and achievement. *Child Development*, 1974, **45**, 490–495.

Kissen, A. T., Reifler, C. B., and Thaler, V. H. Modification of thermoregulatory responses to cold by hypnosis. *Journal of Applied Physiology*, 1964, **19**, 1043–1050.

Knopf, I. J., and Mabel, R. M. Vigilance performance in second graders as a function of interstimulus intervals, socio-economic levels, and reading. *Merrill-Palmer Quarterly*, 1975, **21**, 195–203.

Krupski, A., Raskin, D. C., and Bakan, P. Physiological and personality correlates of commission errors in an auditory vigilance task. *Psychophysiology*, 1971, **8**, 304–311.

Kupietz, S. S. Attentiveness in behaviorally deviant and nondeviant children–I. Auditory vigilance performance. *Perceptual and Motor Skills*, 1976, **43**, 1095–1101.

Kupietz, S. S., and Richardson, E. Children's vigilance performance and inattentiveness in the classroom. *Journal of Child Psychology and Psychiatry*, 1978, **19**, 145–154.

Latz, A., and Kornetsky, C. The effects of chlorpromazine and secobarbital under two conditions of reinforcement on the performance of chronic schizophrenic subjects. *Psychopharmacologia*, 1965, **7**, 77–88.

Lidz, T., Blatt, S., and Cook, B. Critique of the Danish-American studies of the adopted-away offspring of schizophrenics. *American Journal of Psychiatry*, 1981, **138**, 1063–1068.

Locke, J. L. Acoustic vigilance in four-year-old children. *Psychonomic Science*, 1970, **2**, 111–112.

Loeb, M., and Binford, J. R. Modality, difficulty and coupling in vigilance behavior. *American Journal of Psychology*, 1971, **84**, 529–541.

Lucaccini, L., Freedy, A., and Lyman, J. Motivational factors in vigilance: effects of instructions on performance in a complex vigilance task. *Perceptual and Motor Skills*, 1968, **26**, 783–786.

Lundberg, P., Warm, J. S., Seeman, W., and Porter, P. *The vigilance performance of the Type A individual: attentive, aroused and able.* Unpublished manuscript, 1979.

Lynn, R. *Attention, arousal and the orientation reaction.* New York: Pergamon Press, 1966.

Mabel, R. M. The effect of instructional set and consequence of responding on vigilance in second and third grade boys from two socio-economic levels. (Doctoral dissertation, Emory University, 1968.) *Dissertation Abstracts International*, 1969, **30**, 850–851b. (University Microfilms No. 69-13,203.)

McDonald, R. D., and Burns, S. B. Visual vigilance and brain damage: an empirical study. *Journal of Neurology, Neurosurgery, and Psychiatry*, 1964, **27**, 206–209.

McGrath, J. J. *The effects of irrelevant environmental stimulation on vigilance performance* Human Factors Research, Inc., Technical Report No. 206-6. Los Angeles, Calif.: Human Factors Research Inc., 1960.

McGrath, J. J., and O'Hanlon, J. Temporal orientation and vigilance performance. In A. F. Sanders (Ed.), *Attention and performance.* Amsterdam: North Holland, 1967.

Mack, C. N. The effects of different schedules of knowledge of results on the vigilance behavior of hyperactive learning disabled children. (Doctoral dissertation, Texas Tech University, 1975.) *Dissertation Abstracts International*, 1976, **36**, 6389b. (University Microfilms No. 76-7376.)

Mackworth, J. F. *Vigilance and attention: a signal-detection approach.* Baltimore: Penguin 1969.

Mackworth, J. F. *Vigilance and habituation: a neuropsychological approach.* Baltimore: Penguin, 1970.

Mackworth, N. H. *Researches on the measurement of human performance.* Medical Research Council Special Report No. 268. London: HM Stationary Office, 1950.

Margolis, J. S. Academic correlates of sustained attention. (Doctoral dissertation, University of California, Los Angeles, 1972.) *Dissertation Abstracts International*, 1973, **33**, 5555–5556A. (University Microfilms No. 73-10,447.)

Medeiros, E. A., and McManis, D. L. Assessment of introversion–extraversion in children: brief report. *Perceptual and Motor Skills*, 1974, **38**, 429–430.

Moore, S. F., and Gross, S. J. Influence of critical signal regularity, stimulus event matrix, and cognitive style on vigilance performance. *Journal of Experimental Psychology*, 1973, **99**, 137–139.

Neal, G. L. *Some effects of differential pretask instructions on auditory vigilance performance.* Paper presented at the Southwestern Psychological Association meeting, Houston, April 1967.

Neal, G. L., and Pearson, R. G. Comparative effects of age, sex, and drugs upon two tasks of auditory vigilance. *Perceptual and Motor Skills*, 1966, **23**, 967–974.

Noland, E. C., and Schuldt, J. Sustained attention and reading retardation. *Journal of Experimental Education*, 1971, **40**, 73–76.

Orzack, M. H., and Kornetsky, C. Attention dysfunction in chronic schizophrenia. *Archives of General Psychiatry*, 1966, **14**, 323–326.

Orzack, M., Kornetsky, C., and Freeman, H. The effects of daily administration of carphenazine on attention in the schizophrenic patient. *Psychopharmacologia*, 1967, **11**, 31–38.

Ozolins, D. A. The effects of knowledge of results on the vigilance performance of hyperactive and hypoactive children with learning disabilities. (Doctoral dissertation, Texas Tech University, 1974.) *Dissertation Abstracts International*, 1975, **35**, 5128–5129b. (University Microfilms No. 75-7426.)

Ozolins, D. A., and Anderson, R. P. Effects of feedback on the vigilance task performance of hyperactive and hypoactive children. *Perceptual and Motor Skills*, 1980, **50**, 415–424.

Parasuraman, R. Consistency of individual differences in human vigilance performance: an abilities classification analysis. *Journal of Applied Psychology*, 1976, **61**, 486–492.

Parasuraman, R., and Davies, D. R. A taxonomic analysis of vigilance performance. In R. R. Mackie (Ed.), *Vigilance: theory, operational performance and physiological correlates*. New York: Plenum, 1977.

Perryman, R. E., Halcomb, C. R., and Landers, W. F. Operant conditioning of mental retardates' visual monitoring. *Perceptual and Motor Skills*, 1981, **53**, 507–512.

Phares, E. J. Differential utilization of information as a function of internal–external control. *Journal of Personality*, 1968, **36**, 649–662.

Pines, H. A., and Julian, J. W. Effects of task and social demands on locus of control differences in information processing. *Journal of Personality*, 1972, **40**, 407–416.

Pope, L. T., and McKechnie, D. F. *Correlation between visual and auditory vigilance performance*. Aerospace Medical Research Laboratory Technical Report No. AMRL-TR-63-57. Wright-Patterson Air Force Base, Ohio: Aerospace Medical Research Laboratory, 1963.

Rapoport, J. L., Buchsbaum, M. S., Zahn, T. P., Weingartner, H., Ludlow, C., and Mikkelsen, E. J. Dextroamphetamine: cognitive and behavioral effects in normal prepubertal boys. *Science*, 1978, **199**, 560–563.

Rapoport, J. L., Buchsbaum, M. S., Weingartner, H. *et al.* Dextroamphetamine: cognitive and behavioral effects in normal and hyperactive boys and normal adult males. *Psychopharmacology Bulletin*, 1980, **16**, 21–23.

Ricks, N. L., and Mirsky. A. F. Sustained attention and the effects of distraction in underachieving second grade children. *Boston University Journal of Education*, 1974, **156**, 5–17.

Rosvold, H. E., Mirsky, A. F., Sarason, I., Bransome, E. D., and Beck, L. H. A continuous performance test of brain damage. *Journal of Consulting Psychology*, 1956, **20**, 343–350.

Rotter, J. B. Generalized expectancies for internal versus external control of reinforcement. *Psychological Monographs*, 1966, **80** (whole no. 609), 1–28.

Rotter, J. B., and Mulry, R. C. Internal versus external control of reinforcement and decision time. *Journal of Personality and Social Psychology*, 1965, **2**, 598–604.

Rugel, R. P., and Mitchell, A. Characteristics of familial and nonfamilial disabled readers. *Journal of Learning Disabilities*, 1977, **10**, 308–313.

Rutschmann, J., Cornblatt, B., and Erlenmeyer-Kimling, L. Sustained attention in children at risk for schizophrenia: report on continuous performance test. *Archives of General Psychiatry*, 1977, **34**, 571–575.

Saccuzzo, D. P., Hirt, M., and Spencer, T. J. Backward masking as a measure of attention in schizophrenia. *Journal of Abnormal Psychology*, 1974, **83**, 512–522.

Sanders, M. G., Halcomb, C. G., Fray, J. M., and Owens, J. M. Internal–external locus of control and performance on a vigilance task. *Perceptual and Motor Skills*, 1976, **42**, 939–943.

Schein, J. D. Cross-validation of the continuous performance test for brain damage. *Journal of Consulting Psychology*, 1962, **26**, 115–118.

Schneider, K., and Eckelt, D. Effects of success and failure on performance of a simple vigilance task. *Zeitschrift für experimentelle und angewandte Psychologie*, 1975, **22**, 263–289.

Semmel, M. I. Arousal theory and vigilance behavior of educable mentally retarded and average children. *American Journal of Mental Deficiency*, 1965, **70**, 38–47.

Shaywitz, B. A., Klopper, J. H., and Gordon, J. W. Methyphenidate in 6-hydroxydopamine-treated developing rat pups. *Archives of Neurology*, 1978, **35**, 463–469.

Siddle, D. A. T. Vigilance decrement and speed of habituation of the GSR component of the orienting response. *British Journal of Psychology*, 1972, **63**, 191–194.

Simon, M. J. Use of a vigilance task to determine school readiness of preschool children. *Perceptual and Motor Skills*, 1982, **54**, 1020.

Sipowicz, R. R., and Baker, R. A. Effects of intelligence on vigilance: a replication. *Perceptual and Motor Skills*, 1961, **13**, 398.

Smith, S. L. Extraversion and sensory threshold. *Psychophysiology*, 1968, **5**, 293–299.

Smyth, L. D. *The relationship between attention and hypnosis with implications for the roles of anxiety and brain asymmetry*. Unpublished doctoral dissertation, Michigan State University, 1977.

Smyth, L. D. *Attention and hypnosis: a review*. Unpublished manuscript, 1979.

Smyth, L. D., and Lowy, D. *Auditory vigilance during hypnosis*. Unpublished manuscript, 1979.

Stanovich, K. E. Information processing in mentally retarded individuals. In N. R. Ellis (Ed.), *International review of research in mental retardation*, Vol. 9. New York: Academic Press, 1978.

Stores, G., Hart, J., and Piran, N. Inattentiveness in schoolchildren with epilepsy. *Epilepsia*, 1978, **19**, 169–175.

Surwillo, W. W. The relation of autonomic activity to age differences in vigilance. *Journal of Gerontology*, 1966, **21**, 257–260.

Surwillo, W. W., and Quilter, R. E. Vigilance, age, and response time. *American Journal of Psychology*, 1964, **77**, 614–620.

Surwillo, W. W., and Quilter, R. E. The relation of frequency of spontaneous skin potential responses to vigilance and to age. *Psychophysiology*, 1965, **1**, 272–276.

Sykes, D. H., Douglas, V. I., Weiss, G., and Minde, K. K. Attention in hyperactive children and the effect of methylphenidate (Ritalin). *Journal of Child Psychology and Psychiatry*, 1971, **12**, 129–139.

Sykes, D. H., Douglas, V. I., and Morgenstern, G. The effect of methylphenidate (Ritalin) on sustained attention in hyperactive children. *Psychopharmacologia*, 1972, **25**, 262–274.

Sykes, D. H., Douglas, V. I., and Morgenstern, G. Sustained attention in hyperactive children. *Journal of Child Psychology and Psychiatry*, 1973, **14**, 213–220.

Talland, G. A. Visual signal detection, as a function of age, input rate and signal frequency. *Journal of Psychology*, 1966, **63**, 105–115.

Teichner, W. H. The detection of a simple visual signal as a function of time of watch. *Human Factors*, 1974, **16**, 339–353.

Thackray, R. I., Jones, K. N., and Touchstone, R. M. Personality and physiological correlates of performance decrement on a monotonous task requiring sustained attention. *British Journal of Psychology*, 1974, **65**, 351–358.

Thackray, R. I., Bailey, J. P., and Touchstone, R. M. Physiological, subjective, and performance correlates of reported boredom and monotomy while performing a simulated radar control task. In R. R. Mackie (Ed.), *Vigilance: theory, operational performance and physiological correlates.* New York: Plenum Press, 1977.

Thompson, L. W., Opton, E. M., and Cohen, L. D. Effects of age, presentation speed, and sensory modality on performance of a 'vigilance' task. *Journal of Gerontology,* 1963, **18**, 366–369.

Tolin, P., and Fisher, P. G. Sex differences and effects of irrelevant auditory stimulation on performance of a visual vigilance task. *Perceptual and Motor Skills,* 1974, **39**, 1255–1262.

Tune, G. S. Errors of commission as a function of age and temperament in a type of vigilance task. *Quarterly Journal of Experimental Psychology,* 1966, **18**, 358–361.

Tyler, D. M., Waag, W., and Halcomb, C. G. Monitoring performance across sense modes: An individual differences approach. *Human Factors,* 1972, **14**, 539–549.

Underwood, B. J. Individual differences as a crucible in theory construction. *American Psychologist,* 1975, **30**, 128–134.

Waag, W. L. Sex differences in monitoring performance. *Journal of Applied Psychology,* 1973, **58**, 272–274.

Waag, W. L., Tyler, D. M., and Halcomb, C. R. Experimenter effects in monitoring performance. *Bulletin of the Psychonomic Society,* 1973, **1**, 381–388.

Ware, J. R. Effects of intelligence on signal detection in visual and auditory monitoring. *Perceptual and Motor Skills,* 1961, **13**, 99–102.

Ware, R., and Baker, R. A. The effect of mental set and states of consciousness on vigilance decrement: a systematic exploration. In R. R. Mackie (Ed.), *Vigilance: theory, operational performance and physiological correlates.* New York: Plenum Press, 1977.

Ware, J. R., Baker, R. A., and Sipowicz, R. R. Performance of mental deficients on a simple vigilance task. *American Journal of Mental Deficiency,* 1962, **66**, 647–650.

Ware, J. R., Kowal, B., and Baker, R. A. The role of experimenter attitude and contingent reinforcement in a vigilance task. *Human Factors,* 1964, **6**, 111–115.

Warm, J. S., Seeman, W., Bean, L. H., Chin, N., and Wessling, N. F. *Meditation and sustained attention.* Paper presented at the meeting of the Psychonomic Society, Washington, D.C., November 1977.

Weiner, B. New conceptions in the study of achievement motivation. In B. Maher (Ed.), *Progress in experimental personality research,* Vol. 5. New York: Academic Press, 1970.

Welford, A. T. Arousal, channel capacity and decision. *Nature,* 1962, **194**, 365–366.

Werry, J. S., and Aman, M. G. Methylphenidate and haloperidol in children. *Archives of General Psychiatry,* 1975, **32**, 790–795.

White, R. W. A preface to the theory of hypnosis. New York: Holt, Rinehart and Winston, 1965.

Wiig, E. H., and Austin, P. W. Visual attention and distraction in aphasic and non-asphasic children. *Perceptual and Motor Skills,* 1972, **35**, 863–866.

Wilkinson, R. T. Comparison of paced, unpaced, irregular and continuous displays in watchkeeping. *Ergonomics,* 1961, **4**, 259–267.

Witkin, H. A., Lewis, H. B., Hertzman, M., Machover, K., Meissner, P., and Wapner, S. *Personality through perception.* New York: Harper and Row, 1954.

Wohlberg, G. W., and Kornetsky, C. Sustained attention in remitted schizophrenics. *Archives of General Psychiatry,* 1973, **28**, 533–537.

York, C. M. Behavioral efficiency in a monitoring task as a function of signal rate and observer age. *Perceptual and Motor Skills,* 1962, **15**, 404.

Zigler, E. The retarded child as a whole person. In D. K. Routh (Ed.), *The experimental psychology of mental retardation.* Chicago: Aldine, 1973.

Sustained Attention in Human Performance
Edited by J. S. Warm
© 1984 John Wiley & Sons Ltd.

Chapter 6

Theories of Vigilance

Michel Loeb and Earl A. Alluisi

Early 'theories' of vigilance were devised primarily to explain the decreases in 'hits' (Hs) or the increases in reaction time (RT) typically observed as a function of time-on-task. Some also dealt with the average or overall values of these parameters for given sessions. Early formulations tended to ignore trends

179

and values of 'false alarms' (FAs), although this has been less true recently due to the influence of signal detection theory and other psychophysical models.

Fashions in vigilance theories have mirrored fashions in psychological model-making generally; indeed, there are few if any vigilance models that apply solely to vigilance behaviors. The principal theories can be classified as reflecting learning, neurological, and psychophysical or information processing models of behavior, and we review the current status of theories of vigilance with that taxonomy.

LEARNING MODELS

Pavlovian and Hullian inhibition

The first really systematic experiments on vigilance were performed by N. H. Mackworth (1950); the increase in missed signals that he measured as a function of time is shown in Figure 1.1, previously discussed in Chapter 1.

Since Hullian conditioning theory was dominant at the time, it was only natural to attribute the observed decrement in part to response 'inhibition', an hypothesized intervening variable producing a tendency not to repeat a response. The decrement was also attributed in part to a conditioned form of inhibition (Hull's 'sIr'), and it is not entirely clear from Mackworth's discussion whether he was referring to inhibition (1) of the overt responses to the detected signals, or (2) of the temporally preceding observing responses necessary for the detection, or both. Adams (1956) also emphasized the Hullian concept of reactive inhibition ('IR'), but again it is unclear whether the inhibition referred to the detection responses or the observing responses. Such theories would appear to be generally more acceptable if the hypothesized inhibition referred to the observing responses, as detections rarely if ever drop to a zero level in an awake subject. This would be expected if inhibition applies to the observing response (see below), for such responses are assumed to be reinforced whenever a signal is presented and recognized and therefore extinction should not typically be complete.

Skinnerian theory (observing responses)

Holland (1958), a pupil of B. F. Skinner, viewed the vigilance situation in terms of Skinner's principles of operant behavior rather than in Hullian terms. Specifically, he suggested that the responses necessary for observation of the signal and non-signal stimuli — eye movements, head movements, etc. — continue to occur if they are reinforced by the occurrence of detectable signals, and they are extinguished in the absence of such signals. In Holland's earlier experiments, subjects were required to make special responses such as lever presses in order to view a display, and the pattern of their responses followed the characteristic operant paradigm. When there were very few reinforcements, i.e. a dearth of detectable signals, the responses tended to extinguish, as shown by a slowing in the rate of responding in Figure 6.1.

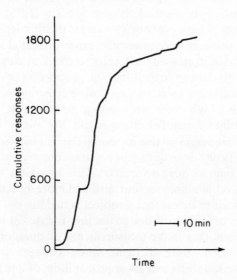

Figure 6.1 Cumulative response curve for observing responses. [Reproduced with permission from Holland, *Science*, **128**, 61–67. Copyright 1958 by the AAAS.]

Holland argued that the pattern of lever-pressing responses permits the inference that natural observing responses are similarly extinguished in the typical vigilance situation. This inference has not been universally accepted. Attempts to measure observing responses directly have met with mixed success; they are generally difficult to measure, especially in ways that do not interfere with the observing or vigilance conditions.

There have been several experiments in which eye movements were measured as indicators of the observing response. In one, Schroeder and Holland (1968) noted a progressive tendency for the subject to observe distracting stimuli, rather than the signal, and this was associated with a progressive decrement in detection responses. Mackworth *et al.* (1964) reported that although some signals were missed with multiple displays when observers were looking at the wrong display, signals were also often missed when the observers' eyes were correctly positioned towards the display on which the signal occurred. Furthermore, Coates *et al.* (1972) found that, for detections of illuminations of small jeweled lights, it was not critical for observers to have their eyes centered on the lights; the better observing strategy in that study was for observers to keep their eyes in a central position rather than to scan continually.

Quality of observing

Even when a special observing response is required, it is not always clearly related in an all-or-none fashion to signal detection. Hockey (1973) found that sleep loss reduced selection of high probability sources of stimulation and increased responses at which subjects were uncertain; noise increased sampling of high probability sources, but decreased tendencies to check sources repetitively. He interpreted beyond his data to suggest that the proportion of definite decisions is increased by noise and decreased by sleep loss. Furthermore, Guralnick (1973) found that although a high event rate reduced detections of signals that were difficult to discriminate, parallel changes did not occur in lever-pressing observing responses. He suggested that increasing the cost of observing (by increasing either or both difficulty or frequency of presentation) may influence the *quality* of observing rather than its mere occurrence. This approach, which stems from Jerison *et al.* (1965), is both more sophisticated and more difficult to check experimentally; it is difficult to detect that a subject is making *pro forma* observing responses when they are 'blurred' due to tearing, focused at infinity, or suffer from other distortions that make measurements of questionable value. The problem becomes even more difficult when changes in observing are accompanied by criterion shifts and lower probabilities of any kind of response.

Neurological responses, which unfortunately are only partially observable — and partially interpretable — with present techniques have also been proposed as indicators of the observing response (see, for example, Wilkinson *et al.*, 1966). To the extent that such models may increase predictive or explanatory power they may be as valid and useful as non-physiological models, or even more so. If, however, the relations between the physiological indicators and the measured performances are merely hypothesized or suggested, then the models suffer from the same defects as the learning models already described; i.e. any model that incorporates unobservable and unmeasurable intervening variables is at best a mere input–output statement, not a testable theory. However, some neurological measurements of 'observing' responses have been associated with vigilance; specifically, a technique to determine which of two signal sources is being monitored (Hillyard *et al.*, 1973). It may well be, however, that neurological correlates of vigilance behavior are best viewed in the context of their indicating central processes, rather than as merely components of observing responses.

NEUROLOGICAL MODELS

Several neurological models have been suggested as being related to vigilance. Generally they involve combinations of hypotheses dealing with arousal, habituation of arousal and sensory habituation.

Arousal

Frankmann and Adams (1962) were among the individuals who first stressed 'arousal' as an explanatory mechanism for vigilance behavior, but the basic concept can be traced back to the work of Hebb (1955), Sharpless and Jasper (1956), Malmo (1959), Berlyne (1960), Duffy (1962), and others. This approach hypothesizes that there is an optimum level of arousal associated with optimum performance, and that either a decrease or increase from the optimum level of arousal produces impairments in performance. Generally the concept has been associated with certain neural mechanisms, notably those of the brainstem reticular formation or the diffuse thalamic projection system, either of which interacts with the cerebral cortex.

The theory is that a given stimulus will produce arousal, but with repetition of the same stimulus or very similar ones (e.g. of non-signal stimuli differing only slightly from signal stimuli), these arousal responses habituate. It has been suggested (Sharpless and Jasper, 1956; Mackworth, 1970) that at least part of the vigilance decrement is due either to a progressive lowering of the arousal level or to habituation of the arousal reaction. Note that these are really two closely related hypotheses; either the decline in the level of arousal or the habituation of the arousal reaction (or both) might be expected to produce similar effects in most cases. (Habituation of arousal is discussed in more detail a little later in this chapter; it is not to be confused with neural habituation, discussed still later.)

The finding that depressant drugs impair vigilance, while stimulants often prevent the usual temporal decrements, is certainly consistent with an arousal hypothesis (Mackworth, 1950; Payne and Hauty, 1954; Loeb *et al.*, 1965; Neal and Pearson, 1966; Mackworth, 1970). However, a change in arousal might also produce changes in expectancy, in the criterion for responding, or in other mechanisms that in turn might influence or mediate changes in vigilance performance (see Mackworth, 1969; see also the relevant sections below). McGrath's finding that irrelevant stimulation enhances vigilance at slow stimulus event rates and impairs it at high event rates (McGrath, 1963) is also interpretable in these terms. So is Davey's (1973) reported finding of an optimal improvement following mild exercise on performance on the Brown and Poulton test (a vigilance task in which the subject reacts to a sequence of odd–even–odd digits) (see Figure 6.2). Randel's (1968) and Davenport's (1974) findings that background stimulation enhances performance, and Kirk and Hecht's (1963) finding that low-level noise acts similarly, also fit into this framework. But care must be exercised in making such interpretations of noise effects, for, as Broadbent (1971) points out, one can argue that steady low-level noise lowers rather than raises arousal because it masks extraneous auditory stimulation.

Recent studies by Corcoran and his colleagues (Mullin and Corcoran, 1977; Corcoran *et al.*, 1977) demonstrated that increasing the intensity of both signals and non-signals by the same amount generally enhances vigilance performance; this also supports an arousal interpretation.

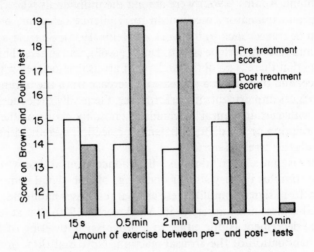

Figure 6.2   Change in performance on the Brown and Poulton vigilance task after mild exercise. [After Davey (1973).]

The evidence from EEG and other physiological measures (such as galvanic skin response, GSR), while generally consistent with the concept of an arousal factor acting to determine both the overall level of performance and the decrement with time on task, is often somewhat equivocal and difficult to interpret. Although Gale (1977) interpreted the changes he found during a vigilance task as indicative of lowered activation, they were frequently not the ones predicted. He concluded that 'there is very little evidence indeed for some central concept of arousal, some unitary state which has straightforward and systematic relationships with measures of behavior or measures of subjective report' (Gale, 1977, p.274). It is clear that the proper use of such physiological techniques in vigilance research requires considerable sophistication not only in these techniques, but also in the literature on vigilance as well!

Other factors

There is evidence that an arousal mechanism could not be solely responsible for all observed vigilance decrements. For one thing, they occur even when subjects are busily involved in several tasks (Hawkes *et al.*, 1964). Although one might argue that distraction and channel overload could more than cancel out any facilitation produced by the arousal of multiple task performances, it is difficult to rationalize the consistent decrement over time as due solely to lowered arousal under conditions that must represent different arousal levels.

Sleeplessness and Arousal

The changes in vigilance behavior following prolonged sleeplessness have been found to differ from those produced by time-on-task alone. Specifically, sleeplessness (which might be expected to produce a low state of arousal) has been observed to produce both decrements in Hs and increases in FAs (Williams *et al.*, 1959) while time-on-task typically produces decreases on both measures. This suggests that while one might talk about 'lowered arousal' under both circumstances, somewhat different states must be involved. Wilkinson (1960) also found that sleep-deprived subjects exhibit a greater decrement in Hs, partly but not totally explained by their tendency to go into a sleep-like state. He has

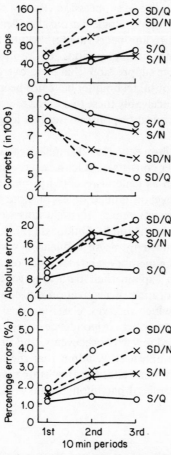

Figure 6.3   Effects of sleep (S) and sleep deprivation (SD) interacting with quiet (Q) and noise (N) on a serial reaction-time task. [After Wilkinson (1969). Copyright (1969) by the American Psychological Association.]

also shown (Wilkinson, 1963) that although noise and sleeplessness individually have detrimental effects, they tend to interact and the effects are not linearly additive (see Figure 6.3). This too, suggests that 'arousal' may not be a unitary concept—at least, not within the context of its applicability to vigilance and vigilance-like situations. An extensive discussion of the interactions of stressors and incentives that might be expected to influence arousal has been written by Wilkinson (1969) (see also Chapter 5).

Varieties of Arousal

As indicated previously, there is some evidence of at least two kinds of waking arousal (and probably more): (a) a cortical arousal evidenced by changes in brain-wave activity such as theta-wave suppression (Beatty *et al.*, 1974; Beatty and O'Hanlon, 1975), and (b) a physiological arousal evidenced by changes in such indices at body temperature and heart rate (cf. Alluisi *et al.*, 1976). Attempts to enhance watchkeeping during periods of prolonged sleeplessness by manipulation of theta-wave suppression (that is, to overcome low physiological arousal with a cortical-arousal technique) have not been completely successful (Morgan *et al.*, 1977). Conceivably these two kinds of activation may be related to the tonic and phasic arousal responses described long ago by Sharpless and Jasper (1956).

In a recent article, Hamilton *et al.* (1977) emphasize that arousal is not a simple unitary concept, but rather consists of at least two or three components having to do with processes such as general receptivity, bias toward certain sources of information (i.e. the novel or familiar or less or more probable), effort extend in responding, etc. Somewhat similar formulations were put forth earlier by Kahneman (1973) and Pribram and McGuinness (1975). Hamilton *et al.* found that the activation produced by noise influenced such diverse processes as guessing behavior, running memory, and efficiency on a task requiring storage and transformations. To explain their data they generated an information-processing model, incorporating two activation states, a system monitor, a bias setter and an executive, which receives, classifies, deals with and responds to signals, depending on degree of correspondence of input to output. The system (as in filter theory) is biased toward novel events, and the output of the monitor also adjusts the bias. Hamilton *et al.* admit that the model is more complex than it need be to explain their data, but they state that 'psychology has been poorly served by the principle of parsimony in this area.' That may be true for vigilance theory in general.

Habituation of Arousal

As indicated above, Mackworth (1969) has suggested that the vigilance decrement is due in part to habituation of the arousal response. There is, in fact, little evidence directly supporting this position, though it is not implausible. Siddle's (1972) finding, that subjects exhibiting more habituation of the galvanic skin response also exhibit more decrement in detections on a vigilance task, can be taken as supporting the arousal-habituation hypothesis. However, this is not the only interpretation possible, since the change in GSR might simply reflect a change in the overall level of arousal, or a change in the anticipatory reaction prior to responding.

As indicated previously, Sharpless and Jasper (1956) identified two components of the neural arousal response: a specific and less rapidly adapting component associated with the diffuse thalamic projection system and a less specific, more rapidly adapting one associated with the ascending reticular activating system. This undoubtedly oversimplifies the case (see also Livington, 1962).

Overview

In general, there appears to be considerable evidence that arousal is associated with both the level of vigilance and the vigilance decrement. At the same time, it appears unlikely either that arousal is an entirely unitary concept or that all of the changes observed in vigilance situations can be accounted for in terms of 'arousal' in any of its forms.

Neural habituation

Results of some experiments might be considered evidence against an arousal-habituation hypothesis, but many of these might also be considered evidence against a neural-habituation hypothesis.

Hernandez-Péon (1961) noted that there is a diminution of the neural response in sensory nuclei with repetition of the same stimulus (often auditory). He explains this phenomenon in terms of inhibition in the descending paths of the recticular formation. Desmedt (1960) has described similar phenomena, which he attributes to actions of inhibitory pathways in or near the classical sensory tracts. Both investigators have also reported that by pairing the habituated stimuli with reinforcing stimuli, the response could be augmented, and that unexpected sensory stimuli also produced such recovery, i.e. had disinhibiting qualities. Jane F. Mackworth (1969) has suggested that the vigilance decrement is partially attributable to neural habituation of this kind; specifically, that the response evoked by the signal lessens with repetition until it falls below the observer's criterion for responding.

The methodology employed in most experiments on neural habituation has been criticised on the grounds of insufficient control, especially over the subjects' orienting responses, and that changes in neural responding obtained with proper experimental control are significantly different (Worden, 1966). The sorts of changes discussed as characterizing neural habituation (such as shifts in the temporal spreading of the responses evoked) would appear to be much more difficult to incorporate into an explanatory concept of changes in vigilance than changes such as those reported by Desmedt and Hernandez-Péon.

Decrements in detections have been found to be greater with irregular than with regular intersignal intervals (Lisper and Tornros, 1974) and shifts in the event rate have been found not to enhance performance (Krulewitz *et al.*, 1975). Both findings suggest that processes other than habituation must be operative but they do not rule out the possibility that habituation might still be operative along with the other processes (e.g. expectancy).

Mackworth (1969) cited the findings of Fox (1964) demonstrating less habituation when the pattern of stimuli observed was temporally irregular. Accordingly, Richter *et al.* (1981) compared the performance of subjects listening for increments in intensity of acoustic pulses presented in a temporally regular or irregular sequence. Performance was superior in the temporally regular condition, which, according to Mackworth, should have produced more habituation and thus poor performance. The implications of this experiment are somewhat attenuated by the fact that there was no vigilance decrement, but according to Warm (see Chapter 2) similar findings were obtained in a later experiment in which a decrement occurred. Richter *et al.* interpreted the superior performance under temporally regular conditions in terms of greater opportunity for relaxation when pulses are temporally regular. It may be that Mackworth's interpretation is not the best in any event. In the Fox paper which she cited it was found that though temporal regularity produced more habituation it was also associated with a higher rate of responding, and Fox associated habituation not with a decrement but rather with the development of proper expectancies for stimulus events. It also should be noted that originally the stimuli to which his animals habituated were cue signals, not neutral events.

Other questions have been raised regarding the habituation hypothesis. In an investigation of the effect of the mode of processing information, Fisk and Schneider (1981) varied the regularity of a complex stimulus pattern. The decrements in a fixed search condition (in which characters were displayed across one diagonal), and in an alternating search condition (in which the characters were displayed alternating on the two diagonals), was greater than in a random search condition (in which the character did not follow on a regular diagonal pattern). Fisk and Schneider argue that an habituation mechanism would call for the alternating search condition to produce the least decrement, since that condition involves the least probability of repetitive stimulation. However, their interpretation is not unique, and therefore is subject to some debate. For example, the alternating search pattern is more predictable and repetitive than a random search pattern, and it clearly appears so perceptually. Also, it is doubtful that the same receptors are repetitively and sequentially stimulated in the usual vigilance situation anyway. With few if any exceptions, there are no experiments on habituation that have employed a regularly alternating pattern, and in view of the more serious objections that have been raised to the habituation mechanism, this one appears to be among the less critical.

As with other mechanisms reviewed, it appears impossible to prove or to disprove the habituation hypothesis solely on the basis of the behavioral data currently available. The most telling evidence against it, in our view, is Worden's (1966) argument that the original experiments were improperly controlled.

PSYCHOPHYSICAL OR INFORMATION PROCESSING MODELS

Under this heading we include recent applications to vigilance of theories that have been developed primarily for cognitive psychology, selective attention, signal detection and general perception.

Filter theory

The extinction concepts in theories of learning described in the first section are quite parallel or similar to the habituation concepts in the section on neurological models immediately preceding. There is also a similarity between the neural habituation hypotheses and Broadbent's filter theory of attention (Broadbent, 1958, 1971). The theory assumes that the monitor's information-handling capacity is limited and that information is selected by a 'filter' biased to receive information from some sources and reject it from others. It is also biased to reject the same or very similar chunks of information repetitively presented and to accept novel information. The net result is a decrement in Hs and an increase in RTs over time when observers are monitoring channels of information where there is considerable repetition or little variation in output. This model also has been applied to the selective attention ('cocktail party') situation.

The theory has been modified (see Broadbent, 1971) to take cognizance of data presented by Moray (1969), Treisman (1969) and others, which indicate that the filter, like most filters in the real world, is relative rather than absolute (i.e. the filter accepts some kinds of information more readily than other kinds, rather than simply accepting and rejecting different kinds of information). The neural habituation model might be viewed as providing a neurological foundation for the filter in filter theory, but it should be noted that both notions are no more than speculative models at this time; neither is as yet an actual description of observed events. While the filter concept can be used to explain a wide variety of data, it is difficult to set up a critical test of its validity as opposed to that of other concepts. Changes in types of observing responses, for example, might also be viewed as equivalent to a filter mechanism, in that some input channels may become inoperative or less efficient while other input channels may be activated instead.

Expectancy

The expectancy model was first suggested by C. H. Baker (1959), who suggested that subjects typically expect temporal patterns very different from those than they actually encounter, and that the discrepancy between their expectations and the schedule actually encountered is the principal cause of the results in a vigilance experiment. The theory predicts that expectation, and therefore performance, should be optimal at the mean intersignal interval. Indeed, Mowrer (1940) had demonstrated much earlier in a simple RT situation that RT was least at the mean intersignal interval where the foreperiod was varied over a number of trials. However, Baker (1959) has demonstrated that subjects may have expectations regarding the mean intersignal interval and its variability, but the expectations may be unrelated to the level of vigilance performance. Baker also suggested that KR may act to inform subjects about the signal schedule. Signal-detection performance has been found to be better when signals occur with greater regularity (that is with less variability around the mean intersignal interval), but generally only when the intersignal interval is quite short — of the order of a few seconds (Smith *et al.*, 1966). This is consistent with findings that man is not a very precise estimator of time except at very short intervals. There are exceptions to this; Warm *et al.* (1974) found a regularity effect at 100 second intervals. One suspects that counting may be occurring in such cases. In any event, beneficial effects of KR and false KR did not differ, even when signals were regular, an effect hard to reconcile with Baker's interpretations of KR effects in terms of expectancy.

Where signal rates have been switched within sessions, without the subjects being informed, the greatest decrement has been associated with the signal density being switched from high to low; the decrement was even greater than when the rate was continuously low, although the final levels of performance were not much different. This effect was shown by Colquhoun and Baddeley (1964). Their results are described in Chapter 2, Figure 2.9. Krulewitz *et al.* (1975) have reported similar effects with event-rate shifting; specifically, when switched from a high to a low event rate, the probability of detection increased, and when switched in the opposite direction, the subject's probabilities of detections decreased. These might be viewed as contrast effects, analogous to the Crespi–Zeeman effect noted in learning experiments.

There are other examples of this sort of effect. For example, Bevan and Turner (1965) have found that a shift from positive to negative reinforcement — or the converse — has a greater effect on vigilance performance than continuous positive or negative reinforcement. Unfortunately, in this case, the negative reinforcer was shock and the subjects could anticipate the shift. However, the same effect was found by these investigators in a later experiment (Bevan and Turner, 1966) in which the reinforcers were verbal and no anticipation was possible.

Although it is clear that expectancy effects do occur, the mechanisms through which they occur are not at all clear. For example, the effects could be identified with a change in observers' criteria for responding (see the next section on theory of signal detection), with probability matching (see Craig, 1978; also discussed below), or with a change in the level of adaptation to a specific stimulus or set of stimuli (Bevan and Turner, 1966).

Theory of signal detection (TSD)

Egan *et al.* (1961) are usually credited with being the first to suggest that the vigilance 'decrement' is due to a change to a more conservative criterion for responding, which results in a decline in both Hs and FAs. An earlier suggestion that the vigilance decrement is in fact a criterion shift was made by Howland (1958), but his formulation was less quantified and formalized than that of Egan *et al.* In any event, a change in criterion should be analyzable in terms of the theory of signal detection (TSD) (Green and Swets, 1966).

One reason why TSD had not been applied earlier to the analysis of vigilance was that TSD experiments typically delimit the intervals during which subjects are allowed to respond, while vigilance experiments do not. Egan *et al.* (1961) suggested that by observing the 'operant rate' of responding at intervals following signal presentation, the times during which responses should be considered Hs could be effectively determined, as could the times when they should be considered FAs. Still another approach could be to use data of this kind to determine the interstimulus intervals at which to present stimuli.

Numerous experiments have attempted to apply TSD methodology to the vigilance situation. In experiments by Broadbent and Gregory (1963a,b) and by Loeb and Binford (1964), observers rated their confidence that signals were being detected. The findings regarding both the certainty ratings and the computed TSD indices (d' and β) indicated that there was a progressive increase in conservatism in responding as a function of time-on-task. This result could be taken as evidence for a TSD theory of vigilance and against other theories (e.g. filter theory, observing response theory, and neural habituation theory), though it could be argued, and often has been, that these other mechanisms mediated changes in performance as measured by TSD indices. It is not entirely clear just why a criterion shift should occur as a function of time-on-task. Possibly observers come to realize that they are often responding to non-signals and raise their criteria accordingly.

Changes in the form of the receiver operating characteristic (ROC) cumulated over increasingly stringent response categories have been noted for individual data from several earlier experiments in a recent article by Craig (1977). Craig concluded that the data supported TSD in a majority of the cases, but not in all, and he suggested that the remaining data might better be explained either by other signal detection models, such as those of Luce and Green (1972) or

McGill (1967), or by the lack of reliability of vigilance data. Loeb (1978) has suggested that the latter alternative is much the more probable; i.e. relatively high reliability should not be expected given (a) the small number of signals presented, (b) the small amount of training as compared with typical TSD experiments, and (c) the very low degree of certainty of subjects in typical vigilance experiments.

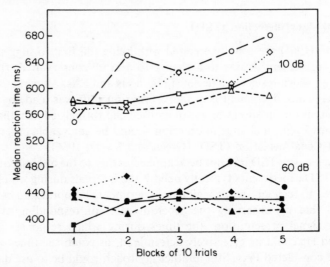

Figure 6.4   Median reaction time in milliseconds when subjects were given feedback △------▲ , pseudofeedback □———■ , no feedback or other stimulation ○----● , or mere acknowledgement of responses ◇·········◆ . [After Loeb and Schmidt (1963).]

Nevertheless, TSD interpretations have been suggested in other studies. For example, Williges (1976) manipulated parameters such as signal probability, payoff, and knowledge of results; he found performance consistent with TSD and the ideal observer hypothesis. According to his idea (see also Williges, 1969), an observer initially adopts some intermediate β and later shifts it in the direction of an optional criterion. If signal probability is less than 0.5, which is almost always true in the vigilance situation, this should result in an increase in β, as it did in his studies.

Other experiments on the effects of differential payoff and feedback on performance have yielded ambiguous and complex data. Payoff has been found to influence β, but not d', and increasing costs for FAs impaired performance, while changing payoff for Hs had no effect (Levine, 1966). It may be that the symmetrical payoff matrix employed is better suited to a conventional detection situation (where signal and non-signal stimuli are equal in probability) than to the vigilance situation (where the signal events are much lower in probability than non-signal events). Also, since human detectors can be expected to have their own values (not entirely monetary), their performance may not be totally determined by the differential (but typically unscaled) payoff set by the experimenter.

Experiments on feedback have also had superficially peculiar results that are understandable when the multiple effects of feedback are considered. For example, even false feedback may improve performance (Loeb and Schmidt, 1960, 1963; Baker *et al.* 1962); a reasonable interpretation is that any feedback provides a general incentive or increased motivation regardless of the content of the feedback *per se* (see Figure 6.4). Chinn and Alluisi (1964) reported that information about misses decreased FAs, that information about correct detections decreases misses, and that information about false responses increased RT and decreased FAs. The results regarding the latter two effects are perhaps best explained by a TSD approach, and the results regarding misses-feedback by a reinforcement hypothesis. This statement, however, may not do full justice to the complex findings of the experiment, and it is recommended that readers sufficiently interested read the original experiment.

Other Criticisms of TSD

The application of TSD to the vigilance situation has been criticized by a number of writers, and these criticisms have recently been summarized by Swets (1977), Craig (1979), Caldeira (1980) and Long and Waag (1981), among others. Many of the objections are methodological. It has been noted that the most common TSD measures of sensitivity and criterion, d' and β, may not be appropriate if calculated in the usual way, as they assume underlying normal distributions and equal variances of effects of signal and non-signal events — conditions not likely to be met in vigilance situations.

It has also been noted that subjects in vigilance experiments or vigilance situations have been exposed to many fewer signal and non-signal events with less feedback than those in the typical detection experiment for which TSD was devised. Swets (1977) notes that this latter observation describes not necessarily a deficiency, but rather an application to a different case. Considering the objections of those who feel TSD is a poor technique in view of the non-normal distributions and unequal variances of noise and signal-plus-noise distributions typically encountered in vigilance experiments, he suggests the use of rating curves to estimate distributional parameters. He further suggests, as does Craig (1979), that alternative TSD measures should be employed, especially nonparametric estimates of sensitivity. Caldeira (1980), on the other hand, indicates that these may be misleading, and that some of the nonparametric measures of sensitivity may in fact be influenced by response bias, especially when the probability of one kind of error is zero.

Another objection is on the grounds of interpretation of the TSD index changes. There is, in fact, considerable confusion about this. Several writers, including the present authors, have evaluated the application of TSD by stating that its predictions to the vigilance situation are or are not confirmed. As Swets (1977) has rightly pointed out, the theory itself makes no predictions about vigilance. However, some advocates of TSD have suggested that changes in criterion or in sensitivity would occur under certain circumstances. Critics have sometimes said that TSD predictions were not upheld when, in fact, they meant that the predictions of these advocates were not confirmed; obviously this is sloppy terminology. A more basic question is whether there are TSD indices which will truly be descriptive of subjects' behavior in TSD terms. For example, if a subject merely fails to respond a great deal of the time (perhaps dozes off), then both Hs and FAs will decline and the computed β would be greater. It would be foolish, however, to say that the subject is in any real sense more conservative in responding. Similarly, if an observer were to fall off in FAs not only because of a criterion shift, but also because of learning the character of non-signal stimuli, then estimating TSD parameters in the usual ways will not provide an accurate description as to what is happening.

An experiment which relates to this has been reported by Binford and Loeb (1966a,b). Performance, which was measured over nine successive sessions (following an initial practice session), was characterized by the usual decline in Hs and FAs within sessions, but between sessions FAs also declined substantially whereas Hs slightly increased. This suggests that the change in FAs *within* sessions may be attributable, like the decline *between* sessions, to some mechanism other than an increase in observers' criteria, e.g. to some sort of learning about the task and the nature of the stimuli — especially the non-signal stimuli. This notion, which we might term a 'stimulus learning hypothesis', essentially requires learning with implicit rather than explicit feedback, and suggests that the changes observed, especially in FAs, are not entirely due solely to criterion shifts (see Loeb, 1978, for an expansion of this argument). Quite recently, Long and Waag (1981) have presented data demonstrating undesirable correlations of sensitivity and criterion indices on vigilance, visual search and an auditory detention task, as well as 'unrealistic' values of TSD indices on the first two of these tasks. They conclude that for many practical applications the use of TSD may be impracticable.

All in all, though it may be reasonable to conceptualize vigilance in terms of changes in signal detection theory indices, the actual use of the usual TSD indices in analysis of vigilance data is fraught with difficulty.

Let us recapitulate. Subjects in vigilance experiments are engaged in detection, and it would be surprising if models for detection could not be applied at least in part to this case. However, there is some question as to whether the data permit reliable TSD indices to be measured, and there may be several processes operating so that the procedures for computing TSD indices may be misleading. Nevertheless, on at least some occasions, the application of TSD may yield some insights into the nature of these operative processes if the application is critically and thoughtfully performed.

Probability matching

Recently, Craig (1976, 1978) has extrapolated from psychophysical probability-matching models (e.g. Atkinson *et al.*, 1964; Green and Luce, 1967) to suggest that subjects start responding at a rate higher than the signal rate, but later tend to match the response rate to the signal rate. The explanation advanced is that there really is no decline in efficiency; rather, the apparent declines in Hs and FAs are entirely attributable to the hypothesized decline in the overall response rate.

The data presented are not broken down into H and FA categories, so the plausibility of the hypothesis cannot be readily determined. However, it is hard to see how this concept, based entirely on within-session data, can be reconciled with the previously cited data of Binford and Loeb (1966a,b) in which there were declines in Hs and FAs in early sessions, declines in FAs and increases in Hs over all sessions, and decreases in Hs with small (non-significant) decreases in FAs in late sessions.

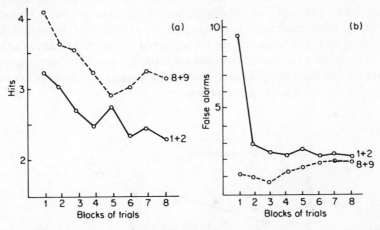

Figure 6.5   Hits (a) and false alarms (b) averaged for first and second sessions (1 + 2) and eighth and ninth sessions (8 + 9). [After Binford and Loeb (1966b). Copyright (1966) by the American Psychological Association.]

The idea of a probability-matching mechanism is ingenious, and it may be viewed as still another restatement, in more explicit terms, of the expectancy hypothesis. Certainly it is possible that subjects may gradually reduce their responding in accordance with the observed ratio of signals to total stimuli or signals to non-signals. However, the real question is whether this is all that occurs. Is such a reduction in overall responding simply a reflection of subjects behaving in accordance with TSD predictions, or because they are occasionally going into states of nonobserving or reverie, as Jerison and Pickett (1964) suggest, or because they are slightly increasing their hit rate and considerably reducing their false alarm rate over sessions, as was observed by Binford and Loeb (1966a,b) (see Figure 6.5).

Information theory and channel capacity

The vigilance situation may be viewed as a choice reaction-time task, with relatively infrequent 'signals' to which the subject responds actively by pushing a button or a key, and relative frequent 'non-signals' for which the subject's expected response is to do nothing. If this is the case, then other models of signal processing, such as those derived from information theory (see Dember and Warm, 1979), may be employed to explain some facets of vigilance behavior. For instance, Kulp and Alluisi's (1967) finding that vigilance performance is a decreasing function of S-R uncertainty fits into this framework. Similarly, both signal rate and regularity effects have been explained in terms of a metric of subjective uncertainty (Smith *et al.*, 1966) as shown in Figure 6.6 (see also Chapter 2, Figure 2.8). This sort of interpretation might also partially explain the previously cited findings of Hawkes *et al.* (1964) that overall detection was poor and a decrement in Hs occurred when a vigilance task was part of a complex of tasks, since channel capacity may have been approached or exceeded on their complex task, and any facilitating effect of greater arousal might thereby have been counteracted.

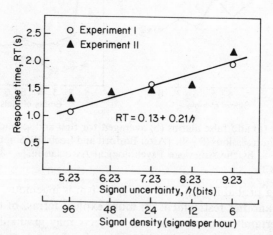

Figure 6.6   Response time in seconds as a function of temporal uncertainty (surprisal). Signal rates are also shown. [After Smith *et al.* (1966) and Dember and Warm (1979).]

Similarly, the findings of Binford and Loeb (1963) that addition of a simple auditory monitoring task degraded performance on a Mackworth clock task and that increasing the auditory load still further improved clock task performance might be interpreted as indicating that the auditory task has both detrimental (channel overloading or distracting) and facilitating (altering) properties, with the latter increasing more rapidly than the former over the ranges of the parameters employed.

Two recently proposed explanations of the vigilance decrement are based on memory load and processing mode; these are described here.

Memory Load

Parasuraman (1979), after surveying the literature and attempting a systematic classification, has suggested that situations in which a true decrement (a decline in d') occurs generally involve a memory load for the subject. Presumably, such a load imposes a continuous strain in that it requires a sustained effort; the result is a cumulative decrease. In an experiment (Parasuraman, 1979) in which subjects either detected increments in a stimulus that was present or a stimulus that was different from a previous one, a decrement was observed only in the latter situation, especially at higher event rates. The outcome is in line with Parasuraman's hypothesis.

Processing Mode

Fisk and Schneider (1981), taking a different tack, also invoke the mechanism of search capacity. It involves the hypothesis that there are two kinds of information processing—an 'automatic' mode, involving parallel search, not limited by short-term memory, and a 'controlled-processing' mode, involving high attentional effort and limited comparison rate serial search, which is quite susceptible to the effects of task load (Schneider and Shiffrin, 1977; Shiffrin and Schneider, 1977). (Similar distinctions have, of course, been made by others.) Fisk and Schneider suggest that a vigilance decrement should occur only in the latter, 'controlled-processing', situation.

In the investigation cited, Fisk and Schneider first set up a situation presumably involving automatic processing, in which stimuli were consistently used as stimuli and non-stimuli, and a situation, presumably involving controlled processing, in which the use of stimuli as signals or non-signals generally was varied. A decrement in sensitivity occurred only in the latter situation (see Figure 6.7). In a subsequent experiment involving a different frame size, a larger memory set and longer interstimulus interval, essentially the same effects were obtained. While the decrement was less, this does not contradict Parasuraman, as several variables were manipulated. (A third experiment, involving controlled processing and variations in the regularity of spatial presentations, has been described previously in the section on habituation.)

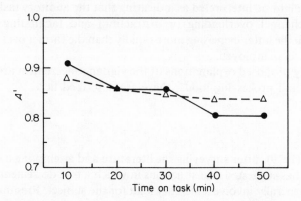

Figure 6.7   Sensitivity (in terms of the nonparametric measure A') when stimuli are variably mapped ●———●, producing controlled processing, and consistently mapped △- - - - -△, producing automatic processing. [From Fisk and Schneider, *Human Factors*, **23**, 737–750. Copyright by The Human Factors Society, Inc., and reproduced by permission.]

Adaptation Level

Still another general information-processing model—Helson's adaptation-level (AL) theory—has been applied by Bevan (1965) to the vigilance situation. According to this view, vigilance depends upon both a subject's state of arousal *and* his expectancies in rather complex interactions: (a) to some extent, his expectancies determine his arousal, which is maximum when expectation is ambiguous, and (b) both arousal and expectancy influence the effects of stimulus variables, situational background variables, and personal residual variables, as in other applications of AL theory (see Helson, 1964). This model incorporates both arousal and expectancy, but it combines them in a way not entirely predictable from their usual formulation.

   In general, then, one might say that to the extent a vigilance task may be considered a special case of the more general information-processing situation, identical factors should be expected to operate the same way in both situations. These factors could be expected to interact further with any other factors that might specifically influence the vigilance situation.

Combined effects of possible mechanisms

Total failures to respond at times could occur because of periods of inadvertent sleep *or* by failures to observe *or* by occasional habituation to a level below criterion. The result, regardless of 'cause', would be recorded as a reduction in both Hs and FAs. An increase in criterion for responding should also reduce Hs and FAs within a session. Occasional blurred observing *or* a change in a different state of arousal (e.g. due to loss of sleep) might produce fewer Hs and more FAs, as would a reduction in probability matching; this should also reduce d' and perhaps lower β.

A mixture of two such processes might produce a lowering of computed d' and an increase in β. Learning about non-signals and signals within a session (and over sessions) should produce effects even more suggestive of β lowering, but also an increase in d'. The resultant d' produced by these various effects is not readily predictable, but it might be expected to remain relatively constant within early sessions and increase to a higher value overall in later sessions.

Overall levels of performance will also reflect the influence of variables that affect other information-processing situations, such as subjects' objective and subjective uncertainties and expectancies, based partially on previous experience. The receiver operating characteristics (ROCs) that will result from the interaction of these various processes cannot really be specified in advance, but there is no reason to assume that the curves will be classically symmetrical, since they need not reflect equal noise and signal-plus-noise variance. There is every reason to believe that numerous qualitatively different processes are operating simultaneously. These may differentially influence EEG and evoked potentials, heart rate, GSR and other physiological indices, so that examinations of these indices are unlikely to resolve our confusion readily.

We are taught to be 'parsimonious' and accordingly to explain as many phenomena as possible in terms of the operation of as few specific mechanisms as possible—a single mechanism being most 'parsimonious'. But this may not be truly parsimonious for vigilance or for many other behavioral phenomena for which the 'one-mechanism' explanation exceeds the limits of credibility. We believe it highly probable that in the final analysis, successful models of vigilance will necessarily incorporate more than one explanatory principle.

A recent example of this kind of combined-mechanism approach is that adopted by Corcoran and his colleagues (Mullin and Corcoran, 1977; Corcoran *et al.*, 1977). They simultaneously manipulated the levels of both signals and non-signals, within sessions at different times of day, and examined the effects on the levels of performance and the decrements within sessions. They interpreted the results in terms of changes in arousal and shifts in TSD indices. Two levels of task sound were employed—90 dB (SPL) signals against an 85 dB background 'pink noise', and 70 dB against a 65 dB background. The results were complex, but in general Hs and FAs were more frequent with the higher sound levels. In addition, there was somewhat less decline in FAs, d' was higher, and β lower at the higher level. Switching from 70/65 to 90/85 dB within a session produced an increase in Hs, an almost stable level of FAs, an increase in d', and a decrease in β.

In the earlier experiment (Mullin and Corcoran, 1977), a higher sound level was associated with a higher H rate in the morning (08.30), but not in the evening (20.30); sound level did not significantly influence the FA rate in this case. The authors concluded that there are complex interactions between arousal state (determined by variables such as the level of stimulation, expectations, time of day and personality) and tendencies to shift sensitivity and criteria for response as a function of time-on-task. While one could quarrel with some of the assumptions underlying their analyses and their interpretations, multifactor approaches of this kind would appear to be the most promising for establishing a valid and credible theory of vigilance phenomena.

CONCLUSION

The evidence clearly leads to the conclusions that (1) vigilance behavior probably is not explicable in terms of a single mechanism; (2) supposedly alternative models often make the same or very similar predictions; (3) most of the models are really not well formulated in quantitatively predictable and verifiable terms; and (4) there are serious difficulties in the application of *all* of the models, though each may explain certain facts of the findings, some better than others.

REFERENCES

Adams, J. A. Vigilance in the detection of low-intensity visual stimuli. *Journal of Experimental Psychology*, 1956, **52**, 204–208.

Alluisi, E. A., Coates, G. D., and Morgan, Ben B., Jr. Effects of temporal stresses on vigilance and information processing. Paper presented at NATO International Symposium on Vigilance, St Vincent, Italy, 3–6 August, 1976.

Atkinson, R. C., Carterette, E. C., and Kinchla, R. A. The effect of information feedback upon psychophysical judgments. *Psychonomic Science*, 1964, **1**, 83–84.

Baker, C. H. Attention to visual displays during a vigilance task: II. Maintaining the level of vigilance. *British Journal of Psychology*, 1959, **50**, 30–36.

Baker, R. A., Ware, J. R., and Sipowicz, R. R. Vigilance: a comparison in auditory, visual, and combined audio-visual tasks. *Canadian Journal of Psychology*, 1962, **16**, 192–198.

Beatty, J., and O'Hanlon, J. F. EEG-theta regulation and radar-monitoring performance of experienced radar operators and air traffic controllers. In E. A. Alluisi (Chairman), *Biofeedback, self-regulation, and performance*. Symposium presented at the Annual Meeting of the Southern Society for Philosophy and Psychology, New Orleans, March 1975.

Beatty, J., Greenberg, A., Deibler, W. P., and O'Hanlon, J. F. Operant control of occipital theta rhythms affects performance in a radar monitoring task. *Science*, 1974, **183**, 871–873.

Berlyne, D. E. Attention, perception, and behavior therapy. *Psychological Review*, 1951, **58**, 137–146.

Berlyne, D. E. *Conflict Arousal and Curiosity*. New York: McGraw-Hill, 1960.

Bevan, W. Behavior in unusual environments. In H. Helson and W. Bevan (Eds), *Contemporary approaches to psychology*. Princeton, N.J.: Van Nostrand, 1967, pp.385–418.

Bevan, W., and Turner, E. D. Vigilance performance with a qualitative shift in reinforcers. *Journal of Experimental Psychology*, 1965, **70**, 83–86.

Bevan, W., and Turner, E. D. Vigilance performance with a qualitative shift in verbal reinforcers. *Journal of Experimental Psychology*, 1966, **71**, 467–468.

Binford, J. R., and Loeb, M. Monitoring readily detached auditory signals and detection of obscure visual signals. *Perceptual and Motor Skills*, 1963, **17**, 735–746.

Binford, J. R., and Loeb, M. Changes in criterion and effective sensitivity observed on an auditory vigilance task over repeated sessions. Sensory Research Laboratories, University of Louisville, Kenty, January 1966 (a).

Binford, J. R., and Loeb, M. Changes within and over repeated sessions in criterion and effective sensitivity in an auditory vigilance task. *Journal of Experimental Psychology*, 1966, **72**, 339–345 (b).

Broadbent, D. E. *Perception and communication.* New York: Pergamon Press, 1958.

Broadbent, D. E. *Decision and stress.* New York: Academic Press, 1971.

Broadbent, D. E., and Gregory, M. Division of attention and the decision theory of signal detection. *Proceedings of the Royal Society B*, 1963, **158**, 222–231 (a).

Broadbent, D. E., and Gregory, M. Vigilance considered as a statistical decision. *British Journal of Psychology*, 1963, **54**, 309–323 (b).

Caldeira, J. D. Parametric assumptions of some 'nonparametric' measures of sensory efficiency. *Human Factors*, 1980, **22**, 119–120.

Chinn, R. McC., and Alluisi, E. A. Effect of three kinds of knowledge-of-results, information on three measures of vigilance performance. *Perceptual and Motor Skills*, 1964, **18**, 901–912.

Coates, G. D., Loeb, M., and Alluisi, E. A. Influence of observing strategies and stimulus and variables on watchkeeping performances. *Ergonomics*, 1972, **15**, 379–386.

Colquhoun, W. P., and Baddeley, A. D. The role of pretest expectancy in vigilance decrement. *Journal of Experimental Psychology*, 1964, **68**, 156–160.

Corcoran, D. W. J., Mullin, J., Rainey, T. M., and Frith, J. The effects of raised signal and noise amplitude during the course of vigilance tasks. In R. R. Mackie (Ed.), *Vigilance: theory, operational performance, and physiological correlates.* New York: Plenum Press, 1977, pp.645–663.

Craig, A. Signal recognition and the probability-matching decision rule. *Perception and Psychophysics*, 1976, **20**, 157–162.

Craig, A. Broadbent and Gregory revisited: vigilance and statistical decision. *Human Factors*, 1977, **19**, 25–36.

Craig, A. Is the vigilance decrement simply a response adjustment toward probability matching. *Human Factors*, 1978, **20**, 441–446.

Craig, A. Nonparametric measures of sensory efficiency for sustained monitoring tasks. *Human Factors*, 1979, **21**, 69–77.

Davenport, W. G. Arousal theory and vigilance: schedules for background stimulation. *Journal of General Psychology*, 1974, **91**, 51–59.

Davey, C. P. Physical exertion and mental performance. *Ergonomics*, 1973, **16**, 595–599.

Dember, W. N., and Warm, J. S. *Psychology of Perception* (2nd ed.). New York: Holt, Rinehart and Winston, 1979.

Desmedt, J. Neurophysiological mechanisms controlling acoustic input. In G. L. Rasmussen and W. F. Windle (Eds), *Neural mechanisms of the auditory and vestibular systems.* Springfield, Ill.: Charles C. Thomas, 1960, pp.152–184.

Duffy, E. *Activation and behavior.* New York: John Wiley, 1962.

Egan, J. P., Greenberg, G. L., and Schulman, A. I. Operating characteristics, signal detectability, and the method of free response. *Journal of the Acoustical Society of America*, 1961, **33**, 993–1007.

Fisk, A. D., and Schneider, W. Controlled and automatic processing during tasks requiring sustained attention: a new approach to vigilance. *Human Factors*, 1981, **23**, 737–750.

Fox, S. S. Evoked potential habituation rate and sensory pattern preference as determined by stimulus information. *Journal of Comparative and Physiological Psychology*, 1964, **58**, 225–232.

Frankmann, J. P., and Adams, J. A. Theories of vigilance. *Psychological Bulletin*, 1962, **59**, 257–272.

Gale, A. Some EEG correlates of sustained attention. In R. R. Mackie (Ed.), *Vigilance: theory, operational performance and physiological correlates*. New York: Plenum, 1977, pp.262–283.

Green, D. L., and Swets, J. A. *Signal detection theory and psychophysics*. New York: John Wiley, 1966.

Green, D. M., and Luce, R. D. Detection of auditory signals presented at random times. *Perception & Psychophysics*, 1967, **2**, 441–450.

Guralnick, M. J. Effects of event rate and signal difficulty on observing responses and detection measures in vigilance. *Journal of Experimental Psychology*, 1973, **99**, 261–265.

Hamilton, P., Hockey, G. R. J., and Rejman, M. The place of the concept of activation in human information processing theory: an integrative approach. In *Attention and performance VII*, New York: Pergamon Press, 1977, pp.463–486.

Hawkes, G. R., Meighan, T. W., and Alluisi, E. A. Vigilance in complex task situations. *Journal of Psychology*, 1964, **58**, 223–236.

Hebb, D. O. Drives and the CNS (conceptual nervous system). *Psychological Review*, 1955, **62**, 243–254.

Helson, H. *Adaptation-level theory*. New York: Harper and Row, 1964.

Hernandez-Péon, R. Reticular mechanisms of sensory control. In W. A. Rosenblith (Ed.), *Sensory communication*. New York: MIT Press–John Wiley, 1961.

Hillyard, S. A., Hink, R. F., Schwent, V. L., and Picton, T. W. Electrical signs of selective attention in the human brain. *Science*, 1973, **182**, 177–180.

Hockey, G. R. J. Changes in information-selection patterns in multisource monitoring as a factor of induced arousal shifts. *Journal of Experimental Psychology*, 1973, **101**, 35–42.

Holland, J. G. Human vigilance. *Science*, 1958, **128**, 61–67.

Howland, D. An investigation of the performance of the human monitor. Wright Air Development Center Technical Report No. WADC-TR-57-431. Wright-Patterson Air Force Base, Ohio: Wright Air Development Center, 1958.

Hull, C. L. *Principles of behavior: an introduction to behavior theory*. New York: Appleton, 1943.

Jerison, H. J. Vigilance: biology, psychology, theory and practice. Paper presented at NATO International Symposium on Vigilance, St Vincent, Italy, 3–6 August, 1976.

Jerison, H. J., Pickett, R. M., and Stensen, H. H. The elicited observing rate and decision processes in vigilance. *Human Factors*, 1965, **7**, 107–128.

Jerison, H. J., and Pickett, R. M. Vigilance: the importance of the elicited observing rate. *Science*, 1964, **143**, 970–971.

Kahneman, D. *Attention and effort*. New York: Prentice-Hall, 1973.

Kirk, R. E., and Hecht, E. Maintenance of vigilance by programmed noise. *Perceptual and Motor Skills*, 1963, **16**, 553–568.

Krulewitz, J. E., Warm, J. S., and Wohl, T. H. Effects of shifts in the rate of repetitive stimulation on sustained attention. *Perception and Psychophysics*, 1975, **18**, 245–249.

Kulp, R. A., and Alluisi, E. A. Effects of stimulus–response uncertainty on watchkeeping performance and choice reactions. *Perception and Psychophysics*, 1967, **2**, 511–515.

Levine, J. M. The effects of values and costs on the detection and identification of signals in auditory vigilance. *Human Factors*, 1966, **8**, 525–537.

Lisper, H. O., and Tornos, J. Effects of inter-signal regularity on increase in reaction time in a one-hour auditory monitoring task. *Acta Psychologica*, 1974, **33**, 455–460.

Livington, R. B. Central control of receptors and sensory transmission systems. In J. Field, H. W. Magoun and V. E. Hall (Eds), *Handbook of physiology, Vol. I, Neurophysiology*. Baltimore, Md: Williams and Wilkins, 1962.

Loeb, M. On the analysis and interpretation of vigilance. Some remarks on two recent articles by Craig. *Human Factors*, 1978, **20**, 445–451.

Loeb, M., and Alluisi, E. A. Influence of display, task, and organismic variables on indices of monitoring behavior. In A. F. Sanders (Ed.), *Attention and performance III*. Amsterdam: North-Holland, 1970, pp.343–366. Also *Acta Psychologica*, 1970, **33**, 343–366.

Loeb, M., and Alluisi, E. A. An update of findings regarding vigilance and a reconsideration of underlying mechanisms. Paper presented at NATO International Symposium on Vigilance, St Vincent, Italy, 3–6 August, 1976. Reprinted in R. R. Mackie (Ed.), *Vigilance: theory, operational performance, and physiological correlates*. New York: Plenum, 1977.

Loeb, M., and Binford, J. R. Vigilance for auditory intensity change as a function of preliminary feedback and confidence level. *Human Factors*, 1964, **6**, 445–458.

Loeb, M., and Schmidt, E. A. Influence of time on task and false information on efficiency of responding to pure tones. US Army Medical Research Laboratory Report Number 426. Fort Knox, Kenty: US Army, 1960.

Loeb, M., and Schmidt, E. A. A comparison of the effects of different kinds of information in maintaining efficiency on an auditory monitoring task. *Ergonomics*, 1963, **6**, 75–81.

Loeb, M., and Van Loo, J. The relationship of stimulus predictability, duration, and patterning and of eye movements to quality of watchkeeping performance. Unpublished manuscript.

Loeb, M., Hawkes, G. R., Evans, W. O., and Alluisi, E. A. The influence of *d*-amphetamine, benactyzine and chlorpromazine on performance in a auditory vigilance task. *Psychonomic Science*, 1965, **3**, 29–30.

Long, G. M., and Waag, W. L. Limitations on the practical applicability of d' and β measures. *Human Factors*, 1981, **23**, 285–290.

Luce, R. D., and Green, D. M. A neural timing theory for response times and the psychophysics of intensity. *Psychological Review*, 1972, **79**, 14–57.

McGill, W. J. Neural counting mechanisms and energy detection in audition. *Journal of Mathematical Psychology*, 1967, **4**, 351–376.

McGrath, J. J. Irrelevant stimulation and vigilance performance. In D. N. Buckner and J. J. McGrath (Eds), *Vigilance: a symposium*. New York: McGraw-Hill, 1963, pp.3–19.

Mackworth, N. H. *Researches on the measurement of human performance*. Medical Research Council Special Report Series No. 268. London: HM Stationary Office, 1950. Reprinted in H. W. Sinaiko (Ed.), *Selected papers on human factors in the design and use of control systems*. New York: Dover, 1961, pp.174–331.

Mackworth, J. F. *Vigilance and habituation*. Baltimore, Md: Penguin Books, 1969.

Mackworth, J. F. *Vigilance and attention*. Baltimore, Md: Penguin Books, 1970.

Mackworth, N. H., Kaplan, I. T., and Metlay, W. Eye movements during vigilance. *Perceptual and Motor Skills*, 1964, **18**, 397–402.

Malmo, R. B. Activation: a neuropsychological dimension. *Psychological Review*, 1959, **66**, 367–386.

Moray, N. Attention: selective processes in vision and hearing. London: Hutchinson Educational, 1969.

Morgan, B. B., Coates, G. L., Kirby, R. H., and Corson, D. L. Efficacy of self-regulation in the enhancement of sustained performance. *JSAS Catalogue of Selected Documents in Psychology*, 1977, **7**, 91 (Ms. no. 1622).

Mowrer, O. H. Preparatory set (expectancy)—some methods of measurement. *Psychological Monographs*, 1940, **52** (whole no. 233).

Mullin, J., and Corcorcan, D. W. J. Interaction of amplitude with cicardian variation in auditory vigilance performance. *Ergonomics*, 1977, **20**, 193–200.

Neal, G. L., and Pearson, R. G. Comparative effects of age, sex, and drugs upon two tasks of auditory vigilance. *Perceptual and Motor Skills*, 1966, **23**, 967–974.

Parasuraman, R. Memory load and event rate control sensitivity decrements in sustained attention. *Science*, 1979, **205**, 924–927.

Payne, R. B., and Hauty, G. T. The effect of experimentally induced attitudes upon task proficiency. *Journal of Experimental Psychology*, 1954, **47**, 265–273.

Pribram, K. H., and McGuinness, D. Arousal, activation, and effort in the control of attention. *Psychological Review*, 1975, **81**, 116–149.

Randel, J. M. Attenuation of the vigilance decrement through stimulation in a second modality. *Human Factors*, 1968, **10**, 505–514.

Richter, D. G., Senter, R. J., and Warm, J. S. Effects of the rate and regularity of background events on sustained attention. *Bulletin of the Psychonomic Society*, 1981, **18**, 207–210.

Schneider, W., and Shiffrin, R. M. Controlled and automatic human information processing: I. Detection, search, and attention. *Psychological Review*, 1977, **84**, 1–66.

Schroeder, S. R., and Holland, J. G. Operant control of eye movement during human vigilance. *Science*, 1968, **161**, 292–293.

Sharpless, S., and Jasper, H. H. Habituation of the arousal reaction. *Brain*, 1956, **79**, 655–680.

Shiffrin, R. M., and Schneider, W. Controlled and automatic human information processing: II. Perceptual learning, automatic attending, and a general theory. *Psychological Review*, 1977, **84**, 127–190.

Siddle, D. A. T. Vigilance decrement and speed of habituation of the GSR component of the orienting response. *British Journal of Psychology*, 1972, **63**, 191–194.

Smith, R. P., Warm, J. S., and Alluisi, E. A. Effects of temporal uncertainty on watchkeeping performance. *Perception and Psychophysics*, 1966, **1**, 293–299.

Swets, J. A. Signal detection theory applied to vigilance. In R. R. Mackie (Ed.), *Vigilance: theory, operational performance and physiological correlates*. New York: Plenum, 1977, pp.705–718.

Treisman, A. M. Strategies and models of selective attention. *Psychological Review*, 1969, **76**, 282–299.

Warm, J. S., Epps, B. E., and Ferguson, R. P. Effects of knowledge of results and signal regularity on vigilance performance. *Bulletin of the Psychonomic Society*, 1974, **4**, 272–274.

Wilkinson, R. T. The effect of lack of sleep on visual watchkeeping. *Quarterly Journal of Experimental Psychology*, 1960, **12**, 36–40.

Wilkinson, R. T. Interaction of noise with knowledge of results and sleep deprivation. *Journal of Experimental Psychology*, 1963, **66**, 332–337.

Wilkinson, R. T. Some factors influencing the effect of environmental stressors upon performance. *Psychological Bulletin*, 1969, **72**, 260–272.

Wilkinson, R. T., Morlock, H. C., and Williams, H. L. Evoked cortical response during vigilance. *Psychonomic Science*, 1966, **4**, 221–222.

Williams, H. L., Lubin, A., and Goodnow, J. J. Impaired performance with acute sleep loss. *Psychological Monographs*, 1959, **73**, (whole no. 484).

Williges, R. C. Within-session criterion changes compared to an ideal observer criterion in a visual monitoring task. *Journal of Experimental Psychology*, 1969, **81**, 61–66.

Williges, R. C. The vigilance increment: an ideal observer hypothesis. In T. B. Sheridan and G. Johannsen (Eds), *Monitoring behavior and supervisory control*. New York: Plenum Press, 1976, pp.181–192.

Wörden, F. Attention and auditory physiology. In E. Stellar and J. M. Sprague (Eds), *Progress in physiological psychology*. New York: Academic Press, 1966, p.145.

Sustained Attention in Human Performance
Edited by J. S. Warm
© 1984 John Wiley & Sons Ltd.

Chapter 7

Vigilance and Inspection

Earl L. Wiener

INTRODUCTION

In March 1979 an obscure three-mile stretch of land in an obscure river in Pennsylvania suddenly became the world's best-known island. Preliminary investigation indicates that the accident was due to operator error, compounded by poor decision making. Vigilance researchers may take some satisfaction that a report on nuclear plant inspection was entitled, *Looking but not seeing* (Tye, 1979). Two months later the entire world-wide fleet of 250 DC-10 aircraft was grounded due to post-accident inspections of wing engine mountings that revealed dangerous cracks. It is ironic that the tragic crash of the American Airlines DC-10 in Chicago in May 1979 was the result of such cracks that not only went undetected, but were actually induced by the maintenance and inspection process (NTSB, 1979). That was not the first time that airline accidents have been caused by oversights by human inspectors. For example, the crash of a Lake Central CV-340 was blamed on the failure of manufacturing quality control to detect a missing process (Anon., 1968).

For those who study or investigate accidents, or other man–machine failures, the story never seems to change very much. The accident reports, the eye-witness accounts, the stories of survivors, and victims, are replete with language we have heard before: 'I never saw it'; 'The flight crew failed to exercise proper vigilance'; 'The operator overlooked instrument indications that would have prevented . . .'; 'The inspector should have recognized . . .'. And so it goes, with a remarkable sameness, whether one is dealing with aircraft or automobiles, faulty goods, the performance of medical practitioners, military lookouts, radar controllers, security guards or industrial inspectors. Our mechanized society relies heavily on the human's imperfect ability to gather information from displays, and make a decision as to whether this information indicates a normal or abnormal condition. Furthermore, the cost of failure is ever increasing, as a consequence of such diverse causes as: (1) concentration of energy sources; (2) concentration of population, in living and working habitats, and in passenger vehicles; (3) enormous dollar judgements in civil torts; (4) extremely high capital costs for equipment.

In this chapter we shall attempt to examine in some detail the nature of the task of the monitor and inspector in the real world, and ask whether or not the vast vigilance literature offers any solutions. This discussion must deal with the embarrassing reality that there may be grave differences between those tasks which occupy monitors and inspectors in the work-a-day world, and those which greet subjects in the laboratory. Such questions are difficult enough when they come from outsiders, but now vigilance researchers must confront defectors from their own ranks. The more polite are asking embarrassing questions, while the less restrained are engaged in wholesale denunciations of the entire field. Some have even dared to question the existence of a vigilance decrement (drop in performance over a watch period) in real-world applications, the one significant effect we could almost always count on in laboratory experiments.

Scope of this chapter

This chapter will discuss essentially three areas of vigilant behavior. First, and in the greatest detail, inspection of individual items for the purpose of removing or classifying those which are defective. This includes mostly manufactured (or agricultural) goods, but to a lesser degree other inspection-like tasks such as reading of diagnostic X-rays. This will be contrasted with monitoring of an on-going process, such as a power plant, a patient in an intensive care unit, a radar air traffic control center or a battlefield. Here the monitor is stationary, maintaining a watch over a time-varying system. The systems are usually automatically controlled—the monitor is not concerned with moment-to-moment manipulations or decisions, but remains as a watchkeeper over the displays, on guard against indications of abnormal conditions. There are many similarities and differences between this activity and industrial inspection, but one important difference should be stressed: process control must be conducted in real time, whereas inspection can either exist in real time as items are manufactured, or can be 'batch processed', with the items held in storage, after fabrication, prior to inspection. Finally, the discussion will turn to a special case of monitoring: vehicular control, wherein the monitor is also in motion within his vehicle. He must now monitor two classes of display (1) those inside the vehicle which indicate its internal status, as well as its relation with the outside world; (2) a direct display of the outside world.

INSPECTION

Overview

Let us begin with an iron rule of production: goods that are produced by whatever process are imperfect, and vary considerably among themselves. This may be due to random or non-random variations in the incoming materials, the processing machinery, the environment or, most important, the human operators. Since there is variation, some of the materials will deviate sufficiently from standards and specifications to be out of limits, and must be 'rejected'. A variety of actions are now available to dispose of the rejected goods, as depicted in Figure 7.1. They may be scrapped, or sold as 'seconds' for a lower price (known generally as 'Class B sales'), or brought up to standard (rectified) on the spot by the inspector, or returned to production for rectification. The important point for this chapter is that the human inspector is the ultimate filter of defective goods. While numerous 'automatic' devices are available for inspection, and do certain jobs such as weighing and measuring with near-perfect accuracy, most inspection of finished goods requires the remarkable, and so far irreplaceable, perceptual ability of the human. Most defects are so ill-defined, so subtle, and so often embedded in complex backgrounds, that there is no man-made device with the perceptual ability to recognize the defects and pass judgement on the acceptability of the items. In many applications inspectors must consider not only 'obvious' defects such as cracks, pinholes and broken connections, but very subtle distinctions such as the appearance of painted surfaces, fabrics (such as carpets), or other items that might be rejected because they 'just don't look right'. Thomas (1962) provides an interesting illustration— an inspection line where a female inspector *listened* to each vacuum cleaner as a final check. Those sounding wrong were sent back for rework. This is a rare example of 'auditory inspection'. A sound-level meter had been tried for this task and was found to be insensitive to the defects.

Furthermore, there is an important economic consideration: the human inspector may be able to spot a defect and eliminate or rectify it early in the manufacturing process. To do so later, by electronic inspection, may be far more costly. For example, the human inspector may visually detect a defective connection in a printed circuit board early in its manufacture. An electronic inspection may not be feasible until after the defective board has been installed as a component in a piece of instrumentation, causing the entire assembly to be rejected.

A primer on quality control

This section will serve as an introduction to statistical quality control (SQC), to prepare the reader to consider the problems of the human inspector. Notation is summarized in Table 7.1. Those already familiar with the subject can easily skip this section. Those who might wish a more detailed introduction can find it in many texts on the subject, such as Duncan (1965) or Besterfield (1979). This introduction will deal only with 'attribute' inspection, where goods are classified usually accept/reject based on the presence or absence of specified attributes such as cracks, holes, off-coloration, surface blemishes, improper shape, etc. We shall not be concerned here with measurement of continuous variables such as size, weight or electrical conductivity, as this can often be relegated to automatic devices.

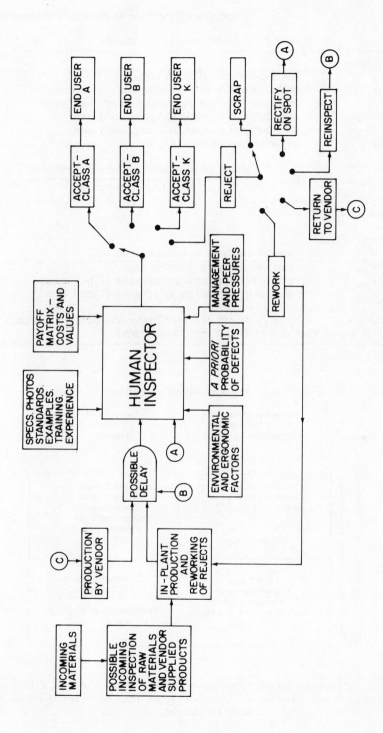

Figure 7.1 Production, inspection and disposition of items with K acceptance categories (classifications) and one rejection category. Upon rejection, numerous courses of action are available.

Table 7.1 . Notations used in this chapter

Probabilities

p'	fraction defective (fault or signal density)
p_1	probability of Type 1 error (rejecting good item)
p_2	probability of Type 2 error (accepting faulty item)
$1 - p_1$	probability of correctly accepting good item
$1 - p_2$	probability of correctly rejecting faulty item
p'_a	apparent fraction defective, i.e.

$$p'_a = \frac{\text{no. of items rejected (defective + effective)}}{\text{no. of items inspected}}$$

Assume $p' < < 1 - p'$

Costs and values

$V_{A\overline{D}}$	value of accepting an effective item
V_{RD}	value of rejecting a defective item
V_{AD}	value (cost) of accepting a defective (Type 2 error)
$V_{R\overline{D}}$	value (cost) of rejecting an effective (Type 1 error)

Assume $\mid V_{AD} \mid > \mid V_{R\overline{D}} \mid$; the cost of a Type 2 error (missed defect or signal) is usually greater than that of Type 1 error (false alarm)

STATE OF PRODUCT (SYSTEM)

	Effective (normal) (no critical signal) probability = $(1 - p')$	Defective (abnormal) (critical signal) Probability = p'
Accept (no response)	Correct acceptance (continue monitoring) Probability = $(1 - p') (1 - p_1)$ Value = $V_{A\overline{D}}$	Type 2 error (missed signal) Omissive error Consumer's risk Probability = $p' p_2$ Cost = V_{AD}
Reject (respond)	Type 1 error Commissive error Producer's risk Probability = $(1 - p') p_1$ Cost = $V_{R\overline{D}}$	Correction rejection (hit, detection) Probability = $p' (1 - p_2)$ Value = V_{RD}

INSPECTOR'S (MONITOR'S) RESPONSE

Figure 7.2 Terminology for the binary accept/reject decision. Note that Type 1 and Type 2 errors can refer to either decisions about single items or inferences about lots, based on samples.

A middle ground is known as 'go/no-go' testing, where an item is fitted to a gauge (or meter) and it either fits specifications or does not, and on that basis is either accepted or rejected. This bears a striking resemblance to the typical laboratory vigilance task, where the monitor observes a long sequence of stimuli that are within tolerance, interspersed with occasional stimuli that are outside of go/no-go limits. These are the 'signals' for which he watches.

In brief, SQC makes use of sampling, rather than 100% inspection, to characterize manufactured lots. Based on an inspected sample, inferences are made concerning the entire lot, which may be accepted or rejected. In attribute sampling, each item is classified as defective or effective, and if the number of defectives exceeds a critical value, the entire lot is rejected. In statistical terms, the null hypothesis of suitable quality is rejected. As always in statistical inference, the decision maker runs the risk of two types of error, rejecting a good lot (Type 1) or accepting a faulty lot (Type 2), as summarized in Figure 7.2. Each imposes its own cost penalties. Dodge and Romig (1929) referred to the Type 1 error as the 'producer's risk', as the manufacturer would be loath to scrap, reinspect or otherwise dispose of a good lot; the Type 2 error is considered the 'consumer's risk', as he would receive goods from a substandard lot, erroneously judged to be suitable. These terms are somewhat confusing, as realistically there are cost penalties accruing to both parties for both types of error. The aim of statistical quality control is to minimize the total of three costs: Type 1 errors, Type 2 errors, and sampling. The cost of Type 1 errors and sampling can readily be obtained or estimated by standard cost accounting methods. The cost of the consumer's risk is somewhat more subtle, as it contains not only accountable terms such as government penalties, warranty repairs and transportation, but also intangibles such as loss of good will, and perhaps defection of customers to a competitor.

The human inspector

This brings us back to the human inspector, for we must now answer the following question: why not perform 100% inspection and avoid sampling errors? The justification for statistical sampling is generally one or more of those listed below:

(1)   Inspection is expensive, and 100% inspection would increase one cost while removing two others, perhaps not economical in the long run. This would especially be true in producing large numbers of very inexpensive items which presumably do not produce critical failures when defective. For example, Penny *et al.* (1956) have demonstrated the use of attribute sampling of raw peanuts: 100% inspection of truckloads of peanuts would be unreasonable, to say the least.

(2)   The inspection is destructive, as for example life testing of electrical

components, environmental or drop testing, taste or chemical testing of food products.

(3) The inspector is fallible, and a better estimate of lot quality could be obtained from careful inspection of the sample than with 100% inspection. For a recent test of this, see Tsao *et al.* (1979).

It was the third reason that brought quality control engineers to at least consider the fact that the human inspector himself is capable of commissive and omissive errors (Juran, 1935). But they naively believed that inspector errors could be eliminated by sampling, and a folklore emerged around the professional inspector. He was seen as essentially perfect; at worst, he might miss about 10% of the defects, and make very few commissive errors. Studies to be cited later shatter this myth. Reliance on the putative perfect ability of the inspector is readily apparent in the sampling plans, for they contain a glaring deficiency: they assume that if a defect exists in the sample, it will be detected on inspection, and further, no false defects will be counted. Ample evidence indicates that inspectors make far more omissive than commissive errors, so one could conclude that in general, the defects in the sample have been historically undercounted, and thus the fraction defective of the lot underestimated, leading to far too many low quality lots being accepted (Type 2 errors). This means that more defective goods are shipped to the consumer than the sampling plans were designed to allow.

The recognition and solution of the problem awaited the post-war human factors movement, wherein a commerce finally developed between psychology and industrial engineering. Today the problem is well recognized, and sampling plans that include corrections for inspector error have emerged in the writings of Wallack and Adams (1970), Bennett (1975), Dorris (1977), Dorris and Foote (1978), and Drury (1978).

Inspector errors and costs

Whether the human operator inspects a sample or an entire lot, the principle remains the same: what he classifies as 'effective' will contain both effective and defective items (Type 2 errors), and likewise his classification of 'defectives' will contain a mixture of true defectives and some effectives (Type 1 errors), as depicted in Figure 7.3. There is a cost penalty attached to both types of error. In some processes the items are classified not simply accept/reject, but are graded into more than two quality classes. The highest quality items would bring the best price, lower quality classes may go to Class B sales, or may even be converted to other forms suitable for lower quality production, but always at a cost penalty to the producer. For example, agricultural products are graded, and priced according to the grade. The lowest quality may be scrapped, or sold for animal feed. Also, lower quality items may be processed, rather than sold as whole

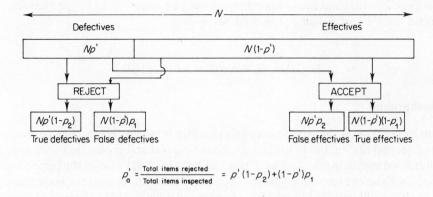

$$p_a' = \frac{\text{Total items rejected}}{\text{Total items inspected}} = p'(1-p_2)+(1-p')p_1$$

Figure 7.3 The accept/reject decision of N items with probabilities.

goods. For example, in Moder and Oswalt's (1959) study of peanut inspection, lots deemed to have greater than 7% fraction defective were considered inedible, but could be converted to peanut oil. In quality control parlance, the 7% figure is known as a 'lot tolerance per cent defective' (LTPD). As in the two-way classification, both types of error can be made, as displayed in Figure 7.4. The principal diagonal represents correct decisions, and off-diagonal entries are classification errors. The upper echelon would represent over-rating (analogous

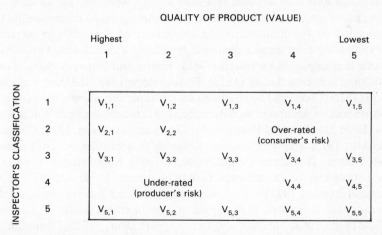

Figure. 7.4 Utility matrix for the K-state product with K response categories. Note that the first $K - 1$ classifications may be graded acceptances and the Kth (here fifth) may be the reject decision. Diagonal entries show the value of assigning product of quality level j correctly to category i; off-diagonal entries show the cost of misclassification of product of level j to category i. For $i < j$, product is over-rated; for $i > j$, product is under-rated.

to Type 2 errors) and the lower echelon would be under-rating (Type 1 errors), again with a cost penalty presumed for each.

VIGILANCE AND INSPECTION

Background

Juran (1935) was the first to recognize certain inspector errors, not so much in detection ability, but in his being subject to social and production pressures. Industrial psychologists such as Tiffin and Rogers (1941) studied the inspection task, with an eye toward developing personnel selection devices for inspectors, a problem still unsolved today (for a review, see Wiener, 1975). There was little, if any systematic research on the ability of the human inspector to perform his task. By the end of World War II, vigilance research was very much in vogue, and the early work of Mackworth, Broadbent and others in Great Britain had spread to the USA.

The vigilance research was mainly concerned with real time processes, as described in the previous section, with only a glancing recognition of industrial inspection as a vigilance task. Mackworth (1956) probably was the first to view inspection in vigilance terms. The confluence of the two fields appeared in the work of Colquhoun (1957, 1959, 1960, 1964) more than that of any other person. At about the same time McKenzie (1958) published an outstanding paper on how the social and interpersonal relations affect inspectors' performance. In the USA, major contributions in experimental approaches to the inspection task were impelled by the miniaturization movement of the 1960s in electronic circuitry, creating even greater demands for highly accurate visual inspection. This work is exemplified by Harris (1966), Harris and Chaney (1969), Teel *et al.* (1968) and Schoonard *et al.* (1973). The development of the theory of signal detection (TSD) (Green and Swets, 1966) stirred numerous investigators to collect data on inspection accuracy, to determine if this model applied (Wallack and Adams, 1969; Sheehan and Drury, 1971; Drury and Addison, 1973; Chapman and Sinclair, 1975; and many more). Research in schedules of reinforcement motivated others (Badalamente and Ayoub, 1969). Some studies were fairly faithful simulations of an industrial task (Colquhoun, 1959; Teel *et al.*, 1968; Williges and Streeter, 1971). Others were conducted in industrial settings, using regular industrial inspectors, under actual or experimental conditions (Jamieson, 1966; Teel *et al.*, 1968; Sheehan and Drury, 1971; Drury, 1975; Chapman and Sinclair, 1975; Zunzanyika and Drury, 1975; Sprague *et al.* 1976).

The literature contains relatively few studies of actual shop floor inspection, due to the difficulty of collecting data of this type, particularly data on missed defects (Fox and Haslegrave, 1969; Drury and Addison, 1973; Moraal, 1975). Moraal discusses the familiar problem of the tradeoff of experimental flexibility with fidelity of conditions, as one considers real world versus laboratory experimentation.

Finally, we note that a marriage of a sort took place between the laboratory world and the industrial world at the International Symposium on Human Factors in Quality Control at Buffalo in 1974. The papers from this meeting (Drury and Fox, 1975a) are a mixture of statistical theory and models, experimental studies of inspector accuracy and industrial examples. It remains to be seen whether the Buffalo symposium will spark the kind of shop floor research that is so badly needed.

Vigilance tasks

Vigilance tasks are defined elsewhere in this volume as well as in the works of numerous authors (Kibler, 1965; Teichner, 1974; Parasuraman and Davies, 1977; Warm, 1977), but in order to explore the similarities and differences between typical vigilance tasks and inspection, and their differing perceptual demands, it is necessary to further examine the nature of the task.

In the typical vigilance experiment, the subject attends to one (usually visual) display, which presents a stream of regularly paced, identical stimuli. At random intervals, unpredictable by the monitor, a palpably different stimulus is presented, and this is the 'signal' for which the monitor watches. He must then respond within an arbitrary time, which Wiener (1975) referred to as the 'fertile period'. Responses not within a fertile period are scored as false alarms (commissive errors). Just how different the signal is from the non-signal is a matter of psychophysical scaling, usually the result of trial-and-error pilot runs. Generally the signal is different from the non-signal in only one aspect— it is longer, shorter, brighter, louder, of higher frequency, slightly different in shape or orientation. The subject is usually required to make successive, single-stimulus judgements, comparing each stimulus event to his stored image of non-signal and signal. In a few experiments, subjects are able to make comparison judgements, observing two or more stimuli simultaneously (Parasuraman, 1979).

In the blank display task, the display is essentially blank until a stimulus event appears. The monitor awaits the appearance of a stimulus of sufficient strength to make him believe a signal is present. A rough analogy would be a radar scope that is blank until a target appears. Of course, anyone who has seen a radar scope is well aware that it is never blank, for even in the absence of signals (returns) it contains noise, false returns, ground clutter and other stimuli. One further problem emerges in the use of the blank scope display: since there are no discrete non-signal events, there is no adequate way to define the false alarm rate. TSD would despair.

Yet a third type of monitoring task bears a resemblance to a hypothesis testing model. This could be called inferential monitoring. The task of the monitor here is one of collecting data from his display, the values being regarded as a sequential sample from a population of known parameters. The monitor, like the quality control engineer, essentially entertains a rolling null hypothesis that the parameters have not changed. At any time he believes that one or more parameters have shifted, he responds (rejects the null hypothesis). This type of task is highly analogous not only to SQC, but to various forms of process control, where trouble is reflected not in a single value, but in an apparent shift, or drift in a population mean (Howland and Wiener, 1963). The inferential monitor can make the usual Type 1 or Type 2 errors. Inferential tasks were first studied by Howland (1958), but have not received the attention that their practical importance deserves. Recently, inferential monitoring has enjoyed a recrudescence among systems analysts concerned with man's ability to detect subtle failures in automatic control systems (Curry and Gai, 1976; Sheridan and Johannsen, 1976).

Signal rate and fault density

The typical vigilance experimental session lasts about 1 hour, during which about 30–60 signals are presented. The experimenter is torn between scheduling frequent signals so as to provide ample data, and a very low signal rate which is more representative of the real world, at least as pertains to process monitoring (Craig and Colquhoun, 1975). Rare examples of lower than usual signal rates are found in Hartnett (1975) and, in the extreme, Warrick *et al.* (1965), who used secretaries actually working at their desks as monitors, receiving 48 signals over a 6-month period. Over this vigil the response time to the signal (a buzzer) decreased steadily. Now if we can further assume that typically the stimulus rate is about one per second in serial tasks, then the fault density (p') would be between 1/120 and 1/60.

This is quite realistic as it pertains to inspection, in fact it would represent relatively high quality production. On the other hand, when comparing experiments to continuous, real-time process monitoring, the studies seem seriously flawed by an unrealistically high signal rate, for in the real-time applications the rate of critical signal appearance would be virtually zero in an hour's vigil. Indeed, it may be virtually zero over a much longer period, for real world monitoring typically involves keeping watch for extremely rare events such as engine failures in aircraft, enemy attacks, nuclear power plant breakdowns, prison breaks, weapons in hand luggage, heart failures and security intrusions. For example, pilots are taught to check for a split-flap condition (asymmetric wing flaps) each time they lower or raise the flaps. It would be a rare pilot who ever sees a split flap in a lifetime of flying: p' is so close to zero as to be incalculable.

Multi-attribute defects

Few experimenters have examined monitoring for more than one type of signal and, where this was done, it was usually confined to two types (Craig and Colquhoun, 1977; Craig, 1979). Here inspection parts company with the vigilance experiment, for in the inspection of manufactured goods, the types of defects are diverse and numerous. Craig and Colquhoun (1975) find this the most serious criticism that could be leveled at the relevance of vigilance experiments. Examples of multi-attribute faults have been reported in the inspection literature, as summarized in Table 7.2.

Table 7.2 Number of types of defects in manufactured items

Author and date	Product	Number of types of defects possible
Chapman and Sinclair (1975)	Jam tarts	5 general types
	Chicken carcasses	Numerous types
Gillies (1975)	Glass sheets	32[†]
Rigby and Swain (1975)	'Complex devices'	41 categories
Moraal (1975)	Steel sheets	> 50[‡]
Fox and Haslegrave (1969)	Steel screws	Up to 6[§]
Sheehan and Drury (1971)	Metal parts	32
Zunzanyika and Drury (1975)	Semiconductors	14
Fox (1964)	Coins	4

[†] 20% of fault types accounted for 80% of the defects detected.
[‡] Nine of those accounted for 75% of defects detected.
[§] Photographs showing defects included in paper.

With this in mind, the perceptual demands of the detection task must be seen in a different light. Each item must be regarded as a potential host for possible defects—it may harbor more than one defect of a certain type, or defects of a variety of types. Flaws may vary also in magnitude (Geyer *et al.* 1979). Each defect type has its own probability distribution, though we will continue to define p' as the probability that an item is defective *per se* (contains at least one rejectable fault). The perceptual process now becomes one of scanning, or searching, for multiple defects occurring in multiple locations on each time. This search process has been modeled by Drury (1978), Spitz and Drury (1978) and Morawski *et al.* (1980) as time-bound search procedure. The inspector examines each item until he either (a) detects a rejectable flaw or (b) runs out of time allocated for the item and turns to the next item. Tsao *et al.* (1979) showed that in a self-paced task, subjects adopt a near-optimal policy of when to stop searching an item and proceed to the next one. Harris (1966) has shown experimentally that as the complexity of the item increases, probability of fault detection decreases in a linear manner, but Corcoran (1964) found no influence of target complexity on detections. Recently, Czaja and Drury (1981) have examined a neglected area, training for multi-attribute inspection, and Gallwey (1982) has found correlated performance on multi-attribute inspection with various prediction tests. Particularly promising is a test of embedded figures.

Inspection tasks

It is now necessary to examine the inspection task in greater detail, noting how it differs from the typical vigilance experiment. Readers who desire more detailed analysis of the inspection task can find it in Harris and Chaney's book (1969), Harris's summary paper (1969), various chapters in Drury and Fox (1975a), and papers by Colquhoun (1957), McKenzie (1958) and Fox (1964).

One way of classifying the task would be to divide it into static and dynamic inspection. In static inspection, the goods are in a fixed position. They may be delivered to the inspector in batches, or one at a time, or he may travel to the site of the product, especially if it is a large item such as a computer, aircraft or the like (see Jamieson, 1966, for an example). The inspector may or may not physically handle the item. The work is unpaced, except for the general pressure to keep up with production. There is another important perceptual feature of static inspection: comparison, rather than absolute judgements, may be possible. The advantage to inspectors, if any, has never been established experimentally, in fact, Brown and Monk (1975) have shown that non-targets, in the vicinity of targets, increased search time. Static inspection of a batch allows the operator to view them as a whole. Perhaps even their spatial patterning would be a visual enhancement; they may arrive, or the inspector may place them, in an orderly geometric pattern. Unfortunately, there is little research on this topic.

In dynamic inspection, the operator is stationary and the goods are transported, usually by some mechanical conveyence such as a belt or monorail, past his view. The inspector is usually on station in a serial flow line: the output from some stage of production becomes his input; and his output goes to the next stage, e.g. Fox's studies of coins that pass the inspector on a conveyor belt (Fox, 1964). In some cases, the manufactured goods are continuous, and pass the inspector in an unbroken flow: for example, carpets, rolled steel, rolled paper and sheet glass (see Gillies, 1975; Moraal, 1975). In these cases, one cannot think in the usual terms of accepting and rejecting items—the task of the inspector is usually to mark faulty *areas* of the product. These areas could be removed (rejected) if and when the product is cut into discrete lengths, or could result in an entire batch (roll) being rejected, or at least down-graded. The perceptual demand on the operator is rather different from that in inspection of individual items: the task is machine-paced in the extreme, and there exists only a weak analogy to the laboratory vigilance task. If continuous product inspection resembles any vigilance paradigm, it would have to be the 'blank display' task. The operator's frame of reference, with conforming product

Figure 7.5   First inspection and minor rectification of injection-molded tennis shoes. Shoes arrive from injection process on a conveyor belt, and are visually inspected. The inspector also 'cleans up' the shoe, removing threads and surplus PVC on the soles. Rejects are placed on the rack (left) and are sold *en masse* to a purchaser for Class B sales; he in turn grades them. Acceptable shoes next are delivered to a second inspector who can also do minor clean-up before packing. (Photo by author, courtesy of Suave Shoe Corp. of Miami.)

flowing by, could be thought of as a blank display—it remains blank until an area containing non-conforming material enters his view. As the defective portion passes, the display again 'goes blank'.

Paced tasks

The more typical inspection situation presents individual items on a conveyance, passing the viewing area of the inspector. Due to the variety of possibilities of arrangements of the goods, a general description of the perceptual demands is almost impossible. The goods could arrive scattered on a conveyor belt, in no particular pattern (see Fox, 1964; Lion *et al.* 1968), requiring the operator to scan items, located helter-skelter, as they pass by (see Figure 7.5). Eye movement patterns and scanning strategies have only recently been studied (see Bloomfield, 1975a,b; Buck, 1975; Noro, 1980). Alternatively, the goods could be either arranged in an orderly geometric pattern on the belt or arranged in 'frames'; for example, Chapman and Sinclair's (1975) inspectors viewed trays of jam tarts, arrayed in rows and columns. Lion *et al.* (1975) found higher detections when items on a conveyor belt passed the inspectors in three rows, rather than one row. In the three-row condition, the belt ran at one-third speed, so that the stimulus rate was the same for the two conditions. p' was 0.10 in their study. These tasks are roughly analogous to those vigilance experiments in which patterns of stimulus figures are displayed, and the subject required to pick out 'faulty' items (Colquhoun, 1959). Eskew and Richie (1982) found an interesting interaction between pacing and personality variables, in particular Rotter's 'Locus of Control'.

In the simplest dynamic task, items pass the inspector's viewing station one at a time (for example, microcircuit boards, glass bottles, TV tubes). An item appears, is scanned for defects, and passes as the next appears. This type of inspection has a stronger analogy to the perceptual activities of a vigilance task than any of the previous. If the goods are uniformly spaced on the conveyor, and the conveyor runs at uniform speed, there is an indisputable resemblance to the typical discrete-stimulus monitoring task. We have said nothing about any perceptual demands stemming from the fact that the target is in motion, but this question has been examined by Williams and Borow (1963), Fox (1964) and Buck (1975), and reviewed by Drury (1973). The critical feature of the dynamic task is probably not that the item is in motion, but that the task is line-paced.

In summary, the dynamic inspection task presents the following properties and problems:

(1)   It is machine-paced. The inspector has limited time to spend on each item, and if he does not reject it, then it is 'gone forever'.

(2)   The items are either rejected (that may mean tagged, or physically

removed from the conveyor), or they are accepted by default. Any lapse of attention on the part of the inspector would lead to 'accept' decisions.

(3) Since the time to inspect is limited, scanning strategies, eye movements and perceptual organization of the task are critically important, though not well researched as yet.

(4) If time versus accuracy relationships can be established (see Fox, 1964; Smith and Barany, 1970; Purswell *et al.*, 1972; Drury, 1973, 1978; Astley and Fox, 1975; Gillies, 1975; Megaw, 1979; Geyer and Perry, 1982), then management must make an economic decision that trades off inspection time (and labor costs) against the cost of Type 1 and Type 2 errors. In one study (Chapman and Sinclair, 1975), the authors advised doubling the number of inspectors as the only way to obtain adequate inspection. We are not told how management greeted the suggestion. On the other hand, Astley and Fox (1975) were able to reduce the number of inspectors needed by 25%. Lion *et al.* (1975) showed that two inspectors working in unison, face-to-face across a conveyor belt, have higher detection rates and fewer Type 1 errors than a single inspector, with equal per-inspector stimulus rates.

Probability of signals

One of the most pervasive findings of vigilance experiments is that the probability of detecting a signal varies directly with the probability of the signal (Jenkins, 1958; Colquhoun, 1961; McGrath and Harabedian, 1963; Wiener, 1963; Baddeley and Colquhoun, 1969). If this holds true in industrial inspection, not only have we established a link between experimental and shop floor results, but have established, as well, an important practical conclusion: the higher the quality of production, the more difficult to detect the rare, faulty items.

It is impossible to characterize a typical defect rate in production, since there is such extreme variation in the nature of the product, the quality of production standards, and the specifications (based on consumer needs) that define a defect. Studies of actual production find p' ranging from 0.01% (Rigby and Swain, 1975) for atomic weapon components, through 0.2% for coins (Fox, 1964) and 4% for certain defects in jam tarts (Chapman and Sinclair, 1975), to McCornack's report (1961) that he observed control charts on shop floors indicating p' values from 5% to 40%. Chapman and Sinclair further report that a certain type of defect occurred only about three times in one million tarts. Values of 1–10% might be thought of as typical in most production. As noted earlier, when discussing discrete-stimulus vigilance tasks, the typical schedules are programmed with fault densities in the neighborhood of 1–2%. Since this is fairly typical of quality production, so we have no problem going from experimental to industrial values of p'.

Several studies have verified the probability effect using inspection-like tasks.

Harris (1968) employed naive subjects (students) to inspect printed sheets for defective patterns, with $p' = 0.25, 1, 4$ and 16%. As p' increased, detections $(1 - p_2)$ increased, and false reports (p_1) decreased. Fox and Haslegrave (1969) performed three experiments in inspection of metal screws. In the first, which was machine-paced, there was no significant difference in detections as p' ranged from 0.5% to 5%. In the two experiments using batch (unpaced) inspection, detections increased with increasing values of p'. There is no clear explanation as to why the probability effect did not hold in the machine-paced task. The probability effect was also found by Drury and Addison's (1973) study of on-line inspectors.

In conclusion, it seems a safe bet that further shop floor research will confirm the probability effect. In one extreme, the three-in-a-million defect reported by Chapman and Sinclair, it is doubtful if such defect would ever be detected, though we are not told its psychophysical properties. It could be a rare, but highly conspicuous defect. In the other extreme, the 40% defect rate observed by McCornack, management might well direct its attention not to inspection, but to production, heeding the old quality control maxim that states, 'quality should be produced into an item, not inspected into it'.

Inspector accuracy

Accuracy of inspection is, of course, the heart of this discussion. Here we cannot hope to review the entire field and all of the factors affecting the inspectors' accuracy, but can only present some data and touch lightly on some of the important aspects of the problem. The reader is referred to excellent works by Jacobson (1952), McKenzie (1958), McCornack (1961), Sinclair (1979), and case studies in Drury and Fox (1975a).

Let us first examine Jacobson's extensive data. In his experiment, 39 industrial operators each inspected 1000 solder connections into which 20 defects had been inserted ($p' = 0.2\%$). The data are shown in Table 7.3. This array indicates that the inspectors caught about 83% of the faults, while making a trivial number of Type 1 errors. The apparent detection rate $p'_a = 0.0172$. In order to compare these results to modern studies, we have computed TSD measures: $d' = 4.25$, and $\beta = 55.00$. The detection rate $(1 - p_2)$ is typical of both

Table 7.3   Jacobson's data on 39 000 inspections (Jacobson, 1952)

Inspector's action	Product					
	Defective		Effective		Total	
Accept	134	(0.0034)	38 195	(0.9793)	38 329	(0.9828)
Reject	646	(0.0166)	25	(0.0006)	671	(0.0172)
Total	780	(0.0200)	38 220	(0.9800)	39 000	(1.0)

inspection and vigilance studies. The low value of p_1 is not even that rare—actually we do not know how rare in vigilance studies, since so few authors even bother to report it. Another example is provided by Schoonard *et al.* (1973) on visual inspection by professionals of integrated circuit chips with $p' = 0.18$. Computation by this reviewer yields $d' = 2.8$, $\beta = 6$.

Additional examples of inspector error rates can be found in McCornack (1961), conveniently tabled. McCornack also develops four measures of inspector accuracy. His A_3 measure is simply percentage of defects rejected $(1 - p_2)$, ranging from a low of about 0.30 to a high of 0.91. Most of the values lie in the 0.60–0.80 range. Numerous other studies confirm these figures. For example, Chaney and Teel (1967) report values between 0.30 and 0.50 for experienced inspectors examining machined parts, Sheehan and Drury (1971) found 0.57–0.85 in their experiment on metal hooks, and Teel *et al.* (1968) report very low detection rates, Fox (1964) found rates of 55%. Harris and Chaney (1969, Chap. 1) suggest that detection rates of 0.50–0.60 are commonplace for experienced electronic inspectors, and Jamieson (1966) found rates of 0.42–0.70 for telephone equipment inspectors. Rigby and Swain (1975) speak of 0.30–0.90. So much for the myth of the near-perfect industrial inspector!

Payoff matrices and decision criteria

So far we have not discussed the role of the subjects' perceived costs of errors. Evidence on the ability of instructions and payoff matrices to influence the rate of Type 1 and Type 2 errors is contradictory. The previous discussion of balancing the values of errors and correct decisions implied that management could set a reject criterion according to an economic model that would minimize total costs. Numerous experimenters have investigated how sensitive the human operator is to changes in the payoff matrix. Much of the research has been encouraged by TSD, which holds that changes in payoffs should move the operators' decision criterion along iso-d' contours, the particular contour determined by the discriminative properties of the task. The results are complex, and defy a simple review. Levine (1966), Wallack and Adams (1968), Smith and Barany (1970) and Williges (1971, 1973) have found some success in manipulating criterion levels, but Levine reported that only costs, not rewards, affected performance. Smith (1975) found slight differences in criteria based on two sets of instructions. Recent discussion of TSD's contribution to vigilance can be found in Chapter 2 of this book and in Swets (1977).

Social and economic pressures

The industrial inspector does not perform his duties in a social or economic vacuum. While his decisions, in theory, are based strictly on the products and standards, it would be foolish to overlook the pressures upon him and their effect on his decision (Sheehan and Drury, 1971). What are the effects of these pressures? Generally they push him toward leniency in his inspection — to pass doubtful goods, and therefore to commit more Type 2 errors. The sources of these pressures are fellow workers, who sometimes bear the burden of management opprobium and even wage or time penalties for rejected items, and the sales department, eager to fill customers' needs on schedule. The only countervailing pressure is from quality control and production supervisors, who are eager to ship high quality items. Regrettably, the function of the inspector and the importance of that function to the welfare of the firm and its employees, not to mention the customers, is vague. The consequences of shipping poor quality goods are far less immediate than the consequences of the rejection decision.

This was first recognized by Juran (1935), who named two common inspector biases 'censorship' and 'flinching'. Censorship refers to excluding unacceptable findings. Juran showed that an inordinate number of samples (far greater than statistical models would predict) contained exactly the maximum allowable number of defects. Flinching means accepting items that are only slightly defective — but still, by strict definition, defective. Belbin (1957), McKenzie (1958), Thomas and Seabourne (1961) and Rigby and Swain (1975) have also written extensively on the social environment of inspection, and Bergum and Lehr (1963) and others (reviewed in Wiener, 1975) have shown the effect of direct supervision of monitors by authority figures. Furthermore, as Juran observed, the inspector quickly learns that in addition to creating problems with fellow workers, rejecting items simply makes trouble for himself. Rejected items generate paperwork and aggravation; accepting a lot is no trouble at all. Swets (1977) has also pointed out that when an inspector rejects an item, he lays himself open to being proven wrong. The rejects may be reinspected and found to be conforming. On the other hand, his Type 2 errors cause him little trouble — they become problems for the customer and the reputation of the firm, but are seldom traced back to the inspector. The same may be said for the process monitor: he creates trouble for himself by sounding an alarm which might soon be proven to be false. This may be embarrassing, or could even result in managerial sanctions. The reader may recall the scene in the popular film *The Caine Mutiny*, when the green junior officer sounds the alert for Japanese planes. The seasoned captain takes one look and sourly remarks, 'Mr Keith, those Japanese planes are seagulls'. If reinforcement theory tells us anything, Ensign Keith's criterion for response was no doubt pushed upward, as his personal Type 1 error costs increased. What about his utility for a missed signal? It would seem very large — one is tempted to say infinite, since his life was at stake. Practical experience seems to dispute this, for, like the industrial inspector who can seldom be blamed directly for a missed fault, the process monitor may place surprisingly low utility on missed signals. The consequences, though large, may appear remote, compared to the obvious and immediate consequences of commissive errors.

The Smith and Barany model (1970) also includes the personal utility (cost) to the inspector of the effort of inspecting, a factor considered in vigilance by Jerison and Pickett (1963). In these models, the expected value of inspecting (observing) must exceed the cost of observing, or the display will go unattended

By contrast, in medical decision making, the values in the payoff matrix may be reversed. The diagnostician places an extremely high value on misses, partly out of concern for the welfare of the patient, partly due to his own vulnerability to civil liability in the event that he overlooks a pathological state. The cost of a Type 1 error is relatively modest, at least to the diagnostician: more tests for the patient, more consultations, higher hospitalization costs and, in the extreme, perhaps unnecessary therapeutic procedures. The physician is seldom at risk due to an initial Type 1 error — he has ample opportunity to reinspect, to gather corroborating information, or to try other diagnostic procedures before committing the patient to a costly, dangerous or painful course of treatment. At any time during the diagnostic chain of events that he finds that the patient is actually not in a pathological state, he need only admit to being very 'cautious' at first, and the patient is only too happy. Type 1 errors, unless someone is rushed into unnecessary surgery, seldom leads a patient to his attorney's office. Likewise, Colquhoun (1964) cautions that if management pays an inspector by the defect detected (with presumably no penalty for Type 1 errors), they should expect p_1 to increase, as the inspector sets a lax criterion for rejection. For a discussion of operator characteristics in medical diagnosis, see Lusted (1968).

Feedforward and feedback

The expectancy theory of vigilance, proposed by Deese (1955) and Baker (1963), and tested extensively by Colquhoun (Colquhoun, 1961; Colquhoun and Baddeley, 1964, 1967; Craig and Colquhoun, 1977) holds that, with experience, the monitor forms an expectation about the stochastic structure of the signal schedule. The theory does not explain just how he is able to estimate p' without knowledge of results, if his Type 1 errors are responses to what he genuinely perceived as signals. Numerous authors (reviewed by Wiener, 1968; Warm, 1977) have shown beneficial effects of knowledge of results (KR) and, furthermore, the benefits have been shown to transfer to later sessions when KR has been removed (Wiener, 1963; Wiener and Attwood, 1968; Attwood and Wiener, 1969). There are, to be sure, rare examples where KR did not influence detection behavior (Montague and Webber, 1975; Murrell, 1975).

The question is whether these findings can be applied to industrial inspection. The evidence is scanty. In feedforward (FF), inspectors would be informed about established (or presumed) levels of p', which may be fairly stable in some production, or vary considerably in others, where the quality of raw materials may not be consistent, or labor forces may be in flux. In the food industry, product quality varies widely over time as a result of seasons and weather.

In most studies which report FF as an experimental variable, it is confounded with other techniques. The reader is unable to assess its individual effectiveness, and will have to be content to say that a 'package' of management techniques which included FF was beneficial. Drury and Sheehan (1969) and Zunzanyika and Drury (1975) report improvements in inspection accuracy when p' is fed forward to inspectors. Sheehan and Drury (1971) report reducing p_2 from 17% to 7.5% with FF, which consisted solely of informing the inspectors which of 32 possible defects would possibly appear in the sample. This differs considerably from FF in the usual sense of relating the fault density—it completely altered the perceptual nature of the task, and in Warm's terminology (1977), reduced to zero uncertainty about the nature of the critical signal. As Murrell (1965, p.425) has pointed out, an inspector builds up 'norms' about multiple faults. If the number of faults is large, he may actually limit the ones he looks for.

In other experiments, Hayes (1950) has shown that inspectors who believe a lot to be good will tend to pass many more defects than from identical lots that they believe to be of poor quality. One might be tempted to recommend that inspectors be given unrealistically low estimates of product quality in order to avoid this effect. This may succeed in the short term, but would no doubt rebound as inspectors form their own, more realistic, estimates of fault density, and as Colquhoun's work suggests, readjust their responding behaviour. In summary, there is an indication, but certainly not a well documented case, favoring the feedforward of fault density information. Experiments in this area are badly needed especially when p' varies considerably from lot to lot, as in the food industry, since there is evidence that operators have difficulty adjusting to changing values of p' (Embrey, 1975; Vickers *et al.*, 1977).

Implementing feedback

In vigilance experiments, where the task was essentially open-loop, the experimenter might provide KR orally (Mackworth, 1950), with lights (Wiener, 1963) or with computer-generated verbal messages (Wiener, 1974). On the shop floor, a wide variety of feedback (FB) techniques are available, including management-supplied information fed back to the inspector, or information inherent in the work arrangement, where production workers receive rejected goods, make the necessary corrections, and pass the reworked items to the inspector (see Figures 7.6 and 7.7). This would provide him with KR, albeit delayed, on the correctness of his reject decisions. What would be absent is feedback on missed defects. Unless there are additional inspectors in series (Thomas, 1962), or unless the next station in the process (e.g. assembly, packing) can return rejectable items to the inspector (Chapman and Sinclair, 1975; Sprague *et al.*, 1976), there is little opportunity for detection and FB of Type 2 errors.

The experimental evidence, while generally favoring FB, is not in good array.

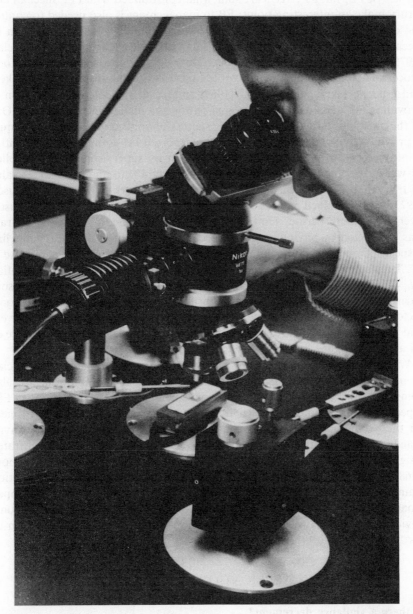

Figure 7.6 Microinspection of incoming LSI circuits before they are assembled on printed circuit boards. This inspection is an accept/rejection decision—rejects are returned to the vendor, who scraps them. (Courtesy of Racal-Milgo, Inc. of Miami.)

Sheehan and Drury (1971) and Zunzankiya and Drury (1975) both recommend the use of FB, but its effects are somewhat confounded with FF. Sheehan and Drury make an interesting point: FB to management is also needed to control the quality of inspectors, so that those with deviant p_1 and p_2 rates can be 'recalibrated' (see also Thomas and Seaborne, 1961). Chapman and Sinclair (1975) provide an example of FB, a production–inspection serial line in food processing, where missed defectives are returned to the inspector by packers and graders. Harris and Chaney (1969) emphasize the role of supervision in providing FB, and link it to group goal-setting as a management technique. One of the most interesting and apparently successful applications of FB techniques is provided by Sprague *et al.* (1976) who reported FB combined with positive reinforcement (praise and displays of interest by supervisors) in a controlled 15-week experiment, brought p' down from over 4% to under the target value of 1%. Another strong case for FB comes from the work of Drury and Addison (1973), who examined records of performance of inspectors in the glass industry over a 10 month period. During 12 weeks of this time, a rapid FB program was conducted by having special inspectors go over the work of regular line inspectors, and give immediate FB. This resulted in a considerable increase in d'. The authors caution, however, that the FB represented not only information by which the inspectors could recalibrate, but a change in supervisory environment, which could also be responsible. This could be due to motivational factors (the familiar 'Hawthorne effect'), or to what Fraser (1950) first observed, and Bergum and Lehr (1963) and others later confirmed: the mere presence of an authority figure increased detections.

We tentatively conclude that FB to the inspector would probably be beneficial, from the point of view of motivation, learning and recalibration; see also comments by Megaw (1979). The management and implementation of FB, especially regarding missed defectives, is not as inexpensive or easy to instrument on the production line as in vigilance laboratories. Nevertheless, we invite management's attention to those vigilance experiments that have demonstrated a significant training effect (Annett, 1966; Wiener, 1967; Wiener and Attwood, 1968; Colquhoun and Edwards, 1970). There seems little reason why inspection training devices, with automatic feedback provision, could not be developed along the lines of Attwood and Wiener's (1969) automated vigilance instructional device, or Warner and Budkin's (1968) 'Link trainer' for self-instruction of cardiologists in pattern recognition.

PROBLEMS IN APPLICATION OF VIGILANCE FINDINGS

Is there a vigilance decrement?

From the early work of Mackworth to the present, almost all simple monitoring experiments have shown a drop in detection performance (increase in p_2) over

Figure 7.7 Inspectors perform a visual check of small transformers, followed by a meter check for electrical characteristics. If the item is accepted, it is stamped with the inspector's number; if not, it is tagged and returned to production. Inspectors are not allowed to rectify—in fact, no tools are permitted at the inspection station. (Courtesy of Racal-Milgo, Inc. of Miami.)

the length of the vigil. The explanations are various, and are discussed elsewhere in this volume. As Craig and Colquhoun (1977) have stated, no unique explanation for the cause of time decrements has yet been offered. Furthermore, vigilance decrement is by no means universal. Numerous experiments have shown no loss in performance over time, especially those involving complex tasks (Teichner, 1974), time-sharing requirements (Alluisi *et al.* 1977), and in some cases auditory monitoring. Some investigators have suggested that decrements have been masked by learning effects—that both are occurring simultaneously, counteracting each other (Beatty *et al.*, 1977).

However, beginning with Elliott (1960), a broader attack has been made on the applicability of vigilance findings to real world situations involving watchkeeping. Kibler (1965), Chapanis (1967), Smith and Lucaccini (1969) and Alluisi *et al.* (1977) have charged that vigilance decrements are not found in real world monitoring. Smith and Lucaccini seem willing to dismiss the relevance of vigilance experiments altogether.

The picture is not at all as clear as the critics would like their readers to believe. First, there are numerous cases of complex tasks that yield time decrements (e.g. Craig and Colquhoun, 1977; Riemersma *et al.*, 1977). Colquhoun *et al.* (1968) showed that as late as the 48th session of a lengthy experiment, time decrements appeared. We cannot resolve this issue by citing evidence pro and con: there are ample amounts of each (see Chapter 8 in this volume). Granted, we are lacking examples from real world applications that exhibit a true decrement, perhaps for good reasons that will be discussed shortly. More constructive would be to heed the call of Swets and Kristofferson (1970) to try to spell out the display characteristics of those tasks which do and do not produce a time decrement. Teichner's (1974) paper was movement in this direction, as was the task taxonomy proposed by Parasuraman and Davies (1977) (and in Chapter 2 in this volume).

Time decrements in inspection

It would seem instructive to turn to the world of industrial inspection for some answers about time decrements. The results are disappointing, mainly because so few authors have ever bothered to look. Indeed, the classic 1932 work of Wyatt and Langdon, which Smith and Lucaccini (1969) dismiss, is one of the few studies we can find where inspectors' performance is measured over a duty period. Another was Chapman and Sinclair (1975), who report an initial warm-up effect, which has also been found in the laboratory (Jerison and Wallis, 1957; Wiener, 1973), followed by a 'steady decrease' during the 1.5 hour vigil. The drop in detection rate is slight, about 10%. Many authors speak of time decrements in inspection: Drury and Fox (1975b) uncritically accept the existence of time decrements, and other authors also uncritically recommend rapid rotation of inspectors to avoid the (presumed) decrements (Belbin, 1957; Gillies, 1975; Rigby and Swain, 1975). Fox (1964) states that 15 minutes is the longest a coin inspector can work before efficiency drops. The reader cannot tell whether their recommendations were simply based on the experience and complaints of inspectors, which are certainly worthy of consideration, or on extrapolations from the vigilance literature.

Where do we stand on vigilance decrement in inspection? There is no satisfactory answer for a variety of reasons:

(1)   The appropriate study has yet to be done.
(2)   There is a widespread practice of rotating operators rapidly between inspection and other tasks during a work day. Vigilance decrements may not have appeared on the shop floor because they are already being effectively avoided.
(3)   Even when inspecting, the operators are usually performing secondary active tasks at the same time (e.g. materials handling, minor rectification, tagging defectives, paperwork and communication), all of which may allay time decrements, though perhaps at the cost of overall performance (see Figure 7.5).
(4)   The social and physical atmosphere is not as severe as one finds in vigilance experiments. Inspectors talk to other workers, have some

freedom of movement, and observe other activities in their environment. Vigilance researchers have learned by now exactly how to produce time decrements: by making the experimental environment as physically and socially confining as possible.

The literature simply does not indicate whether or not time decrements occur on the shop floor. If they do not occur, it may be because management and the worker have already discovered, with or without benefit of vigilance research, the very countermeasures that human factors practitioners would recommend. Whether time decrements exist in the real world will only be resolved by careful and costly experiments, whose design will tax the ingenuity of experimenters and the patience of production line supervisors. As such experiments appear in the literature, we will probably end up exactly where we are today: some will show time decrements, some will not.

OTHER APPLICATIONS

Driving

In driving an automobile or truck (or operating any other vehicle for that matter), the operator must serve as both an active process controller and a passive monitor of a system operating in real time. The driver must time-share, allocating his attention 'simultaneously' to various sub-tasks, including tracking (steering and maintaining a desired speed), decision making, navigation, adherence to regulations and warnings, tending environmental and mechanical systems (and entertainment systems) within the cab, and communicating, all the while maintaining a watch for various events that may occur inside or outside the vehicle. Like the pilot, he must keep watch over instrumentation within the car for extremely rare events, such as a low oil pressure indication.

The windshield of the car is also a display. This, incidentally, is exactly what military pilots are taught—that in instrument approaches, the cockpit window is merely one more 'instrument' to be brought into their scan. It would seem obvious that failures of vigilance play a large part in vehicle accidents (Harris, 1977), but even that remains to be proven. One would think that with the vast amount of research that has been directed toward road safety, that a body of knowledge about the driver-monitor would have emerged. Unfortunately, this does not seem to be the case. While much of the research has been imaginative and interesting, there is little known about the ability of the vehicle operator to detect 'signals' inside or outside the cab.

Some insights have come from experiments where subsidiary watchkeeping tasks have been included in the auto cab (or simulator). In these designs, the operator was required to perform the usual driving task in a roadway, test track or simulated roadway, and at the same time maintain watch over a display, usually some form of pilot light. Dobbins *et al.* (1961), Brown (1967), Laurell and Lisper (1976) and others have used such a design to study not vigilance *per se*, but as a measure of the 'spare capacity' of the driver under various levels of task-induced stress, for example, traffic density. Brown has reasoned that performance on the subsidiary task could be taken as a measure of the information processing capacity of the operator untapped by the primary task of driving, and thus could measure, indirectly, the primary task demands. In a review, Brown (1979) points out that very easy tasks, such as driving in low density traffic, may lead to low levels of arousal, with the following consequences:

(1) The driver may not be able to cope with an emergency when it occurs (see Loeb and Alluisi's discussion of the arousal theory of vigilance in Chapter 6 in this volume).

(2) The driver may be induced to engage in irrelevant activities to counteract the monotony of the task.

Brown wisely cautions against simply making the task easier, which has all too often been a goal of human factors scientists. McBain's (1970) laboratory study, using line truck drivers, lends insights into professional drivers' mechanisms for dealing with monotony. Boadle (1976) reports something of a novel twist: her subjects seemed to be using the subsidiary vigilance task to allay the boredom of simulator driving.

Several reports of on-the-road driving experiments appear in the collected papers of the NATO symposium on vigilance (Mackie, 1977). Most of these dealt with measurement (both behaviorally and physiologically) of fatigue effects. Several employed tasks or measures that are questionably vigilance studies. Riemersma *et al.* (1977) had subjects drive for over 8 hours with two secondary tasks to be attended. One was reporting when a counter reached multiples of 20, which could hardly be called a vigilance task, since the event was entirely predictable. However, the other task required monitoring a display for changes in color of a light. The authors reported that, over the driving period, the missed signal rate (p_2) increased, with no change in p_1. There were mixed outcomes on reaction time to a subsidiary monitoring task during a 3.5 hour drive. There was a greater increase under silent control conditions than when music or voice programs were played in the car. Harris provides an interesting discussion on fatigue and truck accidents, but fails to make more than the 'obvious' case for the importance of vigilance. Mackie and O'Hanlon's study of heat stress in drivers included a secondary monitoring task, and found performance inversely related to measures of driver performance. The authors do not provide information on missed signals, if any, or performance over time. Finally, this reviewer takes exception to O'Hanlon and Kelley's reasoning that lane drift frequency is a measure of driver vigilance. To argue this is to regard any performance error as a failure of vigilance. Maintenance of lateral position of a vehicle within a lane is clearly a tracking task — the lane markers are not improbable, unpredictable events occurring during a vigil. If the term vigilance is to mean anything at all, then experimenters must resist the temptation to redefine any task in vigilance terms.

Some studies have stretched the vigilance–driving connection in the other direction, by taking what might be a perfectly respectable laboratory vigilance task and likening it to driving. For example, Baker and Theologus (1972) employed a task wherein subjects monitored two horizontally-separated red lights — a change in distance between them was the critical signal. The authors claim that this task is analogous to following another car at night, watching for changes in distance. It may well be, but it is doubtful whether this type of analogy will help much in understanding the role of vigilance in traffic safety. Others may have stretched a point by labeling as 'driving' tasks those that bear no resemblance to the actual perceptual activities of driving a vehicle. Mast and Heimstra (1964, and later works) required subjects to detect a light signal while 'driving'. Driving consisted of a penny arcade type task of controlling a model car over a winding road, at best a pursuit tracking task where the controlled cursor was a model car, an 'outside-in' display to say the least.

In conclusion, the diverse experiments on driving and vigilance do not answer the important questions. Weighing the evidence from the on-the-road studies, it certainly appears that a time decrement occurs. Whether this is the vigilance decrement in the usual sense, or is due to the vaguely defined term 'driver fatigue', cannot be answered at this time. Perhaps there is no difference. The critics of 'real world relevance' may well point out that the vigilance tasks were all synthetic, superimposed on the driving environment. What remains to be shown is whether or not conventional vigilance findings would apply to the real driving task — to the detection of unexpected signals appearing in the roadway, a pedestrian dart-out, for example.

Perhaps it is expecting too much of experimenters to develop designs to answer these questions in the roadway. A more practical, certainly safer, approach lies in simulation. With computer-driven displays, and even better, with the ability to optically mix computer-generated images and closed-circuit TV images, it is possible to instrument simulator displays into which realistic, unexpected events could be programmed. If the results show vigilance decrements, signal probability effects, and other familiar laboratory findings, we can then anticipate another round of 'relevance' discussions.

Flying

Our knowledge about vigilance during flying is no more developed than it is with driving, despite vast research on pilot performance. The subject of vigilance arises, usually, not as a result of research or task analysis, but in post-accident investigations. Like the driver, the pilot is required to perform vigilance sub-tasks, monitoring displays both inside the cockpit and outside it. But, unlike the driver, except for collision avoidance, most of the displays he must monitor are inside the cockpit, and relatively little temporally unpredictable information comes through the cockpit window. There is more commentary than hard evidence on how flight crews perform their monitoring sub-tasks. Some information and a lot of speculation comes from task analysis, accident reconstruction and pilot interviews. A higher grade of information might come from simulator studies, but this is extremely expensive research, especially when airline or military quality simulators and experienced air crews are employed, and incidentally, highly experienced and knowledgeable experimenter/observers are required. An outstanding example is a study in a Boeing 747 simulator using 18 airline crews (Ruffell Smith, 1979).

This chapter is not the place for a thorough task analysis of flying. Suffice it to say that flying consists of sub-tasks which include manual control, monitoring displays (including the cockpit window), communication, crew coordination, decision making, paperwork and resource management. Aircrews perform a visual scan of their displays, and to a lesser extent maintain an auditory vigil for warning tones of a great variety (Elson, 1979; Wiener and Curry, 1980). Warning signals can also come from the olfactory sense (electrical smoke) or tactile sense (vibrations), but it would be stretching a point to declare that flight crews consciously maintain an olfactory or tactile vigil.

Certain features of the flying-monitoring task can be generalized. First, the 'signals' are extremely diverse, and p' is extremely low. The split-flap condition has already been mentioned as an example. Flying requires maintaining alertness for dozens, perhaps hundreds of display indications, many of which crew members may never see in a lifetime, but for their simulator training. The perceptual demand upon the pilot combines multi-dimensionality of signals with infinitesmal values of p', and, added to that, a time-sharing requirement that allows only a small portion of the crew capacity to be allocated to monitoring. As the active workload increases, even less time may be available for monitoring. Furthermore, the task is not free of Type 1 errors. A collision between two airliners in 1965 was due, in part, to a visual illusion which led one flight crew to think that a collision was imminent, and take erroneous evasive action that actually brought the aircraft together (Civil Aeronautics Board, 1966). Ruffell Smith's study (1979), gives us rare insight into the extreme variations in signal detection (response time) in a highly realistic simulation of an air carrier flight.

Automation has been proposed by many as the answer to cockpit vigilance. The entire flightdeck task is changing due to automatic flight control, navigation and systems management devices, brought on largely by microcomputer hardware. As Sheridan (1978) observed, the pilot of an advanced aircraft is becoming essentially a systems manager. His input–output device is a computer, which stands as an interlocutor between him and the actual aircraft systems.

Just what effect this degree of automation will have on the aircrews and their ability to deal with emergency situations, not to mention their job satisfaction, is a matter of great concern to human factors scientists (Edwards, 1976; Sheridan, 1976; Wiener, 1977; Wiener and Curry, 1980).

Questions of pilot vigilance have arisen in analysis of 'controlled flight into terrain' accidents, where aircraft under the control of the crew strike the ground (or water) with the crew having no anticipation of the impending crash (Ruffell Smith, 1968; Wiener, 1977). In one dramatic, highly publicized accident, a Lockheed L-1011, assigned to fly at 2000 feet (in clear weather), suffered autopilot disengage while the crew was attempting to diagnose possible landing gear problems, and descended into the Everglades with no intervention on the part of the crew. There were ample indications of the descent in the cockpit, as well as extra-cockpit cues. It is also interesting to note that the descent was observed by an air traffic controller in Miami, using advanced radar equipment that digitally displayed the target's altitude. His puzzling response was analyzed by Wiener (1977).

These accidents have resulted in a US Congressional mandate for a ground proximity warning system (GPWS) for transport aircraft, which in theory would warn the flightcrews of impending terrain strikes. The interesting point is that the GPWS seems to substitute one form of vigilance and decision-making problem for another, a phenomenon familiar to human factor specialists. The GPWS is highly subject to Type 1 and Type 2 errors itself; the Type 1 errors being not only vexing to the crew, but a potential source of accidents. If an erroneous signal induces a pilot to pull up, he may climb into another aircraft. Furthermore, due to excessive Type 1 errors, GPWS alerts lose their credibility and pilots learn to ignore them ('cry wolf' phenomenon). This is discussed by Wiener (1977), and examples of pilot reports of false GPWS alerts are detailed in a special report (NASA, 1978a). In another commentary on a different type of altitude alert system, 20 of 32 pilot reports involve failure to observe the warning (NASA, 1978b). As this author has cautioned before, we cannot 'electronicize' our problems away—warning devices merely trade one vigilance problem for another, and add a few of their own along the way.

Aircraft collision must also be included in any consideration of flying and vigilance. The subject is far too complex to cover here: the interested reader is directed to a discussion by Wiener (1980) and appropriate National Transportation Safety Board (NTSB) accident reports; for example, the collision in Memphis of a Falcon jet and a light aircraft (NTSB, 1978), or the collision of an airliner and a USMC jet over Los Angeles (NTSB, 1979). Runway incursions and near-collisions on the ground are discussed by Billings and O'Hara (1978).

As a result of the Hughes Air West DC-9/USMC F-4 collision in 1971, the NTSB looked into company training on visual scanning, found it non-existent, and recommended that it be added to training and supervision. Other analyses have shown that extra-cockpit scanning is the lowest priority duty—it is the first to be sacrificed when the workload increases. Ironically, but not surprisingly, it is most needed precisely when workload is normally increased—in terminal areas. As we learned from the recent mid-air collisions in Memphis and San Diego, no air traffic control system, radar-based or not, can absolutely guarantee aircraft separation in visual flying conditions. The NTSB report on the Memphis crash discusses the role of the human as a 'backup system' when air traffic control procedures fail.

Again one is tempted by the lure of automation. For many years the aviation industry has sought an electronic collision avoidance system (CAS) for the cockpit. At this writing, several competing systems are waiting in the wings for a decision that is mired in politics. However, there is still reasonable doubt in the industry as to whether such a system would be effective where it is needed the most, in a high-density terminal area. In that environment, there would probably be an unacceptable number of Type 1 errors; the flight crews would be bombarded by spurious alerts, and would probably quickly adapt by ignoring the system. Away from an airport area, it could be effective. A CAS might have prevented the Hughes Air West DC-9/USMC F-4 collision; it is questionable whether it could have prevented the accidents in the San Diego and Memphis terminal areas. The author cautions again, as with the GPWS, that an alerting device is nothing more than a substitute vigilance task.

In summary, there is a growing awareness on the part of accident investigators and regulatory agencies of the importance of human vigilance in flying. What is lacking is a practical means of keeping aircrew alertness at the high level that the task demands. We cannot even begin to grapple with the question of the applicability of laboratory findings until we better understand what goes on in flight-deck monitoring, especially in the highly automated modern aircraft (Ropelewski, 1979). At this time we do not even know if there is a 'vigilance decrement' during a flight. If there is, it would be of critical importance, for the most perceptually demanding portion of any flight occurs at its end: descent, approach and landing.

CONCLUSION

We have seen that human monitoring activities abound, from simple visual inspection of manufactured goods, to the complexity of watchkeeping in a nuclear power plant. The costs of failures range from the annoying to the catastrophic. Reviews of this type usually end with the mandatory call for more research. But the vigilance literature already contains over 1000 citations. What appears to be needed most at this stage is not more laboratory research, though that is always welcome to add new insights and sharpen old ones, but a more concerted effort to apply research findings to real world affairs. The problems are growing more severe—as the consequences of error are rapidly becoming intolerable. Microprocessors are not going to make the problems go away; indeed, they may contribute some of their own. The critics of real world relevance have had their say, and their misgivings are well taken. But further waiting, and further research, does not assure that some day a *deus ex machina* will be lowered to center stage to show us how to deal with inspection and vigilance. The answers will come from a cautious, judicious application of laboratory findings, task analysis and new technologies to the real world of stimulus uncertainty. It is time to put vigilance research to work, even if it means an occasional commissive error.

REFERENCES

Alluisi, E. A., Coates, G. D., and Morgan, B. B. Effects of temporal stressors on vigilance and information processing. In R. R. Mackie (Ed.), *Vigilance: theory, operational performance, and physiological correlates.* New York: Plenum, 1977.

Annett, J. Training for perceptual skills. *Ergonomics,* 1966, **9,** 459–468.

Anon. Crash tied to inspection lapse. *Aviation Week and Space Technology,* 1968, 117–128.

Astley, R. W., and Fox, J. G. The analysis of an inspection task in the rubber industry. In C. G. Drury and J. G. Fox (Eds), *Human reliability in quality control.* London: Taylor and Francis, 1975.

Attwood, D. A., and Wiener, E. L. Automated instruction for vigilance training. *Journal of Applied Psychology,* 1968, **53,** 218–223.

Badalamente, R. V., and Ayoub, M. M. A behavioral analysis of an assembly line inspection task. *Human Factors,* 1969, **11,** 339–352.

Baddeley, A. D., and Colquhoun, W. P. Signal probability and vigilance: a reappraisal of the signal-rate effect. *British Journal of Psychology,* 1969, **60,** 169–178.

Baker, C. H. Signal duration as a factor in vigilance tasks. *Science,* 1963, **141,** 1196–1197.

Baker, W. J., and Theologus, G. C. Effects of caffeine on visual monitoring. *Journal of Applied Psychology,* 1972, **56,** 422–427.

Beatty, J., Ahern, S. K., and Katz, R. Sleep deprivation and the vigilance of anesthesiologists during simulated surgery. In R. R. Mackie (Ed.), *Vigilance: theory, operational performance, and physiological correlates.* New York: Plenum, 1977.

Belbin, R. M. New fields for quality control. *British Management Review,* 1957, **15,** 79.

Bennett, G. K. Inspection error: its influence on quality control systems. In C. G. Drury and J. G. Fox (Eds), *Human reliability in quality control.* London: Taylor and Francis, 1975.

Bergum, B. O., and Lehr, D. J. Effects of authoritarianism on vigilance performance. *Journal of Applied Psychology,* 1963, **47,** 75–77.

Besterfield, D. H. *Quality control: a practical approach.* Englewood Cliffs, N.J.: Prentice-Hall, 1979.

Billings, C. E., and O'Hara, D. B. Human factors associated with runway incursions. In NASA aviation safety and reporting system: eighth quarterly report. Technical Memorandum 78540. Moffett Field, Calif.: NASA, 1978.

Bloomfield, J. R. Studies on visual search. In C. G. Drury and J. G. Fox (Eds), *Human reliability in quality control.* London: Taylor and Francis, 1975 (a).

Bloomfield, J. R. Theoretical approaches to visual search. In C. G. Drury and J. G. Fox (Eds), *Human reliability in quality control.* London: Taylor and Francis, 1975 (b).

Boadle, J. Vigilance and simulated night driving. *Ergonomics*, 1976, **19**, 217–225.

Brown, B., and Monk, T. H. The effect of local target surround and whole background constraint on visual search times. *Human Factors*, 1975, **17**, 81–88.

Brown, I. D. Measurement of control skills, vigilance, and performance on a subsidiary task during 12 hours of car driving. *Ergonomics*, 1967, **10**, 665–673.

Brown, I. D. Can ergonomics improve primary safety in road transportation systems? *Ergonomics*, 1979, **22**, 109–116.

Buck, J. R. Dynamic visual inspection: task factors, theory and economics. In C. G. Drury and J. G. Fox (Eds), *Human reliability in quality control*. London: Taylor and Francis, 1975.

Chaney, F. B., and Teel, K. S. Improving human performance through training and visual aids. *Journal of Applied Psychology*, 1967, **51**, 311–315.

Chapanis, A. The relevance of laboratory studies to practical situations. *Ergonomics*, 1967, **10**, 557–577.

Chapman, E. D., and Sinclair, M. A. Ergonomics in inspection tasks in the food industry. In C. G. Drury and J. G. Fox (Eds), *Human reliability in quality control*. London: Taylor and Francis, 1975.

Civil Aeronautics Board, TWA B-707 and EAL Lockheed Constellation, Carmel, NY, December 4, 1965. Report No. SA-389. Washington, D.C.: Civil Aeronautics Board, 1966.

Colquhoun, W. P. Vigilance and the inspection problem. *Nature*, 1957, **180**, 1331–1332.

Colquhoun, W. P. The effect of a short rest-pause on inspection efficiency. *Ergonomics*, 1959, **2**, 367–372.

Colquhoun, W. P. Temperament, inspection efficiency, and time of day. *Ergonomics*, 1960, **3**, 377–378.

Colquhoun, W. P. The effect of unwanted signals on performance in a vigilance task. *Ergonomics*, 1961, **4**, 41–51.

Colquhoun, W. P. Recent research in the psychology of inspection. *Textile Institute and Industry*, 1964, **1964**, 252–255.

Colquhoun, W. P., and Baddeley, A. D. Role of pretest expectancy in vigilance decrement. *Journal of Experimental Psychology*, 1964, **68**, 156–160.

Colquhoun, W. P., and Baddeley, A. D. Influence of signal probability during pretraining on vigilance decrement. *Journal of Experimental Psychology*, 1967, **73**, 153–155.

Colquhoun, W. P., and Edwards, R. S. Practice effects on a visual vigilance task with and without search. *Human Factors*, 1970, **12**, 537–545.

Colquhoun, W. P., Blake, M. J. F., and Edwards, R. S. Experimental studies of shift work, II: Stabilized 8-hour shift systems. *Ergonomics*, 1968, **11**, 527–556.

Corcoran, D. W. J. The influence of task complexity and practice on performance after loss of sleep. *Journal of Applied Psychology*, 1964, **48**, 339–343.

Craig, A. Vigilance for two kinds of signal with unequal probabilities of occurrence. *Human Factors*, 1979, **21**, 647–653.

Craig, A., and Colquhoun, W. P. Vigilance: a review. In C. G. Drury and J. G. Fox (Eds), *Human reliability in quality control*. London: Taylor and Francis, 1975.

Craig, A., and Colquhoun, W. P. Vigilance effects in complex inspection. In R. R. Mackie (Ed.), *Vigilance: theory, operational performance, and physiological correlates*. New York: Plenum, 1977.

Curry, R. E., and Gai, E. G. Detection of random process failures by human monitors. In T. B. Sheridan and G. Johannsen (Eds), *Monitoring behavior and supervisory control*. New York: Plenum, 1976.

Czaja, S., and Drury, C. G. Training programme for inspection. *Human Factors*, 1981, **23**, 473–484.

Deese, J. Some problems in the theory of vigilance. *Psychological Review*, 1955, **62**, 359–368.

Dobbins, D. A., Tiedemann, J. G., and Skordahl, D. M. Field study of vigilance under highway driving conditions. Technical Research Note No. 118. Washington, D.C.: US Army Personnel Research Office, 1961.

Dodge, H. F., and Romig, H. G. A method of sampling inspection. *Bell System Technical Journal*, 1929, **8**, 613–631.

Dorris, A. L. The effects of inspector error on the operation of a *c*-chart. *AIIE Transactions*, 1977, **9**, 312–315.

Dorris, A. L., and Foote, B. L. Inspector errors and statistical quality control: a survey. *AIIE Transactions*, 1978, **10**, 184–192.

Drury, C. G. The effect of speed of working on industrial inspection accuracy. *Applied Ergonomics*, 1973, **4**, 2–7.

Drury, C. G. Human decision making in quality control. In C. G. Drury and J. G. Fox (Eds), *Human reliability in quality control*. London: Taylor and Francis, 1975.

Drury, C. G. Integrating human factors models into statistical quality control. *Human Factors*, 1978, **20**, 561–572.

Drury, C. G., and Addison, J., An industrial study of the effects of feedback and fault density on inspection performance. *Ergonomics*, 1973, **16**, 159–169.

Drury, C. G., and Fox, J. G. (Eds), *Human reliability in quality control*. London: Taylor and Francis, 1975 (a).

Drury, C. G., and Fox, J. G. The imperfect inspector. In C. G. Drury and J. G. Fox (Eds), *Human reliability in quality control*. London: Taylor and Francis, 1975 (b).

Drury, C. G., and Sheehan, J. J. Ergonomic and economic facts—an industrial inspection task. *International Journal of Production Research*, 1969, **7**, 333–341.

Duncan, A. J. *Quality control and industrial statistics*. Homewood, Ill.: Irwin, 1965.

Edwards, E. Some aspects of automation in civil transport aircraft. In T. B. Sheridan and G. Johannsen (Eds), *Monitoring behavior and supervisory control*. New York: Plenum, 1976.

Elliott, E. Perception and alertness. *Ergonomics*, 1960, **3**, 357–364.

Elson, B. M. Cockpit alert standardization urged. *Aviation Week and Space Technology*, 21 May, 1979, 99.

Embrey, D. E. Training the inspector's sensibility and response strategy. In C. G. Drury and J. G. Fox (Eds), *Human reliability in quality control*. London: Taylor and Francis, 1975.

Eskew, R. T., and Richie, C. V. Pacing and locus of control in qualiity control inspection. *Human Factors*, 1982, **24**, 411–415.

Fox, J. G. The ergonomics of coin inspection. *The Quality Engineer*, 1964, **28**, 165–169.

Fox, J. G., and Haslegrave, C. M. Industrial inspection efficiency and the probability of a defect occurring. *Ergonomics*, 1969, **12**, 713–721.

Fraser, D. C. The relation between angle of display and performance in a prolonged visual task. *Quarterly Journal of Experimental Psychology*, 1950, **2**, 176–181.

Gallwey, T. J. Selection tests for visual inspection on a multiple fault type task. *Ergonomics*, 1981, **25**, 1077–1092.

Geyer, L. H., Patel, S., and Perry, R. F. Detectability of multiple flaws. *Human Factors*, 1979, **21**, 7–12.

Geyer, L. H., and Perry, R. F. Variation in detectability of multiple flaws with allowed inspection time. *Human Factors*, 1982, **24**, 361–365.

Gillies, G. J. Glass inspection. In C. G. Drury and J. G. Fox (Eds), *Human reliability in quality control*. London: Taylor and Francis, 1975.

Green, D. M., and Swets, J. A. *Signal detection theory and psychophysics.* New York: John Wiley, 1966.

Harris, D. H. Effect of equipment complexity on inspection performance. *Journal of Applied Psychology,* 1966, **50,** 236–237.

Harris, D. H. Effect of defect rate on inspection accuracy. *Journal of Applied Psychology,* 1968, **52,** 377–379.

Harris, D. H. The nature of industrial inspection. *Human Factors,* 1969, **11,** 139–148.

Harris, D. H., and Chaney, F. D. *Human factors in quality assurance.* New York: Wiley, 1969.

Harris, W. Fatigue, circadian rhythm, and truck accidents. In R. R. Mackie (Ed.), *Vigilance: theory, operational performance, and physiological correlates.* New York: Plenum, 1977.

Hartnett, O. M. Error in response to infrequent signals. *Ergonomics,* 1975, **18,** 213–223.

Hayes, A. S. Control of visual inspection. *Industrial Quality Control,* 1950, **6,** 73–76.

Howland, D. An investigation of the performance of the human monitor. Wright Air Development Center Technical Report No. WADC-TR-57-431. Wright-Patterson Air Force Base, Ohio: Wright Air Development Center, 1958.

Howland, D., and Wiener, E. L. The system monitor. In D. N. Buckner and J. J. McGrath (Eds), *Vigilance: a symposium.* New York: McGraw-Hill, 1963.

Jacobson, H. J. A study of inspector accuracy. *Industrial Quality Control,* 1952, **9,** 16–25.

Jamieson, G. H. Inspection in the telecommunications industry: a field study of age and other performance variables. *Ergonomics,* 1966, **9,** 297–303.

Jenkins, H. M. The effect of signal rate on performance in visual monitoring. *American Journal of Psychology,* 1958, **71,** 647–661.

Jerison, H. J., and Pickett, R. M. Vigilance: a review and re-evaluation. *Human Factors,* 1963, **5,** 211–238.

Jerison, H. J., and Wallis, R. A. Experiments on vigilance: II: One-clock and three-clock monitoring. Wright Air Development Center Technical Report No. WADC-TR-57-206. Wright-Patterson Air Force Base, Ohio: Wright Air Development Center, 1957.

Juran, J. M. Inspectors' errors in quality control. *Mechanical Engineering,* 1935, **57,** 643–644.

Kibler, A. W. The relevance of vigilance research to aerospace monitoring tasks. *Human Factors,* 1965, **7,** 93–99.

Laurell, H., and Lisper, H. O. Changes in subsidiary reaction time and heart rate during car driving, passenger travel and stationary conditions. *Ergonomics,* 1976, **19,** 149–156.

Levine, J. M. The effects of values and costs on the detection and identification of signals in auditory vigilance. *Human Factors,* 1966, **8,** 525–537.

Lion, J. S., Richardson, E., and Browne, R. C. A study of the performance of industrial inspectors under two kinds of lighting. *Ergonomics,* 1968, **11,** 23–34.

Lion, J. S., Richardson, E., Weightman, D., and Browne, R. C. The influence of the visual arrangement of material, and of working singly or in pairs, upon performance at simulated industrial inspection. *Ergonomics,* 1975, **18,** 195–204.

Lusted, L. B. *Introduction to medical decision making.* Springfield, Ill.: Charles C. Thomas, 1968.

McBain, W. N. Arousal, monotony, and accidents in line driving. *Journal of Applied Psychology,* 1970, **54,** 509–519.

McCornack, R. L. Inspector accuracy: a study of the literature. Sandia Corp. Report No. 53-61(14). Albuquerque, N.M.: Sandia Corporation, 1961.

McGrath, J. J., and Harabedian, A. Signal detection as a function of intersignal-interval duration. In D. N. Buckner and J. J. McGrath (Eds), *Vigilance: a symposium.* New York, McGraw-Hill, 1963.

McKenzie, R. M. On the accuracy of inspectors. *Ergonomics,* 1958, **1**, 258–272.

Mackworth, N. H. *Researches on the measurement of human performance.* Medical Research Council Special Report Series No. 268. London: HM Stationery Office, 1950. Reprinted in H. W. Sinaiko, (Ed.), Selected papers on human factors in the design and use of control systems. New York: Dover, 1961.

Mackworth, N. H. Work design and training for future industrial skills. The 1955 Sir Alfred Herbert Paper, London, 1956.

Mackie, R. R. (Ed.). *Vigilance: theory, operational performance and physiological correlates.* New York: Plenum, 1977.

Mackie, R. R., and O'Hanlon, J. F. Combined effects of extended driving and heat stress on driver arousal and performance. In R. R. Mackie (Ed.), *Vigilance: theory, operational performance and physiological correlates.* New York: Plenum, 1977.

Mast, T. M., and Heimstra, N. W. Effects of fatigue on vigilance performance. *Journal of Engineering Psychology,* 1964, **3**, 73–79.

Megaw, E. D. Factors affecting visual inspection accuracy. *Applied Ergonomics,* 1979, **10**, 27–32.

Moder, J. J., and Oswalt, J. H. An investigation of some factors affecting the hand quality picking of small objects. *Journal of Industrial Engineering,* 1959, **10**, 213–218.

Montague, W. E., and Webber, C. E. Effects of knowledge of results and differential monetary reward on six uninterrupted hours of monitoring. *Human Factors,* 1965, **7**, 173–180.

Moraal, J. The analysis of an inspection task in the steel industry. In C. G. Drury and J. G. Fox (Eds), *Human reliability in quality control.* London: Taylor and Francis, 1975.

Morawski, T., Drury, C. G., and Karwan, M. H. Predicting search, performance for multiple targets. *Human Factors,* 1980, **22**, 707–718.

Murrell, G. A. A reappraisal of artificial signals as an aid to a visual monitoring task. *Ergonomics,* 1975, **18**, 693–700.

Murrell, K. F. H. *Human performance in industry.* New York: Reinhold, 1965.

National Aeronautics and Space Administration. NASA aviation safety reporting system: fifth quarterly report. Technical Memorandum No. 78476. Moffett Field, Calif.: NASA, 1978 (a).

National Aeronautics and Space Administration. NASA aviation safety reporting system: sixth quarterly report. Technical Memorandum No. 78511. Moffett Field, Calif.: NASA, 1978 (b).

National Transportation Safety Board. American Airlines DC-10-10, Chicago–O'Hare International Airport. Report No. NTSB-AAR-79-17. Washington, D.C.: NTSB, 1979.

National Transportation Safety Board. Hughes Air West DC-9 and US Marine Corps F-4B, near Duarte, Calif., June 6, 1971. Report No. NTSB-AAR-72-26. Washington, D.C.: NTSB, 1972.

National Transportation Safety Board. Midair collision involving a Falcon jet and Cessna 150, Memphis, Tenn., May 18, 1978. Report No. NTSB-AAR-78-14. Washington, D.C.: NTSB, 1978.

National Transportation Safety Board. Pacific Southwest Airlines B-727 and Gibbs Flite Center Cessna 172, San Diego, Calif., September 25, 1978. Report No. NTSB-AAR-79-5. Washington, D.C.: NTSB, 1979.

Noro, K. Determination of counting time in visual inspection. *Human Factors,* 1980, **22**, 43–55.

O'Hanlon, J. F., and Kelley, G. R. Comparison of performance and physiological changes between drivers who perform well and poorly during prolonged vehicular operation. In R. R. Mackie (Ed.), *Vigilance: theory, operational performance and physiological correlates.* New York: Plenum, 1977.

Parasuraman, R. Memory load and event rate control sensitivity decrements in sustained attention. *Science,* 1979, **205,** 924–927.

Parasuraman, R. and Davies, D. R. A taxonomic analysis of vigilance performance. In R. R. Mackie (Ed.), *Vigilance: theory, operational performance and physiological correlates.* New York: Plenum, 1977.

Penny, N. M., Elliot, T. A., Moder, J. J., and Carmichael, B. W. Sampling, grading, and cleaning farmers' stock peanuts. Bulletin No. 21. Atlanta: Georgia Institute of Technology Engineering Experiment Station, June 1956.

Purswell, J. L., Greenhaw, L. N., and Oats, C. An inspection task experiment. Paper presented at the meeting of the Human Factors Society, Los Angeles, 1972.

Riemersma, J. B. J., Sanders, A. F., Wildervanck, C., and Gaillard, A. W. Performance decrement during prolonged night driving. In R. R. Mackie (Ed.), *Vigilance: theory, operational performance, and physiological correlates.* New York: Plenum, 1977.

Rigby, L. V., and Swain, A. D. Some human-factor applications to quality control in a high technology industry. In C. G. Drury and J. G. Fox (Eds), *Human reliability in quality control.* London: Taylor and Francis, 1975.

Ropelewski, R. R. L-1011 cockpit automation cuts crew workload. *Aviation Week and Space Technology,* 18 June, 1979, 46–48, 53.

Ruffell Smith, H. P. Some human factors of aircraft accidents involving collision with high ground. *Journal of the Institute of Navigation,* 1968, **21,** 1–10.

Ruffell Smith, H. P. A simulator study of the interaction of pilot workload with errors, vigilance, and decisions. Technical Memorandum No. 78482. Moffett Field, Calif.: NASA-Ames Research Center, 1979.

Schoonard, J. W., Gould, J. D., and Miller, L. A. Studies of visual inspection. *Ergonomics,* 1973, **16,** 365–379.

Sheehan, J. J., and Drury, C. G. The analysis of industrial inspection. *Applied Ergonomics,* 1971, **2,** 74–78.

Sheridan, T. B. Preview of models of the human monitor/supervisor. In T. B. Sheridan and G. Johannsen (Eds), *Monitoring behavior and supervisory control.* New York: Plenum, 1976.

Sheridan, T. B. The changing role of the pilot from manual controller to computer supervisor. In *Proceedings of Symposium on Man–System Interface: Advances in Workload Study.* Washington: Air Line Pilots Association, 1978.

Sheridan, T. B. and Johannsen, G. (Eds), *Monitoring behavior and supervisory control.* New York: Plenum, 1976.

Sinclair, M. A. The use of performance measures on individual examiners in inspection schemes. *Applied Ergonomics,* 1979, **10,** 17–25.

Smith, G. L. Inspector performance on microminiature tasks. In C. G. Drury and J. G. Fox (Eds), *Human reliability in quality control.* London: Taylor and Francis, 1975.

Smith, L. A., and Barany, J. W. An elementary model of human performance on paced visual inspection tasks. *AIIE Transactions,* 1970, **2,** 298–308.

Smith, R. L., and Lucaccini, L. F. Vigilance research: its application to industrial problems. *Human Factors,* 1969, **11,** 149–156.

Spitz, G., and Drury, C. G. Inspection of sheet materials — test of model predictions. *Human Factors,* 1978, **20,** 521–528.

Sprague, D. A., Zinn, B., and Kreitner, R. Improving quality through behavior modification. *Quality Progress,* 1976, **1976,** 22–24.

Swets, J. A. Signal detection theory applied to vigilance. In R. R. Mackie (Ed.), *Vigilance theory, operational performance and physiological correlates.* New York: Plenum, 1977.

Swets, J. A. and Kristofferson, A. B. Attention. *Annual Review of Psychology*, 1970, **21**, 339–366.

Teel, K. S., Springer, R. M., and Sadler, E. E. Assembly and inspection of microelectronic systems. *Human Factors*, 1968, **10**, 217–224.

Teichner, W. H. The detection of a simple visual signal as a function of time of watch. *Human Factors*, 1974, **16**, 339–353.

Thomas, L. F. Perceptual organization in industrial inspectors. *Ergonomics*, 1962, **5**, 429–434.

Thomas, L. F., and Seaborne, A. E. M. The socio-technical context of industrial inspection. *Occupational Psychology*, 1961, **35**, 36–43.

Tiffin, J., and Rogers, H. B. The selection and training of inspectors. *Personnel*, 1941, **18**, 14–31.

Tsao, Y.-C., Drury, C. G., and Morawski, T. B. Human performance in sampling inspection. *Human Factors*, 1979, **21**, 99–105.

Tye, L. S. *Looking but not seeing: the federal nuclear power plant inspection program.* Cambridge, Mass.: Union of Concerned Scientists, 1979.

Vickers, D., Leary, J., and Barnes, P. Adaptation of decreasing signal probability. In R. R. Mackie (Ed.), *Vigilance: theory, operational performance, and physiological correlates.* New York: Plenum, 1977.

Wallack, P. M., and Adams, S. K. The utility of signal-detection theory in the analysis of industrial inspector accuracy. *AIIE Transactions*, 1969, **1**, 33–44.

Wallack, P. M., and Adams, S. K. A comparison of inspector performance measures. *AIIE Transactions*, 1970, **2**, 97–105.

Warm, J. S. Psychological process in sustained attention. In R.R. Mackie (Ed.), *Vigilance: theory, operational performance and physiological correlates.* New York: Plenum, 1977.

Warner, H. R., and Budkin, A. A. 'Link trainer' for the coronary care unit. *Computers and Biomedical Research*, 1968, **2**, 135–144.

Warrick, M. J., Kibler, A. W., and Topmiller, D. A. Response time to unexpected stimuli. *Human Factors*, 7, 1965, 81–86.

Wiener, E. L. Knowledge of results and signal rate in monitoring: a transfer of training approach. *Journal of Applied Psychology*, 1963, **47**, 214–222.

Wiener, E. L. Transfer of training from one monitoring task to another. *Ergonomics*, 1967, **10**, 649–658.

Wiener, E. L. Training for vigilance: repeated sessions with knowledge of results. *Ergonomics*, 1968, **11**, 547–556.

Wiener, E. L. Adaptive measurement of vigilance decrement. *Ergonomics*, 1973, **16**, 353–363.

Wiener, E. L. An adaptive vigilance task with knowledge of results. *Human Factors*, 1974, **16**, 333–338.

Wiener, E. L. Individual and group differences in inspection. In C. G. Drury and J. G. Fox (Eds), *Human reliability in quality control.* London: Taylor and Francis, 1975.

Wiener, E. L. Controlled flight into terrain accidents: system-induced errors. *Human Factors*, 1977, **19**, 171–181.

Wiener, E. L. Midair collisions: the systems, and the realpolitik. *Human Factors*, 1980, **22**, 521–533.

Wiener, E. L., and Attwood, D. A. Training for vigilance: combined cueing and knowledge of results. *Journal of Applied Psychology*, 1968, **52**, 474–479.

Wiener, E. L., and Curry, R. E. Flight-deck automation: promises and problems. *Ergonomics*, 1980, **23**, 995–1011.

Williams, L. G., and Borow, M. S. The effect of rate and direction of display movement upon visual search. *Human Factors*, 1963, **5**, 139–146.

Williges, R. C. The role of payoffs and signal ratios in criterion changes during a monitoring task. *Human Factors*, 1971, **13**, 261–267.

Williges, R. C. Manipulating the response criterion in visual monitoring. *Human Factors*, 1973, **15**, 179–185.

Williges, R. C., and Streeter, H. Display characteristics in inspection tasks. *Journal of Applied Psychology*, 1971, **55**, 123–125.

Wyatt, S., and Langdon, J. N. Inspection processes in industry. *Industrial Health Research Board Report* No. 63, London: HMSO, 1932.

Zunzanyika, X. K., and Drury, C. G. Effects of information on industrial inspection performance. In C. G. Drury and J. G. Fox (Eds), *Human reliability in quality control.* London: Taylor and Francis, 1975.

Sustained Attention in Human Performance
Edited by J. S. Warm
© 1984 John Wiley & Sons Ltd.

Chapter 8

Human Engineering: The Control of Vigilance

Angus Craig

INTRODUCTION AND OVERVIEW

The aim of the present chapter is to describe procedures for the control of vigilance in real operations. Inevitably, since the procedures are based on principles which derive from laboratory research findings, this aim will require some evaluation of the operational relevance and applicability of these findings.

Although contemporary research on vigilance is of a predominantly theoretical nature, its roots are firmly entrenched in real operational issues. As Mackworth commented to Jerison: 'the essential feature of the vigilance story was that its origins were without any theoretical background' (Jerison, 1970, p.130). Close links can be traced between the problem topic studied today and early observations concerning the effects of 'industrial fatigue' and boredom on the efficiency of quality checkers, examining for defective product (Wyatt and Langdon, 1932; Baker, 1964). Above all, the major impetus for laboratory research on vigilance arose out of the practical problems encountered during World War II, when the frequency of reports of failures to detect various types of military target either by unaided vision or via the use of radar and similar devices reached the point at which research was commissioned to investigate the causes of what at the time was ascribed to 'mental fatigue' (Ditchburn, 1943; Lindsley, 1944; Mackworth, 1950).

In the nearly four decades since World War II, approximately one thousand reports have been published, including five hundred in the last ten years alone, with progress reviews at periodic intervals, outlining the theoretical and empirical advances contributing to a better understanding of vigilance (e.g. Broadbent, 1958; Frankmann and Adams, 1962; Jerison and Pickett, 1963; Loeb and Alluisi, 1970, 1977). On occasion, demurring voices have also been raised, questioning whether, despite the vast amount of research on the topic, much of practical value had emerged which could usefully be employed to control the watchkeeping behaviour of human operators in real man–machine systems (e.g. Elliott, 1960; Kibler, 1965; Smith and Lucaccini, 1969; Nachreiner, 1977). This same question will also be addressed in the course of the present chapter.

The chapter begins by describing the nature of vigilance tasks and the associated efficiency problems which have to be overcome. It then proceeds to assess the incidence and scope of these problems in real situations. Next, principles of control emerging from the research work are specified, and evaluated in terms of their operational relevance and practicability. Finally, an attempt is made to identify unexplored avenues for research and to assess future trends and needs.

IDENTIFYING THE PROBLEM AND THE ENGINEERING GOALS

It seems useful to start by offering a definition of the term 'vigilance', and none has yet surpassed that given by N. H. Mackworth who pioneered so much of vigilance research. He stated that '*vigilance could be regarded as a state of readiness to detect and respond to certain specified small changes occurring at random time intervals* in the environment' (Mackworth, 1957a, pp.389–390).

This statement not only provides some idea as to what vigilance means, but also provides an indication of the type of task to which it is relevant. The industrial inspector knows (or at least he should know) what to look for in the way of faulty product, but he does not know when a fault will appear. Similarly, the sonar or radar operator knows what a target looks like (or sounds like) but, although in certain circumstances he may expect it, he does not know precisely when it will occur. Some may quibble over minor details of the definition, arguing, for example, that the specified changes may not be all that small and that some military targets are really rather gross in relation to the background against which they are seen (e.g. Kibler, 1965), or that the changes are not truly random in their occurrence, that, for example, industrial processing faults usually produce defects in bunches, rather than sporadic defects spread over the whole working period (e.g. Nachreiner, 1977). In the main, however, Mackworth's statement provides an acceptable working definition of vigilance.

In the laboratory, there are fewer discrepant examples, owing primarily to a tendency to constrain the type of task used within fairly narrow limits. This may, in part, derive from early attempts to define the characteristics of tasks in which vigilance was likely to arise, as, for example, McGrath (McGrath *et al.*, 1959; McGrath, 1963b), who cites 10 criteria whose characteristics include: (a) a weak brief signal to be detected; (b) infrequent, irregular occurrence of the signal, with no more than 36 signals per hour; (c) the subject or operator responds to the signal only, making no response to alternative, non-signal events, and is not required to make an interpretive identification; (d) performance at the task is sustained for at least 1 hour; (e) the subject's motor involvement is slight; (f) he makes a simple decision about the presence of a signal, and is not required to sort, interpret or classify. Such constraints naturally invite attack from those who are concerned with the practical relevance of vigilance research, and who rightly point out the discrepancies between these characteristics and those of real tasks. Kibler (1965), for example, critically compares them with the requirements of aerospace monitoring tasks, inescapably concluding that the laboratory tasks have low face validity, and Nachreiner (1977) highlights some major differences in regard to industrial inspection tasks.

However, the above criteria are not included here as a prescription for setting up a vigilance task. Instead, they are presented because they convey some impression of the typical task used in laboratory research. Exceptions to each of the criteria can be found in the literature on vigilance, some reported experiments requiring the identification of events which occur much more frequently (e.g. Wilkinson, 1957); others requiring sustained performance for considerably less than an hour (e.g. Davies, 1968, whose task lasted for 5 minutes only); and yet others demanding that the subject responds not only to the occurrence of the signal, but to non-signal occurrences as well (e.g. Whittenburg *et al.*, 1956), or that he makes an evaluative or classificatory response (e.g. Adams *et al.*, 1961; Broadbent and Gregory, 1963, 1965). But on the whole, a task conforming to the above-listed characteristics remains typical of those used in research, even today.

Rather than become mired in specious argument about what is or is not an appropriate vigilance task, the present course adopted is to accept that vigilance applies equally to the laboratory tasks and to the various monitoring tasks encountered in real operations. Whether or not the same problems of efficiency as found in the laboratory (and specified below) also arise in real operations is a separate issue, and questions of face validity, regarding the (usually) greater complexity of the real tasks, reduce to elementary empirical questions which can to some degree be answered by laboratory experimentation (e.g. Craig and Colquhoun, 1977).

In practice, whether in the laboratory or in the field, the extent of an operator's vigilance, his/her readiness to detect and respond, is usually assessed by measuring the proportion of signals (targets, defects) which he/she correctly detected. (Alternatively, one could use the complement of detection rate, namely the proportion of signals which were missed, and went unreported.) Sometimes, his/her alertness is indexed by the degree to which the signal has to be increased (in size, loudness, brightness) before he/she detects it (e.g. Wiener, 1973) and sometimes by the speed with which he/she responds to the occurrence of the signal (e.g. Buck, 1966). In the laboratory, at least, the operator's vigilance is usually assessed over consecutive periods of time (e.g. every 10–15 minutes in a 1-hour session).

A characteristic vigilance function obtained from a laboratory experiment is depicted in Figure 8.1. This illustrates quite clearly the dual problems of vigilance which have been identified by the research effort:

(i)   Overall, efficiency is at a suboptimal, impoverished level.
(ii)   There is a decrement function over time applying to this level.

It is important to realize, here, that the subjects in the experiment whose results are presented in Figure 8.1 had previously shown themselves capable of near 100% detection efficiency, when signals were presented under alerted conditions. This pattern is, incidentally, very similar to that which was provided by those wartime operational reports on military target-spotting and which was replicated by Mackworth in his original simple simulation studies (Mackworth, 1950).

There can be little doubt that, in recent years at least, the research effort has focused almost entirely on the 'vigilance decrement', paying somewhat less attention to the problem of the generally low level of overall efficiency. Jerison and Pickett (1963), for example, argue that even the problem of an initially low level of detections is merely a measurement artefact; that the initial decrement is masked because performance is usually averaged over the first 15–30 minutes of the task. (Reference to Figure 8.1, however, clearly indicates that in the first 3 minutes alone, a serious efficiency problem exists which could

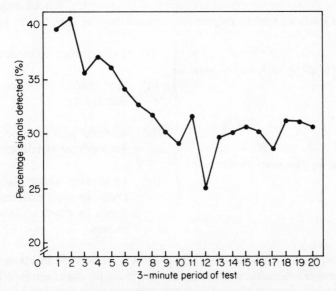

Figure 8.1 The 'vigilance decrement': mean percentage of signals detected by a group of 36 subjects in a 1-hour session of simple visual inspection, as a function of time on task. [After Craig and Colquhoun (1975).]

not have resulted from mere averaging of the data over these 3 minutes.) They stated quite categorically that 'The decrement function is the source of the vigilance problem in man–machine systems' (Jerison and Pickett, 1963, p.223). Unfortunately, it is just this view, apparently prevalent among contemporary vigilance workers, which has been attacked most vehemently by the critics of the laboratory research. To a degree, such criticism is justified since there is not one vigilance problem, but two, and they need not both occur. But, if only one of them should present itself, then it is unquestionably the problem of an inefficient overall level, rather than of a decline in the level over time (Self and Rhodes, 1964; Schoonard *et al.*, 1973; Nachreiner *et al.*, 1975). Almost twenty years ago, the point was firmly put by Elliott (1960), who claimed that, in his considerable experience with closely simulated radar or asdic military watchkeeping tasks, a decrement was never found (although see Colquhoun, 1977, for a counterexample), and that the major source of the problem, found also in real military watchkeeping, was the low efficiency level which was already apparent during the first half-hour on watch. His views had been expressed previously, when Mackworth had commented: 'I agree, however, with Elliott that the emphasis in research should no longer be on this decline with prolonged work, but rather on why the operator does not do what he can do' (Mackworth, 1957a, p.391). In other words, the focus should be on the suboptimal detection level which persists from the beginning of the work period.

Having defined the problems encountered in vigilance, it is an easy task to define the goals of human engineering. These may be specified as follows:

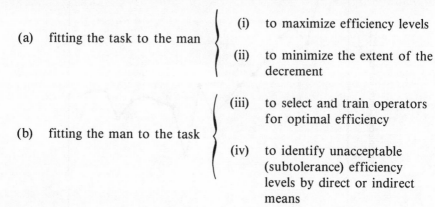

(a)   fitting the task to the man

    (i)   to maximize efficiency levels

    (ii) to minimize the extent of the decrement

(b)   fitting the man to the task

    (iii) to select and train operators for optimal efficiency

    (iv) to identify unacceptable (subtolerance) efficiency levels by direct or indirect means

Suggested means for achieving these goals will be detailed in a later section. For the moment it suffices to note that the bulk of the research effort has concentrated on the task-related factors pertinent to the first pair of goals (the second, in particular), and it is in relation to these that research has met with greatest success, in terms of the reliability of obtained effects. Reliable evidence pertaining to devices for selecting operators (e.g. personality questionnaires) or to indirect ways of assessing the level of vigilance (e.g. by using physiological measures) has been less forthcoming, and the research effort accordingly less successful.

Before presenting and discussing principles for the control of vigilance which have emerged from the research work, it seems appropriate to consider evidence on the incidence and extent of vigilance problems in real operations. This forms the content of the next section.

INCIDENCE OF VIGILANCE SITUATIONS AND PROBLEMS IN REAL OPERATIONS

The emphasis here is largely on industrial inspection, with some mention of sonar and radar devices. This merely reflects the relative availability of the evidence, since, for rather obvious reasons, many studies of military watchkeeping are classified, and hence hard data in the form of detections and missed signals are seldom provided in unrestricted or published reports. There have, of course, been numerous studies involving closely simulated radar or sonar monitoring (e.g. Wallis and Samuel, 1961; Adams, 1963), but only a representative few which provide hard data obtained from experienced operators are cited in this section. Vehicle driving, which many consider to be a task involving vigilance (e.g. O'Hanlon and Kelly, 1977), is also excluded from consideration in this section, again because of the unavailability of hard, congruent, evidence on the vigilance component. Although some evidence is available on a fatigue effect in prolonged driving (e.g. Harris, 1977), as in comparable tasks involving tracking (e.g. Siddall and Anderson, 1955), other studies have found no evidence of impaired driving over as long a period as 11 hours (Fuller, 1978).

Task duration

The length of time for which continuous attention to the task is demanded is generally regarded as one of the key features of a vigilance task, and it will be remembered that a duration of 1 hour was mentioned in the characteristic features listed earlier, although, to reiterate, there is nothing sacrosanct about that duration.

Some indication of the duration demanded in inspection tasks is provided by the results of a survey conducted by Megaw (1977), who had sent a questionnaire on inspection procedure and problems in industry to 151 firms in the UK. One of the questions asked approximately how long an inspector was expected to work at visual examination without taking a break, either to rest or to work on another activity. From the replies received, the percentage frequency for various duration categories were

Duration (min)	0–30	31–60	61–120	120–240
Percentage of firms (%)	25	14	19	42

These figures, which show a considerable range, are, of course, for the duration expected of the worker, and may differ quite considerably from the duration he/she actually works. Fox (1977), for example, points out that in coin inspection, only 14 minutes out of each 24 minute inspection-cycle was actually spent in examining coins. Similarly, Hermann (1977) observed that, at sea, operating bridge look-outs normally spent only 48 minutes out of each hour on duty actually watching the sea area, and that when distractions from superior officers were present the actual look-out time fell to as low as 32 minutes per hour. Belbin (1957b) mentions that in viewing radiographs of light alloy castings, examiners spent no more than 10–15 minutes on continuous inspection. Nachreiner (1977) reported that the modal period of continuous attention actually paid to various monitoring tasks was of only 5 minutes' duration, and that periods as long as 20 minutes were rarely observed. His observations are depicted graphically in Figure 8.2.

It would appear, therefore, that although typical industrial and military tasks apparently demand relatively prolonged periods of continuous attention varying between somewhat less than half-an-hour's duration and a duration of about 4 hours, the actual time spent attending continuously is likely to be relatively

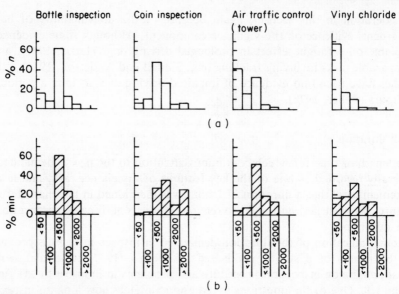

Figure 8.2   Distribution of duration of periods of continuous information processing for operators in different monitoring jobs for one complete working day. Duration of information processing periods is 0.01 min. (a) Distribution of durations as percentage of total number of periods. The number per cent (% *n*) is measured relative to the number of information processing periods. (b) Percentage distribution of total information processing time (% min) over periods of different duration. [After Nachreiner (1977).]

short. Real tasks differ in this latter respect from most laboratory situations of vigilance, where the task demands are usually quite rigidly adhered to, so that an hour demanded is, in practice, an hour spent. However, although the following comment is not supported by an abundance of evidence, it seems doubtful that the vigilance problems are eradicated merely because operators only attend intermittently to the task in hand (see, for example, Jenkins, 1958). One can see in Figure 8.1 that efficiency problems already exist during the first few minutes of the task. It may even be that intermittent release from the task is simply one of the ways operators cope with the demands for sustained vigilance (Bills, 1931; Broadbent, 1958; Jerison *et al.*, 1965).

Signal rate

A second characteristic listed in the earlier features of a typical vigilance task is that signal events have a relatively infrequent occurrence. In the laboratory, the signal rate is usually held to a moderately low level (frequently of the order of 2–5% of the total event occurrence), but not too low as to preclude the possibility of obtaining reliable estimates of detection rate (see Craig and Colquhoun, 1975). Elliott (1960), among others, has complained that these typical

Table 8.1 Incidence of signals (percentage occurrence) in normal operating conditions in a number of real monitoring and inspection tasks

Authors	Product or task type	Defect or target rate (%)
1. Astley and Fox (1975)	Rubber seals	25
2. Carter (1957), cited in McCornack (1961)	Acoustic tiles	14
3. Chapman and Sinclair (1975)	Jam tarts	4
	Chicken carcasses	15
4. Drury and Addision (1973)	Glassware	25–60
5. Elliott (1960)	Sonar/radar	1 target per week or per month
6. Fox (1975)	Rubber seals	1
7. Fox (1977)	Coins	0.17
8. Fox and Embrey (1972)	Metal parts	1
9. Mills and Sinclair (1976)	Knitwear	49
10. Nachreiner et al. (1975)	Coins	2.5
11. Raphael (1942)	Fabric	13–53
	Surface finish	20–56
12. Rigby and Swain (1975)	Electronic modules	
	(a) Complex	6
	(b) Simple	1.4
13. Wyatt and Langdon (1932)	Cartridges	1–3
14. Yerushalmy (1969)	(a) Pulmonary photofluorograms	3.2
	(b) Pulmonary roentgenograms (X-rays)	1.5

signal rates are still far in excess of the rates observed in real sonar or radar operations. However, as Table 8.1 reveals, monitoring tasks actually encompass a wide range of defect or target (i.e. signal) rates, among which it even appears that Elliott's (1960) sonar target rates are atypically low. Mackworth (1957a) previously commented on this dissimilarity between the signal rates encountered in military and non-military situations, pointing out that in the fastest operation he had observed, lighter flint inspection, inspectors dealt with between 35 000 and 40 000 flints per hour, which, with a 10% incidence of rejects, would represent 350–400 signals per hour! He also observed that, in the pharmaceutical industry, inspectors of intravenous ampoules typically considered only about 3500–4000 ampoules per hour. Thus, one can see that not only is there a considerable range in the percentage frequency of occurrence of real signals, but also a very wide range in their rate of occurrence over time. The differences in range between these real rates and those employed in vigilance research would seem merely to be that the latter are somewhat more constrained.

On balance, therefore, considering both task duration and signal rate, there can be little doubt that situations likely to involve problems of vigilance are prevalent in real operations in both the industrial and the military spheres.

Performance assessment

In the absence of some objective measurement of performance, it is impossible to determine whether a vigilance problem exists, even although the situation may appear conducive to it. Before the reader comments on the apparently trivial nature of this statement, he would do well to reflect on the observation that, in the survey carried out by Megaw (1977), not one single case was reported in which objective performance measurement was carried out. All too frequently, reliance is placed on the foreman's or supervisor's opinion as to how efficiently the job is being done (Mitchell, 1935; McKenzie, 1958), with occasional feedback in the form of customers' complaints (Belbin, 1957a), and frequently also, when an objective assessment is made, management are rather surprised to discover just how inefficient their workers are (Mills and Sinclair, 1976; Fox, 1977). With inspection tasks at least, performance can be estimated by checking, post-inspection, the proportion of rejects still remaining in the accepted batch, and the proportion of good product erroneously scrapped (Drury and Addison, 1973; Mills and Sinclair, 1976); by inserting, and later checking on the sort, a batch containing a known number of good and defective product (Fox, 1975); or by occasionally injecting known faults which have been marked with a fluorescent dye so that they are subsequently retrievable (Belbin, 1957a). Even although the post-inspection checking may itself be imperfect, the effects of this are relatively minor, but do tend to overestimate the inspector's detection accuracy (McCornack, 1961). Despite the availability of these techniques, the

Author	Product or task type	Misses (%)	Decrement
1. Assenheim (1969)	Glassware		
	(a) Foremen	<10	—
	(b) Inspectors	>20	—
2. Astley and Fox (1975)	Rubber seals	8	—
3. Belbin (1957a)	Ball-bearings	37	—
4. Belbin (1963)	Tin cans	42	—
5. Carter (1957) cited in McCormack (1961)	Acoustic tiles	21	—
6. Chapman and Sinclair (1975)	Jam tarts	23	—
	Chicken carcasses	34–44	Yes
7. Drury and Addison (1973)	Glassware	5–22	—
8. Fox (1975)	Metal fasteners	17	—
	Rubber seals	49	Yes
9. Fox (1977)	Coins		
	(a) Before ergonomic redesign	45.5	—
	(b) After ergonomic redesign	26	—
10. Fox and Haslegrave (1969)	Screws	30–40	—
11. Gillies (1975)	Glass sheets	9	—
12. Harris (1966)	Electronic equipment	25–80	—
13. Hayes (1950)	Piston rings	36	—
14. Jacobsen (1952)	Solder connections		
	(a) Solderless	16	—
	(b) Loosely soldered	18	—
15. Kelly (1955), cited in McCormack (1961)	TV panels	9	—
16. Rigby and Swain (1975)	Electronic modules		
	(a) Complex	7	—
	(b) Simple	1	—
17. Schoonard et al. (1973)	Silicon chips	25	No
18. Self and Rhodes (1964)	Side-looking radar	35	No
19. Tiffin and Rogers (1941)	Tinplate		
	(a) Appearance 1	41	—
	(b) Appearance 2	24	—
	(c) Appearance 3	65	—
	(d) Weight	27	—
20. Yerushalmy (1969)	X-rays	20	—

problem for the reviewer remains that of uncertainty regarding the incidence of vigilance problems owing to the paucity of available data.

Efficiency problems

From the limited reports which have been published, a sample of the findings is provided in Table 8.2. This sample, although by no means exhaustive, is representative of those available, and convinces that considerable problems do exist. In most, but not all, cases, the data were gathered under conditions in which the operators knew their performance was being assessed, but in fact it is well known that this is likely to result in the acuteness of the efficiency problems being underestimated rather than overestimated (Fraser, 1953; McKenzie, 1958). It should be noted too, that in a majority of the tasks listed in Table 8.2 the defects or targets are glaringly obvious under alerted conditions. For example, in Jacobsen's (1952) study, when alerted to their presence, the solderless connections, in which the wires hang loose, are not confusable with properly soldered joints, yet one in six of these faults was overlooked by experienced inspectors. There is, therefore, clear scope for engineering tasks like those listed in order to improve operator efficiency.

The final column in Table 8.2 lists the incidence of reported decrements, or the absence of these, in sustained performance, and it is notable that few studies choose to report on this aspect of performance. Of the four which do, however, two studies reported a decrement in detection rate, from which one can conclude that a decrement function *may* exist in real operations. On the basis of the available evidence, one cannot begin to ascertain the probable incidence of the decrement function in real operations, but neither can one dismiss it out of hand (Elliott, 1960; Teichner, 1974). The observation that few studies mention presence or absence of a decrement may well arise from the practical difficulties encountered in assessing real performance over time, and to speculate on other reasons does not seem worthwhile (Smith and Lucaccini, 1969).

It is well known that, in industrial inspection at least, the detection rate achieved by an inspector can be influenced considerably by his standards as to what constitutes a rejectable fault (McKenzie, 1958), and that when standards are low, insufficient faults are rejected, while when standards are high, a high detection rate is achieved, but only at the cost of falsely scrapping a high proportion of good product (Sheehan and Drury, 1971). Similar effects occur in target detection with a sonar device (Rizy, 1972). Thus, the percentages of missed signals listed in Table 8.2 could be due to either low standards or task difficulty. Although, as already mentioned, most of the tasks listed involve targets or defects which are inherently easy to detect under alerted conditions, it does not necessarily follow that the system as a whole presents an easy task to the operator. An indication of the range of task difficulties in some typical operations is given in Table 8.3.

Table 8.3 Estimates of signal discriminability (d') in a number of real monitoring and inspection tasks

Authors	Product or task type		Estimated d'
1. Assenheim (1969)	Glassware	(a) Inspectors	1.4
		(b) Foremen	2.5
2. Astley and Fox (1975)	Rubber seals		3.3
3. Carroll (1969)	Printed circuits		3.2
4. Carter (1957), cited by McCormack (1961)	Acoustic tiles		2.5
5. Chapman and Sinclair (1975)	Jam tarts		2.6–3.1
6. Drury and Addison (1973)	Glassware		
		(a) Without feedback	2.5
		(b) With addition of feedback	3.2
7. Gillies (1975)	Glass sheets		3.4
8. Jacobsen (1952)	Solder joints		4.1
9. Kelly (1955), cited in McCormack (1961)	TV panels		2.5
10. Rigby and Swain (1975)	Electronic modules		
		(a) Complex	2.4
		(b) Simple	4.3
11. Rizy (1972)	Sonar		2.0–3.0
12. Schoonard et al. (1973)	Silicon chips		2.7
13. Sheehan and Drury (1971)	Machine parts		
		(a) Single defect	3.2
		(b) Paired defects	3.0
14. Yerushalmy et al. (1950)	Pulmonary photofluorograms		2.6
15. Zunzanyika and Drury (1975)	Semiconductors		1.2–2.2

The difficulty index is the familiar d' measure of discriminability from signal detection theory (Green and Swets, 1966), and is based in the usual manner on the proportion of signals (defects or targets) correctly detected *and* the proportion of non-signals (good product, non-targets) incorrectly classified as signals (usually termed 'false positives') according to the formula

$$d' = Z(\text{Proportion false positives}) - Z(\text{Proportion detected}),$$

where $Z(x)$ signifies the normal deviate corresponding to the proportion, x (see Chapter 2 in this volume for a more extensive treatment of signal detection theory).

The d' measure as used here provides an index, independent of operator standards, of the degree to which signals are discriminable within the operational system, whether in inspection (Sheehan and Drury, 1971; Drury and Addison, 1973; Chapman and Sinclair, 1975) or in sonar monitoring (Rizy, 1972). The usefulness of d' in vigilance research has been amply demonstrated (Mackworth, 1970; Swets, 1977). The following provides a useful, 'rule-of-thumb' guide to interpreting the values listed in Table 8.3:

d'	<1.5	1.5–2.5	2.5–3.5	>3.5
Task difficulty	Very difficult	Moderately difficult	Moderately easy	Very easy

As can be seen, common operations encompass the full range, from the prohibitively difficult, as in Assenheim's (1969) study of glassware inspectors, to the exceedingly easy, as in Jacobsen's (1952) report on solder inspection. It is instructive to note that systems in which the individual signals are clearly conspicuous may nevertheless present difficulties for the operator (e.g. Schoonard *et al.*, 1973), and that numerous factors such as lighting (Belbin, 1963), pacing (Chapman and Sinclair, 1975) and display size or configuration (Fox, 1977) can influence the operational level of efficiency. These issues will be elaborated on further, in a later section.

It may also be noted here that the values listed in Table 8.3 are not atypical of those obtained with simplified systems in the laboratory, where tasks also range from the very difficult (e.g. Craig and Colquhoun, 1977, Experiment II, mean $d' = 1.2$) to the very easy (e.g. McGrath, 1965, Group I, auditory pretest, mean $d' = 3.9$).

This section has demonstrated that real operations contain an abundance of situations conducive to vigilance problems and that efficiency problems, sometimes of a fairly serious nature, do exist. It was also apparent that, at an empirical level, sufficient parallels exist between performance in the laboratory and performance in real operations to suggest that the research effort may have a useful contribution to make towards reducing these problems in the field. This potential contribution in the form of principles for the control of vigilance provides the content for the next section.

EMERGENT ENGINEERING PRINCIPLES
FOR THE CONTROL OF VIGILANCE

It may seem that to elevate research findings, not all of which have withstood the test of consistent repeatability, to the status of 'principles' defies justification. Nevertheless, with the inclusion of some necessary provisos, the attempt is made in this section. The empirical rules which are identified and described provide guidelines for improving vigilance, i.e. for reducing or minimizing errors. This directional focus distinguishes the present course from previous surveys or reviews of factors which influence vigilance, either to the betterment or to the detriment of performance (e.g. Craig and Colquhoun, 1975; Loeb and Alluisi, 1977; Warm, 1977). In addition, a second source of distinction lies in the present emphasis on not simply vigilance *during* performance at a task, but on the *results* of such vigilance. Generally, research interests lie in specifying vigilance levels during sustained task performance; however, in practical situations, it is more frequently the case that one is interested in the *consequences* of vigilance performance, rather than in the performance itself, in, for example, the remaining risks consequent on a sonar operator's performance, or in the outgoing quality of product after it has been inspected. As will be seen, on occasions there is an apparent paradox between performance and its consequences such that manipulations which are held to improve the former actually degrade the latter.

Fitting the Task to the Man

Reduce uncertainties

Inherent in any task are several sources of uncertainty which can have a detrimental influence on performance. A first general principle is therefore to reduce the levels of uncertainty. There are two major sources: uncertainty about what constitutes a signal (target/defect) and uncertainty about where the signal will occur. The enhancement of efficiency (reduction in both errors of omission and of commission) by specifying the signal in advance (hence ensuring that the operator knows precisely what he is looking for) was amply demonstrated by Gundy (1961) and the benefits are revealingly discussed by McKenzie (1958) in his report on inspector accuracy. Prior specification is also beneficial when applied to tolerance limits, in contexts such as fabric inspection, where deviations from a norm occur (Raphael, 1942); even the accuracy of go–not go gauging is improved by the provision of tolerance specifications (Lawshe and Tiffin, 1945). Sheehan and Drury (1971) have also demonstrated that when there is more than one kind of signal to be detected and when circumstances are such that advance warning can be given of the particular signal mix to expect, efficiency is improved, (see also also Childs, 1976; Megaw and Richardson, 1979).

There is also a generally held belief that uncertainty may be reduced to the benefit of performance by the provision of a reference standard against which events/items can be compared. But this view seems decidedly suspect, and it is doubtful whether much attention is paid to the standard (Baker and O'Hanlon, 1963; Colquhoun and Edwards, 1970; Drury, 1975), although in the special circumstances where ample time is available and use of the standard actively encouraged (Chaney and Teel, 1967), or where comparison with the standard is the natural strategy imposed by the structure of the task (Parasuraman and Davies, 1977), improvements in efficiency have been observed.

It does, however, seem pertinent to mention here that the provision of reference standards can reduce uncertainties about category boundaries in classification tasks, where the examiner's job is to sort or grade material into appropriate classes, rather than merely to detect presence or absence of a signal. Indeed, according to some (e.g. Colquhoun, 1963), the troubles associated with the running of an inspection department most often appear to arise from alleged failures in fault classification (rather than in detection). Gatherum *et al.* (1959, 1960, 1961) demonstrated that the provision of visual references helped to maintain classification standards in judgments of the quality of meat, improved the consistency between different examiners, and reduced the visual drifts in standards consequent on changes in batch quality (judges tending to be more critical when batch quality is high). But it should be pointed out that the judges in that study had ample time to refer to the standards.

Another technique which helps to reduce uncertainty, and which usually results in improvements in detection efficiency and in the speed of reactions, is to provide additional (redundant) information about items/events in a second sensory modality (e.g. looking *and* listening, instead of just looking alone). Colquhoun (1975) summarizes much of the evidence from monitoring studies. The technique, although sometimes difficult to engineer, can have a marked effect on detections, as, for example, in the study reported by Craig *et al.* (1976) in which a combined audio-visual presentation yielded a 50% improvement over the visual mode alone. Although similar benefits have been claimed both in the laboratory and in the field, when the condition of redundancy is effected by employing multiple monitors operating on a single source of information (as opposed to a single individual monitoring multiple sources) (e.g. Yerushalmy *et al.*, 1950; Konz and Osman, 1977), the advantages have not proved sufficiently reliable across different studies to endorse the practice (Davies and Tune, 1970).

In this context, one might also consider that increased signal conspicuity reduces uncertainty, and there is ample research evidence that such an increase does indeed reduce errors, both of omission and of commission, and also reduces the signal response time (e.g. Binford and Loeb, 1963). Throughput also improves (Drury, 1975). Thus, any image-enhancement techniques are likely to increase the efficiency of radar/sonar operation, while in inspection, the general rule should be that the more conspicuous the fault, the better, as might be achieved, for example, by improved lighting, or by contrast (Astley and Fox, 1975; Faulkner and Murphy, 1975). This directly implies that improvements in processing which merely reduce the severity of defects, without reducing their incidence, are not to be recommended, since they will simply make the operator's task more difficult, degrade his efficiency, and slow him down. It is noted that this suggestion contrasts markedly with that of Arnborger *et al.* (1954), who advocated improving production to the point at which a defect was so difficult to see that it could be spotted less than 50% of the time (they also advocated dispensing with the examiner's services when this point was reached). Signal conspicuity can also be increased by allowing more time for the examination of each item or event (Drury, 1973), an effect which is simple to engineer, but which can make a very considerable impact on operating costs (see, for example, Chapman and Sinclair, 1975).

Spatial uncertainty refers to the inevitable absence of specification about where, within the field of view, a signal is likely to appear. Numerous research studies, dating back notably to those of Nicely and Miller (1957), of Bergum and Lehr (1963) and of Adams and his colleagues (Adams, 1963), have indicated that when spatial uncertainty exists, vigilance performance is usually degraded, with a reduction in the level of correct detections, and a slowing in the speed of reacting to signals. In one laboratory study (Baker and Harabedian, 1962), the mere introduction of spatial uncertainty reduced detections from 100% to 87%; in another study (Howell *et al.*, 1966), reducing the spatial uncertainty by compressing the display into a smaller area significantly reduced the time taken to react to signals. Similar effects are found in practical situations. For example, Wallis and Samuel (1961), using trained operators in a very close simulation of prolonged 'plan position indicator' (PPI) airborne radar, observed that detections were less reliable at long ranges which required a larger search area on the PPI scope, and Harris (1966) demonstrated that, in the inspection of electronic equipment by experienced inspectors, fault detections were inversely related to the number of component parts in which a fault could occur and which therefore had to be examined, in each item of equipment. Fox (1977), in his study of coin inspection, similarly demonstrated the practical effects of spatial uncertainty by varying the size of the display aperture through which the coins were viewed: detections were significantly increased by reducing the size of the aperture, and although this tended to lower the total throughput, the improved efficiency of inspection more than compensated in terms of cost-effectiveness. Teel *et al.* (1968) reduced the spatial uncertainty inherent in the photomasters of electronic circuit boards by providing inspectors with a visual aid in the form of an overlay matrix mask. This simple procedure decidedly improved detections of one kind of defect (although not of another); and reduced the inspection time; the resultant reduction in scrappage costs was estimated to be in excess of $10 000 per year. In some instances, a further means of reducing spatial uncertainty may lie in the possibility of implementing computer assistance, to specify, with some degree of reliability, the location of a probable signal on the display. Murrell (1977), for example, has shown that efficiency in a simulation study is reliably improved by such an aid.

Uncertainties about what to look for, and where to look for it, may be regarded as related to task difficulty, and, in general, reducing the difficulty increases the efficiency of the operator. There are, in addition, uncertainties about how many to look for, or when to look for them, but it is not clear that the principle of uncertainty reduction applies unequivocally to these. For example, telling the operator what proportion of the events will be signals (e.g. Williges, 1969), or telling him that this proportion will change to a new (and specified) level (Williges, 1973; Embrey, 1975) alters his standards for reporting signals, but does not affect his actual efficiency: errors of omission and of commission shift in opposite directions. The effect is similar to that produced by appropriate pretest 'expectancy' training (Colquhoun and Baddeley, 1964). In inspection operations, the information (or training) is likely to leave outgoing quality at an unchanged level, and the only real advantage would seem to be that in radar/sonar operations (or any other situation where detections are at a premium) detection levels might be improved, although at the cost of increased false alarms. But this will only happen if the true signal rate is higher than the operator expects, a circumstance which apparently seldom arises in practice. Indeed, the more usual effect will be that the operator becomes more conservative, with an attendant reduction in detections, as a result of the information. Experienced operators are, in any case, likely to have built up appropriate expectancies about the frequency or proportion of signals in any familiar situation (Wyatt and Langdon, 1932, 1932; Bakwin, 1954), and in an unfamiliar or novel context it seems probable that the information to be imparted is simply not available.

The last-mentioned comment also applies to temporal cueing: if one knew when the signal was due, the operator could be dispensed with. However, were such information available (even if only in a probabilistic form, as in computer-assisted monitoring), it is doubtful whether any real benefit would accrue (Colquhoun, 1966; Murrell, 1977), although lasting advantages have been claimed when temporal cueing is provided during the initial stage of training an inexperienced operator (e.g. Annett and Clarkson, 1964). Detections may be increased, the reaction time to signals reduced, if temporal uncertainty is reduced by arranging that the interval between signals is more regular (Baker, 1959; Smith, 1961; Adams and Boulter, 1964). Thus, in inspection, where faults tend to occur in bunches, so that some batches contain several while others have none at all, some improvement might be achieved by mixing the material prior to inspection, to create a more uniform distribution of faults over the period of work (Wyatt and Langdon, 1932; Baker, 1964).

The occurrence of a signal is less unexpected when signals are frequent than when they are infrequent. Thus, increasing the signal frequency, or the proportion of events which are signals, is a means for reducing temporal uncertainty, and since the early studies by Deese (1955) demonstrating the importance of signal frequency, and by Colquhoun (1961), on signal probability, has proved one of the most reliable ways to increase the proportion of signals detected. There is, for example, some evidence that the mere insertion of artificial signals can improve detections of true signals (Garvey *et al.*, 1959), and that adding extra signals can increase the speed of reacting to signals (Faulkner, 1962). However, it does seem that the improvement in detections is bought at the price of increased commissive errors, so that the insertion of the artificial signals does not, in fact, improve overall efficiency (Wilkinson, 1964; Murrell, 1975). Indeed, an examination of data from studies showing an improved detection rate consequent upon an increased signal frequency or signal probability, reveals that the improvement is seldom sufficient to compensate for the increased signal rate; the number of signals remaining undetected is the same or even greater than before, and outgoing quality is the same or even less (Anonymous, 1956; Drury and Addison, 1973). An example to illustrate this important point is provided in Table 8.4. The data are from the much quoted study by Baddeley and Colquhoun (1969). Thus, there is no real gain from an increased signal rate. However, the practical point has been made by Jerison and Pickett (1963) that the effective signal rate can be increased without the addition of more signals, simply by instructing monitors to regard less critical events or items as signals. The same point has been put more recently by Rizy (1972), who indicated that in sonar monitoring detections could be improved by considering not only target reports made with high confidence, but also low confidence reports as well. Rizy (1972) suggests that the reports (at different confidence levels) could then be filtered at the command level, the filtering being appropriate to suitable courses of action, depending on the situational risks. In general, however, it would seem that reducing uncertainties about signal frequency or about the timing of signal occurrence is of little real merit.

Table 8.4 Effects of increased proportion of signals on performance: percentage detections, number of misses and outgoing quality

Percentage signals (%)	Average percentage detections (%)	Average number missed	Average outgoing quality (% signals)
2	34.3	15.8	1.3
6	34.6	47.1	4.0
18	44.2	120.5	11.1
24	47.1	152.4	14.8
36	51.8	208.2	22.2

One final source of uncertainty remains: uncertainty on the part of the operator as to how well he is performing his job. This can also be reduced by practical means, by feeding back information following a post-inspection audit, or by signalling to the operator his performance in respect of artificial signals. The effects of immediate or delayed feedback are due to motivational as well as instructional influences (Wiener, 1975; Warm, 1977), and are generally beneficial: efficiency is improved (reduction in both errors of omission and of commission) in the real situation (e.g. Drury and Addison, 1973; Gillies, 1975) as in the laboratory (Wilkinson, 1964; Williges and North, 1972), and reactions are generally quicker too (McCormack, 1959). However, since the feedback need not be veridical (Weidenfeller *et al.*, 1962; Warm *et al.*, 1974), there is reason to believe that the facilitative effects are primarily motivational in character, and that the instructional influence is slight (McCormack, 1967; Mackworth, 1970; Warm, 1977). Thus, although it does seem worthwhile to reduce performance uncertainty, the effect may not be due to that reduction *per se*.

Motivate or Stimulate the Operator

One advantageous means of doing so has just been mentioned. Another effective way of increasing motivation (at least in the short term) is by verbal instruction. Lucaccini *et al.* (1968) showed that detections were significantly better for monitors who had been instructed that the vigilance task was 'challenging', than for those who had been told it was 'monotonous'. Nachreiner (1977) obtained a similar improvement by subjects who perceived the task as a selection test for a job, rather than as a vigilance experiment. Although false alarm data were not presented in either case, they were reported to be negligible in the earlier study, thereby indicating that a genuine improvement in efficiency had been achieved. Drew (1940), in his study of pilot fatigue, found that performance was significantly improved when instructions of a manoeuvre to be undertaken were perceived as difficult, rather than easy.

Where primary interest lies in the achieved level of detections, research has shown that improved levels can be attained by verbal encouragement to do better (e.g. Mackworth, 1950), or to be less cautious about reporting signals (Colquhoun, 1967). These manipulations, it now seems, affect the operator's standards of judgment, although they do not appear to influence his overall efficiency (i.e. the improved detections are usually paralleled by increased commission errors). Nevertheless, motivating the operator to detect a greater proportion of signals is clearly advantageous in, for example, radar operation or X-ray examination, where the costs of a miss greatly outweigh those of a false alarm. Unfortunately, artificial manipulation of the pay-off structure (by, for example, financial incentives) is not invariably successful in achieving that end: some results have been encouraging (Levine, 1966; Davenport, 1968, 1969) while others have proved disappointing (Smith and Barany, 1970; Williges, 1971;

Guralnick, 1972). However, Rizy's (1972) elegant study of sonar monitoring, in which he achieved a convincing simulation of the conventional problem environment, with trained operators who had considerable experience of operational conditions, leaves no room for doubt that detections can be readily manipulated in a predictable manner, *so long as one employs realistic, credible pay-offs* (although Rizy does suggest that the determination and operation of pay-offs could be postponed to the command level, if the operators could be encouraged to report targets with varying degrees of confidence; low confidence reports could then be attended to or not, as the situation demanded).

It is, of course, well known that money can be used to motivate greater effort or concentration, although McKenzie (1958) injects a cautionary note when he points out that financial incentives can differentially influence judgments and throughput, depending on whether the bonus is applied to the volume of work handled, work passed or work which has been finally packaged. In addition, in the study reported by Mitten (1952), inspection speed showed only meagre improvement as a result of financial incentives, but increased considerably when the incentive was 'time off' on completion of a weekly quota. Mitten's study demonstrates not only the importance of motivation, but also the need to make a proper investigation of the operator's value systems, in order to determine which particular incentive scheme to employ.

Monitoring jobs are intrinsically boring and, in industry, they are often of rather low status. As a consequence, in the short term at least, changes which relieve task boredom, or which indicate an interest in or concern for the monitors, often have a beneficial, motivating influence on performance. For example, Fraser (1953) provided experimental evidence that the mere presence of a silent supervisor could elevate detections, an effect which seems to parallel observations in industry, as in the Hawthorne studies (Roethlisberger and Dickson, 1939), and perhaps also in Drury and Addison's (1973) study, where the supervisor's presence was necessary to provide the information feedback to the inspectors. Chapman and Sinclair (1975) report a similar effect, an increase in inspection speed by inspectors who knew they were being observed.

Where a task is sufficiently complex and interesting in itself, there may be little problem with motivation, and, indeed, Adams and his coworkers (Adams, 1963) suggest that in such cases human operators prove remarkably efficient and reliable. However, where boredom is a problem, the task can be made more interesting by breaking it up into segments and interpolating periods of activity of some other kind. This was demonstrated to improve the accuracy of repetitive vernier gauge setting in an experiment by Saldanha (1957), and has subsequently been shown to benefit performance in the field. For example, Fox (1977) found that batch inspection of coins, with interpolated periods of fetching and loading/unloading the conveyor belt hopper, resulted in a significantly higher percentage of fault detections than was observed with continuous inspection. Rigby and Swain (1975) report a similar improvement when inspection (of

X-rays of components in an assembled unit), instead of being continuous, was limited to periods of 30 minutes, separated by an hour spent on another job. Similarly, Wallis and Samuel (1961) found that radar performance was significantly inferior when continuous than when interrupted by 5–10 minutes of navigation. It is often the case that such job enlargement or enrichment schemes can be applied to a team whose functions rotate at fairly frequent intervals, without reducing the final output level (see, for example, Wyatt and Langdon, 1932; Baker, 1964). Despite Jenkins' (1958) finding that 15 minute vigils separated by 10 minute rest breaks still showed some decrement, laboratory studies have indicated that the provision of rest pauses of as little as 5 minutes' duration, facilitates overall detection levels (Mackworth, 1950; Colquhoun, 1959). The effect, which appears to relieve boredom, is largely due to the arrest of the decrement, and has led to the recommendation that the break should be given within the first half-hour, the period of maximal decrement (see Figure 8.1). This is apparently a fairly common practice in industrial tasks requiring sustained attention (Hanhart, 1954; Belbin, 1957b; Bhatia and Murrell, 1969) and may be one of the reasons why decrements are seldom found or reported. One can also stimulate visual monitors to achieve better detection levels by providing them with a programme of background music, the more varied the better. The beneficial effects of 'varied auditory stimulation' have been observed in a number of laboratory experiments (e.g. Tarriere and Wisner, 1962; McGrath, 1963a; Poock and Wiener, 1966), and have also been successfully demonstrated in an application to industrial inspection (Fox and Embrey, 1972). In the laboratory, McGrath (1963a) has shown that the same principle extends to the use of varied visual stimulation in elevating detection performance on a listening task.

In this present context, one might also recommend that, where possible, monitors should be allowed to progress at their own rate, rather than being subject to machine pacing. Primarily, the reason for making this recommendation is that operators usually prefer a self-paced task and find it more interesting (McFarling and Heimstra, 1975; Fox, 1977). Evidence based on a performance evaluation is equivocal: some laboratory studies have found little difference between paced and unpaced conditions (e.g. Wilkinson, 196?; Colquhoun, 1962), while others point to the superiority of the self-paced condition (e.g. Broadbent, 1953; Williges and Streeter, 1971), although the superior detection efficiency may be at the expense of a reduction in speed (McGarling and Heimstra, 1975). A similar ambivalence is found in practice: Mitten (1952) reports that the introduction of a variable-speed control actually led to improvements in both quality and throughput, whereas Fox (1977) found that detections could be degraded by self-pacing, without any compensating advantages of increased speed.

Generally, it would seem that motivating or stimulating the monitor does have a facilitating effect on detections, at least in the short term. What is not yet so clear, is whether such changes are lasting, and also, whether they reliably improve overall efficiency.

Moderate Environmental and Other Stresses

Since vigilance tasks are characteristically boring, it is often the case that mild stress will have an alerting effect on the monitor, improving his vigilance. Poulton (1973, 1977), for example, in his excellent summaries, indicates that mild discomfort produced by heat, noise, vertical vibration or physical exercise may increase detections, work rate and response speed, although he does warn that satisfactorily reliable evidence of a genuine improvement in overall efficiency (i.e. a reduction in commission errors accompanying the increased detection) is not yet generally available. As a practical example, Drew (1940) found that fatigue errors in pilots could be counteracted to some extent by a short period of discomfort in seating. However, when the stressors induce too great a degree of discomfort, vigilance apparently suffers, as was found by Poulton *et al.* (1965) in their study of ship look-outs operating under either freezing Arctic conditions, or under wet and windy conditions in a temperate zone, the discomfort of which is only too familiar. The effects on vigilance of a combination of adverse stressors are somewhat unpredictable. They may even neutralize each other, as in the experiment by Poulton and Edwards (1974) in which loud noise, which had a mildly depressing influence on efficiency, cancelled out most of the significantly detrimental effect of heat stress.

In summary, it would seem that, on the basis of present research evidence, one can put forward three basic engineering principles which aid in fitting the (vigilance) task to the man: (a) reduce uncertainties, particularly those pertaining to signal characteristics and to spatial factors; (b) motivate or stimulate the operator, to make the task more challenging or interesting; and (c) optimize the operating conditions by including a moderate degree of stress.

Fitting the man to the task

Although seldom spoken of in other than hushed voices, it is generally acknowledged that in vigilance experiments the performance differences between the subjects who participate exceeds those between the experimental conditions (see, for example, Buckner *et al.*, 1960). Thus the potential benefits from choosing the right personnel for the job may well be in excess of those to be achieved by, for example, reducing signal uncertainties. It is therefore exasperating that guiding principles for selecting and training operators remain, on present evidence, somewhat obscure. One can at best provide a few rough pointers, although it is realized that their immediate practical value is slight. This rather pessimistic view is shared by Wiener (1975), who presents an excellent summary of relevant findings.

Selection

There is no single criterion for distinguishing between good and bad inspectors, and the best advice one can offer is to nibble away at the uncertainties in an attempt to reduce them (as in the first principle offered). It should be clear that, in a search which has been going on now for at least 40 years, if any of the more obvious criteria such as age, sex or sensory acuity had proved dependable, there would be little contemporary problems in selection. Sex differences have been obtained (e.g. Waag *et al.*, 1973), but not with sufficient reliability or consistency to favour male or female operators. Nor is age a reliable guide, for, despite the observation that aging is generally associated with a deterioration in abilities (Welford, 1958), such detrimental effects are too easily offset by the facilitative effects of experience. Sheehan and Drury (1971) did find a significant negative correlation between age and inspection efficiency, but this seems to be the exception rather than the rule. McCornack (1961), for example, cites four earlier industrial studies which had found no relation, or only a very weak one, between age and performance, and Jamieson (1966) actually found that *errors* made during the inspection of electromagnetic switches were negatively correlated with age. The latter finding is in agreement with at least some studies of industrial and aircraft accidents caused by a failure of vigilance, or by fatigue (Thorndike, 1951). The only case in which age seems likely to be a reliably decisive factor is where a rapid motor response or handling action is called for. One might, therefore, recommend that older personnel be limited to slow or unpaced tasks, and not employed on high speed, machine-paced jobs, often associated with automation (see Conway, 1955). Particular instances like this can be avoided by preliminary abilities screening (for vision, hearing, motor functioning, etc.) to ensure that there are no basic defects which would render the person physically or mentally incapable of doing the job. Beyond this, one can, with only slight confidence, use standard tests of abilities, such as those to measure static or dynamic visual acuity (e.g. Nelson and Barany, 1969) to reduce the uncertainty in selection, for although encouraging associations have been obtained, there is no guarantee that the person with the most acute vision or hearing, as measured by one of these tests, will prove to be the best monitor (Megaw, 1978); Baker (1960) claims that detection efficiency of radar operators is unrelated to visual acuity, and Tiffin and Rogers (1941) make a similar observation in regard to the accuracy of inspectors.

Alternative approaches to selection, using aptitude tests, have on the whole proved disappointing. As Wiener (1975) points out, correlations with actual efficiency have generally proved too low to be of practical value; high correlations with supervisor's ratings have been obtained, but are to be discounted owing to the notoriously poor validity of the latter as an index of actual efficiency (see, for example, Mills and Sinclair, 1976); and despite some encouraging results (e.g. Harris, 1964; Embrey, 1978) none has yet withstood the test of demonstrating consistent reliability. The use of personality tests (almost exclusively limited to laboratory studies) has proved equally disappointing, and despite some findings of theoretical interest, the practical benefits seem, at present, virtually non-existent.

A final approach, recommended by some, disparaged by others, is to base selection on performance at a sample of the task itself. The justification for this rests on observations made in both laboratory and industrial contexts, that the relative performance levels for the individuals in a group are reliably consistent from one session or period of time, to another (Lockwood, 1958; Buckner *et al.*, 1960; Gunn and Loeb, 1967; Chapman and Sinclair, 1975). Jerison and Pickett (1963) state that the session-to-session reliability coefficient is generally of the order 0.6–0.9 (maximum = 1.0), and Wallis and Samuel (1961) report a high reliability (>0.7) between radar performance under an 'alerted' condition and that observed under the normal vigilance test conditions. However, as yet, evidence is equivocal as to whether these 'consistent' individual differences are maintained over extended periods of time. Moraal (1975), for example, reports that in sheet steel inspection, the reject percentages (averaged over 3 months) of 10 inspectors were highly correlated between periods separated by a full year; Mills and Sinclair (1976), on the other hand, could find no correspondence for either detection levels or work rate of eight examiners, between a sample of normal production inspection (of knitted garments) and inspection of a test batch administered 6 weeks later. Until sufficient evidence has been accumulated to offer a satisfactory conclusion on this issue, doubts must remain about the efficacy of the task-sample approach to selection (or indeed, about any approach to selection). A further problem for the task-sample approach is that, in time, the person selected may be employed on a different task, as in the change from PPI to B-scan sonar displays. Unfortunately, there is general consensus (from laboratory and field) that correlations of performance between different tasks (or even between different signals within one task) are low (e.g. Wyatt and Langdon, 1932; Tiffin and Rogers, 1941; Buckner *et al.*, 1960; Pope and McKechnie, 1963; Moraal, 1975) the only major exceptions appear to be in laboratory studies comparing visual and auditory vigilance (e.g. Gunn and Loeb, 1967; Craig *et al.*, 1976). In other words, a task-sample will probably be too specific to guarantee future dividends, but may help to reduce some of the uncertainty of selection in the short term.

Training

There seems little doubt that, whether operators are carefully selected or not, the performance achieved by a naive operator on a vigilance task can benefit from training. The uncertainty reducing techniques discussed earlier, of signal specification, immediate feedback or knowledge of results (KR), and cueing, have all been shown to be effective ways of rapidly attaining a satisfactory, high plateau of efficiency, and it has also been shown that the beneficial effects of KR and cueing transfer to later sessions or possibly even to different tasks, when these training aids are withdrawn (Gundy, 1961; Annett, 1966; Wiener, 1967). However, as already noted, there is at least some evidence (e.g. Colquhoun, 1966; Colquhoun and Edwards, 1970) which suggests that, beyond the initial stage in training, experience at the task is as effective as any training aids in elevating performance. Wiener (1975) does point out, though, that in contexts where the experiential factor is at a minimum, as, for example, where the signal is barely discriminable and rarely occurs, advantages will almost certainly accrue from the employment of training aids or from a training programme designed to elevate experience of the signal; he also cites a number of industrial case studies which claim to have successfully applied training aids (particularly KR) to the economic and ergonomic advantage of the companies concerned. In addition to training for signal detectability, there is evidence that subjects can be trained, by instruction, to adopt a more efficient scanning strategy for visual search (Coates *et al.*, 1972). But one is ultimately forced to admit that the research contribution to the development of a 'good' monitor is comparatively slight, and limited to the short term, and that the major development arises through the acquisition of experience, often gained only after many years. This is exemplified in Thomas's (1962) discussion of the development of perceptual skills by industrial inspectors, the development involving not only the ability to 'detect', but also the enhancement of this as a result of an increased understanding of the underlying causal relationships in the work situation (often itself the result of paying attention over many years to the cueing effects of systematic faults in production). Thomas describes, for example, the inspector of domestic vacuum cleaners, who could better an audiometric device, and could tell by the sound of the cleaner not only whether it was faulty, but also could specify the production source of the fault; and the elderly female inspector of castings, who was so skilled in distinguishing between surface blemishes which would disappear when painted, and those which would not, that her performance could not be approached by a successor, even after an intensive, three-month, training programme. However, as a token of encouragement to the research workers, one should point out that such exceptional skills are probably rare, and that the trainee monitor may well be as efficient as his more experienced senior, as indicated in a number of the studies cited by McCornack (1961), and in the more recent study by Mills and Sinclair (1976).

Identifying Unacceptable Efficiency Levels

The three principal techniques for identifying unacceptably low levels of efficiency have already been specified. These are, where appropriate: by re-inspection, by examining efficiency on an inserted sample, and by checking the detection of occasionally inserted artificial signals. These techniques offer relatively direct indications of efficiency, and may be as unobtrusive as the effort expended in applying them permits. Where their application is not practicable, because of interference with the task, it may nevertheless prove possible to identify potential substandard levels by indirect means. For example, the quest for a physiological alertness indicator, as earlier sought in muscle tonus by Kennedy and Travis (1947), appears to be closing in on its goal, as evidenced by a number of reports (particularly that of Carriero, 1977) in the vigilance symposium edited by Mackie (1977). No-one would claim an identity between level of physiological function and vigilance, but the correspondence seems sufficiently close to justify the use of a physiological indicator, in the absence of any direct measure of vigilance. Recent advances in telemetric recording of activity in central and autonomic nervous systems bring the use of such measures within the realms of practicability. There is also some correspondence between vigilance efficiency and certain behavioural measures (e.g. critical flicker fusion frequency, binocular near-point accommodation, accuracy of tracking onto a stationary target), which suggests that very brief inserted tests might have a role to play as indirect indicators of unacceptable vigilance levels (Saito and Tanaka, 1977; Takakuwa, 1977). However, if one can disrupt performance to insert such a test, then presumably a sample batch, or some artificial signals, could be inserted instead.

The general principle which emerges is therefore, once more, that of reducing uncertainty about performance. This time, however, the emphasis is placed on obtaining even a crude indication of substandard levels, rather than focusing as before on the effects of relatively fine-grained information feedback to the operator.

OVERRIDING INFLUENCES

The principles described in the preceding section all emerged from research studies, the majority of which were conducted under carefully controlled laboratory conditions. However, despite the correspondence which has already been noted between some of the research findings and the results of practical, operational studies, there is more than a suspicion that real task demands and influences have not been (or cannot be) replicated in an experimental or laboratory context (Chapanis, 1967; Nachreiner, 1977). The problem is not so much one of physical characteristics of the job (which could be studied in the laboratory) as of the social environment in which the work takes place.

The literature on inspection operations is replete with examples illustrating the social influences on operator performance. A useful summary is provided by McKenzie (1958). These social influences can operate in a number of ways. One can have, for example, accept/reject biases arising out of social pressures (e.g. Schwartz, 1957). The operator may adopt a bias towards conservatism because management are favourably disposed towards low rejection rates (e.g. Belbin, 1957a), or a bias may be imposed by peer pressure in the inspection group not to deviate too far from the established group norm for percentage rejects; from either source, performance is not likely to be questioned if it comes within acceptable limits of the social norm. Similar chronic biases may also exist with regard to the classification of items close to the tolerance limit, when one may observe either a tendency towards 'censorship' or towards 'flinching' (Juran, 1935, 1951). On the whole, these biases seem to influence the rejection standards rather than the actual efficiency of inspection, and may be sufficiently powerful to over-ride any other inducements, including financial incentives, or the usual effects of changes in defect rate (Mitchell, 1935). Other biases, sometimes of a less chronic form, although no less effective, may well influence efficiency also, and appear to stem from the general rule of not upsetting other people, applied to a situation in which the development of interpersonal relations between inspector and process operator or repairman is inevitable. The inspector is not likely to report many faults (even if they are detected) in the work of a friend, particularly if that friend will be penalized for faulty work (Belbin, 1963). Alternatively, when the repairman (perhaps paid for work done) has little work to do, faults will be found for him (i.e. deliberate errors of commission), and when he is already harassed, no more faults will be found (i.e. deliberate errors of omission) (McKenzie, 1958). Rigby and Swain (1975) observe that the inspector may also deliberately miss defects when he himself has to do the re-working, or when each reject involves some overly bothersome paperwork. Typically, one can view the inspector's performance as a compromise or equilibrium between opposing forces: on the one hand, to do his job by detecting faults (this, characteristically, is how his role is perceived), and on the other, to find few faults lest he incur the hostility of the production personnel, or even of management (Belbin, 1957a). The problem is exacerbated in direct relation to the degree of social involvement, and also the extent to which objective standards for inspection remain undefined; it is minimized, for the individual, when standards are clearly defined and when inspection is carried out in relative isolation from production (Jamieson, 1966), although the latter may have an adverse effect on the social status of inspectors as a group, and may give rise to the development of a lenient group norm.

Thus, to underline the point previously stressed by McKenzie (1958), a major difference between laboratory and factory is that the real inspector operates in a social context, in full awareness that he is examining someone else's work; these social influences, from which the laboratory subject is effectively cocooned, can even inhibit the operational influence of other factors whose effects have been consistently demonstrated in the research environment, to the extent that inspectors are often influenced more by other people than by the quality of the product (McKenzie, 1958; Harris, 1969). Similar influences undoubtedly afflict the sonar operator who is at pains to detect any 'target-like' image, but who may be reprimanded (officially or unofficially) if he makes too many commissive errors. Considering the pressures to conform, there is little surprise in Elliott's (1960) claim that the manipulation of target frequencies over a wide range does not appreciably affect behaviour in military watchkeeping tasks, where social isolation is not a relevant condition.

OPERATIONAL RELEVANCE

The issues discussed to this point have been premised on the efficiency problems which were defined at the beginning of the chapter. These problems, studied in so much detail over the years, are largely as specified by the research worker, and, although they are also of concern to the quality-control manager or to his military equivalent, it does seem that there is some disparity between the views of researcher and practitioner. The most obvious case in point is the difference in emphasis placed on the 'vigilance decrement'; as discussed previously, this is of paramount importance to the research worker, yet it seems to be of only slight concern in practice (and for this reason was relegated to a minor role in this chapter). The essayed function of this current section is to present the real and significant problems of monitoring as perceived by the practitioner, and, by so doing, to arrive at an evaluation of the operational relevance of the research effort which has so far been expended.

The goal is undoubtedly that of detecting all signals, be they military targets or production defects; the problem is that signals are missed. Often, these errors are held to imply inefficiency on the part of the observer, but although this may be true to an extent where the task involves visual scanning, inefficiencies in which can contribute to errors (e.g. Wallis and Samuel, 1961; Coates *et al.*, 1972), the view is generally open to question. The demonstration, primarily through the illuminating influence of signal detection theory (Green and Swets, 1966), that signal detection is a limited process and that even optimal efficiency is not necessarily free from errors of omission, is one of the major contributions of the research effort. The limits on signal discriminability are determined by the resolving power of the sensory system, visual auditory or other, and are such that even for what may be termed an easy discrimination, some modicum of confusion between signal and non-signal exists, so that some degree of error, no matter how small, is ultimately inevitable. (This is equivalent to saying that the discriminability index (d') for most tasks falls within a finite, measurable range.) Given this confusability, the only guarantee that no signals will be missed would be if the monitor reported everything as a signal, scrapping every item of production, or reporting a contact on each sweep of the scope, behaviour which would obviously be quite unacceptable. Thus some proportion of omission errors must be tolerated. The question is how much?

The relative incidence of errors of omission and of commission, the balance between them, is at the discretion of the operator, and depends on his standards for deciding to report a signal. At one extreme, as in providing the above 'guarantee', he could produce an overwhelming abundance of commission errors, but with zero misses, while at the other, he could emit no false alarms, but miss every signal that occurred. The optimum standard to employ will depend on the particular goal being pursued. Green and Swets (1966, pp.18–25) define optimizing rules in respect of various decision goals, such as minimizing overall error rates or maximizing expected value when pay-offs are operable, and research studies have shown that the standards employed by monitors are often adjusted to approximate these ideals (e.g. Williges, 1969, 1973; Rizy, 1972); some evidence is also consistent with the goal of equalizing the frequency of errors of each type (sensible when pay-offs are symmetric), which results in behaviour known as probability matching (e.g. Craig, 1978). Decision goals, and behaviour appropriate to them, are not necessarily compatible with each other, as the hypothetical example in Table 8.5 illustrates. The example lists a range of possible behaviours for a situation (military or industrial) in which only a small, fixed proportion of events/items are signals, and in which signal discriminability is maintained at a constant level. The list shows, for instance, that although the goals of keeping missed signals and outgoing quality at some tolerable level (less than 1%, say) are compatible, they cannot coexist with the goal of maintaining an acceptably low scrap level (less than 10%, say). Similarly, the desire to hold overall errors to a minimum is clearly not consistent with the demand for a low proportion of missed signals, and neither of these goals is compatible with the optimum when decisions about signals are held to be 10 times more critical than decisions about non-signals.

Thus one can regard this aspect of research work as contributing to an understanding of goal compatability. A rational basis is provided for demonstrating what *can* be achieved, and for resolving the dilemma of the quality-control manager who is charged with minimizing both costs and errors. In addition, for a specified set of circumstances, it is apparent that one can integrate the behavioural decisions (with their consequent balance of errors) with the costs of production, inspection and replacement, to determine the optimum decision rule for a minimum cost sampling plan (Bennett, 1975; Drury, 1978; Megaw, 1978). Actual, achieved performance may then be compared to the optimum to determine whether there is a need for more or less conservatism in inspector standards.

A related efficiency problem for the practitioner is the lack of consistency in the judgments by a single operator. In research studies, consistency is usually expressed in terms of the agreement between percentage detections or percentage correct judgments from one testing time to another. In the field, however, consistency usually implies that the same judgment (pass–fail, target–non-target) will be made about an item on consecutive occasions. To the author's knowledge, no laboratory study has indexed consistency in this way, although numerous field studies have done so (e.g. Hayes, 1950; Lockwood, 1958; McKenzie, 1958;

Table 8.5 Effects of decision standards on balance of errors and other aspects of performance, assuming constant levels of signal discriminability ($d' = 3.0$) and signal probability ($= 0.05$)

	Percentage missed (%)	Percentage false alarms (%)	Overall error (%)	Percentage affirmative (i.e. signal) reports (%)	Average outgoing quality (% signals)
	30.15[†]	0.66	2.13	4.12	1.57
	22.96[‡]	1.19	2.28	4.98	1.21
	20.00	1.54	2.46	5.46	1.06
	10.00	4.27	4.56	8.56	0.55
	9.85[§]	4.36	4.63	8.65	0.54
Increasing	5.00	8.69	8.51	13.01	0.29
conservatism	2.00	17.11	16.35	21.15	0.13
	1.00	25.14	23.93	28.85	0.07

[†] Optimum to minimize overall error.
[‡] Probability matching (equalize error frequencies).
[§] Optimum to maximize net value when decision pay-offs are as follows: hits ($+ 10$), misses ($- 10$), correct non-detect ($+ 1$), false alarm ($- 1$).

Meadows *et al.*, 1959; Yerushalmy, 1969). Although this problem of inconsistency is enhanced by instability in the standards of judgment and by the spatial uncertainty when an element of visual search is involved, it does seem an inevitable consequence of signal–non-signal confusability; on the signal detection analogue, momentary fluctuations in the internal noise in the sensory system, or, alternatively, momentary fluctuations in standards (Eijkman and Vendrik, 1963), are liable to give rise to misleading sensations on some occasions, but not on others. One would expect inconsistencies to be greater for borderline items/events in the neighbourhood of the accept–reject (detect–not detect) boundary, but reliable evidence of this has not yet been obtained from monitoring studies. Occasionally, these very inconsistencies are utilized by, for example, asking inspectors to re-examine work which they have already passed, to remove defects missed on a previous check (e.g. Belbin, 1957a; Kennedy, 1957; Harris, 1969; Nachreiner *et al.*, 1975). However, it should be realized that such a practice is likely to augment considerably the proportion of commissive errors, due to the examiner's set to find signals. This is well illustrated in Bakwin's (1954) classic report of the multiple screening of 1000 American children, to select those requiring tonsillectomy. By the end of a third screening, only 65 unselected children remained!

An additional form of inconsistency which is of concern to the practitioner, but which has been virtually absent from research considerations, is that between the detection rates for different kinds of signal. Tiffin and Rogers (1941), for example, reported a mean correlation of only 0.20 between detection rates for different defects in tinplate inspection, and Tiffin (1943) later stated that the highest observed inter-fault correlation was only 0.35. One would, of course, expect differences in detection rates due to differences in signal discriminability and in the relative incidence of the signals; however, the major problem posed by these low correlations is their implication that the person who is good at detecting one kind of signal is not necessarily equally good at detecting signals of some other kind. Industrial inspection offers many examples of this kind of inconsistency (although the pattern of detection rates for different signals may nevertheless be consistent within a single individual, as indicated by Moraal (1975)). This is a problem which research workers have not even begun to tackle.

The reason for the failure of research on this issue is largely a pragmatic one: it is easier to gain an understanding of the fundamental vigilance process when the task is simplified to the barest elements of only one kind of signal. However, it is abundantly clear that in the military and in industry, in particular, signals of many different types can occur within the constraints of one task. Jamieson (1966) cites one particular inspection task in which different kinds of signal numbered in the thousands. Rigby and Swain (1975) usefully illustrate the attendant problems by tabulating the frequency of usage in one task of 41 different defect categories, nine of which were not used at all (i.e. no defects reported), while seven of them accounted for 77% of all defects reported; the frequency of usage bore no relation to the incidence of defects. According to the latter authors, their observations suggest that the practical limits on what an inspector can look for are nine very easy defects, or three very difficult ones, which is reminiscent of the information processing limits observed in laboratory research outside the monitoring field (Miller, 1956). As mentioned, vigilance research has not yet examined this multiple-fault situation in sufficient detail, and the few studies which have done so recently (e.g. Craig and Colquhoun, 1977; Konz and Osman, 1977; Geyer *et al.*, 1979; Megaw *et al.*, 1979) have been rather more concerned with the questions as to whether efficiencies are altered by the presence of other signal types, and whether it is more efficient to employ one person to look for all signals, or different persons each looking for one kind only. On these issues, findings are generally encouraging (in terms of efficiencies and labour economies) when only a couple of different signals are involved, which agrees with observations in real situations (e.g. Fox and Haslegrave, 1969; Sheehan and Drury, 1971). That, however, is still a long way from the majority of real tasks with their more numerous kinds of signal.

Mention was made at an earlier point in this chapter that the problems associated with the running of industrial inspection departments most often appear to arise from alleged failures in fault classification, rather than in simple fault detection (Colquhoun, 1963). Indeed, as Thomas and Seaborne (1960) point out, it is unusual to find industrial tasks in which faults are simply present or absent: most faults occur in varying degrees with the attendant problems of flinching, censorship and drifting standards. And, as Gillies (1975) confirms, from his study of glass inspection, most incorrect decisions are associated with discretionary faults. An equivalent problem exists in military watchkeeping, where it has long been acknowledged that a major source of confusion lies in the occurrence of 'target-like' non-targets. Laboratory-based research has not as yet made any significant contribution to these problems, although preliminary attempts have been made (e.g. Craig and Colquhoun, 1977). The nature and seriousness of the practical problem is exemplified in Belbin's (1957a) account of hosiery inspection (which also illustrates the influence of social pressures): faults were graded into 'menders' (for which the knitters were paid a slightly reduced price) and 'seconds' (which were paid at only half price), the standards being passed by word-of-mouth; pressure from the knitters had led over time to a reduction (almost to zero) in the incidence of faults classified as 'seconds'; management, unaware of the drift in standards, could happily point to the apparent reduction in fault severity as evidence that production standards had improved; they had not. It seems clear that the possibility of such changes in standards of fault (i.e. signal) classification poses additional difficulties for evaluating the merits of a system, or of any proposed alterations to it, a problem set which has been conveniently absent from laboratory studies focusing on a simple presence/absence classification.

In conjunction, the presence of multiple signals, and the existence of a dimension of 'signalness', define a task which is seldom seen in the laboratory context (a notable exception being the study reported by Craig and Colquhoun, 1977). One may additionally point to the fact that these signals often tend to occur in bunches, or not at all, which is rather different from the standard laboratory task in which signals occur at random over the whole session, with a constant probability of occurrence at any moment (although see Williges, 1973, and Embrey, 1975, for exceptions in which signal probability changed to a new level during the task). Research work therefore has little to offer in the way of directly combating the problems specific to this type of task, a task which is prevalent in real operations. Yet despite this, as has already been noted earlier in this chapter, numerous parallels exist between laboratory-based findings and observations made in real situations. These parallels are sufficient to consider that the research effort, based on tasks of a simpler nature, has made at least some contribution to the solution of real problems, and to suggest that issues of face validity of the task are not of primary importance.

Throughout this chapter, in describing detection performance, the emphasis has been on judgments about individual items. While these are recognized as fundamental, it is the case that in many industrial inspection jobs, judgments about the quality of a batch are based, not on 100% inspection of the batch, but on a sample only (or on several samples) drawn from it. Thus the batch is accepted or rejected according to whether some critical count of defects is found in inspecting a small, sampled proportion (e.g. 10%). Sampling plans are readily available for relating the likelihood of an acceptable batch to the number of defects found in a sample (e.g. Bennett, 1975). So far, only one laboratory study (Tsao *et al.*, 1979) has even considered the issue of performance differences between sampling and 100% inspection; the study found no reliable difference in detections or inspection speed between 60 items viewed as a sample (of a 1000 item batch) or 60 items viewed as a complete batch; but the study is flawed, and the issue remains open, since no comparison was made between decisions about the 1000 item batch based on a sample, and decisions based on complete inspection of all 1000 items. It follows, from what has just been said, that there has not been any systematic research on the effects of knowledge of the critical count level on the inspector's standards of judgment, although clearly it would be valuable to know whether there were conditions particularly conducive to the problems of censorship and flinching, and whether there were consistent, individual predispositions to these modes of behaviour. Just as earlier it was pointed out that a disparity may exist between the research worker's predeliction for assessing performance in terms of proportion of signals detected, and an assessment in terms of outgoing quality, so too here a similar disparity may exist, and performance might better be assessed in terms of the correctness of judgments about the whole batch, given the inspected sample.

The preceding examples, supplemented by acknowledgment of the difficulties in trying to correct undesirable tendencies in the judgments of operators whose task experience often exceeds that of the manager or watch officer, are sufficient to indicate that the problems confronting the practitioner can differ quite considerably from those perceived by the research worker; the latter is perhaps rather more concerned with the issue of the decrement shown by naive subjects performing on a simple task than real operations warrant.

CONCLUSIONS: DIAGNOSIS AND PROGNOSIS

Throughout the chapter, repeated demonstrations were made of similarities between effects found in the laboratory and those observed in the context of a real operation. These indicate that the research effort has made a substantial contribution, and that the 'principles' outlined previously are in fact applicable. Whether the contribution is significant in relation to the volume of research, and whether similar or even greater gains would have accrued from the same amount of effort applied to field studies is an open question. It is clear that research has provided a number of useful guidelines for improving vigilance performance, but it is equally clear that it has only just scratched the surface of the problems which exist.

It is becoming obvious that, with the advent of the current microprocessor revolution, monitoring tasks are gradually changing in form, and many new ones are being introduced, as older processes give way to automation. The skilled lathe operator of a year or two back is, today, the monitor who minds the automated machining process; and increasingly, the monitor is being called upon to make judgments of a complex, cognitive nature, rather than of a predominantly perceptual kind. If present trends continue, there will shortly be a preponderance of complex tasks, rather similar to those encountered in aerospace monitoring (Kibler, 1965) (though probably without the specific problem of occasional bursts of signals creating periods of information overload), in which the operator has to detect signals (varying in kind, location and modality), integrate the perceptual information and interpret its significance, then decide on and select an appropriate course of action. The requirements of the older, classic vigilance paradigm were: if detect signal, then report 'signal'; progressively, it seems, the typical requirements will be of the form: if see signal A and see signal B but do not hear signal C, then pursue plan X, otherwise ignore or take some other course of action. No doubt many will recognize this as an abstracted description of some current monitoring task. One can expect to encounter more of them in future.

Paradoxically, it is not at all evident that research on vigilance will mirror the trends in real tasks. There are still many unresolved issues surrounding performance on the simpler tasks, and equally many avenues which have not yet been systematically explored. Although vigilance was originally introduced into the research domain as a genuine practical problem, most of the research on it is conducted by academics working in universities and other research establishments, and their interests naturally focus on theoretical issues rather than on applied aspects, in an attempt to clarify understanding of the fundamental vigilance process. One might expect, for example, further research to determine whether the basic problem of low and declining detection rates is indeed primarily and simply due to the subject setting, or adjusting towards, an appropriately conservative standard of report for signals whose occurrence is rare, as some investigators have suggested (e.g. Williges, 1969; Craig, 1978). At the same time one would hope to see more studies employing multiple-signal tasks, either in the visual search mode or in the single-source mode, and more tasks using multidimensional signals or tasks incorporating a dimension of 'signalness'. There is little doubt that these do pose interesting theoretical problems for research, as well as approximating that little bit more closely to the tasks encountered in real situations.

A major qualification, which applies to most of the findings which have been discussed, is that research studies are usually conducted within a relatively short period of time, and the subjects whose performance is studied rarely serve for more than one or two sessions. As Poulton (1973) emphasizes, one's confidence in the reliability of such evidence and in its suitability for application is not high. Since existing evidence on whether performance improves or deteriorates with practice is, at best, inconclusive (Mackworth, 1970), there is a need for further studies, with repeated observations on performance over several sessions, although one has to realize that these protracted studies are inevitably more time-consuming and costly than those lasting only one or two sessions. There is much to be gained, however, not least in terms of the necessary, additional investigation of the consistency of individual differences, perhaps fruitfully linking this up with the continued quest for some reliable personality (or other) correlate of performance.

Perhaps one should conclude on a note of optimism, by suggesting that vigilance research has already made a valuable contribution and will continue to do so, gradually building the foundations on which to bridge the chasm between real and laboratory tasks and problems. But the author cannot help feeling that, throughout, he has merely been echoing and paraphrasing similar views expressed more than 25 years ago (e.g. Mackworth, 1957b).

REFERENCES

Adams, J. A. Experimental studies of human vigilance. United States Air Force ESD Technical Documentary Report No. 63-320, 1963.

Adams, J. A., and Boulter, L. R. An evaluation of the activationist hypothesis of human vigilance. *Journal of Experimental Psychology*, 1962, **64**, 495–504.

Adams, J. A., and Boulter, L. R. Spatial and temporal uncertainty as determinants of vigilance performance. *Journal of Experimental Psychology*, 1964, **67**, 127–131.

Adams, J. A., Stenson, H. H., and Humes, J. M. Monitoring of complex visual displays: II. Effects of visual load and response complexity on human vigilance. *Human Factors*, 1961, **3**, 213–221.

Annett, J. Training for perceptual skills. *Ergonomics*, 1966, **9**, 459–468.

Annett, J., and Clarkson, J. K. The use of cueing in training tasks. US Navy Technical Report NAVTRADEVCEN 3143-1. US Naval Training Device Centre, 1964.

Anonymous. Vigilance—the nature of alertness and the problem of its maintenance during long spells of work. *Nature*, 1956, **178**, 1375–1377.

Arnborger, A., Fors, M., and Sandell, K. Production of ampoules and control by inspection. *Farmaceuteste Revy*, 1954, **53**, 490–496.

Assenheim, G. Etude d'un systeme au travers d'une centre privilegie: un poste de controle en cristallerie. *Le Travail Humain*, 1969, **32**, 1–12.

Astley, R. W., and Fox, J. G. The analysis of an inspection task in the rubber industry. In C. G. Drury and J. G. Fox (Eds), *Human factors in quality control*. London: Taylor and Francis, 1975, pp.253–272.

Baddeley, A. D., and Colquhoun, W. P. Signal probability and vigilance: a reappraisal of the signal-rate effect. *British Journal of Psychology*, 1969, **60**, 169–178.

Baker, C. H. Attention to visual displays during a vigilance task: II. Maintaining the level of vigilance. *British Journal of Psychology*, 1959, **50**, 30–36.

Baker, C. H. Factors affecting radar operator efficiency. *Journal of the Institute of Navigation*, 1960, **13**, 148–163.

Baker, C. H. Industrial inspection considered as a vigilance task. Los Angeles: Human Factors Research Inc., 1964.

Baker, C. H., and Harabedian, A. A study of target detection by sonar operators. Report No. 206-16. Los Angeles: Human Factors Research Inc., 1962.

Baker, C. H., and O'Hanlon, J. The use of reference signals in a visual vigilance task. I. Reference signals continuously displayed. Report No. 750-1. Los Angeles: Human Factors Research Inc., 1963.

Bakwin, H. Pseudoxia pediatrica. *New England Journal of Medicine*, 1954, **232**, 691–697.

Belbin, R. M. New fields for quality control. *British Management Review*, 1957, **15**, 79 (a).

Belbin, R. M. Compensating rest allowances. *Work Study and Industrial Engineering*, 1957 (b).

Belbin, R. M. Inspection and human efficiency. *Ergonomics for Industry*, 1963, **4**, 13.

Bennett, G. K. Inspection error: its influence on quality control systems. In C. G. Drury and J. G. Fox (Eds), *Human reliability in quality control*. London: Taylor and Francis, 1975, pp.1–10.

Bergum, B. O., and Lehr, D. J. Vigilance performance as a function of task and environmental variables. Research Report No. 11. US Army Air Defense Human Research Unit, 1963.

Bhatia, N., and Murrell, K. F. H. An industrial experiment in rest pauses. *Human Factors*, 1969, **11**, 167–174.

Bills, A. G. Blocking: a new principle in mental fatigue. *American Journal of Psychology*, 1931, **43**, 230–245.

Binford, J. R., and Loeb, M. Monitoring readily detected auditory signals and detection of obscure visual signals. *Perceptual and Motor Skills*, 1963, **17**, 735–745.

Broadbent, D. E. Noise, paced performance and vigilance tasks. *British Journal of Psychology*, 1953, **44**, 295–303.

Broadbent, D. E. *Perception and communication*. London: Pergamon Press, 1958.

Broadbent, D. E., and Gregory, M. Vigilance considered as a statistical decision. *British Journal of Psychology*, 1963, **54**, 309–323.

Broadbent, D. E., and Gregory, M. Effects of noise and of signal rate upon vigilance analysed by means of decision theory. *Human Factors*, 1965, **7**, 155–162.

Buck, L. Reaction time as a measure of perceptual vigilance. *Psychological Bulletin*, 1966, **65**, 291–304.

Buckner, D. N., Harabedian, A., and McGrath, J. J. A study of individual differences in vigilance performance. Report No. 206-2. Goleta, Calif.: Human Factors Research Inc., 1960.

Carriero, N. J. Physiological correlates of performance in a long duration repetitive visual task. In R. R. Mackie (Ed.), *Vigilance: theory, operational performance and physiological correlates*. New York: Plenum, 1977, pp.307–330.

Carroll, J. M. Estimating errors in the inspection of complex products. *Transactions of Industrial Engineering*, 1969, **1**, 229–238.

Chaney, F. B., and Teel, K. S. Improving human performance through training and visual aids. *Journal of Applied Psychology*, 1967, **51**, 311–315.

Chapanis, A. The relevance of laboratory studies to practical situations. *Ergonomics*, 1967, **10**, 557–577.

Chapman, D. E., and Sinclair, M. A. Ergonomics in inspection tasks in the food industry. In C. G. Drury and J. G. Fox (Eds), *Human reliability in quality control*. London: Taylor and Francis, 1975, pp.231–251.

Childs, J. M. Signal complexity, response complexity and signal specification in vigilance. *Human Factors*, 1976, **18**, 149–160.

Coates, G. D., Loeb, M., and Alluisi, E. A. Influence of observing strategies and stimulus variables on watchkeeping performance. *Ergonomics*, 1972, **15**, 379–386.

Colquhoun, W. P. The effect of a short rest pause on inspection efficiency. *Ergonomics*, 1959, **2**, 367–372.

Colquhoun, W. P. The effect of 'unwanted' signals on performance in a vigilance task. *Ergonomics*, 1961, **4**, 41–51.

Colquhoun, W. P. Effects of a small dose of alcohol and certain other factors on the performance of a vigilance task (in French). *Bulletin du Centre d'Etudes et Recherches Psychologiques*, 1962, **11**, 27–44.

Colquhoun, W. P. The reliability of the human element in a quality control system. *Glass Technology*, 1963, **4**, 94–98.

Colquhoun, W. P. Training for vigilance: a comparison of different techniques. *Human Factors*, 1966, **8**, 7–12.

Colquhoun, W. P. Sonar target detection as a decision process. *Journal of Applied Psychology*, 1967, **51**, 187–190.

Colquhoun, W. P. Evaluation of auditory, visual and dual-mode displays for prolonged sonar monitoring in repeated sessions. *Human Factors*, 1975, **17**, 425–437.

Colquhoun, W. P. Simultaneous monitoring of a number of auditory sonar outputs. In R. R. Mackie (Ed.), *Vigilance: theory, operational performance and physiological correlates*. New York: Plenum, 1977, pp.163–188.

Colquhoun, W. P., and Baddeley, A. D. Role of pretest expectancy in vigilance decrement. *Journal of Experimental Psychology*, 1964, **68**, 156–160.

Colquhoun, W. P., and Edwards, R. S. Practice effects on a visual vigilance task with and without search. *Human Factors*, 1970, **12**, 537–545.

Conway, J. Labor's stake. In *The challenge of automation*. Washington, D.C.: Public Affairs Press, 1955.

Craig, A. Is the vigilance decrement simply a response adjustment towards probability matching? *Human Factors*, 1978, **20**, 441–446.

Craig, A., and Colquhoun, W. P. Vigilance: a review. In C. G. Drury and J. G. Fox (Eds), *Human reliability in quality control*. London: Taylor and Francis, 1975, pp.71–88.

Craig, A., and Colquhoun, W. P. Vigilance effects in complex inspection. In R. R. Mackie (Ed.), *Vigilance: theory, operational performance and physiological correlates*. New York: Plenum, 1977, pp.239–262.

Craig, A., Colquhoun, W. P., and Corcoran, D. W. J. Combining evidence presented simultaneously to the eye and the ear: a comparison of some predictive models. *Perception and Psychophysics*, 1976, **19**, 473–484.

Davenport, W. G. Auditory vigilance: the effects of costs and values on signals. *Australian Journal of Psychology*, 1968, **20**, 213–218.

Davenport, W. G. Vigilance for simultaneous auditory and cutaneous signals. *Canadian Journal of Psychology*, 1969, **23**, 93–100.

Davies, D. R. Age differences in paced inspection tasks. In G. A. Talland (Ed.), *Human aging and behavior: recent advances in research and theory*. New York: Academic Press, 1968, pp.217–238.

Davies, D. R. and Tune, G. S. *Human vigilance performance*. London: Staples Press, 1970.

Deese, J. Some problems in the theory of vigilance. *Psychological Review*, 1955, **62**, 359–368.

Ditchburn, R. W. Some factors affecting the efficiency of work by lookouts. Admiralty Research Laboratory Report No. ARC/R1/84/46/0. London, 1943.

Drew, G. C. An experimental study of mental fatigue. Air Ministry FPRC/227. London, 1940 (reissued 1962).

Drury, C. G. The effect of speed of working on industrial inspection accuracy. *Applied Ergonomics*, 1973, **4**, 2–7.

Drury, C. G. Human decision making in quality control. In C. G. Drury and J. G. Fox (Eds), *Human factors in quality control*. London: Taylor and Francis, 1975, pp.45–53.

Drury, C. G. Integrating human factors models into statistical quality control. *Human Factors*, 1978, **20**, 561–572.

Drury, C. G. and Addison, J. C. An industrial study of the effects of feedback and fault density on inspection performance. *Ergonomics*, 1973, **16**, 159–169.

Eijkman, E. and Vendrik, A. J. H. Detection theory applied to the absolute sensitivity of sensory systems. *Biophysics Journal*, 1963, **3**, 65–78.

Elliott, E. Perception and alertness. *Ergonomics*, 1960, **3**, 357–364.

Embrey, D. E. Training the inspector's sensitivity and response strategy. In C. G. Drury and J. G. Fox (Eds), *Human reliability in quality control*. London: Taylor and Francis, 1975, pp.123–131.

Embrey, D. E. The selection and training aspects of industrial inspection. In *Ergonomics of visual inspection*. Department of Engineering Production, University of Birmingham, and Ergonomics Society, 1978.

Faulkner, T. W. Variability of performance in a vigilance task. *Journal of Applied Psychology*, 1962, **46**, 325–328.

Faulkner, T. W., and Murphy, T. J. Lighting for difficult visual tasks. In C. G. Drury and J. G. Fox (Eds), *Human reliability in quality control*. London: Taylor and Francis, 1975, pp.133–147.

Fox, J. G. Vigilance and arousal: a key to maintaining inspectors' performance. In C. G. Drury and J. G. Fox (Eds), *Human reliability in quality control*. London: Taylor and Francis, 1975, pp.89–96.

Fox, J. G. Quality control of coins. In E. S. Weiner and H. G. Maulle (Eds), *Case studies in ergonomics practice*, Vol. 1: *Human factors in work, design production*. London: Taylor and Francis, 1977, pp.101–130.

Fox, J. G., and Embrey, D. E. Music: an aid to productivity. *Applied Ergonomics*, 1972, **3**, 202–205.

Fox, J. G., and Haslegrave, C. M. Industrial inspection efficiency and the probability of a defect occurring. *Ergonomics*, 1969, **12**, 713–721.

Frankmann, J. P., and Adams, J. A. Theories of vigilance. *Psychology Bulletin*, 1962, **59**, pp.257–272.

Fraser, D. C. The relation of an environmental variable to performnace in a prolonged visual task. *Quarterly Journal of Experimental Psychology*, 1953, **5**, 31–32.

Fuller, R. G. C. Effects of prolonged driving on heavy goods vehicle driving performance. US Army Research Institute Liaison Office, Europe, 1978.

Garvey, W. G., Taylor, F. V., and Newlin, E. P. The use of 'artificial signals' to enhance monitoring performance. US Naval Research Laboratory, Engineering Psychology Branch, Applications Research Division NRL Report 5269. 1959.

Gatherum, D. P., Harrington, G., and Pomeroy, R. W. Visual judgments of quality in meat. *Journal of Agricultural Science*, 1959, **52**, 320–331.

Gatherum, D. P., Harrington, G., and Pomeroy, R. W. Visual judgments of quality in meat. *Journal of Agricultural Science*, 1960, **54**, 145–157.

Gatherum, D. P., Harrington, G., and Pomeroy, R. W. Visual judgments of quality in meat. *Journal of Agricultural Science*, 1961, **57**, 401–417.

Geyer, L. H., Patel, S., and Perry, R. F. Detectability of multiple flaws. *Human Factors*, 1979, **21**, 7–12.

Gillies, G. J. Glass inspection. In C. G. Drury and J. G. Fox (Eds), *Human reliability in quality control*. London: Taylor and Francis, 1975, pp.273–287.

Green, D. M., and Swets, J. A. *Signal detection theory and psychophysics*. New York: John Wiley, 1966.

Gundy, R. F. Auditory detection of an unspecified signal. *Journal of Acoustical Society of America*, 1961, **33**, 1008–1012.

Gunn, W. J., and Loeb, M. Correlation of performance in detecting visual and auditory signals. *American Journal of Psychology*, 1967, **80**, 236–242.

Guralnick, M. J. Observing responses and decision processes in vigilance. *Journal of Experimental Psychology*, 1972, **93**, 239–244.

Hanhart, A. *Die Arbeitspause im Beitrieb*. Zurich: Oesch-Verlag, 1954.

Harris, D. H. Development and validation of an aptitude test for inspectors of electronic equipment. *Journal of Industrial Psychology*, 1964, **2**, 29–35.

Harris, D. H. Effect of equipment complexity on inspection performance. *Journal of Applied Psychology*, 1966, **50**, 236–237.

Harris, D. The nature of industrial inspection. *Human Factors*, 1969, **11**, 139–148.

Harris, W. Fatigue, circadian rhythm and truck accidents. In R. R. Mackie (Ed.) *Vigilance: theory, operational performance and physiological correlates*. New York: Plenum, 1977, pp.133–146.

Hayes, A. S. Control of visual inspection. *Industrial Quality Control*, 1950, **6**, 73–76.

Hermann, R. Two studies for optimising operating bridges and their application in inland—and sea-navigation. In D. Anderson, H. Instance and J. Spencer (Eds), *Human factors in the design and operation of ships*. London: Taylor and Francis, 1977, pp.58–68.

Howell, W. C., Johnston, W. A., and Goldstein, I. L. Complex monitoring and its relation to the classical problem of vigilance. *Organizational Behavior and Human Performance*, 1966, **1**, 129–150.

Jacobsen, H. J. A study of inspector accuracy. *Industrial Quality Control*, 1952, **9**, 16–25.

Jamieson, G. H. Inspection in the telecommunication industry: a field study of age and other performance variables. *Ergonomics*, 1966, **9**, 297–303.

Jenkins, H. M. The effect of signal rate on performance in visual monitoring. *American Journal of Psychology*, 1958, **71**, 647–661.

Jerison, H. J. Vigilance: a paradigm and some physiological speculations. In A. F. Sanders (Ed.), *Attention and performance III*. Amsterdam: North Holland, 1970, pp.367–380.

Jerison, H. J., and Pickett, R. M. Vigilance: a review and re-evaluation. *Human Factors*, 1963, **5**, 211–238.

Jerison, H. J., Pickett, R. M., and Stenson, H. H. The elicited observing rate and decision processes in vigilance. *Human Factors*, 1965, **7**, 107–128.

Juran, J. M. Inspectors' errors in quality control. *Mechanical Engineering*, 1935, **57**, 643–644.

Juran, J. M. (Ed.) *Quality-control handbook*. New York: McGraw-Hill, 1951.

Kennedy, C. W. *Inspection and gauging*. New York: Industrial Press, 1957.

Kennedy, J. L., and Travis, R. C. Prediction of speed of performance by muscle action potentials. *Science*, 1947, **105**, 410–411.

Kibler, A. W. The relevance of vigilance research to aerospace monitoring tasks. *Human Factors*, 1965, **7**, 93–99.

Konz, S., and Osman, K. Team efficiencies on a paced visual inspection task. *Journal of Human Ergology*, 1977, **6**, 111–119.

Lawshe, C. H., and Tiffin, J. The accuracy of precision instrument measurement in industrial inspection. *Journal of Applied Psychology*, 1945, **29**, 413–419.

Levine, J. M. The effects of values and costs on the detection and identification of signals in auditory vigilance. *Human Factors*, 1966, **8**, 525–537.

Lindsley, D. B. (Ed.) Radar operator 'fatigue': the effects of length and repetition of operating periods on efficiency of performance. Office of Scientific Research and Development Report No. OSRD 3334. 1944.

Lockwood, V. M. Evaluation of tube screening procedures: Part I. Engineering evaluation. *ASQC Convention Transactions*, 1958, **1958**, 421–430.

Loeb, M., and Alluisi, E. A. Influence of display, task, and organismic variables on indices of monitoring behavior. *Acta Psychologica*, 1970, **33**, 343–366.

Loeb, M., and Alluisi, E. A. An update of findings regarding vigilance and a reconsideration of underlying mechanisms. In R. R. Mackie (Ed.), *Vigilance: theory, operational performance and physiological correlates*. New York: Plenum, 1977, pp.719–749.

Lucaccini, L. F., Freedy, A., and Lyman, J. Motivational factors in vigilance: effects of instruction on performance in a complex vigilance task. *Perceptual and Motor Skills*, 1968, **26**, 783–786.

McCormack, P. D. Performance in a vigilance task with and without knowledge of results. *Canadian Journal of Psychology*, 1959, **13**, 68–71.

McCormack, P. D. A two-factor theory of vigilance in the light of recent studies. In A. F. Sanders (Ed.), *Attention and performance I*. Amsterdam: North Holland, 1967.

McCornack, R. L. Inspector accuracy; a study of the literature. Sandia Corp. Technical Memorandum 53-61(14). Los Angeles: Sandia Corp.

McFarling, L. H., and Heimstra, N. W. Pacing, product complexity and task perception in simulated inspection. *Human Factors*, 1975, **17**, 361–367.

McGrath, J. J. Irrelevant stimulation and vigilance performance. In D. N. Buckner and J. J. McGrath (Eds), *Vigilance: a symposium*. New York: McGraw-Hill, 1963, pp.3–19 (a).

McGrath, J. J. Some problems of definition and criteria in the study of vigilance performance. In D. N. Buckner and J. J. McGrath (Eds), *Vigilance: a symposium*. New York: McGraw-Hill, 1963, pp.227–237 (b).

McGrath, J. J. Performance sharing in an audio-visual vigilance task. *Human Factors*, 1965, **7**, 141–153.

McGrath, J. J., Harabedian, A., and Buckner, D.N. Review and critique of the literature on vigilance performance Technical Report No. 206-1. Goleta, Calif.: Human Factors Research Inc., 1959. Reprinted in *Studies of human vigilance: an omnibus of technical reports*. Goleta, Calif.: Human Factors Research Inc., 1968.

McKenzie, R. M. On the accuracy of inspectors. *Ergonomics*, 1958, **1**, 258–272.

Mackie, R. R. (Ed.). *Vigilance: theory, operational performance and physiological correlates*. New York: Plenum, 1977.

Mackworth, J. F. *Vigilance and attention*. Harmondsworth: Penguin Books, 1970.

Mackworth, N. H. *Researches on the measurement of human performance*. Medical Research Council Special Report Series No. 268. London: HM Stationery Office. Reprinted in H. W. Sinaiko (Ed.), *Selected papers on human factors in the design and use of control systems*. New York: Dover, 1961, pp.174–331.

Mackworth, N. H. Some factors affecting vigilance. In N. H. Mackworth (Ed.) *Vigilance, The Advancement of Science*, 1957, **53**, 389–393 (a).

Mackworth, N. H. (Ed.) Vigilance. *The Advancement of Science*, 1957, **53**, 389–410 (b).

Meadows, A. W., Lovibond, S. H., and John I. D. The establishment of psychophysical standards in the study of fruit. *Occupational Psychology*, 1959, **33**, 217–221.

Megaw, E. D. The analysis of visual search strategies to improve industrial inspection. Science Research Council Contract B/RG/7380, Second Progress Report. London: Science Research Council, 1977.

Megaw, E. D. Some factors affecting inspection accuracy. In *Ergonomics of visual inspection*, Department of Engineering Production, University of Birmingham, and Ergonomics Society, 1978.

Megaw, E. D., and Richardson, J. Target uncertainty and visual scanning strategies. *Human Factors*, 1979, **21**, 303–315.

Megaw, E. D., Richardson, J., and Alexander, J. Fault mix and inspection performance. *International Journal of Production Research*, 1979, in press.

Miller, G. A. The magical number seven, plus or minus two: some limits on our capacity for processing information. *Psychological Review*, 1956, **63**, 81–97.

Mills, R., and Sinclair, M. A. Aspects of inspection in a knitwear company. *Applied Ergonomics*, 1976, **7**, 97–107.

Mitchell, J. H. Subjective standards in inspection for appearance. *Human Factors*, London, 1935, **9**, 235–239.

Mitten, L. G. Research team approach to an inspection operation. In C. W. Churchman, R. L. Ackoff and E. L. Arnoff (Eds), *Introduction to operations research*. New York: John Wiley, 1952.

Moraal, J. The analysis of an inspection task in the steel industry. In C. G. Drury and J. G. Fox (Eds), *Human reliability in quality control*. London: Taylor and Francis, 1975, pp.217–230.

Murrell, G. A. A reappraisal of artificial signals as an aid to a visual monitoring task. *Ergonomics*, 1975, **18**, 693–700.

Murrell, G. A. Combination of evidence in a probabilistic visual search and detection task. *Organizational Behavior and Human Performance*, 1977, **18**, 3–18.

Nachreiner, F. Experiments on the validity of vigilance experiments. In R. R. Mackie (Ed.), *Vigilance: theory, operational performance and physiological correlates*. New York: Plenum, 1977, pp.665–678.

Nachreiner, F., Klimmer, F., Knauth, P., Lange, W., and Rutenfranz, J. Untersuchungen über leistungsbegrenzende Bedingungen bei einer optischen Kongrollaufgabe. *Internationales Archiv für Arbeitsmedizin*, 1975, **34**, 247–268.

Nelson, J. B., and Barany, J. W. A dynamic visual recognition test for paced inspection tasks. *Transactions of Industrial Engineering*, 1969, **1**, 327–332.

Nicely, P. E., and Miller, G. A. Some effects of unequal spatial distribution on the detectability of radar targets. *Journal of Experimental Psychology*, 1957, **53**, 195-198.

O'Hanlon, J. F., and Kelley, G. R. Comparison of performance and physiological changes between drivers who perform well and poorly during prolonged vehicular operation. In R. R. Mackie (Ed.), *Vigilance: theory, operational performance and physiological correlates*. New York: Plenum, 1977, pp.87-109.

Parasuraman, R., and Davies, D. R. A taxonomic analysis of vigilance performance. In R. R. Mackie (Ed.), *Vigilance: theory, operational performance and physiological correlates*. New York: Plenum, 1977, pp.559-574.

Poock, G. K., and Wiener, E. L. Music and other auditory backgrounds during visual monitoring. *Journal of Industrial Engineering*, 1966, **17**, 318-323.

Pope, L. T., and McKechnie, D. F. Correlation between visual and auditory vigilance performance. Aerospace Medical Research Laboratory Technical Report No. AMRL-TR-63-57. Wright-Patterson Air Force Base, Ohio: Aerospace Medical Research Laboratory, 1963.

Poulton, E. C. The effect of fatigue upon inspection work. *Applied Ergonomics*, 1973, **4**, 73-83.

Poulton, E. C. Arousing stresses increase vigilance. In R. R. Mackie (Ed.), *Vigilance: theory, operational performance and physiological correlates*. New York: Plenum, 1977, pp.423-459.

Poulton, E. C., and Edwards, R. S. Interactions and range effects in experiments on pairs of stresses: mild heat and low-frequency noise. *Journal of Experimental Psychology*, 1974, **102**, 621-628.

Poulton, E. C., Hitchings, N. B., and Brooke, R. B. Effects of cold and rain upon the vigilance of lookouts. *Ergonomics*, 1965, **8**, 167-168.

Raphael, W. S. Some problems of inspection. *Occupational Psychology*, 1942, **16**, 157-163.

Rigby, L. V., and Swain, A. D. Some human-factor applications to quality control in a high technology industry. In C. G. Drury and J. G. Fox (Eds), *Human reliability in quality control*. London: Taylor and Francis, 1975, pp.201-216.

Rizy, E. F. Effect of decision parameters on a detection/localization paradigm quantifying sonar operator performance. ONR Engineering Psychology Program R 1156. Washington, D.C.: Office of Naval Research, 1972.

Roethlisberger, F. J., and Dickson, W. J. *Management and the worker*. Cambridge, Mass.: Harvard University Press, 1939.

Saito, M., and Tanaka, T. Visual bottle inspection performance in highly paced belt-conveyor systems. *Journal of Human Ergology*, 1977, **6**, 127-137.

Saldanha, E. Alternating an exacting visual task with either rest or similar work. Medical Research Council Applied Psychology Research Unit Report No. 289/57. London: Medical Research Council, 1957.

Schoonard, J. W., Gould, J. D., and Miller, L. A. Studies of visual inspection. *Ergonomics*, 1973, **16**, 365-379.

Schwartz, D. H. Statistical 'sleuthing' to detect bias in visual inspection. *Industrial Quality Control*, 1957, **3**, 14-17.

Self, H. C., and Rhodes, F. The effect of simulated aircraft speed on detecting and identifying targets from side-looking radar imagery. Aerospace Medical Research Laboratories Technical Development Report No. AMRL-TDR-64-40. Wright Patterson Air Force Base, Ohio: Aerospace Medical Research Laboratories, 1964.

Sheehan, J. J. and Drury, C. G. The analysis of industrial inspection. *Applied Ergonomics*, 1971, **2**, 74-78.

Siddall, G. J., and Anderson, D. M. Fatigue during prolonged performance on a simple compensatory tracking task. *Quarterly Journal of Experimental Psychology*, 1955, **7**, 159–165.

Smith, L. A., and Barany, J. W. An elementary model of human performance on paced visual inspection tasks. *AIIE Transactions*, 1970, **2**, 298–308.

Smith, R. L., and Lucaccini, L. F. Vigilance research: its application to industrial problems. *Human Factors*, 1969, **11**, 149–156.

Smith, R. P. The effects of signal intensity and signal variability in the efficiency of human vigilance. PhD Dissertation, Emory University, 1961.

Swets, J. A. Signal detection theory applied to vigilance. In R. R. Mackie (Ed.), *Vigilance: theory, occupational performance and physiological correlates*. New York: Plenum, 1977, pp.705–718.

Takakuwa, E. The function of maintaining concentration (TAF): an approach to the evaluation of mental stress. In R. R. Mackie (Ed.), *Vigilance: theory, operational performance and physiological correlates*. New York: Plenum, 1977, pp.217–238.

Tarriere, C., and Wisner, A. Effets des bruits significatifs ou non significatifs au cours d'une epreuve vigilance. *Le Travail Humain*, 1962, **25**, 1–28.

Teel, K. S., Springer, R. M., and Sadler, E. E. Assembly and inspection of microelectronic systems. *Human Factors*, 1968, **10**, 217–224.

Teichner, W. H. The detection of a simple visual signal as a function of time of watch. *Human Factors*, 1974, **16**, 339–353.

Thomas, L. F. Perceptual organisation in industrial inspectors. *Ergonomics*, 1962, **5**, 429–434.

Thomas, L. F., and Seaborne, A. E. M. Subjective judgment in inspection and quality control. DSIR sponsored project, Progress Report, 1959–1960.

Thorndike, R. L. The human factor in accidents with special reference to aircraft accidents. USAF School of Aviation Medicine Report No. 21-30-001. 1951.

Tiffin, J. *Industrial psychology*, War Department Educational Manual EM 490. New York: Prentice-Hall, 1943, pp.262–279.

Tiffin, J., and Rogers, H. B. The selection and training of inspectors. *Personnel*, 1941, **18**, 14–31.

Tsao, Y.-C., Drury, C. G., and Morawski, T. B. Human performance in sampling inspection. *Human Factors*, 1979, **21**, 99–105.

Waag, W. L., Halcombe, C. G., and Tyler, D. M. Sex differences in monitoring performance. *Journal of Applied Psychology*, 1973, **58**, 272–274.

Wallis, D., and Samuel, J. A. Some experimental studies of radar operating. *Ergonomics*, 1961, **4**, 155–168.

Warm, J. S. Psychological processes in sustained attention. In R. R. Mackie (Ed.), *Vigilance: theory, operational performance and physiological correlates*. New York: Plenum, 1977, pp.623–644.

Warm, J. S., Epps, B. D., and Ferguson, R. P. Effects of knowledge of results and signal regularity on vigilance performance. *Bulletin of the Psychonomic Society*, 1974, **4**, 272–274.

Weidenfeller, E. W., Baker, R. A., and Ware, J. R. Effects of knowledge of results (true and false) on vigilance performance. *Perceptual and Motor Skills*, 1962, **14**, 211–215.

Welford, A. T. *Ageing and human skill*. Oxford: Oxford University Press, 1958.

Whittenburg, J. A., Ross, S., and Andrews, T. G. Sustained perceptual efficiency as measured by the Mackworth 'clock' test. *Perceptual and Motor Skills*, 1956, **6**, 109–116.

Wiener, E. L. Transfer of training from one monitoring task to another. *Ergonomics*, 1967, **10**, 649–658.

Wiener, E. L. Adaptive measurement of vigilance decrement. *Ergonomics*, 1973, **16**, 353–363.

Wiener, E. L. Individual and group differences in inspection. In C. G. Drury and J. G. Fox (Eds), *Human reliability in quality control*. London: Taylor and Francis, 1975, pp.101–122.

Wilkinson, R. T. The effects of lack of sleep. Medical Research Council Applied Psychology Unit Report No. 323. London: Medical Research Council, 1957.

Wilkinson, R. T. Comparison of paced, unpaced, irregular and continuous display in watchkeeping. *Ergonomics*, 1961, **4**, 259.

Wilkinson, R. T. Artificial 'signals' as an aid to an inspection task. *Ergonomics*, 1964, **7**, 63.

Williges, R. C. Within-session criterion changes compared to an ideal observer criterion in a visual monitoring task. *Journal of Experimental Psychology*, 1969, **81**, 61–66.

Williges, R. C. The role of pay-offs and signal ratios in criterion changes during a monitoring task. *Human Factors*, 1971, **13**, 261–267.

Williges, R. C. Manipulating the response criterion in visual monitoring. *Human Factors*, 1973, **15**, 179–185.

Williges, R. C., and North, R. A. Knowledge of results and decision making performance in visual monitoring. *Organizational Behavior and Human Performance*, 1972, **8**, 44–57.

Williges, R. C., and Streeter, H. Display characteristics in inspection tasks. *Journal of Applied Psychology*, 1971, **55**, 123–125.

Wyatt, S., and Langdon, J. N. Inspection processes in industry. Medical Research Council IHRB Report No. 63. London: HM Stationery Office, 1932.

Yerushalmy, J. The statistical assessment of the variability in observer perception and description of roentgenographic pulmonary shadows. *Radiological Clinics of America*, 1969, **7**, 381–392.

Yerushalmy, J., Harkness, J. T., Cope, J. H., and Kennedy, B. R. The role of dual reading in mass radiography. *American Review of Tuberculosis*, 1950, **61**, 443–464.

Zunzanyika, X. K., and Drury, C. G. Effects of information on industrial inspection performance. In C. G. Drury and J. G. Fox (Eds), *Human Reliability in Quality Control*. London: Taylor and Francis, 1975.

Sustained Attention in Human Performance
Edited by J. S. Warm
© 1984 John Wiley & Sons Ltd.

Chapter 9

Search

Timothy H. Monk

INTRODUCTION

The essence of search

It is often forgotten that the title of Mackworth's (1948) classic paper, which introduced the field of vigilance, referred to the 'clock task' as a 'visual search task'. Nowadays this description might seem a little surprising in view of the predominance of temporal, rather than spatial, aspects to the task and the very transitory nature of the 'target'. On closer inspection, however, it is clear that the 'Mackworth clock' task has two properties that are characteristic of visual search studies. First, the task required of the observer is to eliminate spatial uncertainty, i.e. to answer the question 'Where did the target (signal) occur?' Due to the mechanics of the task, this is equivalent to '*when* did the target occur?', but both questions are equally valid ways of stating the task. Secondly, Mackworth's task has the property of 'target certainty'. The target certainty property is that by which, if the spatial uncertainty is eliminated for the observer (e.g. by its position being pointed out by the experimenter), there is no doubt in his mind that he is looking at the target, and it is, thereafter, 'obvious' to him. Thus it is only the presence of spatial uncertainty that is preventing the observer from detecting the target. The essence of the search task is the elimination of this spatial uncertainty. Having eliminated that uncertainty, the decision part of the task is very often trivial. This property is illustrated in Figure 9.1; once the target has been found, it is very hard to lose it again.

The general lack of consensus about the definition of the term 'visual search', and the widely differing aims of those working in the field (see below), has meant that a variety of different tasks have all been given that label. Tachistoscopic recognition (Cavanagh and Chase, 1971), card sorting (Pomerantz and Garner, 1973), letter cancelling (Kaplan *et al.*, 1966; Gordon, 1968), list search (Neisser, 1963) and free-search, both with and without non-targets (Green and Anderson, 1956; Ford *et al.*, 1959) have all been described by their authors as 'visual search' tasks.

Depending upon the nature and purpose of the task, different dependent variables (e.g. search time, reaction time, search rate, detection rate, fixation density) have been used to measure the observer's performance. However, all these tasks have the properties of 'spatial uncertainty reduction' and target certainty to a greater or lesser extent. The author will thus adopt these two properties as a working definition of visual search for the purposes of the present chapter.

Search as an aspect of attention

Having adopted this working definition of visual search, it is clear that most of us are doing it all the time. Although one has some memory of where the

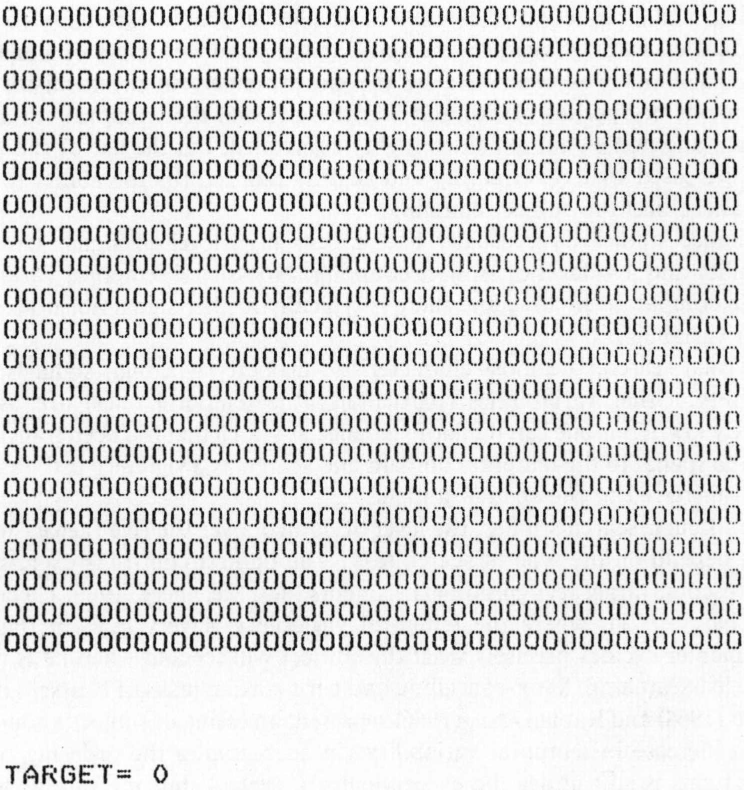

```
OOOOOOOOOOOOOOOOOOOOOOOOOOOOOOOOOOOOOOOOOOO
OOOOOOOOOOOOOOOOOOOOOOOOOOOOOOOOOOOOOOOOOOO
OOOOOOOOOOOOOOOOOOOOOOOOOOOOOOOOOOOOOOOOOOO
OOOOOOOOOOOOOOOOOOOOOOOOOOOOOOOOOOOOOOOOOOO
OOOOOOOOOOOOOOOOOOOOOOOOOOOOOOOOOOOOOOOOOOO
OOOOOOOOOOOOOO◇OOOOOOOOOOOOOOOOOOOOOOOOOOOOO
OOOOOOOOOOOOOOOOOOOOOOOOOOOOOOOOOOOOOOOOOOO
OOOOOOOOOOOOOOOOOOOOOOOOOOOOOOOOOOOOOOOOOOO
OOOOOOOOOOOOOOOOOOOOOOOOOOOOOOOOOOOOOOOOOOO
OOOOOOOOOOOOOOOOOOOOOOOOOOOOOOOOOOOOOOOOOOO
OOOOOOOOOOOOOOOOOOOOOOOOOOOOOOOOOOOOOOOOOOO
OOOOOOOOOOOOOOOOOOOOOOOOOOOOOOOOOOOOOOOOOOO
OOOOOOOOOOOOOOOOOOOOOOOOOOOOOOOOOOOOOOOOOOO
OOOOOOOOOOOOOOOOOOOOOOOOOOOOOOOOOOOOOOOOOOO
OOOOOOOOOOOOOOOOOOOOOOOOOOOOOOOOOOOOOOOOOOO
OOOOOOOOOOOOOOOOOOOOOOOOOOOOOOOOOOOOOOOOOOO
OOOOOOOOOOOOOOOOOOOOOOOOOOOOOOOOOOOOOOOOOOO
OOOOOOOOOOOOOOOOOOOOOOOOOOOOOOOOOOOOOOOOOOO
OOOOOOOOOOOOOOOOOOOOOOOOOOOOOOOOOOOOOOOOOOO
OOOOOOOOOOOOOOOOOOOOOOOOOOOOOOOOOOOOOOOOOOO
OOOOOOOOOOOOOOOOOOOOOOOOOOOOOOOOOOOOOOOOOOO
```

TARGET= ◇

Figure 9.1   An example of a typical visual search task. Note that once the target has been found, it is very hard to 'lose' it again.

objects in our visual world are located, additional search processes are always needed for the total elimination of spatial uncertainty. Thus the process of attention has a strong search component, and study of the areas of 'search' and 'attention' are intimately bound up.

In studying the phenomenon of attention in the laboratory, the various factors involved in the process must first be isolated and controlled. The five factors requiring control can be categorized as (i) signal spatial variability, (ii) signal temporal variability, (iii) non-signal spatial variability, (iv) non-signal temporal variability, and (v) the degree to which the observer is forced to attend. The fifth factor represents the relative freedom of the observer to avoid the (visual or auditory) 'display' and was termed 'subject coupling' by Loeb and Alluisi (1970). Different approaches to the study of attention can be characterized by levels of these five factors and the degree of control exerted over them.

In Broadbent's (1958) auditory studies, the degree of control was high on all five factors. The use of auditory signals and non-signals caused close subject coupling, and a reduction of signal and non-signal spatial variability to three positions (left ear, right ear, both ears). The temporal variability of signal and non-signal input was controlled by the experimenter. In the tachistoscopic experiments of Sperling (1960) and Sternberg (1966) the temporal variability of signal and non-signal remained highly controlled, but the use of the visual mode increased spatial variability and slightly reduced (by the ability to look away and blink) the subject coupling.

Vigilance studies have usually had a very high level of signal temporal variability and low level of subject coupling. Non-signal temporal variability is often comparatively low, and there is typically neither signal nor non-signal spatial variability.

In visual search, the most characteristic property is a high signal spatial variability. Other variabilities (particularly the temporal ones) are usually relatively low. Thus one can think of vigilance as search that has been transferred from the spatial to the temporal domain and search as a vigilance task that has been transferred to the spatial domain.

In particular search studies, the level of control over the five factors will of course depend on the type of search task. The tightest control is exercised in tachistoscopic target recognition experiments (e.g. Sternberg, 1966; Cavanagh and Chase, 1971), where the temporal variability is very low, in that the experimenter decides precisely what the subject will see and when he is to see it. The list-searching, letter-cancelling and card-sorting tasks of Neisser (1963), Rabbitt (1964) and Kaplan *et al.* (1966) represent an easing of subject's coupling, and an increase in temporal variability. In such studies the ordering of the search items is still under the experimenter's control, but the rate at which the information is scanned is dependent upon the subject. In normal 'free search' (e.g. Ford *et al.*, 1959) the subject is even permitted to choose his scan-path, and thus has control over the order in which the information is received. Free search thus represents the condition of minimum control over the five factors.

The close relationship between search and attention has meant that visual search tasks have been used quite extensively to answer general, theoretical questions about information processing and pattern recognition. Probably the best known such application is that of Neisser (1967), whose model of pattern recognition arose directly from observations made in visual search experiments. This has resulted in a division of the search field into studies answering two very different types of research question. A detailed discussion of this dichotomy will be given later; first, however, will follow a brief introduction to the concepts, methods and vocabulary of the search field.

The concepts, methods and vocabulary of visual search

A *search trial* starts when the observer begins looking for a target and ends when he indicates either that he has found it or that he is sure it does not appear in the display. The duration of the search trial, the *search time* is usually taken as the major dependent measure, although in some paradigms the search time is held constant and accuracy used as the dependent measure. In searching for the *target* the observer typically covers the display with a sequence of *fixations*, each lasting about 350 ms. Between the fixations are *saccades*, moving the eye to the next position, and typically lasting about 50–60 ms. The pattern described by the sequence of fixations is known as the *scan-path*, which can be measured by a variety of devices and procedures (see Laycock, 1979, for an excellent review).

The *display* can vary in complexity from a blank screen containing a small patch of light to a whole passage of text. Displays for which the target is the only item present are known as *impoverished*. *Cluttered* displays are characterized by the presence of confusing *non-targets* in the display leading to *competition search*. The non-targets can be arranged in a variety of ways. In *list-searching* tasks, the observer is forced to work his way through the material in a well-defined order. This results in the use of over-learned reading habits, and a correspondingly regular scan-path. This knowledge of the scan-path can be used to create a more sensitive measure of search performance (Neisser, 1963). By plotting search time against position of target in list (for a set of lists) the experimenter can obtain a measure of 'search rate' that is independent of reaction time.

In *free search* the non-targets (if present) are arranged in a way that does not encourage or enforce one particular scan-path through the items. They can either be arranged in a *regular array* or spread randomly over the display in an *irregular array*. The observer is free to use any scan-path that he cares to construct. This results in a wide range of variability both between and within individuals. Indeed, it is almost impossible to predict exactly what sort of scan-path will occur on a given trial. There are, however, four patterns of scan-path that occur slightly more frequently than most; the horizontal zig-zag, the vertical zig-zag and inward and outward spirals.

Clearly, in a free search paradigm, the search time will depend not only upon target and non-target characteristics, but also upon whereabouts along the scan-path the target happens to lie. Thus, if the observer happens to use a scan-path that starts in the top left corner, then targets occurring in that area will tend to have shorter search times than those, say, occurring in the bottom right. To overcome this inherent variability, a large number of trials are typically used, with the target positioning determined by some pseudo-random process. The distribution of search times that is produced is usually highly skewed, approximating to a negative exponential distribution. This latter result has been much used by those constructing mathematical models of search performance (see later section).

Because of the large amount of skew present in search-time distributions, it is often thought preferable either to use non-parametric statistics, and the median as the reported measure, or to transform the data logarithmically prior to analysis of variance. In the latter case, it is often better to use the geometric, rather than the arithmetic, mean as a measure of central tendency.

A major theoretical concept is that of the *lobe*. Broadly speaking, this is the area of display around the centre of a fixation, within which a target would be detected. The size of the lobe is thus *not* a constant, equivalent, for example, to that of the fovea, but varies according to factors such as the target/non-target difficulty, observer acuity, etc. In practice, the size and shape of the lobe for a particular observer/display combination is usually determined in a separate experiment. The observer is asked to fixate a point, and targets are introduced at varying distances from it. This results in a series of contours around the point, representing the probability of target detection. Then, according to the sophistication of the model, either the 50% contour is simply taken as the 'edge' of the lobe (*'hard shelled'*) or all the probability information is retained (*'soft shelled'*). In the hard shelled case, it is assumed that any target occurring inside the lobe will always be found. The lobe is discussed further in the section on mathematical models.

Historical perspective: two types of search study

The earliest roots of visual search as an experimental field date back to the work of Donders in the last century (republished as Donders, 1969). Donders' 'C-reaction' represents the precursor to the search process, in that only one of the ensemble of possible stimuli required a response to be made. There was, however, no spatial uncertainty to be reduced. Blumenfeld (1925) was the first to categorize search as involving the reduction of position uncertainty. He pointed out that abstraction and search were interrelated processes, with the former needed to recognize the target from the features that had been specified.

As with attention and vigilance, it was World War II that provided the impetus for modern studies of visual search. The problems of locating aircraft from the ground or targets from the air, and the use of sonar and radar, all resulted in the need for visual search studies designed to answer specific design problems. The best known studies of this type are those of Blackwell (1946), whose contrast thresholds are still being used to this day. Military applications in visual search are still the most prevalent, and one of the major problems of the field is the secrecy that often thus prevails.

Concurrent with the development of search as a behaviour warranting investigation *per se* has been a use of visual search experiments simply as a tool to study the more general processes of attention and pattern recognition. Although studies using visual search in this way have also given important insights into the actual search task itself, and will thus be cited in later sections, the different emphasis of such tasks, and the restricted nature of their search processes, require that a distinction be made between these tasks and those which are primarily concerned with the search behaviour itself. Such tasks will thus be labelled 'cognitive search' tasks, the description 'visual search' being reserved for studies that are mainly concerned with the search task *per se*.

Since the physical details of the material to be searched have not had to correspond to specific 'real life' situations, cognitive search tasks have usually used alphanumeric search material which is easy to generate and standardize. Following Neisser's use of letter and word lists (Neisser, 1963; Neisser and Beller, 1963), many cognitive search tasks have concentrated on alphanumeric list-searching for presentation of their search material (e.g. Kaplan *et al.*, 1966).

In contrast, the consideration of visual search as a part of human behaviour warranting investigation for its own sake has generated a wide variety of different search tasks. Much research has been generated and financed by bodies requiring the solution of a particular display problem, and some visual search studies have thus been primarily addressed to a particular type of display—e.g. sonar displays (Vallerie and Link, 1968), aerial maps (Enoch, 1959), air to ground search (Williams, 1966). Many studies have been less specific in intent, however, (e.g. Green and Anderson, 1956; Baker *et al.*, 1960), and all have usually contributed knowledge that has been of general use. Many studies have put forward mathematical models of search performance (e.g. Krendel and Wodinsky, 1960), but as Howarth and Bloomfield (1971) remark, such models are usually highly specialized in intent, and an acceptable overall model of visual search has yet to emerge. Some of the concepts involved in mathematical modelling are considered in a later section.

The division of visual search experiments into two groups as outlined above is obviously an over-simplification. Much overlap exists and most studies have provided information that can be used, at least partially, to further both aims. Most of the visual search studies to be described in this chapter are, however, concerned with visual search processes *per se*, rather than the information processing that underlies them. Indeed, the main bias of this chapter is towards 'applied' rather than 'pure' research.

The focus of this chapter

In the remainder of this chapter, the author aims to provide a general overview of the area and summary of pertinent research findings for those interested in vigilance and inspection. In doing this there is a very real danger of the text degenerating into an almost unreadable annotated bibliography. In seeking to avoid such a pitfall, the author is aware that the resulting coverage is far from comprehensive, but hopes that this has been compensated for by a slightly more fluent text than would otherwise have appeared.

The area has been divided into sections concerned with display variables, observer variables, temporal effects and mathematical models. Each section will start with an outline giving the general 'feel' for the problem, followed by a slightly more detailed description of the results that have been found.

DISPLAY VARIABLES

In discussing the 'display' in a visual search task, one must be careful to remember that the term can often be used in a rather abstract way. A display can be anything from a few square miles of forest viewed through an airplane window (Stager and Angus, 1978) to a pair of underpants (Megaw, 1979). Thus, although the more conventional displays, occurring on screens or panels, may be the first to spring to mind when the term is used, it must be realized that trays of jam tarts, photographs and maps are equally valid examples of visual search displays.

In the laboratory, most studies have been forced to resort to the simplicity of artificial displays presented on TV screens or via a slide projector. Although having a certain cost in the form of a lack of realism, such artificial displays have the advantage of increased levels of control over the target and non-target elements. Obviously, it would be impossible for a visual search study to quantify and control the whole richness and complexity of most 'real life' displays. Indeed, the vast majority of studies to be described are concerned simply with the effect of manipulation of a single display variable. Clearly, in 'real life', where a large number of display variables may be changing, these factors may interact to produce very different effects to those predicted from simple summation of the individual factors. Unfortunately, as in many other fields of human performance, the 'state' of the art' is insufficiently advanced for these interactions to be predictable.

Display contents

The simplest forms of display are those in which the target is effectively the only element present. Impoverished displays such as these have no confusing non-target elements to clutter them, and are characteristic of, for example, ground to air search, or quality inspection in glassmaking. Tasks using such displays often have targets that are closer to threshold than usual, and thus tend to exhibit less of the 'target certainty' property mentioned earlier. Indeed, for glassmaking quality inspection, Drury (1975) has put forward a model incorporating both search and signal detection components.

The lack of any non-targets to impose structure on to the scan-path means that impoverished displays probably represent the free-est of 'free search' conditions. Ford *et al.* (1959) used such displays to demonstrate the 'edge effect' (see below).

Cluttered displays are obviously harder to search through than impoverished ones. As one would expect, the function linking search time and number of non-targets (display density) is a monotonically increasing one. Some studies (e.g. Eriksen, 1955; Green and Anderson, 1956; Smith, 1962; Gordon and Winwood, 1973) suggest a linear function, although for large numbers of non-targets it is probably more accurate to follow Bloomfield (1970) in postulating a power function. More specifically, Bloomfield suggested that search time was proportional to the square root of non-target density.

As both Bloomfield (1970) and Drury and Clement (1978) have pointed out, the three factors of display density, display size and number of non-targets are always confounded. Thus, one can only change two of the three factors independently, since the level of the third factor will be dictated by those of the other two. Drury and Clement (1978) studied the three factors as independently as possible and found that although all three were important determinants of search time, that of number of non-targets appeared to be the most pronounced. They also found that, for a constant number of non-targets, the effect of reducing the search area (and thus increasing the non-target density) was to enhance search performance, presumably by reducing the number of fixations needed to cover the display. Such an interpretation is in agreement with the results of Gordon and Winwood (1973), who found that merely enlarging the whole display (by moving the slide projector further away from the screen) had little beneficial effect on search performance. In that case, it would appear that any benefits in terms of detectability had been swamped by the increase in fixations needed to cover the display. Thus, in practical terms, the advantages to be gained by simply 'scaling up' the whole display are probably minimal.

Unless the non-targets are totally homogeneous, the particular 'mixture' of the various types of non-targets will obviously have an important effect. The most important variable in this respect is that of colour, which will be considered in detail in a later section. Other factors are the similarity of various subsets of non-targets in size, shape or contrast.

Not only the form that the non-targets take, but also their respective positions in the display, will govern the way in which they influence search performance. There is a whole range of ways in which the individual non-targets can be positioned. At one end of the range is the regular array, where a homogeneous set of non-targets are ordered in a fixed matrix of possible positions (corresponding, for example, to a set of jam tarts on a tray). Regular displays tend to produce rather different search strategies to those used in irregular displays, particularly when the latter exhibit changes in the configuration of non-targets from one trial to the next. Search in regular displays is often more passive, with the observer detecting a flaw in the display as a whole, rather than actively seeking out the particular target element. This difference in

302

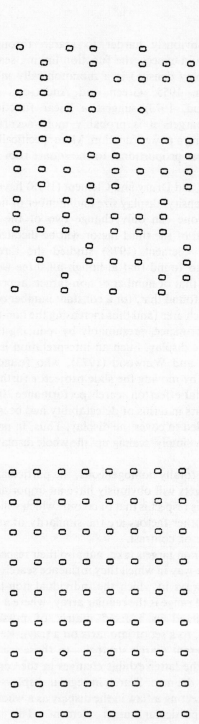

Figure 9.2 Examples of search in regular and irregular displays (see text). Both displays have the same number of non-targets.

TARGET= O

strategy—which often leads to better performance in regular displays (Bloomfield, 1970)—is illustrated in Figure 9.2.

The irregular spacing of non-targets can produce problems of camouflage. Unlike that in a regular array, a target in an irregular array can either be emphasized by isolation or camouflaged by being surrounded by the non-targets that happen to be in its vicinity. In particular, Brown and Monk (1975) showed that specific configurations of surrounding non-targets could have marked effects on search time. More generally, Monk and Brown (1975) showed a linear relationship between search time and target surround density, with high densities producing poorer search performance. Since the process of increasing *overall* non-target density will also tend to increase target surround density, this latter result will clearly be confounded with (and might indeed markedly contribute towards) the overall display density effect mentioned above.

Obviously, it is rather artificial to concentrate on a simple dichotomy between 'regular' and 'irregular' displays. In real life, display regularity represents a whole continuum stretching from the pattern of tiles on a wall to the entropy of a busy street scene. Even in the laboratory, Brown (1976) was able to demonstrate a continuum of display regularity (with computer-generated displays) that corresponded to an equivalent simple ordering of search times. Moreover, apart from the more abstract effects of display regularity, the inherent structure of a display can often tell the observer where to look first. Thus bridges cross rivers, and vehicles usually run on roads, and observers will clearly use this information when it is of advantage. Even in chest X-rays, trainee radiographers have been shown gradually to settle in to the scan-path that most optimally covers the display (Thomas and Lansdown, 1963). Thus, to conclude, display structure can influence both search performance *per se* and the particular scan-path shown by the observer.

Display movement

There are many situations in which the display is moving relative to the observer's frame of reference. The most obvious is the military one of air-to-ground search from a swiftly moving aircraft. Others include the industrial inspection of items on a conveyor belt or material being produced in a continuous, moving sheet (e.g. textiles, glass).

In target conspicuity experiments without a search component, Ludvigh and Miller (1958) and Burg and Hulbert (1961) have shown visual acuity to drop as target velocity increased. Erickson (1964) examined the effect of display movement in situations where there was a strong search component. Erickson used three display velocities (5, 7 and 10 deg s^{-1}) and, as one would expect, found the detection rate to drop as the speed was increased. He also found that the edge effect (see below) was particularly marked with higher velocities (i.e. more centrally-located targets were found than those nearer to the edge).

This, he interpreted, was the result of a tendency to give up trying to move the eyes, the observer instead merely fixating the centre of the 'window', at these higher display velocities. In agreement with this interpretation was his finding that, at higher display velocities, foveal acuity was a better predictor of performance than peripheral acuity, whilst at slower display velocities the reverse was true.

Thus in practical terms, apart from the obvious result that display movement degrades performance, there is the effect of high velocities tending to cause simple fixation of the middle of the display. This latter effect should be taken into account when designing the optimum inspection system for situations in which high display velocities necessarily occur.

The edge effect

Because of the freedom of choice given to the observer in a free search task, there are bound to be irregularities in the coverage of the display by the observer's scan-path. Thus some areas of the display will tend to be neglected in terms of average fixation density. Clearly, the particular areas that are neglected will depend upon the individual variability of the observer's choice of scan-path. However, generalizations can be made, the most important of which is the *edge effect*, which can account for comparatively large differences in search time.

The edge effect was first described in two papers appearing consecutively in the 1959 volume of the *Journal of the Optical Society of America*. Both studies used eye-movement recording, and neither study measured search time. Enoch (1959) used circular displays of various sizes (3°, 6°, 9°, 18° and 24°) comprising aerial map backgrounds on which were superimposed 'Landolt C' targets. For all display sizes, Enoch found that more fixations fell in the central part of the display than at the edge. Whilst there was little interaction between the edge effect and display size for displays subtending more than 9°; with the smallest displays more fixations appeared to fall outside the display altogether. Ford *et al.* (1959) used a very different type of experiment. Their displays subtended 30°, and were impoverished, the target consisting of a small patch of light that occasionally appeared. The session was divided into 5 second intervals, and fixation data taken from the intervals during which no target occurred. Ford *et al.* found an annular effect, whereby areas at the very centre and at the very edge of the display tended to be neglected.

Both Enoch and Ford *et al.* were primarily interested in fixation density rather than search time, and merely hypothesized the expected relationship between the two. The edge effect in terms of search time was first demonstrated by Baker *et al.* (1960), who showed that, for various sized circular displays, search times for centrally-located targets were significantly faster than for those located near the edge. Interestingly, Baker *et al.* also found an annular effect similar to that of Ford *et al.*, with optimum performance occurring slightly 'off centre'.

Edge effects accounting for a change in search time of up to 25% have since been found by the present author in displays subtending 5°, 6°, 7.5° and 20° at the subject's eye (Monk, 1974, 1976, 1977, 1979).

Quadrant effects

Quadrant effects have been found in both fixation density and search time, but in contradictory ways. Enoch (1959) divided each circular display into four quadrants by the intersecting vertical and horizontal diameters. He found that in terms of fixation density, the upper left quadrant appeared to be consistently neglected. In a square display, however, Gould and Schaffer (1965) found that more fixations occurred at the top of the display than the bottom, and at the right of the display than the left.

In terms of search time, however, Baker *et al.* (1960) (whose displays were circular) found that it was the lower quadrants (particularly the lower right) that had the longer search times. Gordon and Winwood (1973) also found the lower quadrants to have longer search times (in rectangular displays) than the upper ones, although no consistent left–right bias emerged. Other studies have failed to show any consistent quadrant effect (e.g. Ford *et al.*, 1959), and quadrant effects would thus appear to be much less important or robust than edge effects.

Target and non-target uncertainty

In order to find the target at all, the observer must, of course, be aware of at least one attribute that distinguishes it from all the non-targets in the display. There may, however, be several possible elements that 'fit the bill' as a target, and the observer might be asked to search for any one of these, rather than for a single specified target. Thus in a glassmaking quality control task, for example, the inspector might be asked to search, not just for bubbles, but also for lumps of grit and areas of discoloration. The target uncertainty effect (or target set size effect) is the difference in search time between a task with a single specified target, and an equivalent one in which the target is one of a set of n possible targets. The crucial question is that of whether or not there is a target uncertainty effect, i.e. whether or not searching for one of a set of n possible targets necesarily takes longer than searching for a single target.

In the area of search that the author has referred to as 'cognitive search' (see above), much research has been stimulated by the pioneering work of Neisser and his associates (Neisser, 1963; Neisser *et al.*, 1963). These studies indicated that given enough practice (in a list-searching task), there was no target uncertainty effect. They were, however, criticized (see, for example, Rabbitt, 1971) for allowing inordinately high error rates, and even Neisser (1974) would now agree that under more reasonable error rates there is an effect of target uncertainty.

In the more applied visual search area, studies of target uncertainty effects are much less common, despite the obvious practical ramifications. Bloomfield (1970) did provide some evidence of a target uncertainty effect, but his main conclusion was that further work was needed. Monk (1976) studies the effect using a task in which all of the (four possible) targets differed from the non-targets along a single dimension (i.e. they were all brighter than the non-targets, but to a differing degree). This situation thus favoured a strategy independent of target uncertainty. A target uncertainty effect in the order of 10% was still found, however. This effect appeared to be independent of target difficulty or target position.

A related question (studied by Schoonard and Gould, 1973) is whether certainty about a target being present on every trial has any effect on search times. The evidence suggests that it does not.

Non-target uncertainty is probably more accurately described as non-target heterogeneity, in that it represents the size of the 'alphabet' from which the non-target items are chosen. This effect has been studied extensively by Gordon and his associates (Gordon, 1968, 1969; Gordon *et al.*, 1971) who found that search time was proportional to the size of the non-target 'alphabet' (for both letters and nonsense figures). This appeared to be primarily due to an increase in the number of fixations for high non-target uncertainties. This result is important from an applied viewpoint, since it indicates that the items to be ignored can have as large an effect on search time as the target itself.

Colour

The fact that the blending of target and background colours is one of the major components of camouflage reinforces the importance of colour in the visual search process. Camouflage has been a particularly difficult phenomenon to study, however, and laboratory studies have thus concentrated on fairly simple displays in which colour is merely introduced as a factor.

The pioneering study of colour in visual displays is probably that of Green and Anderson (1956), who studied the effect of colour on search through a rectangular matrix of two-digit numbers. As mentioned earlier, search time is usually porportional to the number of non-target items in the display. Green and Anderson, however, found that when the observer was told the colour of the target, search time became proportional to the number of non-targets *of that colour*. This meant that observers were able to ignore all display items of a different colour, with minimal 'cost' in terms of search time; and that colour could thus be used as a powerful aid to the observer.

This research was followed up by Smith (1962) who studied the effects of number of colours (up to five), display density and target colour specification on search time. Smith confirmed that the effect of colour, either in target or background, was non-significant *per se*, but when knowledge of target colour was given there was an advantage in terms of search time, in the way suggested by Green and Anderson (1956). Cahill and Carter (1976) studied the effect of having up to 10 different colours in the display, and found that benefits in search time still appeared with up to nine colours, but above that, particularly for high denisty displays, the patches of colour became too diffuse for any advantage to be gained.

Apart from enabling the subject to ignore whole sets of non-targets, there are other benefits, either real or apparent, that accrue from the use of colour in visual displays. For a comprehensive review and evaluation of all such effects, the reader is referred to Christ (1975). A more detailed evaluation of the complexities of colour vision itself can be obtained from Hunt (1979).

OBSERVER VARIABLES

As in the case of vigilance (Wiener, 1975), much less attention in the visual search area has been paid to the 'soft' observer variables, such as age, than to the 'hard' display variables, such as display density, which can be better counted on to give significant results. Partly as a consequence of this, and partly to avoid too much overlap with Chapter 5, the present section will be rather limited in extent.

Obviously, the most important observer variable in a visual search task is eyesight. As Bloomfield (1975a,b) points out, the two aspects of eyesight that are crucial to the observer are his visual acuity and the way in which he distributes his fixations over the display (i.e. his search strategy). It is probably true to say that other observer variables, such as age, sex and experience, are mediated through these two aspects of eyesight, and this section will thus be divided into two subsections accordingly.

Visual acuity factors

As mentioned earlier, little or no useful information can be taken in during saccades, when the eye is moving from one position to the next (Volkman, 1962). The main 'business' of search thus takes place during the fixations (which last on average from 200 to 350 milliseconds), and the main determinant of search time is thus the number of fixations needed to find the target (or, on average, to cover the display). Clearly, the more information that can be taken in during a fixation the larger will be the lobe size, and thus the fewer the fixations needed to cover the display. Observers who have good peripheral acuity should, as a consequence, be faster searchers. A study by Schoonard *et al.* (1973) gives an indication of whether fast observers (or inspectors) are fast because they make fewer fixations (perhaps due to better peripheral acuity) or fast because they have shorter fixations (indicating an ability to process the information from a given fixation more quickly). The evidence suggests that it is the former, since the fastest (and most accurate) observers relied on far fewer fixations than the slowest, whilst modal fixation times appeared remarkably constant between individuals. Indeed, constancy of fixation time appears to be a striking phenomenon in visual search (see also Gould and Schaffer, 1965), and one which is most useful to the constructors of mathematical models (see later sections).

That visual acuity is affected by extremes of age is obvious. However, more subtle changes in visual field size were detected by Burg (1968) who, in a study of over 17 000 subjects, found that visual field size appears, on average, to rise at first, achieving a maximum at about 35 or 40 years of age, before showing the expected decline into old age. Because of the nature of this function, it is not surprising that Erickson (1964) found no correlation between age and search performance in a group aged between 23 and 41 years. Also, any detrimental effects of advanced age may be overwhelmed by enhancements due to experience and motivation (Jamieson, 1966).

Burg, (1968) also found that women had consistently larger visual fields than men. This would suggest that on average women might prove to be better inspectors. However, a survey of inspection studies by Wiener (1975) suggested that there was no consistent evidence that they were; a conclusion which is shared by Bone (1978) in her laboratory study of visual search performance.

Overall, the enormous range of individual differences in visual acuity make these negative results unsurprising. Any effect of age or sex would tend to be masked by such 'noise', unless enormous samples of subjects were studied. In conclusion, the most useful practical advice would thus be to ensure adequate visual acuity in the observer, but to avoid generalizations about individuals' acuity from their age or sex.

Search strategy effects

The particular choice of scan-path typically adopted by the observer will have an important effect on search efficiency. The problem of obtaining an optimum scan-path is the old one of reconciling the competing demands of speed and accuracy. Thus if inter-fixation distances are too small, the scan-path will be unrealistically slow and conservative, whilst if they are too large, targets might be missed, necessitating the re-scanning of the display. Outside the laboratory, the problem of taking into account the inherent structure and target location biases of the display also have to be taken into account.

The major observer variable with respect to search strategy effects is that of experience. Practice effects are discussed in a later section ('Within- and between-session effects'), and it is probable that many of the effects reported there result from the gradual adoption of more efficient search strategies. One only has to spend a few mintues in the field watching a skilled observer at work to realize the benefits in search efficiency that experience can bring. It would appear, however, that it is generally *not* helpful to dictate a particular scan-path by the superimposition of a grid.

Other search strategy effects will spring from the 'type' of person the observer is. The most obvious individual differences in this respect are intelligence and 'perceptual style'. The effect of intelligence level on search performance appears to be minimal (Wiener, 1975), unless one considers the audio-visual checking task of Kappauf and Powe (1959) to be a search task, in which case higher intelligence might be considered to be beneficial.

The effect of perceptual style was studied by Bone (1978) who measured the 'field independence' of her subjects by the Witkin embedded figure test. This measure gave an indication of their ability to pick out a figure from a confusing background. It was found to correlate with search performance, but only when the display was structured, with the non-targets appearing in 'clumps' (thus explaining conflicting results in the literature).

As a general conclusion to the discussion of subject variables, it seems clear to the author that people matched on peripheral visual acuity and level of experience are unlikely to show any differences due to their age, sex, intelligence or personality. It is thus to these two major factors that attention should be given.

TEMPORAL EFFECTS

Temporal effects in visual search are taken to be those that result from (a) the time at which the search trial takes place (either within the session or within the day) or (b) the duration of a particular search trial (and/or that of its neighbours). This section will thus be divided into three fairly distinct subsections, namely within- and between-trial effects, within- and between-session effects, and time of day effects.

Within- and between-trial effects

Individual search trials often last several seconds, and there are thus changes in strategy and efficiency that can occur actually within the search trial itself. Thus the duration of an on-going search trial can govern the efficiency with which the observer performs. The question clearly arises as to whether lengthening the search trial will cause the observer to perform more efficiently or less so. Indirect evidence for enhanced efficiency is provided by Kreuger's (1970) finding that familiarity with search material aids performance, and for reduced efficiency by Boynton's (1960) finding that his observers felt like 'giving up' after 12 seconds of search.

The question was addressed directly by Monk (1977), who systematically controlled perceived search time whilst still having a measure of search time as a dependent variable. This apparently contradictory design was accomplished by the surreptitious insertion of time lags between the start of the search trial and the actual presence of the target in the display. Thus by lengthening the lag, perceived search time could be lengthened at will, with post-target search time (perceived search time minus lag) used as the dependent variable. Monk found that the effect of lengthening a search trial was detrimental, increases in post-target search time of 14.6% and 17.9% occurring for 7.5 and 15.0 second lag conditions. This experiment also gave evidence of a 'carry-over' effect, whereby post-target search time was reduced if the same lag had been used on the previous trial as on the present one. This 'repetition' effect paralleled one found earlier (Monk, 1974b), by which trials with a particular target had reduced search times if the previous trial had also had that target.

In conclusion, it would appear that adverse within- and between-trial effects can best be reduced by ensuring that search trials are kept short, and the population of search times relatively homogeneous. This might be achieved either by dividing the targets up between several observers, or (if high accuracy is essential) by having a 'multi-pass' system.

Within- and between-session effects

In all but the most practised of subjects, the greatest within- or between-session effect is the improvement in search time that accrues with practice. Such a practice effect is often quite strong enough, and persistent enough, to obliterate any vigilance decrement that might otherwise occur. Thus, in this section, consideration will first be given to practice effects, before going on to a brief discussion of the effects of vigilance on search performance.

Practice effects in search are described as within- and between-session effects, since they typically last for a number of sessions. The present author found improvements due to practice to last for up to twelve 45-trial sessions (Monk, 1974a). Massive improvements due to practice were also found by Neisser (1963) whose parallel processing results (see 'Target uncertainty' section) only emerged after a considerable number of practice sessions. Gordon (1968) was also able to demonstrate a practice effect in list-search which was independent of familiarity with the actual stimulus material.

In free search, there are, however, some discrepant studies. Baker *et al.* (1960) found a practice effect, but attributed it to acquisition of the skill of matching blurred to non-blurred images rather than search *per se*. Gould and Schaffer (1965) found no reliable practice effects in either search time or eye movement parameters, and Krendel and Wodinsky (1960) found no significant difference between the search times of two groups of subjects, one of whom had 10 hours of preliminary pre-training.

Despite the negative results reported above, it would appear that practice effects are often a strong factor to be reckoned with when studying search tasks in the laboratory, particularly when the material is presented in the form of lists.

Since the bulk of this book is concerned wtih vigilance effects of one sort or another, it would be repetitive to give a detailed discussion of vigilance effects *per se* in the present chapter. For example, Chapter 7 considers many inspection situations in which search is an important factor. From a strictly search-oriented viewpoint, many of these studies are anyway of limited interest, since they are concerned with the effect of search on vigilance, rather than the effect of vigilance (i.e. time on task) on search. This section will thus limit itself to the few studies that have considered the effect of time on task on various search measures.

Although the search component of Colquhoun and Edward's (1970) task was very limited (the display consisted of six discs in a row), they did obtain a distinct 'edge effect' whereby detection rate for outer locations was worse than that for inner ones. Although there was a pronounced 'vigilance decrement' in terms of detection efficiency, Colquhoun and Edwards found no evidence of any reliable within-session change in the edge effect. In a later experiment, using a very wide display, W. P. Colquhoun and S. Folkard (personal communication) did, however, achieve a slight, but statistically reliable, reduction in the edge effect. Clearly, much more work is needed in this area before definite conclusions can be drawn, but at present it would seem that within- and between-trial effects are unlikely to produce major changes in search behaviour, other than the simple improvement in search time due to practice.

Time of day effects

Circadian (i.e. around 24 hours) rhythms have now been found in a range of performance measures (see Hockey and Colquhoun, 1972, for a review). Circadian performance rhythms are not the mere step functions that would result from poor performance at night being contrasted with better performance during the day. They are continuous, gradual fluctuations in efficiency over the whole 24-hour period, and are thus important, even in normal 'dayworking' situations. Moreover, although certain individual (interpersonal) differences do exist, the similarities between individuals' circadian rhythms of performance efficiency at a particular task far outweigh the differences. Thus, for a particular task, it is perfectly feasible to estimate the time at which performance will be at a maximum or minimum for the population as a whole.

Time of day effects in search performance have had comparatively little attention paid to them. The four studies that can be gleaned from the literature have invariably used material in which a strict order of scanning is imposed, with the subject working his way through a printed sheet (or sheets). Figure 9.3 illustrates the observed time of day effects in (i) crossing out all the letters 'E' in a magazine article (Blake, 1967); (ii) finding the tilted zeros in a page otherwise full of upright zeros (Hughes and Folkard, 1976); (iii) searching through sets of dot matrices for those only having four elements (Klein *et al.*,

1972), and (iv) searching through random letters for a pair of identical letters occurring next to each other (Fort and Mills, 1976). The normal daily oral temperature rhythm (Colquhoun *et al.,* 1968) has also been plotted for comparison (see below).

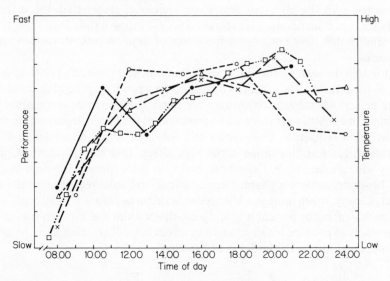

Figure 9.3   The time of day effect in performance efficiency on a range of search tasks (see text), plotted with that of normal body temperature ($N=56$). ●———●, Blake (1967); Δ–·–Δ, Hughes and Folkard (1976); ○————○, Klein *et al.* (1972); ×————×, Fort and Mills (1976); □—···—□, temperature.

From Figure 9.3 it is clear that there is a well-defined time of day effect, common to all four studies, despite important differences in search tasks and subject samples. All four studies used analyses of variance to confirm the statistical significance of their results. On average, the difference between the 'peak' and 'trough' points represents a 10% change in performance and is thus equivalent in magnitude, for example, to the legal limit of alcohol. Figure 9.3 also reveals strong evidence of an apparent parallelism between the circadian rhythms of oral temperature and search performance. Indeed, Kleitman and Jackson (1950) asserted that performance tests were largely unnecessary since time of day effects in performance could be predicted from temperature. This, however, is *not* the case, since a recent study has shown that the correlation between temperature and performance can be changed from a significantly positive value to a significantly negative one, simply by changing the complexity of the same search task (Folkard *et al.*, 1976). This study was crucial in finding that task demands can radically affect the nature of a performance rhythm. Thus, even within a single search task, increases in complexity can move the

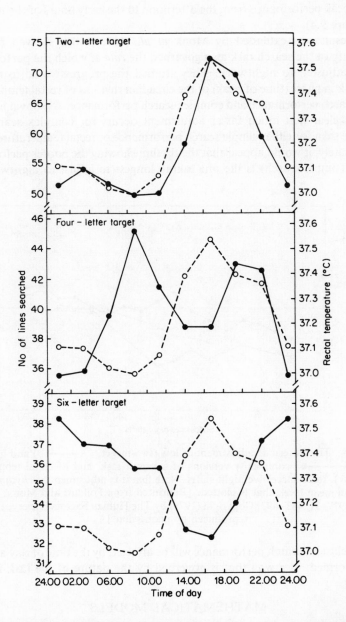

Figure 9.4 The circadian rhythms of performance (●———●) and rectal temperature
(○———○) for low (two-letter), medium (four-letter) and high (six-letter) complexity
versions of a search task. Improvements in performance are represented by a rise.
[Reprinted from Folkard and Monk, *Human Factors*, 1979, **21**, 483–492. Copyright
(1979) by The Human Factors Society, Inc., and reproduced by permission.]

time of peak performance from the afternoon to the early hours of the morning (see Figure 9.4).

The result was extended by Monk *et al.* (1978), who showed that the complexity of the search task also governed the *rate* at which the performance rhythm adjusted to nightwork. They studied the progressive adjustment to nightwork in phase (time of peak) of the circadian rhythms of rectal temperature, simple search performance and complex search performance. As shown in Figure 9.5, it is clear that much faster adjustment occurs for complex search performance than for either simple search performance or rectal temperature. Thus, unfortunately, it would appear that the rhythm showing the poorer performance at night (simple search) is the one taking longest to adjust to nightwork.

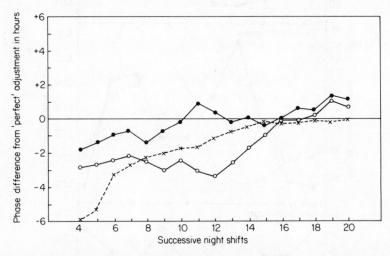

Figure 9.5   The pattern of adjustment of low (two-target, O————O) and high (six-target, ●————●) complexity versions of a search task, and of rectal temperature (×-----×), to 20 successive night shifts. Note that it is adjustment of *rhythm phase*, rather than mean level, that is plotted. [Reprinted from Folkard and Monk, *Human Factors*, 1979, **21**, 483–492. Copyright (1979) by The Human Factors Society, Inc., and reproduced by permission.]

In conclusion, search performance will be affected by the time of day at which it is performed, in a way that is governed by the nature of the task itself.

MATHEMATICAL MODELS

The military importance of visual search is obvious, and almost all mathematical models of search performance have been funded by defence establishments of one sort or another. As a consequence, many are unpublished, but there remains a strong body of search models in the literature. Because of the applied bias, the main aim of most search modellers has been (consciously or unconsciously) to predict search times successfully, i.e. to construct an equation or computer program which, when you tell it the parameters of the task and the observer, will tell you what the search time will be. This aim has resulted in the use of a number of assumptions and hypothetical constructs that are (at best) dubious as descriptions of what is actually going on, though as elements of a purely predictive model, they are, of course perfectly acceptable.

Partly because of this concentration on prediction rather than description, and partly because of the tedium that might result for the mathematically unsophisticated reader, this section will not present a detailed discussion or catalogue of the dozen or so models that have been put forward. Readers who require such details are instead referred to Bloomfield (1975a) or Overington (1979). This section will, however, attempt to give an idea of some of the concepts and techniques that are common to most mathematical models of search behaviour. The text is thus divided into subsections headed 'Scan-path selection', 'Lobes' and 'Frequency distributions'.

Scan-path selection

As mentioned earlier in the chapter, the type of scan-path used varies widely both from one observer to another and within the same observer on different trials. Scan-path selection is thus the most difficult aspect of search to model. As a consequence, modellers have considered the process to be stochastic, rather than deterministic, with the observer randomly sampling various portions of the display with each fixation.

This sampling can either be with or without replacement. In random sampling with replacement, it is assumed that the observer has no memory for where he has searched, but merely continues to take samples at random from the display, with each sample having the same probability of containing the target. Although such a procedure may seem highly unlikely, it does have the advantage of taking into account 'back-tracking to cover old ground' (which certainly does occur), and the occasional occurrence of very long search times, which would be impossible if sampling was without replacement. Moreover, in some situations (see Bloomfield, 1975a), it provides a better fit to the observed data than that provided by sampling without replacement.

In sampling without replacement, it is assumed that the subject has perfect memory for where he has already searched, and only fixates 'new areas'. With each new fixation, the probability of finding the target increases, and eventually he covers the whole display exhaustively. This procedure has the advantage of simulating the case in which the subject does systematically work his way through the whole display. It suffers, however, from the drawbacks mentioned above, and if one is primarily interested in predicting search times, random sampling with replacement is probably the better choice.

The lobe

As mentioned earlier in the chapter, the lobe is *not* a constant parameter of vision like the fovea. It is an artificial construct, dependent on the acuity and motivation of the observer and the target and display characteristics. In fact, the lobe is merely a set of probability contours, mapping out the probability of detecting the target at various eccentricities from the point of fixation. Depending upon the sophistication of the model, lobes can be either 'soft-shelled' or 'hard-shelled'. Soft-shelled lobes are the more sophisticated, representing a complete set of probability contours. As a consequence, they are harder to determine and to incorporate computationally. For the hard-shelled lobe, only the 50% contour is taken, and all targets falling inside it are assumed to be found and those outside it to be lost.

As a predictive tool, there is no doubt that the lobe has been an invaluable construct, particularly since it enables the time variable to be divided into a set of fixations or glimpses, each taking a certain length of time (often assumed to be 333 milliseconds). However, the lobe has severe weaknesses as a descriptive tool, notably (1) its inability to cope with the situation where a target at the 'edge' of one fixation directs the gaze to the target on the next (Howarth and Bloomfield, 1971), and (2) the fact that using his 'eye-marker' camera, Mackworth has repeatedly shown that observers can be looking straight at a target yet totally fail to see it (e.g. Mackworth *et al.*, 1964). These weaknesses make it perhaps unfortunate that the lobe has become so entrenched in the mathematical modelling of search behaviour.

Search time distributions

Earlier in the chapter it was mentioned that the distribution of search times that are obtained in a search experiment are very rarely distributed according to a normal (Gaussian) distribution. Instead, they usually exhibit a distinct positive skew, such that the mean and the standard deviation are correlated. This skew means that when plotted cumulatively (i.e. as the number of search times less than t, for various values of t), the distribution approximates well to a negative exponential distribution of the form

$$P(t) = 1 - e^{-t/\lambda}, \tag{9.1}$$

where $P(t)$ is the probability of detection before time t and λ is the mean search time.

Figure 9.6 illustrates the cumulative distribution of some actual search times, together with equation (9.1) (with an appropriate value of λ fitted).

To the search modeller, the fact that equation (9.1) is equivalent to a simple sampling procedure (being a special case of the Poisson distribution) has been

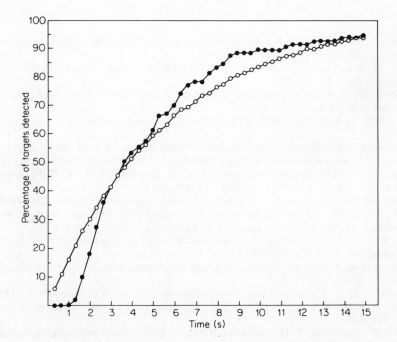

Figure 9.6 Cumulative probability of detection curves. 'Observed' curve (●———●) represents actual data (179 trials) from a single subject. 'Predicted' curve (○———○) results from substitution of the mean search time (5.79s) into equation (9.1) (see text).

invaluable (e.g. Krendel and Wodinsky, 1960) in justifying such procedures in their models. Thus the nature of search time distribution has itself governed the direction which many models of visual search have taken.

GENERAL CONCLUSIONS

Search is one of the most complicated aspects of human behaviour to be studied in the laboratory, involving a welter of decisions and strategies that are beyond the experimenter's control. It is this lack of control that makes the area appealing to the present author, but the lack of control also means that the data is invariably very messy, and the set of answerable research questions rather limited. There are many research questions that have been answered, and hopefully most will have been covered in this chapter. Many are still to be answered, however, and the area is wide open for further exploitation. The author's only caveat is that, although rewarding, search can also be an exacting mistress.

REFERENCES

Baker, C. A., Morris, D. F., and Steedman, W. C. Target recognition on complex displays. *Human Factors*, 1960, **2**, 51–61.

Blake, M. J. F. Time of day effects on performance in a range of tasks. *Psychonomic Science*, 1967, **9**, 349–350.

Blackwell, H. R. Contrast thresholds of the human eye. *Journal of the Optical Society of America*, 1946, **36**, 624–643.

Bloomfield, J. R. Visual search. Unpublished PhD thesis, University of Nottingham, 1970.

Bloomfield, J. R. Theoretical approaches to visual search. In C. G. Drury and J. G. Fox (Eds), *Human reliability in quality control*. London: Taylor and Francis, 1975.

Bloomfield, J. R. Studies on visual search. In C. G. Drury and J. G. Fox (Eds), *Human reliability in quality control*. London: Taylor and Francis, 1975.

Blumenfeld, W. Das Suchen von Zahlen in begrenzten ebenen Felde und das Problem der Abstraktion [The search for numbers in limited plain fields and the problem of abstraction]. *Zeitschrift fur angewandte Psychologie*, 1925, **25**, 58–107.

Bone, K. E. The relation between field dependency, visual search and structure of displays. *Ergonomics*, 1978, **21**, 383–388.

Boynton, R. M. Concluding remarks. In *Visual search techniques*, NAS-NRC Publication No. 712. 1960, pp.231–239.

Broadbent, D. E. *Perception and Communication*, London: Pergamon Press, 1958.

Brown, B. Effect of background constraint on visual search times. *Ergonomics*, 1976, **18**, 441–449.

Brown, B., and Monk, T. H. The effect of local target surround and whole background constraint on visual search times. *Human Factors*, 1975, **17**, 81–88.

Burg, A. Lateral visual field as related to age and sex. *Journal of Applied Psychology*, 1968, **52**, 10–15.

Burg, A., and Hulbert, S. F. Dynamic visual acuity as related to age, sex and static acuity. *Journal of Applied Psychology*, 1961, **45**, 111–116.

Cahill, M., and Carter, R. C. Color code size for searching displays of different density. *Human Factors*, 1976, **18**, 273–280.

Cavanagh, J. P., and Chase, W. G. The equivalence of target and non-target processing in visual search. *Perception and Psychophysics*, 1971, **9**, 493–495.

Christ, R. E. Review and analysis of color coding research for visual displays. *Human Factors*, 1975, **17**, 542–570.

Colquhoun, W. P., and Edwards, R. S. Practice effects on a visual vigilance task with and without search. *Human Factors*, 1970, **12**, 537–545.

Colquhoun, W. P., Blake, M. F. J., and Edwards, R. S. Experimental studies of shift-work. I: A comparison of 'rotating' and 'stabilised' 4 hour shift systems, *Ergonomics*, 1968, **11**, 437–453.

Donders, F. C. On the speed of mental processes (translated by W. G. Koster). *Acta Psychologica*, 1969, **30**, 412.

Drury, C. G. Human decision making in quality control. In C. G. Drury and J. G. Fox (Eds), *Human reliability in quality control*. London: Taylor and Francis, 1975.

Drury, C. G., and Clement, M. R. The effect of area, density, and number of background characters on visual search. *Human Factors*, 1978, **20**, 597–602.

Drury, C. G., and Fox, J. G. *Human reliability in quality control*, London: Taylor and Francis, 1975.

Enoch, J. M. Effect of the size of a complex display upon visual search. *Journal of the Optical Society of America*, 1959, **49**, 280–286.

Eriksen, C. W. Partitioning and saturation of visual displays and efficiency of visual search. *Journal of Applied Psychology*, 1955, **39**, 73–77.

Erickson, R. A. Relation between visual search time and peripheral visual acuity. *Human Factors*, 1964, **6**, 165–177.

Folkard, S., and Monk, T. H. Shiftwork and performance. *Human Factors*, 1979, **21**, 483–492.

Folkard, S., Knauth, P., Monk, T. H., and Rutenfranz, J. The effect of memory load on the circadian variation in performance efficiency under a rapidly rotating shift system. *Ergonomics*, 1976, **19**, 479–488.

Ford, A., White, C. T., and Lichtenstein, M. Analysis of eye movements during free search. *Journal of the Optical Society of America*, 1959, **49**, 287–292.

Fort, A., and Mills, J. N. Der Einfluß der Tageszeit und des vorhergehenden Schlaf-Wach-Susters auf die Leistungsfahigkeit unmittelbar nach dem Aufstehen. In G. Hildebrandt (Ed.), *Biologische Rhythmen und Arbeit*. Berlin: Springer-Verlag, 1976.

Gordon, I. E. Interactions between items in visual search. *Journal of Experimental Psychology*, 1968, **76**, 348–355.

Gordon, I. E. Eye movements during search through printed lists. *Perceptual and Motor Skills*, 1969, **29**, 683–686.

Gordon, I. E., and Winwood, M. Searching through letter arrays. *Ergonomics*, 1973, **16**, 177–188.

Gordon, I. E., Dulewicz, V., and Winwood, M. Irrelevant item variety and visual search. *Journal of Experimental Psychology*, 1971, **88**, 295–296.

Gould, J. D., and Schaffer, A. Eye movement patterns in scanning numeric displays. *Perceptual and Motor Skills*, 1965, **20**, 521–535.

Green, B. F., and Anderson, L. K. Color coding in a visual search task. *Journal of Experimental Psychology*, 1956, **51**, 19–24.

Hockey, G. R. J., and Colquhoun, W. P. Diurnal variation in human performance: a review. In W. P. Colquhoun (Ed.), *Aspects of human efficiency: diurnal rhythm and loss of sleep*, London: English Universities Press, 1972, pp.1–23.

Howarth, C. I., and Bloomfield, J. R. Search and selective attention. *British Medical Bulletin*, 1971, **27**, 253–258.

Hughes, D. G., and Folkard, S. Adaptation to an 8-h shift in living routine by members of a socially isolated community. *Nature*, 1976, **264**, 432–434.

Hunt, R. W. G. Color vision. In J. N. Clare and M. A. Sinclair (Eds), *Search and the human observer*. London: Taylor and Francis, 1979.

Jamieson, G. H. Inspection in the telecommunications industry: a field study of age and other performance variables. *Ergonomics*, 1966, **9**, 297–303.

Kaplan, I. T., Carvellas, T., and Metlay, W. Visual search and immediate memory. *Journal of Experimental Psychology*, 1966, **71**, 488–493.

Kappauf, W. E., and Powe, W. E. Performance decrement at an audio-visual checking task. *Journal of Experimental Psychology*, 1959, **57**, 49–56.

Klein, K. E., Wegmann, H. M., and Hunt, B. I. Desynchronization as a function of body temperature and performance circadian rhythm as a result of outgoing and homegoing transmeridian flights. *Aerospace Medicine*, 1972, **43**, 119–132.

Kleitman, N., and Jackson, D. P. Body temperature and performance under different routines. *Journal of Applied Physiology*, 1950, **3**, 309–328.

Krendel, E. S., and Wodinsky, J. Search in an unstructured visual field. *Journal of the Optical Society of America*, 1960, **50**, 562–568.

Krueger, L. E. Effect of frequency of display on speed of visual search', *Journal of Experimental Psychology*, 1970, **84**, 495–498.

Laycock, J. The measurement and analysis of eye movements. In J. N. Clare and M. A. Sinclair (Eds), *Search and the human observer*. London: Taylor and Francis, 1979.

Loeb, M., and Alluisi, E. A. Influence of display, task, and organismic variables on indices of monitoring behaviour. *Acta Psychologica*, 1970, **33**, 343–366.

Ludvigh, E. J., and Miller, J. W. Study of visual acuity during the ocular pursuit of moving test objects. *Journal of the Optical Society of America*, 1958, 48, 799–802.

Mackworth, N. H. The breakdown of vigilance during prolonged visual search. *Quarterly Journal of Experimental Psychology*, 1948, **1**, 6–21.

Mackworth, N. H., Kaplan, I. T., and Metlay, W. Eye movements during vigilance. *Perceptual and Motor Skills*, 1964, **20**, 549–554.

Megaw, E. D. Factors affecting visual inspection accuracy. *Applied Ergonomics*, 1979, **10**, 27–32.

Monk, T. H., Sequential and spatial effects in visual search. Unpublished PhD thesis, University of Nottingham, 1974(a).

Monk, T. H. Sequential effects in visual search. *Acta Psychologica*, 1974, **38**, 315–321(b).

Monk, T. H. Target uncertainty in applied visual search. *Human Factors*, 1976 **18**, 607–612.

Monk, T. H. Sequential expectancy in visual search. *Human Factors*, 1977, **19**, 601–606.

Monk, T. H. Temporal effects in visual search. In J. N. Clare and M. A. Sinclair (Eds), *Search and the human observer*, London: Taylor and Francis, 1979.

Monk, T. H., and Brown, B. The effect of target surround density on visual search performance. *Human Factors*, 1975, **17**, 356–360.

Monk, T. H., Knauth, P., Folkard, S., and Rutenfranz, J. Memory based performance measures in studies of shiftwork, *Ergonomics*, 1978, **21**, 819–826.

Neisser, U. Decision-time without reaction-time: experiments in visual scanning. *American Journal of Psychology*, 1963, **76**, 376–385.

Neisser, U. *Cognitive psychology*. New York: Appleton–Century–Crofts, 1967.

Neisser, U. Practised card sorting for multiple targets. *Memory and Cognition*, 1974, **2**, 781–785.

Neisser, U., and Beller, K. Searching through word lists. *British Journal of Psychology*, 1963, **56**, 349–358.

Neisser, U., Novick, R., and Lazar, R. Searching for ten targets simultaneously. *Perceptual and Motor Skills*, 1963, **17**, 955–961.

Overington, I. The current status of mathematical modelling of threshold functions. In J. N. Clare and M. A. Sinclair (Eds), *Search and the human observer*, London: Taylor and Francis, 1979.

Pomerantz, J. R., and Garner, W. R. The role of configuration and target discriminability in a visual search task. *Memory and Cognition*, 1973, **1**, 64–68.

Rabbitt, P. M. A. Ignoring irrelevant information. *British Journal of Psychology*, 1964, **55**, 99–113.

Rabbitt, P. M. A. Times for the analysis of stimuli and for the selection of responses. *British Medical Bulletin*, 1971, **27**, 259–265.

Schoonard, J. W., and Gould, J. D. Field of view and target uncertainty in visual search and inspection. *Human Factors*, 1973, **15**, 33–42.

Schoonard, J. W., Gould, J. D., and Miller, L. A. Studies of visual inspection. *Ergonomics*, 1973, **16**, 365–379.

Smith, S. L. Color coding and visual search. *Journal of Experimental Psychology*, 1962, **64**, 434–440.

Sperling, G. Negative after-image without prior positive image. *Science*, 1960, **131**, 1613–1614.

Stager, P., and Angus, R. Locating crash sites in simulated air-to-ground visual search. *Human Factors*, 1978, **20**, 453–466.

Sternberg, S. High-speed scanning in human memory. *Science*, 1966, **153**, 652–654.

Thomas, E. L., and Lansdown, E. L. Visual search patterns of radiologists in training. *Radiology*, 1963, **81**, 288–292.

Vallerie, L. L., and Link, J. M. Visual detection probability of 'sonar' targets as a function of retinal position and brightness contrast. *Human Factors*, 1968, **10**, 403–411.

Volkman, F. C. Vision during voluntary saccadic eye movements. *Journal of the Optical Society of America*, 1962, **52**, 571–578.

Wiener, E. L. Individual and group differences in inspection. In C. G. Drury and J. G. Fox (Eds), *Human reliability in quality control*, London: Taylor and Francis, 1975.

Williams, L. G. Target conspicuity and visual search. *Human Factors*, 1966, **8**, 80–92.

Sustained Attention in Human Performance
Edited by J. S. Warm
© 1984 John Wiley & Sons Ltd.

Chapter 10

Epilogue

Joel S. Warm

Since the pioneering studies of Norman Mackworth (1948, 1950), psychologists have sought to gain insight into the factors which determine the quality of sustained attention. The preceding chapters have provided a comprehensive and critical evaluation of these efforts. In this final chapter, it seems appropriate to summarize briefly some of the accomplishments that have been made and to highlight some possible directions for future research.

TOWARDS DEEPER UNDERSTANDING

Psychophysical considerations

In the introductory chapter, I indicated that research on sustained attention, like that in other areas of science, has followed a dynamic course. More specifically, I suggested that over the years the character of vigilance research has evolved from early phases of discovery and data acquisition to a more mature and perhaps more demanding level of development—a phase in which deeper understanding and exploration are required. This suggestion can serve as a theme for developments in the psychophysics of vigilance and for the other aspects of the vigilance story as well.

From the discussion provided by Jerison and myself in Chapter 2, it is evident that much work has been devoted to studying the stimulus factors which control vigilance performance. Most of the more obvious parameters, such as the sensory modality of signals, signal amplitude and duration, signal density and regularity and the background event rate have been identified and examined intensively. In addition, a major general model in modern psychophysics, the theory of signal detection, has been utilized in vigilance studies and its contributions and limitations have been explored carefully. Much has been learned but much also remains to be learned.

Consider, for example, the issue of multi-task monitoring. Although this topic was not addressed in Chapter 2, data are available to show that intricate cross-task interactions can occur when two or more monitoring tasks are performed together (Davies and Tune, 1969; Hohmuth, 1970; Wickens *et al.*, 1981; Wolk *et al.*, 1983). The multi-task paradigm provides an opportunity for those concerned with the psychophysics of vigilance to examine the interplay of the stimulus characteristics of the tasks involved and, in this way, broaden our understanding of context effects in sustained attention. This is a potentially important issue since operational settings, unlike most laboratory settings, often require observers to monitor several displays simultaneously (see Chapters 6 and 7 in this volume and Cordes, 1983a,b).

The taxonomic analysis of vigilance tasks, particularly the work of Davies and Parasuraman (1982), represents a major innovation. It combines an important psychophysical determinant, background event rate, with the information processing demands of the task to create a new empirical framework in which to view vigilance performance. It also raises many questions. As Jerison and I have noted, they revolve about the manner in which the standard psychophysical parameters in vigilance are related to the kinds of dis-criminations—simultaneous or successive—that subjects must make in a sustained attention task. At this writing, some work along these lines has already begun to appear. Recall that the Davies and Parasuraman taxonomy indicated that the vigilance decrement reflects a decline in perceptual sensitivity (d') only under conditions of a fast event rate coupled with successive (memory-based) discriminations. In a very recent paper, Nuechterlein *et al.* (1983) have demonstrated that when target images are severely degraded, temporal declines in perceptual sensitivity occur with simultaneous (non-memory) discrimination tasks as well.

Finally, the problem of task complexity represents a major unsolved issue in the psychophysics of vigilance. Indeed, it is sort of a 'sleeping giant'. We have known for a long while that some complex tasks may not reflect the vigilance decrement. Instead, the quality of sustained attention in these tasks can remain stable over several hours of watch. These results, however, have not enjoyed the importance, either on an empirical or a theoretical level, that they may deserve. Recently, it has become clear that different ways of increasing the intricacy of the discriminations that subjects must make in separating signals from noise can not only retard the vigilance decrement but can also amplify or reverse it. Clearly, more systematic exploration of the relation between vigilance performance and task complexity is needed.

Psychobiological considerations

Our knowledge of the psychobiology of sustained attention has expanded considerably since the early days of vigilance research. In one of the first and most widely known reviews of vigilance, Frankmann and Adams (1962) addressed physiological issues principally in terms of arousal and its relation to the decrement function. Parasuraman's cogent discussion in Chapter 3 illustrates the substantial gain in information since that time. In addition to early measures involving the galvanic skin response and gross electro-encephalographic activity, a variety of more sophisticated indicies have been employed to probe the physiological basis of vigilance performance. These include pupillary responses, catecholamine levels and event-related electrocortical potentials. In addition, a number of pharmacological agents have been shown to influence the manner in which people can sustain attention for prolonged periods of time. We have learned that early thinking about arousal as a unitary state mechanism was too simplistic, and that while arousal may be related to the overall level of vigilance performance, other factors may underlie the decrement. Moreover, a number of brain systems involving structures such as the mesencephalic reticular formation and the basal ganglia have been nominated to play a part in the control of vigilance and the possibility of hemispheric specialization for sustained attention has been explored.

While advances in the psychobiology of vigilance have been made, the story is far from complete. Parasuraman raises several issues with regard to findings based on measures of autonomic activation and event potentials that are in need of clarification and he has indicated that our knowledge of brain systems and hemispheric specialization in sustained attention has only scratched the surface of what must be involved. He has also pointed out that work along a potentially intriguing line of research, that of relating neurophysiological measures to the information processing demands of vigilance tasks, has only just begun.

Environmental stressors

The impact of environmental stressors—conditions which alter the comfort of the observer—is an important consideration in vigilance research. Intuitively, it would seem reasonable to expect that stressors such as extremes of temperature, vibration, noise and variations in atmospheric conditions would degrade the ability of observers to maintain attention to the task at hand. Hancock's careful examination of this issue in Chapter 4 reveals that while such is sometimes the case, things are not so simple. Under some conditions, acoustic and thermal stressors can facilitate performance while other forms of environmental stress have a surprisingly negligible effect upon performance efficiency.

The picture that seems to emerge is that reactions to environmental stress are complex and depend to a considerable extent upon particular combinations of type of stressor, task demand, and the skill of the monitor. Hancock's review indicates that research on the impact of environmental stress is incomplete at this time. He notes that data with respect to several dimensions of stress are limited or equivocal and that the effects associated with multiple stressors remain to be more thoroughly examined. I might add that efforts to relate the effects of stress to standard psychophysical dimensions and to psychophysiological phenomena other than arousal are also sparse. A recent study by Lysaght (1982) which describes the manner in which the effects of acoustic stress depend upon the kind of noise stimuli employed and the complexity of the discriminations involved in a vigilance task, suggests that this might be a fruitful line of investigation to pursue. Moreover, Hancock's suggestion that the road to further understanding in regard to environmental stress and vigilance may be in a closer examination of the covert strategies and attentional allocation policies utilized by observers warrants careful consideration.

Individual differences

Anyone who has conducted experiments in vigilance cannot help but note the wide individual differences that occur. Indeed, Davies and Parasuraman (1982) have pointed out that such differences are a common finding in vigilance studies (see also Craig's comments in Chapter 7). Even under the same experimental conditions, some subjects detect many of the signals while others detect hardly any at all. Similarly, false alarm rates and response times vary considerably among participants. Furthermore, as Smith (1966) has pointed out, some conscientious subjects strive to perform close to the limit of their capability and maintain a temporally stable level of performance while others, characterized as 'periodic participators', show a strong vigilance decrement. Small wonder that considerable effort has been devoted toward the identification of individual characteristics that are associated with efficient watchkeeping. Berch and Kanter (Chapter 5) have provided a thorough examination of this problem and the whimsical want-ad with which they end their chapter reflects the *mélange* of abilities and personality traits that have been related in some way to watchkeeping efficiency.

The discovery of this broad assortment of psychological characteristics is encouraging but it is also disappointing. As Berch and Kanter have noted, no one factor seems to predominate in accounting for individualization in vigilance and it has not been possible to develop a global selection test that would adequately forecast an observer's monitoring efficiency in different situations. Perhaps a careful examination of the relation between the information processing characteristics of different vigilance tasks and relevant personal attributes would be useful. In this way, it might be possible to bring some order into the picture by determining the precise nature of the tasks in which one or another attribute accounts for a greater proportion of the variance between observers.

One of the most crucial aspects of Berch and Kanter's chapter is their discussion of the use of vigilance tasks to determine attentional deficits in clinical populations. Such use implies that the study of sustained attention has matured in the sense that it is no longer the sole and somewhat esoteric concern of experimental and engineering psychologists. It has developed a broader appeal, and vigilance tasks now serve as tools for investigating other problems.

This development is an exciting new aspect of vigilance. However, it is currently marred by problems in experimental design that may have been overlooked in several experiments. As Berch and Kanter have indicated, much of this work can be indicted on the grounds that little effort was made to show that the clinical groups that were studied could differentiate signals from noise during short-term alerted conditions, or if they could direct attention to the task at hand during such conditions. In situations like this, it is difficult to make a clear interpretation of the meaning of disparities in monitoring efficiency between normal and clinically disordered groups. An outcome favoring the normals could reflect an attentional deficit in the disordered subjects. It could also stem from an initial inability among the disordered individuals to distinguish signals or to focus attention on the task in the first place, or an unwillingness on their part to participate in the experiment. In sum, it could have little to do with sustaining attention. Berch and Kanter have also noted that task durations in several clinical studies were quite brief and that this might play a role in some of the inconsistencies in experimental outcomes that were observed. Clearly, more careful work is necessary to clarify these matters.

Kanter (1983) has recently developed a paradigm for studying vigilance performance in hyperactive (attentional deficit disorder) children which takes account of some of the problems just described and establishes firmly that such children suffer a deficit in sustained attention. His report might serve as a guide for future research with other clinical populations. In addition, the work of Nuechterlein and his colleagues (Nuechterlein, 1982; Nuechterlein *et al.*, 1983) provides a technique which could possibly telescope the time needed to reveal perceptually based vigilance deficits in clinical populations. Together with these newly emerging techniques, efforts to determine comparative differences in perceptual sensitivity and response strategies among normal and clinical groups and to relate the performances of disordered individuals to brain systems in vigilance might further our understanding of the locus of deficits in sustained attention.

Theories of vigilance

The body of data that has accumulated in relation to vigilance is substantial. Is there any way to order and account for this panorama of information? Stated somewhat differently, is there an acceptable general model of vigilance? At this time, the answer to that question is 'No'. In their searching review of vigilance theories, Loeb and Alluisi (Chapter 6) describe the variety of approaches that have been taken toward a unified general position. They point out that each of the several models described seems able to account for some part of the data but no single model is capable of handling it all. Moreover, many of the models can be challenged on several grounds. Loeb and Alluisi's conclusions are echoed in other recent treatments of theories of vigilance (Warm, 1977; Davies and Parasuraman, 1982). At present, we seem to have arrived at a stalemate in theoretical development. This state of affairs poses a serious problem since advancement in any field of science is often predicated on good theoretical ideas.

How can the situation be rectified? One possibility is to seek fresh ideas that might have more power in explaining vigilance performance. Posner's (1978) notion of pathway inhibition (see Chapter 2) and the concepts of controlled and automatic processing used by Fisk and Schneider (1981) (see Chapters 2, 4 and 6) may have promise.

A different type of approach, and one that I find attractive, has been offered by Loeb and Alluisi. They suggest that efforts to build a 'one-mechanism' explanation of vigilance may not be feasible. Instead, they argue that a 'multi-mechanism' view might be more realistic. While deviating from the ideal of parsimony that is commonly used as a criterion in evaluating psychological theories (cf. Allport, 1955), a multi-mechanism view is not necessarily unique to vigilance; it seems to be appropriate in other areas of psychology as well (cf. Dember and Warm, 1979; Ettenberg, *et al.*, 1981). As applied to vigilance, an approach of this sort might dictate the development of a 'multiple regression model' in which different weights are assigned to several theoretical mechanisms on the basis of their ability to account for different sources of variance in vigilance performance. Psychophysical, physiological, environmental and individual determinants would, of course, be included as sources of variance. Along these lines, a taxonomic analysis, like that of Davies and Parasuraman (1982), could be quite helpful since it would separate tasks according to their information processing characteristics and pinpoint situations in which experimental outcomes are more likely to reflect sensory or decision factors.

The operational applicability of vigilance research

The relation between science and technology is currently a source of lively debate in governmental, industrial and university sectors (Adams, 1982; Badia and Runyon, 1982; Mook, 1983). At issue is the value of basic research in resolving important practical problems. Since the study of vigilance was prompted initially by practical concerns, the science/technology issue is especially pertinent here. Has anything emerged from the vast number of laboratory studies of vigilance that would be useful in controlling the monitoring behaviors of human operators in applied settings?

From the thoughtful discussions of Wiener in Chapter 7 and Craig in Chapter 8, the answer to this difficult question seems to be a qualified 'Yes'. While several criticisms have been leveled against the ecological validity of laboratory studies of vigilance, evidence can be marshalled which parries the thrust of these criticisms. For example, as both Wiener and Craig note, the argument that the vigilance decrement does not occur in operational situations can be answered in several ways: (1) careful observations of the decrement function in these situations are sparse; (2) in the data that are available, there is some evidence to show that the decrement does indeed occur in operational tasks; (3) as Craig has indicated, the problem in operational tasks involves more than just the decrement, it includes a low level of overall performance as well. Another form of argument against the operational relevance of laboratory-based vigilance experiments is the approbation that microprocessors will soon obviate the need for human monitoring functions. In response to this point, Wiener has indicated that microprocessors do not eliminate the need for human monitors—they merely require operators to substitute one monitoring task for another.

If one wants to apply laboratory research to practical problems, one must first know what those problems are. From Wiener's description of the monitoring requirements in industrial inspection tasks and in vehicle operation and flying, it is clear that these problems are complex and often involve multi-task situations and multidimensional stimuli. It is also clear, however, that many of the psychophysical dimensions of laboratory vigilance tasks are woven into the fabric of real-world monitoring. Craig has skilfully blended the results from laboratory tasks into an extensive number of carefully worked out recommendations for improving the quality of sustained attention in the workplace. Nevertheless, as both authors suggest, human factors technology for the control of vigilance is still in its infancy. Many issues need answers. As Craig has indicated, they range widely from psychophysical concerns such as assessing detection rates for different mixtures of signals (multiple faults) to determining the effects of social pressures on operator performance.

A final word

In their discussions of operational vigilance problems, both Wiener and Craig mention that monitors must often hunt among displays or within a display for critical stimuli. Clearly, an element of search is an influential factor in many vigilance tasks. In his chapter on search (Chapter 9), Monk points out that Mackworth was aware of this important relation in his early investigations. However, later generations of vigilance researchers may have lost sight of it. Monk's chapter provides a search tutorial that might promote further exploration into the implications of search for vigilance performance. In addition to extending our knowledge of sustained attention, work in this direction can have even broader appeal. Moray (1969) has distinguished among several possible subdivisions of attentive phenomena (see Chapter 1). Search and vigilance are included in these subdivisions. As I have noted elsewhere (Warm, 1977), very little is known about the linkage between different aspects of attention. Perhaps, at last, this bridge will begin to be crossed.

Since the mid 1970s, the pace of research in vigilance has not been as rapid as it once had been. This has led some investigators to conclude that the information to be 'mined', so to speak, had been 'played out'. To the contrary, I think not. While the problems inherent in developing deeper understanding are perhaps more intricate and subtle than those encountered during the first blush of discovery, they are nonetheless challenging. Many of these problems remain to test the ingenuity of researchers who wish to unravel the conundrum of sustained attention.

REFERENCES

Adams, J. A. Research and the future of engineering psychology. *American Psychologist*, 1982, **27**, 615–622.

Allport, F. H. *Theories of perception and the concept of structure.* New York: John Wiley, 1955.

Badia, P., and Runyon, R. P. *Fundamentals of behavioral research.* Reading, Mass.: Addison-Wesley, 1982.

Cordes, C. Human factors and nuclear safety: grudging respect for a growing field. *APA Monitor*, 1983, **14** (5) (a).

Cordes, C. Human factors and nuclear power: nose to grindstone or lip service? *APA Monitor*, 1983, **14**(6) (b).

Davies, D. R., and Parasuraman, R. *The psychology of vigilance.* London: Academic Press, 1982.

Davies, D. R., and Tune, G. S. *Human vigilance performance.* New York: American Elsevier, 1969.

Dember, W. N., and Warm, J. S. *Psychology of perception*, 2nd edn. New York: Holt, Rinehart and Winston, 1979.

Ettenberg, A., Koob, G. F., and Bloom, F. E. Response artifact in the measurement of neuroleptic-induced anhedonia. *Science*, 1981, **213**, 357–359.

Fisk, A. D., and Schneider, W. Control and automatic processing during tasks requiring sustained attention: a new approach to vigilance. *Human Factors*, 1981, **23**, 737–750.

Frankmann, J. P., and Adams, J. A. Theories of vigilance. *Psychological Bulletin*, 1962, **59**, 257–272.

Hohmuth, A. V. Vigilance performance in a bimodal task. *Journal of Applied Psychology*, 1970, **54**, 520–525.

Kanter, D. R. *Attention deficit disorder and vigilance performance*. Unpublished doctoral dissertation, University of Cincinnati, 1983.

Lysaght, R. J. *The effects of noise on sustained attention and behavioral persistence*. Unpublished doctoral dissertation, University of Cincinnati, 1982.

Mackworth, N. H. The breakdown of vigilance during prolonged visual search. *Quarterly Journal of Experimental Psychology*, 1948, **1**, 6–21.

Mackworth, N. H. *Researches on the measurement of human performance*. Medical Research Council Special Report Series No. 268. London: HM Stationary Office, 1950. Reprinted in H. W. Sinaiko (Ed.), *Selected papers on human factors in the design and use of control systems*. New York: Dover, 1961.

Mook, D. G. In defense of external invalidity. *American Psychologist*, 1983, **38**, 379–387.

Moray, N. *Attention: selective processes on vision and hearing*. New York: Academic Press, 1969.

Nuechterlein, K. H. Signal detection in vigilance tasks and behavioral attributes among offspring of schizophrenic mothers and among hyperactive children. *Journal of Abnormal Psychology*, 1983, **92**, 4–28.

Nuechterlein, K. H., Parasuraman, R., and Jiang, Q. Visual sustained attention: image degradation produces rapid sensitivity decrement over time. *Science*. 1983, **220**, 327–329.

Posner, M. I. *Chronometric explorations of mind*. Hillsdale, N.J.: Lawrence Erlbaum, 1978.

Smith, R. L. *Monotony and motivation: a theory of vigilance*. Santa Monica, Calif.: Dunlap and Associates, Inc., 1966.

Warm, J. S. Psychological processes in sustained attention. In R. R. Mackie (Ed.), *Vigilance: theory, operational performance and physiological correlates*. New York: Plenum, 1977.

Wickens, C. D., Mountford, S. J., and Schreiner, W. Multiple resources task-hemispheric integrity, and individual differences in time-sharing. *Human Factors*, 1981, **23**, 211–229.

Wolk, K., Bowers, J. C., Vandenboom, B., Dember, W. N., and Warm, J. S. *Effects of primary task event rate on probe detections in a vigilance task*. Paper presented at the meeting of the Southern Society for Philosophy and Psychology, Atlanta, April 1983.

Author Index

Subject Index